**The Today Show, CNN, Larry King, CNBC,**
**The New York Times, The Chicago Tribune,**
**National Public Radio, The Wall Street Journal**

**. . . are just some of the places you've seen, heard, and read about us.**

## What They Say About Us

D1303799

"One organization with a long record of success in helping people [with t
O'Clock Club."
*FORTUNE*

"Many managers left to fend for themselves are turning to the camaraderie offered by [The Five O'Clock Club]. Members share tips and advice, and hear experts."
*The Wall Street Journal*

"If you have been out of work for some time . . . consider The Five O'Clock Club."
*The New York Times*

"Wendleton has reinvented the historic gentlemen's fraternal oasis and built it into a chain of strategy clubs."
*The Philadelphia Inquirer*

"Organizations such as The Five O'Clock Club are building . . . an extended professional family."
Jessica Lipnack, author, *Professional Teams*

"[The Five O'Clock Club] will ask not what you do, but 'What do you want to do?' . . . [And] don't expect to get any great happy hour drink specials at this joint. The seminars are all business."
*The Washington Times*

"The Five O'Clock Club's proven philosophy is that job hunting is a learned skill like any other. The Five O'Clock Club becomes the engine that drives [your] search."
*Black Enterprise*

"At The Five O'Clock Club, [members] find discipline, direction and much-needed support."
*Modern Maturity*

"On behalf of eight million New Yorkers, I commend and thank The Five O'Clock Club. Keep the faith and keep America working!"
David N. Dinkins, former Mayor,
The City of New York

## What Job Hunters Say About Kate's Other Books

"During the time I was looking for a job I kept Kate's books by my bed. I read a little every night, a little every morning. Her common-sense advice, methodical approach, and hints for keeping the spirits up were extremely useful."

> Harold Levine, coordinator, Yale Alumni Career Resource Network

"I've just been going over the books with my daughter who is 23 and finally starting to think she ought to have a career. She won't listen to anything I say, but you she believes."
Newspaper columnist

"Thank you, Kate, for all your help. I ended up with four offers and at least fifteen compliments in two months. Thanks!"

> president and CEO, large banking organization

"I have doubled my salary during the past five years by using The Five O'Clock Club techniques. Now I earn what I deserve. I think everyone needs The Five O'Clock Club."

> M. S., attorney, entertainment industry

"I dragged myself to my first meeting, totally demoralized. Ten weeks later, I chose from among job offers and started a new life. *Bless You!*

> Senior editor, not-for-profit

"I'm an artistic person, and I don't think about business. Kate provided the disciplined business approach so I could practice my art. After adopting her system, I landed a role on Broadway in *Hamlet*."

> Bruce Faulk, actor

"I've referred at least a dozen people to the Five O'Clock Club since I was there. The Club was a major factor in getting my dream job, which I am now in."

> B.R., Research Head

My Five O'Clock Club coach was a God-Send!!! She is truly one of the most dynamic and qualified people I've ever met. Without her understanding and guidance, I wouldn't have made the steps I've made toward my goals.

> Operating Room Nurse

The Five O'Clock Club has been a fantastic experience for my job search. I couldn't have done it without you. Keep up the good work

> Former restaurant owner who found his dream job with an organization that advises small businesses.

# What Human Resources Executives Say About Five O'Clock Club Outplacement!

"_This thing works_. I saw a structured, yet nurturing, environment where individuals positioned themselves for success. I saw 'accountability' in a non-intimidating environment. I was struck by the support and willingness to encourage those who had just started the process by the group members who had been there for a while."

> Employee Relations Officer, financial services organization

"_Wow! I was immediately struck by the electric atmosphere_ and people's commitment to following the program. Members reported on where they were and what they had accomplished the previous week. The overall environment fosters sharing and mutual learning."

> Head of Human Resources, major law firm

"The Five O'Clock Club program is _far more effective_ than conventional outplacement. Excellent materials, effective coaching and nanosecond responsiveness combine to get people focused on their central tasks. Selecting the Five O'Clock Outplacement Program was one of my best decisions this year."

> Sr. Vice President, Human Resources, manufacturing company

"_You have made me look like a real genius_ in recommending The Five O'Clock Club [to our divisions around the country]!"

> SVP HR, major publishing firm

"Selecting Five O'Clock outplacement was _one of my best decisions this year_."

> SVP, HR, consumer products firm

# YOUR GREAT BUSINESS IDEA

## THE TRUTH ABOUT MAKING IT HAPPEN

- The One-Hour Business Plan: Pre-test Your Ideas for Viability
- Being an Entrepreneur: How to Make Money When You're Not Working
- How to Turn Your Business into Your Career
- Step-by-Step: How to Get From Square One to a Fully Operating Business

## Kate Wendleton

Five O'Clock Books
www.FiveOClockClub.com

The Five O'Clock Club®

For information, please contact:
The Five O'Clock Club®
300 East 40th Street
New York, New York 10016 www.FiveOClockClub.com

Library of Congress Cataloging-in-Publication Data
Wendleton, Kate.
Your great business idea : the truth about making it happen / by Kate Wendleton.
p.  cm.
ISBN 978-0-944054-13-0
1.  New business enterprises. 2.  Small business--Management. 3.
Entrepreneurship. I. Title.
HD62.5.W457 2007
658.1'1—dc22            2007004360

NOTICE TO THE READER
Publisher does not warrant or guarantee any of the products described herein or perform any independent
analysis in connection with any of the product information contained herein. Publisher does not assume, and
expressly disclaims, any obligation to obtain and include information other than that provided to it by the
manufacturer.

The reader is expressly warned to consider and adopt all safety precautions that might be indicated by the
activities herein and to avoid all potential hazards. By following the instructions contained herein, the reader
willingly assumes all risks in connection with such instructions.

The Publisher makes no representation or warranties of any kind, including but not limited to, the
warranties of fitness for particular purpose or merchantability, nor are any such representations implied with
respect to the material set forth herein, and the publisher takes no responsibility with respect to such material.
The publisher shall not be liable for any special, consequential, or exemplary damages resulting, in whole or
part, from the readers' use of, or reliance upon, this material. The authors and The Five O'Clock Club affirm that
the Web site URLs referenced herein were accurate at the time of printing. However, due to the fluid nature of
the Internet, we cannot guarantee their accuracy for the life of the edition.

President, The Five O'Clock Club: Kate Wendleton
Chief Operating Officer: Richard C. Bayer, Ph.D.
SVP, Director of the Guild of Career Coaches: David Madison, Ph.D.
Cover Design: Andrew Newman Design
Interior Design and Production: Bookwrights

*To Richard, my heartbeat and my pal*
*And to my parents*

*The way to achieve success is first to have a definite, clear, practical ideal*
*— a goal, an objective. Second, have the necessary means to achieve your ends —*
*wisdom, money, materials, and methods. Third, adjust all your means to that end.*

Aristotle 384BC-322BC, Greek philosopher and scientist,
student of Plato and teacher of Alexander the Great

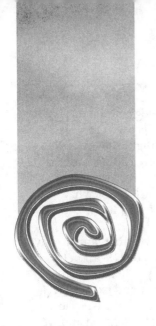

# Preface

This is not "the only book you'll ever need" to run your small business, but it *is* the only book you'll ever need to develop a sound business concept—one that has a good chance of succeeding and is right for your personality. That's what *this* book will do for you. This is a book on small business *concepts and strategy.*

I continually read business books: books about finance, marketing, law, management, business strategy, or other specific business issues. Or books that have to do with the kind of business *we're* in: publishing, seminars, coaching, and so on. Or books about successful entrepreneurs who inspire me to move mountains myself. To be successful, you'll eventually need more than this book. But reading books on financing or marketing won't help you come up with a *good business idea* or tell you the truth about what is involved in *developing a good idea.*

I hear "business ideas" all the time:

- I'll develop my own action toy and develop a movie character and comic book.
- I love eating out. I'll open up a restaurant. How hard can it be?
- I've thought of a $2.00 novelty item I can sell to businesses.

- I'll open up my own (fill in the blank) store.

I've heard them all—and the good ideas, too. Ideas are easy. Most would-be entrepreneurs with an idea think the first thing they should do is incorporate—and maybe get some space. They think the purpose of a business plan is to get financing. But they have not *thought through* their idea, tested it for viability, developed a business plan that helps them to run the business, or figured out the steps it would take to make the idea work.

Here's a hard, cruel fact: Ninety percent of all American small businesses fail within the first three years. But that seems to be the American way: fire and then aim. Yet the local Korean grocery stores or Indian-run motels tend to be successful. Why? They start out with realistic, time-tested plans.

This book helps entrepreneurs develop a business idea and a business plan that have a chance for success. Readers learn that the real purpose of a business plan is not to raise capital but to force the entrepreneur to *think through* the business concept, research the competition, and develop realistic financial projections—all to increase the chance for success.

Some businesses are more complex and more difficult to start than others, but the successful people I've worked with take on average two years from the time they *thought* of having a business until they were ready to start implementing the plan. It can take that much time to develop the right strategies. How do you know whether you have a good idea—one that has a chance for success and will actually satisfy you? How do you know what to do first, second, third? That's what *this* book is about.

I've taught hundreds of people how to decide whether their business idea was worth pursuing (For a glimpse, see the chapter, "The One-Hour Business Plan."). I've saved them time, money and heartache. You too can learn from the mistakes and successes of others. Follow the Five O'Clock Club methodology, and modify it to suit your own situation. *Then* you can read all those other books on selecting the right business structure, raising venture capital, and the like—because by then you'll know that you have a workable business idea. You'll know what it takes to start a business. You will know the *truth* about making it happen.

This book can help you whether you already have an idea, or *wish* you had one. We'll help you flesh out your idea. But you'll also learn that: "Ideas are easy. Planning and execution are everything." You too can live the American dream of being your own boss. Read on and we'll tell you the truth about how to do it.

# Table of Contents

Preface .......................................................................................................................... x

Introduction ............................................................................................................... xv

## Part One: Entrepreneurial Options

Should You Have Your Own Small Business? ............................................................ 3

Is Entrepreneurship For You? .................................................................................. 11

Targeting the Businesses of the Future ................................................................... 15

Case Study: Scott — Targeting the Future .............................................................. 27

## Part Two: Deciding the Kind of Business You Want: Start by Understanding Yourself

How to Choose Your Business ................................................................................. 33

Exercises to Analyze Your Past and Present: The Seven Stories Exercise ..................... 35

- The Seven Stories Exercise Worksheet ............................................................... 40
- Your Current Work-Related Values ................................................................... 45
- Other Exercises: Interests, Satisfiers, and Bosses ............................................. 47
- Your Special Interests ........................................................................................ 49
- Satisfiers and Dissatisfiers in Past Jobs ............................................................. 50
- Your Relationship with Bosses ........................................................................... 51

Looking into Your Future ......................................................................................... 53

- Your Fifteen-Year-Vision and Your Forty-Year Vision ...................................... 55
- Your Fifteen-Year-Vision and Forty-Year Vision Worksheet ............................. 57
- Your Forty-Year Vision…Fifteen Years is a Good Start ..................................... 59

- The Ideal Scene .................................................................................... 62
- The Ideal Scene Worksheet ................................................................. 65
- My Ideal Business ............................................................................... 67
- Describing Your Ideal Business Worksheet ...................................... 69
- Your Ideal Business Environment ..................................................... 71
- Your Ideal Business Envirnment Worksheet ..................................... 73
- Brainstorming Possible Businesses ................................................... 75
- Brainstorming Possible Businesses Worksheet ................................. 78

Case Study: Chiron — Finding a Future ................................................... 79
- Preliminary Business Investigation: Businesses Worth Exploring ............ 88

## Part Three: Getting Yourself Ready

Ambition, Courage, Follow-Through and Other Entrepreneurial Virtues ...................... 93
Your Wealth Goal .................................................................................. 99
Forming the Right Character for Entrepreneurship .............................. 103
Life Takes Time ..................................................................................... 113

## Part Four: Buying an Existing Business (including a Franchise)

Buying an Existing Business ................................................................. 117
Buying a Franchise ................................................................................ 127

## Part Five: Starting Your Own Business (including a high-growth business)

Starting a Growth Business ................................................................... 131
Case Study: Yadira — Determining the Kind of Business She Wants ...................... 137
Case Study: Robert – First, Thirteen Years of Research ......................... 147

## Part Six: Becoming a Consultant in Your Own Field

On Your Own: Becoming a Consultant .................................................. 153
How to Start Your Own Consulting Business ....................................... 155
Creating Your Own Job: Consultants Who Made It Work .................... 167

## Part Seven: Marketing–Making Sure the Right People Know About You

Marketing Your Small Business ............................................................ 173
Researching Your Business Idea ........................................................... 183
Targeting: Becoming an Expert in a Niche ........................................... 191
Your Two-Minute Pitch: The Keystone of Your Marketing .................. 195
Naming Your Business .......................................................................... 207

Developing Your Marketing Literature.................................................... 211
Selling to Organizations (the Corporate Sale)......................................... 215
Getting Lots of Meetings with Organizations.......................................... 223
The Stages of Your Corporate Sales Campaign ....................................... 231
Speeches or Demonstrations: An Important Promotional Technique........ 237
Public Relations Tips for Your Small Business ........................................ 251

## Part Eight: Understanding the Numbers: Making a Profit

Cash is King ......................................................................................... 259
Analyzing the Business ......................................................................... 265
Profits: The Bottom Line ...................................................................... 271
Cost Accounting: Managing for Profitability ......................................... 279
Accounting Basics ................................................................................ 289
15 Helpful Hints for a Profitable Agreement ......................................... 295
Negotiating a Consulting or Freelance Assignment / Pricing a Project ....... 297

## Part Nine: Putting It All Together

The One-Hour Business Plan ................................................................ 309
Developing Your Business Plan ............................................................. 317
Planning the Stages of Your Organization's Growth .............................. 321
Your Exciting Business Idea ................................................................. 329

## Part Ten: What is the Five O'Clock Club?"America's Premier Career Coaching Network"

How to Join the Club............................................................................ 335
Questions You May Have About the Weekly Job-Search Strategy Group ..... 339
The Way We Are.................................................................................... 347
Lexicon Used at The Five O'Clock Club ................................................ 349
Application for Club Membership and Subscription to The Five O'Clock News ........... 352

Bibliography ........................................................................................ 353
Appendix: The New Outplacement Model............................................. 357
    (The Five O'Clock Club's pitch to prospective customers)
Index ................................................................................................... 367

About the Author.................................................................................. 379
About the Five O'Clock Club and the "Fruytagie" Canvas ..................... 381

# Introduction

I started my own small business on the side in 1978. It's not as though I woke up one morning and said, "I want a career-coaching business." The process was lengthier and more angst-ridden than that.

I was 33 years old, and had worked primarily – and happily — for large corporations. My most recent employer had gone through six downsizings, and I escaped each time. The problem was that I did not *want* to escape getting the ax. I wanted the outplacement services so I could figure out what to do with my life. I volunteered to be let go, but they said no.

So I got together six or seven friends – some employed and some unemployed – who wanted a new job, and I found a career coach to help us for six weekly sessions. The first week that George came to us, he was very casual and chatty. This wouldn't do at all. I wanted a syllabus and an organized approach. The next week, he was more serious and organized, and we all learned a lot. After the time was up, we all took George out to dinner, and I brought in another coach to lead the group. Surprisingly, this coach taught us

very different approaches from what George had said. Who was correct?

After this person's six weeks were up, I decided to run the group myself. Being a business person – and a researcher at heart – I asked each group member to try different techniques and report back to the group. I kept meticulous notes and observed what was working and what was not. Over the next 8 years, I ran small groups in my apartment and became more and more methodical about it: groups of 6 engineers, 6 clerks, 6 people who had been unemployed two years or more, 6 executives. I wanted an approach that would work for everyone, no matter what his or her level. In 1986, I published my first book to document my findings, and thus began the Five O'Clock Club approach to job search and career development.

That's the short story, and it's all true. But there's more to the story than that. *Prior* to 1978, I spent many years trying to figure out what to do with my life. I had been in good jobs, jobs I was proud of, but I wanted something more. I thought about what I loved: art, horticulture, and my job-search group. First, I investigated working in the arts field, running seminars and other events. However, when I met people working in the arts field, many were very rich, some were paid only $1.00 a year for a full-time job, and I didn't want to be in a field where they were my competitors. I needed to earn money.

I then investigated my other great love: horticulture. I wrote a business plan, took very serious courses with nurserymen (there happened to be no women in my courses), started growing plants and over-wintering them, went to trade shows, gathered literature on my competition, and finally decided that I didn't have the temperament to weather the bad weather, which could affect business dramatically.

Finally, I spent time during those eight years of research developing the business plan for the Five O'Clock Club, investigating the nuances of small-group processes and what makes them successful or unsuccessful, researching the competition (all big companies) and deciding what my competitive advantages would be. I wanted:

- a name that separated us from the competition,
- job-search materials based on research that would be the best in the market,
- a concern for job hunters that superceded an interest in the bottom line,
- a mantra that "we will always do what is in the best interests of the job hunter," and
- a pragmatic approach to job search rather than the intensely psychological (and often weird) approaches that were common at the time.

For many years, I worked at a job and ran the business on the side. For many additional years, I worked 2 to 3 days a week as a consultant and ran the business the other eight days a week! Eventually, I gave up all outside sources of income and was fully supported by the business. Now, our multi-million-dollar business works with over 200 Five O'Clock Club-certified coaches across the country.

There were many hard times along the way. In the early years, I failed completely three times. That is, there was a problem with my model. I had to completely fold up shop, recover emotionally and financially, and start all over again. Each time I learned from my mistakes. Today, it would be difficult for the business to fold because the momentum is on our side and we have become even stronger, and are worthy competitors against the "big boys" in our industry.

However, just about every week, someone comes to me with an idea for our business. There's a saying around our office: "Ideas are easy. Execution is everything."

It doesn't help you to simply have an idea. That's loser thinking. You have to flesh it out, investigate it, make it happen. Buy yourself a bound notebook, the kind you liked in school, and use it for taking notes about your own business. Many years from now, you'll be glad you captured these ideas. The starting place is right here, right now. Get out your pen and notebook and write down your own truth about making it happen. You too can join the ranks of those who start something, become the boss and meet payroll!

Kate Wendleton
New York City, 2007

# Part One

Entrepreneurial Options

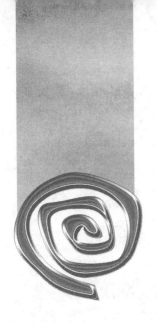

# Should You Have Your Own Small Business?

## The Benefits of Having Your Own Business

According to the SBA, small businesses provide approximately 75 percent of the net new jobs added to the economy and employ 50.1 percent of the private work force. If you decide to have your own small business, you won't be alone and you'll be part of the engine that's driving the U.S. economy.

Having your own small business can mean anything from buying an existing business, opening a retail store, buying a franchise, starting a growth business, or becoming a consultant in your own field. Doctors, lawyers and architects are often in their own businesses. You can work on your own, with others, or have employees. You can work endless hours, or work part-time while keeping your day job. You may need investment capital or you can bootstrap your company—by using your own money and reinvesting profits in the business.

Having your own business can be fun—and sometimes nerve-wracking. There are many advantages:

## 1. You will be your own boss.

You decide the kind of organization you want, the people you want to work with, the values you hold dear, and exactly how you want your small company to operate. You can decide how your employees should dress for work, how they will treat each other and your customers, where the business should be located, and generally how you want to live your life. One very successful entrepreneur said to me, "I always leave at five o'clock. Five to nine is 'mommy time.' Then I'm back on my computer working again and at work early the next day." That's what she valued and that's what she got.

My needs were different. At a certain period in my work-life, I wanted to be able to take a brief afternoon nap when I felt the need, which was not all that often. It was important to me to have that freedom, and I know I produced more because I was well-rested.

A major motivator for entrepreneurs is that we don't want to work for anyone else. We want to be in control of our own futures as much as we can. We want to call the shots. If the business fails, it's our fault. And if it succeeds, it's also because of us.

> You can decide the kind of life you
> want to live, the ideals you value.

## 2. Long hours, maybe.

When you work long hours for a boss, those hours often *feel* long. But when you're working for yourself, you decide the kinds of hours you want to put in, you're doing it for yourself, and the hours just don't seem as long. What's more, you can decide what your hours will be. Some people have businesses that don't get started until 10:00 AM In addition, from time to time, in the early days, I would say that I wanted to leave early to go to the movies. Now, I arrive very early in the morning—way before anyone else—and no one begrudges me this flexibility. The staff has flexibility as well—to do what they consider important.

## 3. Live your ideals.

It's your business. You can decide how you want your business to function. I set the tone for the business, most importantly that the job hunter comes first, that we must always act ethically, pass up business and press coverage that would not be in the best interests of our clients, and so on. Even when times were tough, we turned down press coverage that would negatively impact job hunters or employees. We turned away business from rich companies that wanted to provide their employees with very little help during their career transition. Those who wanted to cheat their employees could work with one of our competitors. We didn't *have* to work with everyone.

It's *your* business. Decide how you want it to work, the kinds of people you want to work with, and the kinds of clients you want to have.

Decide as well how you want to run your shop. Most of our staff has flex-time, and we have no scheduled holidays off. If someone wants to work on Thanksgiving Day and the day after, that's fine. He or she may use the hours off at some other time. When people join the company, they earn two days off a month, which they can use for sick time, vacation, holiday or personal. They don't have to tell us *why* they want the time off. If they want a day off, they can have it. If they're sick, they're sick and they can use a day. We don't have to be "mommy" and decide what's okay for them. It's a fun way to work.

Decide how you want *your* company to operate.

> Small business owners have a
> significantly higher probability of being
> classified as high income and high wealth.

## 4. Earnings and growth potential are far greater than when you work for someone else.

The tax system in America was created for entrepreneurs. When you discuss business over lunch, that lunch is a business deduction. The government is paying for part of it.

The average millionaire in America looks like the person next door—as a famous book described it. That millionaire does not live like Donald Trump or work on Wall Street. He or she lives in a modest house, lets the car get old, and generally lives beneath his or her means. That's how they become millionaires! If they had spent the money, they wouldn't *have* the money. A person who *looks* impressive may be amassing *debt* instead of wealth.

The average millionaire runs a common, small business (makes spiral staircases, soap or cookies, caters or cleans houses) and runs it well. An SBA study concluded definitively that, although small-business ownership is risky, small-business owners had a significantly higher probability of being classified as high income and high wealth. Yes! This country was made for entrepreneurs!

Thomas J. Stanley, the author of "The Millionaire Next Door," (which stayed on the *New York Times* bestseller list for more than 150 weeks), studied thousands of millionaires. He found, unsurprisingly to us, that millionaires choose careers that match their abilities. They are creative and practical. They focus on a goal, take calculated risks and then work harder than most people. Almost none of them credit their success to being smart. They say the keys to success are being honest and disciplined, getting along with people, having a supportive spouse and working hard.

Somehow they figured out what they enjoyed doing and also did well. They decided to be the best at something they love—something that was also marketable.

One of Stanley's case studies is Donald Sonner, the head of Southern Bloomer Manufacturing Co. in Bristol, Tenn. Sonner's only education was a single year of high school, but he was a millionaire by the time he was 24. His company takes scrap cloth and makes gun-cleaning patches and underwear for prisons. He got rich by working hard and capitalizing on an idea no one else had.

Recently, I read where the multi-millionaire son of a former slave ran a limousine service that specialized in meeting the needs of the rich and famous. He had lots of employees, ran a mundane business very well and became very rich by the time he retired.

### 5. Running a company is exciting and endlessly interesting.

Because your business is small, you can notice something that's wrong and fix it without going through a huge bureaucracy. Yes, you need advisors, or a very sharp staff, but it's not the same tedium as trying to convince your boss and your boss's boss and five other departments why this thing should be done.

There is so much to learn! You'll find yourself interested in other small businesses, what they do, and how they're run. As the business grows, your role changes. For 19 years, I ran small groups within The Five O'Clock Club, coaching

people on their searches. But the business grew too large to allow me to indulge myself that way. I had to let go, trust our highly qualified coaches to take care of our clients, and spend more time actually running the business. Essentially, I was kicked upstairs, and I'm now in a new career and loving every minute of it.

## The Downsides of Having Your Own Business

It's not all roses. You have to ride through the rough spots and overcome any obstacles.

### 1. Isolation.

This is the word I've heard most often from people who decided to pack up their business and get a job. Start-ups are hard—and often lonely. Twenty years ago, I hired a temp assistant from time to time just to have someone in the office, which was in my *apartment*. I sometimes needed a kick-start when my energy ran low. Some people rent office space in a temporary office center or at someone's law office just so they can be around other people. I had a part-time day job. On other days, I used to go out to breakfast in the morning—to get up and out, and then go back to my apartment and work.

Join associations so you can be around other entrepreneurs or at least people who are in your field—or people you could sell your products or services to. Find some way around this problem, or tough it out.

Now I'm *surrounded* by people and have to arrive early for a little quiet and thinking time.

> **Live beneath your means. Run a business and run it well.**

### 2. The lean years.

There was a long period when my business was not doing well. No one knew it, but I was forced to move out of my apartment, selling everything I had, and sleep on a sofa in the office. I kept my underclothes in a bag in the bottom drawer of a filing cabinet and told the staff that the few clothes I kept in a closet were there in case I had to do a TV interview. At the end of the workday I'd leave with everyone else, walk around the block, and come back to the office, my new home. Now, with our business booming, I don't live the high life, but it's out of choice, not necessity. I tell you this to let you know that for some years you may feel quite a pinch.

## 3. Meeting payroll.

Small business owners will proudly tell you that the thing that separates them from non-entrepreneurs is that they have to meet payroll. Some even have had to lend money to their companies to meet this obligation.

It's almost the difference between being a child and a parent. Employees are akin to being children: they ask their employers for money, time off and trips. Small business owners are akin to being the parent: they have the responsibility for others, set their own hours, and give permission.

Your family and your employees depend on you. Your customers and vendors depend on you as well. Sometimes panic can set in. You have to get a grip and make sure you don't over-extend yourself.

## 4. Regulations, filings, taxes, licensing.

Do not mess up on filings, taxes and other paperwork. Provide 1099s for consultants and W-2s for employees. There are health-care issues, tariffs, duties, the FDA and other regulators, depending on the kind of business you have. In the early days, when we had little income, the one thing I made sure we spent money on was trademark and copyright protection. Otherwise, we would have no business.

## 5. No steady paycheck.

Working for someone else feels much more secure. Of course, the average American has been in his or her job for only four years, and workers don't know from one day to the next whether they will keep their jobs, so they don't have security either! That can be the reality! But it can be nerve-wracking when you're the one in charge of paying yourself.

## 6. "It would be great if it weren't for the people."

If you want to grow your business, chances are you will have people working for you. One husband-wife team, with a small tree-service business, said they were burnt out and exasperated with the many issues involved with having employees. Some business owners decide they want to quit because they're so tired of irresponsible workers. But the only thing worse than being the boss is *not* being the boss! As the owner, you get to pick the work arrangements that best satisfy your needs. However, the great insight of management comes when you realize that meeting your needs results from figuring out how to better meet the needs of great employees.

The secret is finding employees who have standards that match your own. When we recruit, we ask prospective employees what kind of hours they worked in past jobs. If all of their jobs were straight nine-to-five, they won't be right for us. We don't work long hours, and we want people to have personal lives, but when we land that big contract, we want all hands on deck working overtime for a few weeks. We don't want clock-watchers—those who somehow manage to show up precisely at nine and leave precisely at five.

Employees have to be managed. Everyone can work as a team, but you are still the boss and set the pace. You reward and give kudos to everyone who lives up to their potential, and counsel those who are not performing up to snuff.

> No steady paycheck, lots of reporting, and the big one: Meeting payroll.

## 7. The price of failure.

It's easier to get another job than it is to get another business. And when you lose your job, you won't usually lose your life's savings and your house. But small business owners may put up their house as collateral when taking out a small-business loan. They may use their life's savings (as I did). Try to save money before you start your business so you'll have a cushion.

Fred, one of my clients, had no cushion. His computer business, which he shared with his girlfriend, went bankrupt five years ago, well before I knew him. Now at age 53, he has been working as a realtor. He considers himself a good businessman and would like to have his own business again. However, he can't put away the $15,000 he needs to get the business started while he continues to work as a realtor.

But, in truth, there is little hope for Fred. He recently went on a cruise with his bride-to-be, just months after they bought a new house and furnished it beautifully. They have an extensive wine collection. They are planning a big wedding, although it is the second marriage for both of them, and then another cruise. They are deep in debt and still buy gifts for each other and are thinking about getting a hot tub. I'm not sure why Fred went bankrupt before, but I have an inkling. If they want to live the high life and he can't start saving, his small business has little chance of success.

You must make the same sacrifice for your business as you would for a little baby. You save in advance, pull in your belt, and sacrifice until the child is finally on his or her own. Until the business can comfortably support you, you must live beneath your means.

## Why Small Businesses Fail

The high failure rate for small businesses is well known. And I can see why it's true. Below are some of the most common reasons.

## 1. Lack of planning.

A group of yuppies opened a deli in my neighborhood. They probably figured, "I go to delis all the time. How hard can it be?" Because I'm interested in small businesses, I decided to give them a try. I ordered half of a roasted chicken. They said, "We only sell the roasted chickens whole." I responded, "That's just fine. I'll go right across the street where they'll sell me half a chicken." They were closed within four months.

Yet the Korean grocers who open tend to do well from the first day they open and most tend to succeed. A lot of Indians are attracted to running small motels, and they are successful. Greeks run coffee shops and are successful. That's because they all have a business plan of sorts. They tell each other who to buy from, what to sell, how much to charge. They don't go into it blindly. They are almost like franchisees, following a plan.

But Americans are action-oriented and think they'll figure it out as they go along. I've even heard very famous people brag that they don't have a plan, which adds to the mystique. But those business leaders *do* have a solid strategy, which they follow religiously. Sure, they let someone else figure out their detailed plans, but they are not as haphazard as many would like to pretend.

Still others may be *unaware* of their own effective marketing efforts. I once appeared on a successful person's radio show. In reading over my credentials before the broadcast, the host noticed that I had been on a number of television stations that he wanted to be on. During the commercials, he mentioned people whom he had contacted at those stations, asked me who I knew and asked if I would put in a good word for him. Of course I would.

Almost in the same breath, he said that he had been very lucky in his career in that he had never had to job hunt or market himself. New opportunities just magically came his way. He seemed not to realize that he was continually marketing himself. It had become second nature. If people aspiring to his position in radio had asked him how he had gotten there, he would not have been able to tell them.

I heard a successful children's book author give a speech. People in the audience were dying to know to what she attributed her success. She said it was pure luck, that she rarely got out of her pajamas, and the money kept pouring in. Yet she had many deals for related items, and she wrote four or five books a year. I believe she was far more planful than she appeared, and she simply didn't want to tell us any of her secrets.

Many successful people don't like to admit that they plan. It ruins the aura. But most successful people never rest; they are always aware and always planning—and modifying their plans depending on what they learn.

> My mantra for a dozen years:
> "Keep panic at bay."

## 2. Lack of experience.

Like the deli owner above, many people go into businesses where they have no experience and have done little research. Remember, it takes *two years* of planning and research before you can actually plunge in.

## 3. Lack of financing.

Some people think the first thing they need to do is raise money for their new business. But banks and investors are unlikely to give you money unless you have plenty of experience, a good business plan, a strong management team, and collateral. Many companies, including ours, take the boot-strapping approach. We grew slowly, sometimes too slowly, but with our own money. We put back into the business whatever money we made, and we contributed our own money. This gave us the independence to do what we wanted. Investors are often eager to get a quick return on their investment. But we wanted to do what was in the best interests of the job hunters and those who came to us for career development advice—and not charge them an arm and a leg. Investors would not have tolerated this idealistic approach.

## 4. Weak management team.

You can't know everything yourself. You need advisors or people who work for you who are knowledgeable. Over the years, I have received advice from the SBA, from SCORE, and from various executives who took a special interest in my business. They found it exciting to listen to the business model and comment. I am very grateful to them. At the end of the day, however, you have the responsibility to make sure you are getting the advice you need. You need what is called "bench strength"—a strong management team. You need more brains than you have—others who are strong and knowledgeable.

I once heard the swan song speech of a famous venture capitalist. He had invested in 181 companies, only a handful of which were extremely profitable, and he made himself quite a fortune over the years. Now that he was retiring, he was willing to share his secrets with this eager audience. When someone asked what the successful companies had in common—were they from the same or similar industries, for example—he just rolled his eyes. If it had been that obvious, he would have invested in just those industries. Instead, he had invested in everything from start-up pharmaceutical companies to a limousine service. He said his analysis showed him that it wasn't the kind of *business* they were in that made the difference. *It was the strength of their management team*. He believed he could have taken those same successful managers and given them a completely different kind of business to run and they would have been just as successful.

Most managers tend to hire people who are just like them: the same nationality or race, same age, even similar personalities. In today's economy, you usually need different criteria for who you choose to work with. I've noticed that some of our Five O'Clock Club coaching managers choose for their teams coaches whom they personally like. But whether or not I *like* a coach is irrelevant. What's relevant is the competence of the coach and how well the coach relates to our diverse range of clients. We can't have coaches who are all alike because the clients we service are very different.

Our back office is similar in its diversity. We look like a little United Nations. We want very bright, hard workers, not those who were born with a silver spoon in their mouths, but those who want to work hard and are innovative and do what it takes. These kinds of people come from all nationalities, cultures and personalities. And it makes the workplace interesting. For example, during Ramadan, when Muslims fast for an entire month, we refrained from our monthly employee lunch out of the office until Ramadan was over. Then we "broke fast" with our Muslim colleague, which was interesting for us.

## Other Reasons for Failure
### Location.

Depending on the business, it can fail because of a poor choice of location. One of our clubs doubled in size when we moved it.

### Emphasis on appearances.

Many businesses fail almost immediately because the owner is more interested in the appearance of having a successful business rather than actually having a successful business. For example, rather than operating out of home to start and keep expenses down, some people think it's most important to have an office and two staff members. That may be true in some cases, but often not.

> **Remember: When things seem to be failing, keep panic at bay.**

### Lack of control over expenses.

It's amazing to see a start-up business spend money as if it were extremely successful. As Richard Bayer, our Chief Operating Officer, reminds us, "The profit is at the margins." This means that we watch our pennies, and don't spend money as if it didn't matter. Do you really need the best furniture? Do you need to use FEDEX or UPS rather than the Post Office?

### High growth can kill a business.

You may think you want the business to pour in, but make sure you can handle it. Once, after there was a huge write-up about us in the *New York Times*, we were flooded with people who wanted to attend our groups. We had to explain that it was like a restaurant that got great reviews and then accepted every reservation. It would make for a very unpleasant dining experience. There are only so many tables and so many waitstaff. So, too, with our business. We formed a triage system: those who were most in need (such as those who were unemployed) got priority. Those who were not in a hurry were placed on a waiting list. We had a four-month waiting list for those who were not in a rush, but when the person finally got in, he or she got good service and was treated well. You may think that we could simply add dozens of coaches and serve people that way, but in our old brick-and-mortar days we did not have our Insider Program (by telephone), which allows for the number of groups to ebb and flow.

## Low sales are a major problem.

In addition to having a good product or service, marketing (and pricing) is the key to every business. Over the years, we have been approached by many start-ups who wanted to partner with us. It's interesting listening to their plans for their businesses. But one striking similarity is the number who have developed a great product or service—and perhaps have raised millions in venture capital—but *have given little thought to marketing.* They are of the school of thought: "Build it and they will come." Well, they *don't* come. You've got to get customers in, and you have to know how to market your product or service.

I hope these introductory tips help you to start thinking about whether a small business is right for you.

. . . . . . . . . . . . . . . . . . . . . . . . . . . . .

*The essence of the high-risk society is choice: the choice between embracing uncertainty and running from it.*

Michael Mandel, *The High-Risk Society*

## Having a Job and a Dream

If you *do* want your own business, it may be wise not to quit your day job. Your business will take extensive planning, and it may take a while before your new business can support you financially. Many people work at a day job and start the business on the side. After a while, you can continue to work at your day job, cutting back to two or three days a week, while your business grows. Then gradually, the business supports you more and more and finally you can cut the umbilical cord.

Many people, including myself, hang on to the corporate ties for the security of having an income stream. Small businesses are as unsteady as little babies. It can be a disaster for your business if a major customer takes six months to pay you. What will you do for money? Be sure you have no credit card debt before you go into your business because you may need to run up a little from time to time before you are eligible for bank credit. Be sure to live well beneath your means and take pride in that. You are no longer in the corporate rat race where appearances are so important. Now, cash is king. You need the cash to run your business, *not* to take a cruise or buy new clothes or the latest car.

Work during the day and plan the business on the side. It's best if what you do during the day has something to do with your business idea. If your business idea has to do with food, work around food as your main job. If you want to have your own cleaning business, work in someone else's cleaning business. But work in the office—don't actually serve food or clean. Learn the *business* side of their business—the numbers. Find out who their vendors are, what they pay, how they market, who they see as their competition.

> It takes an average of two years from the time you have a business idea until you're ready to start.

# Is Entrepreneurship for You?

"Start-ups are hard." That's my mantra. There's so much to learn, so many balls to juggle. It's up to you—with the help of your advisors—to figure out what is wrong and what you should be doing next. Another mantra of mine is, "What is the most important thing for me to focus on today? What's second?" And that's what I do. It wasn't always the task I most wanted to do, but the one that most needed to be done or needed my attention. I still do that: make my priority list for the next day—and also my priority list for the next year!

But someday, the business develops a life of its own, money comes in even when you're sleeping, the staff develops the right values and comes up with ideas—and actions—that move the business ahead, rather than thinking of what's best for them personally. Then you have arrived. You are on a different plane and you know it. You have to keep yourself from being cocky. You can guide this ship rather than push it with your own body. Delegate more and hire stronger managers who can take this thing to the next level. You—or your staff—will spend time developing more controls and more thorough documentation.

You'll need better financial advisors and wealth consultants. That's the payoff.

Yes, start-ups are hard, but good planning, insight and research can make a huge difference in your chances for success. Here are a few questions to ask yourself to determine if entrepreneurship is right for you.

## 1. If a really great job comes along with fantastic pay, will you take it?

If so, you'll never make it in your own business. You're ready to sell out and you haven't even started! You don't have the drive or the stamina to ride out the bad times. Better to quit now rather than pretend you want your own business.

## 2. Are you a self-starter?

*You're* the boss now. There's no one breathing down your neck. Even when I worked for others, I acted more like an entrepreneur. In one job, I was the office head at an outplacement firm's branch. The place looked depressing to me, so I got permission from the boss to come in on a Saturday with a few eager clients to paint the office.

It's not hard to spot the owner: he or she is the one who picks up the stray paper on the carpet or in the company parking lot. No one else really notices the paper or feels it has anything to do with them.

Now *everything* is your job. You develop projects, decide what you will work on, organize your own time, and follow through on details. You have no one to report to. There is no mail room. It's all ultimately up to you.

### 3. How well do you plan and organize?

Research indicates that poor planning is responsible for most business failures. Good organization—of financials, inventory, schedules, and production—can help you to avoid many pitfalls. You must be *driven* to develop systems, have others follow those systems, and document what they do. You need a vision and a business plan, of course, and new plans every year. It's your job to keep everyone else organized. Successful entrepreneurs resist the temptation to do what is unimportant or the easiest, and have the ability to think through to what is the most essential.

### 4. How's your physical and emotional health?

Will you buckle under the stress? Another one of my mantras was, "Keep panic at bay." When things are not going according to plan, can you keep your head on straight or do you fall apart? You're the leader. Others are looking to you for the confidence that things will work out, or at least that you'll all be able to survive this.

Are you in good physical health? The business owner cannot afford to get a lot of colds or otherwise be indisposed. Business ownership is fun, rewarding and exciting, but it's also a lot of work. Can you face six or seven 12-hour work-days every week? You may have to do that for a long while. So minding your health is vital!

### 5. What will motivate you to stick with it?

Do you have the drive it takes to run a business? What will make you stick it out despite setbacks, even failures, unruly employees and customers, financial problems, and periods of burnout?

### 6. How self-aware are you?

One of our employees had an idea a day. Most of them were silly and not well thought out. After months of this, I asked him, "Do you see yourself as a person who generally has good ideas?" His answer was a most assured "yes." But he was wrong. Successful people tend to be better at predicting how other people see them. Are you aware of your strengths and weaknesses? Or are you the type who thinks you're a genius simply because you're in a position of power or because your significant other adores you?

### 7. How good are you at making decisions–really?

Small business owners are required to make decisions constantly—often quickly, independently, and under pressure. Are you willing to draw a team around you that can participate in the kind of decision-making where you may be weak? Do you *know* the areas where you are weak?

### 8. Have you ever worked for a small business before?

When you were young, did you have ideas for having your own business? When I was 13, I ran my own baby-sitting business. On a typewriter, one at a time, I typed up "business cards" that said I "proudly announced the formation of my baby-sitting business." I listed the rates and contact information and distributed them everywhere. I was no Bill Gates, but still the drive was there. Over the years, I ran small ventures, and helped my father in his many side businesses. As an adult, I worked for many small businesses (as well as large ones).

If you have had no contact with small businesses, you may be surprised by what you're in for. You may have to unclog the toilet. You are not allowed to disdain menial tasks. Take some pride in them. Later on, you can reminisce about the good old days when you were the one who had to paint the place.

## 9. How will the business affect your family?

Your spouse may be panicky at the thought of your taking this risk rather than simply getting another job. He or she needs to know that it will take time. Make sure your finances are in order so you can weather the storm for the months or years that it may take. You may have to adjust to a lower standard of living or put family assets at risk in the short-term. If you work a day job and plan to start your business on the side, your family needs to understand that you will be preoccupied for some time and not have the time with them that you used to have.

## 10. Do you have a reasonable amount of self-confidence, ambition and drive, a passion for your business idea, and an optimistic attitude?

You'll need all of these to keep yourself and others going, and to convince others to be enthusiastic about your product or service. *Entrepreneurs must demonstrate extreme self-confidence* to cope with all the risks of operating their own business. Entrepreneurs have the need to achieve: Although they keep an eye on profits, this is often secondary to the drive toward personal success.

## 11. Do you have a willingness to learn financials?

You cannot delegate profitability. You must understand the numbers *yourself* and review what the bookkeeper or accountant does. You must keep meticulous records and enjoy analyzing your business numbers. Otherwise, you will not price your product or service properly and will undercharge. You need to have a handle on the *profit margin* of every product or service you offer.

## 12. Are you willing to work hard?

In the beginning, there's no one but you. It's common for founders to work 60- or 80-hour weeks. You will have to be naturally industrious to make this work. If you've always been a slouch, chances are slim that you will now become a workaholic.

Well, now's your chance to back out. Would you rather have a paycheck and not have to worry about all of this? Then you can spend your evenings drinking beer and watching football games! Or do you want to join the group that "has to meet payroll." If you run your company into the ground, there will be nobody else to blame and no excuses will be accepted. If you think you want to pursue this further, let's get started.

Now, to summarize, what does it take to plan and succeed?

- Decide what you want to do (we'll show you how in later chapters),
- Do something, some one thing (don't hedge your bets by starting three businesses at once),
- Do it well,
- Know your competition,
- Work hard,
- Have the discipline to do what needs to be done,
- Use good judgment or rely on the advice of others who have good judgment,
- Have the relentless ambition not to give up,
- Be able to hold out for the long term—such as by working at something else to earn money or having plenty of savings,
- Have well-grounded confidence in your business,
- Want to be your own boss (many people stick to it just because they absolutely do not want to work for someone else),
- and finally, keep panic at bay.

It's my hope that this book will protect you from these pitfalls. It sounds easier to open that deli or start a catering business simply because you like to cook, but it's important to have the right strategies in place, and this is a book about business strategy.

## The Three Most Important Factors in Small Business Success

A lot of factors can influence the success or failure of your business, but three are the most important:

1. *The business idea must be financially feasible.* You must be able to sell the product or service at a price that will lead to profitability. I often think that pricing is the core of the business. Setting the right price means that you understand what the market will pay and understand your business well enough that you know your costs, including overhead.

2. *You must choose a product or service you can be passionate about.* You will have many obstacles to overcome and people to convince. Most often, you will have to stick with the business a very long time to get a good return on the investment of your time and money. So pick something you can be passionate about.

3. *You must be capable of carrying out the idea.* Most successful business owners have previous experience or are willing to devote considerable time to getting experience in the business they want to run. And you must be able to finance the business. If you want to have an experiential hair salon where each customer can decide where she wants to pretend she is—on the beach, in a palace, at a ski resort—but cannot convince venture capitalists to give you the $1 million you think it will take, you don't have a business.

   Ideas are cheap; Execution is everything. Rethink your idea and come up with one that you have a better chance executing.

## Should You Have a Partner?

Many potential small-business owners feel insecure. They don't know all they think they should know and may immediately assume that they should have a partner. I have worked with many people whose small business failed *because* they had a partner. Most often, the partnership failed because the partner stole money (or spent the company's money as if they were rich), or the partner simply stopped working. These partnerships can be very difficult to dissolve.

Before you take on a partner, ask yourself this: Do I need a partner or do I simply need to hire someone who can do the things I need to have done? For example, if you are lacking in marketing expertise, should you have a partner or should you find someone to help you with marketing? If you are lacking in accounting expertise, do you really need a partner to fill this function, or can you hire to have it done?

### Homework:

Write a paragraph or two describing why you think entrepreneurship is right for you.

# Targeting the
# Businesses of the Future

*There is guidance for each of us, and by lowly
listening, we shall hear the right word.*

Ralph Waldo Emerson

Obviously, this is not the best time to open a business tuning pianos or fixing TVs. Those businesses have gone the way of the buggy whip. It's better to pick a business that has a future.

One Five O'Clock Clubber started her own private not-for-profit school for underprivileged children in Harlem. She raised millions of dollars from organizations such as the Bill and Melinda Gates Foundation. Alternative schools are certainly a growth industry.

In 2004, my brother, Robert, started his own very successful nano-technology company when he was 55. He was the oldest founder the venture capital firm had ever invested in. Those investors knew that it took a long time to build the base of information he had. Robert has an engineering degree in materials science, worked in that field for over thirty years in various positions (from scientist to global marketer), and spent thirteen years doing his own research on the side. At the time he started his business, most of the other entrants in the nano-technology field

did not have his expertise or business acumen. Yet nano-technology was a hot area and venture capital was relatively easy to come by. He needed millions in venture capital because the machines cost from $80,000 to $150,000 each, he needed a dozen or so scientists to work on new product development, and it could take years to bring the product to market. He passed up funding from various investors and selected the one that best appreciated his approach to business development and was high in integrity.

Education and nano-technology are industries of the future—industries that are likely to grow. But so are everyday service businesses such as tech consulting, catering, and specialty child care. People are busier, more are two-wage families, children and parents have different schedules, and the need for someone else to fix their computers, cook, or care for their children is increasing. Basic service businesses will always be in demand and cannot easily be outsourced to India, Israel or Russia.

Certain service businesses may be needed every few blocks or miles. These could include home house cleaners, dry cleaners and laundromats, hairdressers, barbers, and so on. There is a great deal of merit in deciding to run a business that is commonly needed, and running it better than others do. No, you don't want to open a beauty salon right next door to another one, but if you research the area, you may find a location that is underserved. Run it well, learn how to market, please your customers, live beneath your means, and you could have a very nice income for yourself.

That may be enough for you: decent income in something you can handle. Or you may be more ambitious and want to expand—maybe even considerably. It's up to you: single operation or high growth.

..........................................

*Believe it is possible to solve your problem.*
*Tremendous things happen to the believer.*
*So believe the answer will come. It will.*

Norman Vincent Peale

## Service Businesses: From Home-Based to High Growth

High-tech or glamorous ideas, such as my brother's, tend to be risky. More ordinary ideas may be steadier, easier to manage and still provide a good income. You can start with a small, home-based business, keep it that size and make a comfortable living, or end up with a growth business employing many people and having multiple locations. It's your choice. Here are a few ideas that focus on people who do not have enough time or expertise to do everything themselves, so you can help them. I'm sure you'll think of other needs and ideas.

- Bookkeeping for small businesses—One of our clients got most of the leads for her thriving business from local banks
- Home Renovation Services—According to AARP, 82 percent of midlife and older Americans wish to remain in their homes

forever. But those homes have to be made more livable.

- Catering Services—You can cater for parties or cater for everyday meals.
- Cleaning Services—Domestic and small business cleaning services are in high demand.
- Clothing Maker—Who has time to shop, shop, shop for that perfect-fitting suit that you saw once and never again? Custom-made clothing will be more in demand.
- Pet Groomer/Walker/Sitter—The sky is the limit on what pet owners will spend.
- Cake Baking & Decorating—for bar mitzvahs, sweet sixteen parties, and, of course, weddings.
- Specialty chocolates/party favors—To be sold to individuals, stores or caterers.
- Caretaking—of older Americans and people with disabilities
- Career Coaching—Careers are too complex to handle just by yourself. Many people get advice from their career coach twice a year just as they see their dentist twice a year. It's a check-up to keep your career on track and handle any problems that may arise.
- Gift basket business—People want items that are new and different. And you can sell them on Ebay!
- Beautician—You can start it from home and then grow it.
- Travel services—for specific categories of people, such as the aged, families, professionals and so on.
- Child Care—Regular day care centers are still needed, but affluent families want day care with something extra, such as second-language skills, computer instruction, dance instruction and crafts.
- Wellness and health. People will buy anything that helps them to look and feel better. Home exercise and massage could lead to a growth business that competes with today's gyms.
- Tech consulting. "Geeks on Demand" and like businesses are a God-send to small

businesses and individuals who don't have the time or expertise to figure out how to hook up their printers, network together the ten computers in an office, or set up security systems.

•••••••••••••••••••••••••••••••••••••••

*Sell where you can, you are not for all markets.*

William Shakespeare

## New Ideas—Or Not

You can come up with a new idea or you can run a common business uncommonly well. We'll take you through exercises to help you better understand what you enjoy doing and also do well. Those enjoyable skills could be the basis for your business. Look at the people around you. What services could they use? Look at a business you like. Can you run one like it but better? The business you noticed on a recent trip: Is there a similar one where you live, and is there a need? Look in your present company. Can you be a service provider to your present employer? Can you start a business doing something your employer isn't or serve a market they are not presently serving? (That's what my brother did.) Look at ideas or programs your company rejects, or tries to do and fails. These are often small-business opportunities. Look at growing ethnic populations and sell what they want the way they want it, such as beauty salons aimed at specific segments, foods prepared the way they had it in the old country, clothing that is specific to an ethnic group but may appeal to other groups. Pay attention to skills-oriented television channels and magazines, and see what the trends are.

If you think you know a better way to give a customer what he or she wants or needs, you're probably correct. Brush off comments or "advice" such as "That's been done before" or "That's already been tried." Those thoughts are idea killers. Ignore them.

But ideas are easy. Execution is everything. You will need to research the market thoroughly to see whether it stands a chance. This book will

help you do that. Later, you can expand your business by looking for complementary markets to those you initially serve.

•••••••••••••••••••••••••••••••••••••••

*In this high-risk society, each person's main asset will be his or her willingness and ability to take intelligent risks. Those people best able to cope with uncertainty . . . will fare better in the long run than those who cling to security.*

Michael Mandel, *The High-Risk Society*

## Temporary Setbacks

Some industries and occupations ebb and flow with supply and demand. When a field is hot, such as during the dot.com or nano-technology eras, or in fields such as contract nursing, contract computer programming, or the staffing industry (search firms), more people enter those fields creating an excess.

For example, during boom times many people decide to have their own recruiting firms. During bust times, the market flushes out as many as two-thirds of those companies. They fold. Some owners know this will happen because they have done their research, and they hedge their bets, offering other services or becoming so entrenched with their customers that they can ride out the hard times. Those who think the boom will last forever are unprepared for the bad times and simply have to get jobs working for someone else—probably in another industry.

Right now, all of the talk is about health care because of the aging baby boomers. There will certainly be room for plenty of entrepreneurs to serve this market, but the chances are good that too many people will be attracted to aspects of this field and only the good will survive. You can plan for that eventuality before you start your business.

The overall economy may also temporarily affect a field or industry. Real estate, for example, may suffer in a down economy and pick up in a strong one. When the real estate market is booming, many people say, "I know. I'll become a realtor, get a license and have my own business." In down real estate markets, it's not so cheery.

Too many people open restaurants without doing research. Yet the failure rate is high—60 percent after three years according to a recent Ohio State University study.

........................................

*Strategy without tactics is the slowest route to victory. Tactics without strategy is the noise before defeat.*

Sun Tzu c. 490 BC, Chinese military strategist

## Ahead of the Market

When the Berlin Wall came down in 1989, there was a rush of companies wanting to capitalize on the potential market in Eastern Europe. Given all they were reading in the papers, entrepreneurs thought it would be a good market for them to explore. But they were ahead of the market. It took a few years before the market caught up with the concept. Now many businesses thrive and many people are employed in Eastern Europe or in servicing that market.

The same may be true for the area that you are in or are trying to get into: The market may not be there because it has not yet developed. Remember that it is much easier to fill a need than it is to create a demand. It's hard to convince people or organizations that they need your service or product when they don't believe they do. It's a lot easier when they think they need something and you are there to fill that need.

## Can You Compete?

*Your most dangerous competitors are those that are most like you. The differences between you and your competitors are the basis of your advantage.*

Bruce Henderson, Founder Boston Consulting Group, *Harvard Business Review* 1989

Before you start your business, decide how you will you be able to compete. If you want to

do something in the medical imaging field, for example, who would your competitors be? How will you be different, better or cheaper?

We had to think through the same issues ourselves. Career coaching as a profession is a commodity business. It is very easy entry: anyone can become a career coach, but few do well at it. Career coaching services are sold primarily to corporations (outplacement services) or to individual consumers (retail services). Until 1998, The Five O'Clock Club had been primarily retail, selling to consumers.

The outplacement side of the business derives its revenues from corporations only. This business is also easy entry, and was flooded with new companies in the 1980's. Predictably, there was a shake-out, and many businesses folded.

Over the years, employers were unwilling to pay the outrageous prices the traditional outplacement firms were asking. As their profit margins have become squeezed, more and more outplacement firms have become seriously interested in other businesses, leaving more room for us because our overhead and prices are dramatically lower than theirs.

Those firms that are purely retail are going after the same retail market that we are. These firms tend to operate the same as each other: they charge heavy up-front fees (in the range of $5000 to $7000 per person), and they are known to lose interest in a client when the client starts to have trouble. They have, therefore, historically been subject to lawsuits from unhappy clients.

The Five O'Clock Club is, at present, the only national firm offering affordable group career coaching services to individuals as well as private counseling on a pay-as-you-go basis.

........................................

*I have always found that my view of success has been iconoclastic: success to me is not about money or status or fame, it's about finding a livelihood that brings me joy and self-sufficiency and a sense of contributing to the world.*

Anita Roddick

# Barriers to Entry

The Five O'Clock Club has always concentrated on developing barriers for competitors intending to enter the retail market. Most of these barriers have helped us in the outplacement market as well. These include:

## A. The Five O'Clock Club Name and Logo

- *Our competitors' names* all sounded like law firms (Lee Hecht Harrison, Drake Beam Morin, Right Associates). We picked the name "The Five O'Clock Club" because it sounded friendly and like a place where employees would want to go to get help with their careers—and socialize to meet other professionals.
- "The Five O'Clock Club" is a good name for the retail market. Clients tell each other that they are "going to the Club." It creates a nice attitude on the part of clients, and they have no trouble remembering it.
- *The brand*. Everything The Five O'Clock Club does is meant to strengthen the brand. In this commodity business, we developed a brand that is to career coaching what Purdue is to chicken (a former commodity product) and Sunkist is to oranges. People across the country ask for The Five O'Clock Club by brand name and only want to work with a Five O'Clock Club coach.
- *The logo*. The logo conjures up images of those comfortable, relaxed times when people get together to exchange information—for job hunting or for getting along in their present jobs, for starting their own small businesses, or for enjoying their leisure time effectively. The message in the logo is both businesslike and sociable. It is elegant, friendly and stable.
- The people associated with today's Five O'Clock Club are just like the people in the original 1880s Five O'Clock Club: they are competent and they are winners. They

are busy people who treat each other with respect, and share their experiences and fellowship.
- The Five O'Clock Club name and logo are registered trademarks.
- *The history*. The original Five O'Clock Club was formed in Philadelphia in 1886. It was made up of the leaders of the day who shared their experiences in a "spirit of fellowship and good humor."
- Today's Five O'Clock Club acquired the name and the rights to it in 1984. Members get a nice feeling belonging to something that has such an interesting history. Competitors will find this history difficult to match in its public appeal.

## B. The Program Content

- *The methodology*. All outplacement firms use the same vanilla approach to job-search counseling. This has helped to keep it a commodity business.
- The firms keep the approach simple: "network a lot; do well in your interviews." However, job search is no longer as simple as it once was. The outplacement firms have not changed or even modified their approach since the early 1970's, when The Five O'Clock Club was started.
- The Five O'Clock Club approach, however, is based on research, and is unlike anything taught at any of the outplacement firms. It would be very difficult for them to develop an approach that is different from what they now do. Yet our methodology is a strong point of differentiation.
- Another competitive advantage is our *ongoing, thorough research* into how people get ahead in their careers and how job hunters got the best jobs fastest. Our competitors were not interested in helping employees so much as they were driven by profit margins, so they did not invest a lot in research. This gave us a distinct

edge—and a good reputation for caring about employees more than profits.

- *Our personal approach*. Our competitors are reducing the emphasis on coaching and increasing the emphasis on technology (webinars, e-learning, databases of outdated job listings). We provide what job hunters need most: the career coaching itself—with a real, live person.
- *The materials*. The books and CDs are the best on the market because they are based on our 25 years of continual research. We decided our materials would be the best on the market—and sold in regular stores—not secretively as our competitors did, seen only by those who were using their services. We thought we would let the market decide how good or bad our product was.
- *The computer system*. Because we are client-centered, The Five O'Clock Club has the best client-tracking system in the business. (Outplacement firms have great systems for tracking the *corporations* who refer business to them). Coaches get reports on the clients in their small groups. And our coaches and/or client services department make sure our clients are making the most of our services. Our competitors, on the other hand, make money only when half the people they get paid for don't use their services.

## C. Pricing and Staff

- *Pricing and ethics*. Our mantra is to do what is in the best interests of the employee or job hunter. The Five O'Clock Club never charges *individuals* heavy up-front fees. Clients are on a "pay-as-you-go" basis. Most pay for ten sessions at $400—as opposed to thousands they would pay at the traditional *retail* firms.
- For our *employer*-paid clients, we do the opposite. We won't accept business from employers who essentially want to give their employees nothing and pretend to

be helping them. We insist that employers provide private as well as group coaching, our materials, and a one-year package to protect the employee against a quick job loss at the next place of employment.

- *The staff*. The Five O'Clock Club is extremely well known within career coaching circles. Because of the strength of our program, we have the pick of the best career coaches around. Our coaches like working for us because they get to do good work. This is another strong competitive advantage.
- *We did not accept investor money*. We wanted to run an ethical business that charged individuals very little ($400 to $700). Our competitors charged heavy up-front fees ($5000 to $7000), and told people how they could take out a loan to pay for the service. If we had investors, they would not allow our pricing practice to continue: they want a quicker return on their money. Others have accepted investor money. This gives them less freedom to run the business the way they want.

We decided on all of these competitive advantages *before* we started the Club. And then during the early years, when competitors from all over the world observed how we were doing (and visited us), we never bragged about our success. Instead, we told them that we thought it was *great* they wanted to enter the market: "People need so much help, but I hope you're not doing this for the money! There's no money in it." That kept quite a lot of them out of the market and bought us some time.

With our completely different business model more suitable to today's market, we compete against relative giants. You too will have to think about how you can compete in your market.

····················································

*If you succeed in judging yourself rightly, then you are indeed a man of true wisdom.*

Antoine de Saint-Exupéry, *The Little Prince*

## What about *Your* Industry or Profession?

Is your dream industry or field growing, permanently retrenching, or in a temporary decline because of supply and demand or other economic conditions? If you are lucky, your idea is in tune with the market. Often, you can find out by reading newspapers, magazines, and trade journals, and talking to people in the industry. (We'll talk about research techniques a lot more in other chapters.)

Most people in permanently retrenching industries, including the leaders, incorrectly think the decline is temporary. You have to decide for yourself. You could perhaps gain insight and objectivity by researching what those outside your industry have to say.

## Retrenching Markets Are All Alike

When an industry retrenches, the results are predictable. A retrenching market, by definition, has more sellers than customers. It becomes more and more difficult to sell your product or service. For example, the video stores that offered tape rentals were once big chains (Blockbuster Video) as well as Mom and Pop stores. Video cassettes were replaced by DVDs, and then they were replaced by other media and many stores closed. Low-fat foods were in, followed by low-carbs, and then a rash of other diet fads replaced low-carbs. Low-fat food stores closed. Later, low-carb foods hit bottom after being all the rage for a few years.

The more a market retrenches, the worse it gets. Those who want to stay in the field have to work harder to get business and must reduce profit margins. Companies in the retrenching industry must downsize or go out of business.

It's easier if you target a growth industry rather than one that is in decline. That may sound obvious, but you'd be surprised how many people select as targets businesses that are likely to decline.

*One doesn't discover new lands without consenting to lose sight of the shore for a very long time.*

André Gide

## The Attributes of a High-Growth Industry

By definition, growth industries have room for outsiders: There are not enough providers inside the industry. Then the new industry attracts new competitors—many of whom will fail because they will be unprepared. But if the industry is still growing, those who got in early are the most knowledgeable and valuable, and may have a slight edge. If the industry does *not* continue to grow, new entrants create a surplus and there will be a shake out.

As long as the industry continues to grow, there is an open window: Those outside the industry can get in. As the industry stabilizes, there will be plenty of experienced people, investors and purchasers will want primarily those with direct experience, and the window will close.

HMOs, cellular technology, for-profit schools—and the Internet—were essentially nonexistent industries just 20 years ago.

*People of my generation, seeking to understand why companies succeed, have spent most of their time hunting an elusive animal called the SCA, or, to give its full name, the sustainable competitive advantage. They've hunted it in the belief it was the embodiment of success; a guarantee, if not of corporate immortality, at least, of a long, healthy, and prosperous business life. But they never found the creature. Or, if they found it, they never caught it. It seems the SCA, once found, becomes sand, running through fingers. There is some evidence of the animal's previous existence in the Great Museum of Corporate Profitability. The IBM exhibit, for instance, shows the company could do no wrong—for a long period. The AT&T*

> *exhibit, the DuPont exhibit, and the Siemens exhibit all suggest these firms domesticated the SCA—for a while. Maybe the SCA is like the Great Awk. It might have existed once, but it became extinct so long ago that no one really knows for sure . . . I hesitate to say it, but I'm beginning to believe strategic agility is more important than strategy—that a firm's ability to make money has more to do with its ability to transform itself, continuously, than whether it has the right strategy.*
>
> Francis Gouillart, Senior vice president, Gemini Consulting, *Journal of Business Strategy*, May 1995.

## Pick a Field You Know

Many professionals decide to become consultants in their old field. Doctors, lawyers and architects are likely to go into their own private practices. That's what they know and (I hope) love. Pick a niche that interests you—something you already know or are willing to learn. I spent from 1978 to 1986 doing research on job hunters and career changers before I was ready to start my business. If you decide you want to have a certain kind of business, pick something you already know or research it so you know it inside out.

A middle-aged actor started a business coaching senior executives in presentation techniques. A sales executive who had spent 30 years in the financial services industry started a search firm that specialized in that industry. His firm is thriving 10 years later. A banker who, through much soul-searching, decided she wanted to be in the food business, studied at the French Culinary Institute and (to make a long story short) started her own dessert and pastry business. You will read Yadira's detailed story later.

If you are not expert in the industry you are targeting, *become* expert. Study the industry. Take a job working for a small to mid-sized business in that industry. Then you can start your business on the side so long as it does not compete directly with your employer. For example, you can start it in another location or offer a different service or serve different markets.

When I decided to get serious about growing The Five O'Clock Club (I had been running it part time), I first took a job as a chief financial officer for a 200-person outplacement firm. That would have been a terrible career move if I had not been clear to myself about why I was there: to learn everything I could about the business from the inside. Much of what I learned there served me well in my own business.

## Expanding Your Target Geographically

Studies show that more jobs and companies are created in the suburbs than in major metropolitan areas, and there is greater job creation in the *new* suburbs than in the *old* suburbs. Oops! It's good to know the facts, because you can think about your business accordingly. If you have been ignoring the suburbs, think about them. Why open a beauty salon in mid-town where the competition is greater when you may have an easier time being the big fish in a smaller market

••••••••••••••••••••••••••••••••••••••••••

> *All our lives we are engaged in the process of accommodating ourselves to our surroundings; living is nothing else than this process of accommodation. When we fail a little, we are stupid. When we flagrantly fail, we are mad. A life will be successful or not, according as the power of accommodation is equal to or unequal to the strain of fusing and adjusting internal and external chances.*
>
> Samuel Butler, *The Way of All Flesh*

## The Bad News Is Good News—If You Are *FLEXIBLE*

Virtually every industry and field has been and will continue to be affected by technological changes. Whether you are in education, mail order, or book publishing, your field will be affected. As Alice said about Wonderland: It takes all the running you can do to stay in the same place.

The good news is that many fields are much easier to enter today than they were in times when industries were more stable. There is room for you if you target properly and stay flexible. If you continue to learn about the field and the areas you are pursuing, you will be able to make changes as the world changes. If your targeted industry or profession is retrenching, it makes sense to investigate some of the growing fields.

.......................................

*Within the next decades education will change more than it has changed since the modern school was created by the printed book over three hundred years ago. An economy in which knowledge is becoming the true capital and the premier wealth-producing resource makes new and stringent demands on the schools for education performance and educational responsibility. . . . How we learn and how we teach are changing drastically and fast—the result, in part, of new theoretical understanding of the learning process, in part of new technology.*

Peter Drucker, *The New Realities*

## Getting More Sophisticated

*Business opportunities are like buses, there's always another one coming.*

Richard Branson, founder of Virgin Enterprises

Whether you are relatively new to the labor force or have been working a while, think past the obvious and think more deeply about the changes that are occurring.

Listed below are a few of the industries business experts project will grow in the near future. Try to discover other areas that may be affected by these or how your own job may be affected by growth in these areas. Each is huge and changing, and can be better defined by your investigating, and can be better defined by your investiga-

tion through networking, as well as Internet and library research.

Here is the list of some of the industries expected to grow:

- Health care and biotech, or anything having to do with them. Health care is considered a sure bet because of the aging population and the advances being made in medical technology.
- Anything high-tech, or the high-tech aspect of whatever field or industry you are in.
- The international aspect of the field/industry you are considering.
- The environmental area; waste management.
- Safety and security (especially since the September 11th attack on the United States). But also the safety of data, such as shredding services, identity theft prevention and recovery services, hosted computer security, data backup, and surveillance cameras.
- Telecommunications, the new media, and global communications (movie studios, TV networks, cable companies, computer companies, consumer-electronics companies, and publishers).
- Education in the broadest sense (as opposed to the traditional classroom), including computer-assisted instruction. (Researchers have found that people who are illiterate learn to read better with computer-assisted instruction than they do in a classroom.) Because all of us will have to keep up-to-date in more areas in order to do our jobs well, technology will play an important part in our continuing education. Further, with America lagging so far behind other countries educationally, both the for-profit and not-for-profit sectors are working hard to revamp our educational system. And with the No Child Left Behind Act on everyone's minds—from

parents to school district officials—it's no wonder. homework help is a hot area, too. Scholastic created Homework Hub, a website designed to help kids—and their busy parents—with things like book reports, math homework, test prep and study skills.

- Alternative means of distributing goods. Instead of retail stores, think not only about direct mail but also about purchasing by TV—or the Internet.
- Anything serving the aging population, both products and services.

In studying the preceding list, think of how you can combine different industries to come up with areas to pursue. For example: Combine the aging population with education, or the aging population with telecommunications, or health care with education, and so on. The more you research, the more sophisticated your thoughts will get.

If you combine education with the new media, you will be thinking like many experts. Students in schools are learning from interactive multimedia presentations on computers—presentations that will be as exciting as computer games and MTV combined, and almost as up-to-date as the morning news (most textbooks are years out of date). Teachers will do what computers cannot do: facilitate the groups, encourage, reinforce learning.

A computer-based approach can be used to train and update the knowledge of the U.S.'s workers: Employees can learn when they have the time and at their own pace, rather than having large numbers of workers leave their jobs to learn in a classroom situation.

When you read predictions that there will be a huge growth in a certain industry, say, home health-care workers, personal and home care aides, and medical assistants, medical secretaries, radiology technologists and technicians, and psychologists, you may think: "I don't want to run any of those businesses." Think more creatively. Companies will have to spring up to supply and train those workers. (Some of the training could

be done on multimedia.) People will be needed to consult to the companies, develop their systems and products to help them run their businesses better. If you read about the tremendous growth in the temporary help business, you *may* run a temporary help business yourself, or decide to compete with that industry by developing a new idea.

Think about the field you are interested in, and how it is being affected by technology. Virtually every job and industry—whether it is publishing, entertainment, manufacturing, or financial services—is being impacted by technology, and by the global marketplace. If you are not aware, you will be blindsided.

·······································

*When there is no vision, the people perish.*

Old Testament, Proverbs 29:18

## Your Age: How Much Longer Do You Want to Work?

*Age puzzles me. I thought it was a quiet time. My seventies were interesting and fairly serene, but my eighties are passionate. I grow more intense as I age.*

Florida Scott Maxwell

Some people think the best age to start your own business is in your mid-twenties—before being saddled with the pressures of a young family. But I started my growth business at age 40; my brother started his growth business at age 55. With the Forty-Year Vision, you will realize that you have the time to start and be successful in a business. And the best news is that entrepreneurs are not forced into retirement as those in corporate America are. We can work as long as we want.

The average life expectancy today in the United States is 29 years longer than it was in 1900. These years have been added to middle age, not old age. You have the time to learn and run a successful business for many, many years. You could have your greatest life accomplishments after the age of 50 or even older. Why give up now?

There's no question that the length of your life has a connection to your career. The more you know now, the better you will be able to plan ahead for your work life. If you follow The Five O'Clock Club's suggestion and make a Forty-Year Vision, or at least a Fifteen-Year Vision, you may live to see every aspect of it come true—even if you're 50 right now.

Culinary expert Julia Child, who died at age 91, is a striking example of those who don't really hit their stride until they are older. She was forced to abandon her first career because she married a fellow civil servant, Paul Child. After several years of searching, she discovered French cooking when her husband was assigned to France as a USIA officer. Starting at about the age of 35, Julia trained as a chef, founded her own cooking school, and worked on a cookbook, *Mastering the Art of French Cooking*. In 1960, when she was almost 50, the couple moved back to the United States, where the book was published. A chance publicity appearance on television led to her famous TV series.

And why not? At age 40, 50, 60, you will find that you are now using everything you have ever learned in your life and bringing it all together. You don't have the pressure of putting the kids through school. You can afford to take risks. Some fields, such as consulting, often favor the older folks. Who wants a twenty-year-old financial advisor?

There is a myth, formed in the dot.com era, that most business start-ups are formed by people in their twenties. Everyone else was considered over the hill. But most of those failed, didn't they? If you are young, you can start a business, but don't exclude yourself simply because of your gray hair.

..........................................

*The trouble with the future is that it usually arrives before we're ready for it.*

Arnold H. Glasow

## Figure It Out

It's your job to figure out how your dream industry or field is being impacted by technology, global competition, and the market in general. Think where you fit into the future. Do research. We are now on the ground floor of many industries, and at an exciting time for those who choose to take advantage of the revolutionary changes that are taking place.

..........................................

*The factory of the future will have only two employees, a man and a dog. The man will be there to feed the dog. The dog will be there to keep the man from touching the equipment.*

Warren Bennis

## Homework:

It's good to go through the process of developing a business idea—even if this is not the business you eventually start. What kind of business idea do you think you want to practice on?

# Case Study: Scott— Targeting the Future

## It's Time to Take Control of Your Own Career

Get in the habit of reading the papers and noticing what news may affect the industry or field you are targeting. Learn about some of the industries of the future.

Even if you already know the kind of business you want to have, do the exercises in the next section. Be sure to include at least the Seven Stories Exercise, Interests, Values, and Fifteen- or Forty-Year Vision. They won't take a long time to do, and they will support your decision, help you to change your mind, or think of something you can truly love.

. . . . . . . . . . . . . . . . . . . . . . . . . . . . .

## Case Study: Scott
## What Should I Be when I Grow Up?

Scott is 38, a lawyer with a varied background. He had worked for the DA's office and a stock exchange, and wrote for a magazine. With his diverse past, he didn't know what to do next.

I know only one way to figure out what a person should be, and it's to use the methodology in this book. So that's what I did with Scott—a shortened version of the exercises.

. . . . . . . . . . . . . . . . . . . . . . . . . . . . .

## Seven Stories Exercise

First, we did the Seven Stories Exercise. I said: "Tell me something you've done that you really enjoyed doing, know you did well, and felt a sense of accomplishment about. It doesn't matter what other people thought, how old you were, whether or not you earned money doing it.

You may want to start with: 'There was the time when I . . .'"

Scott said: "There was the time when I argued my first case before a jury."

I asked him to tell me the details and what he enjoyed about it.

"I liked being independent, I was calling the shots. I had to plan the whole thing myself . . ."

I asked for another story.

Scott said: "I wrote an exposé for a magazine."

I asked Scott to tell me more. He said he enjoyed the same things: being independent, calling the shots, etc. Seemingly, the only time Scott enjoyed a bureaucratic environment was when he broke away from it.

Scott thought that he had a scattered background, and that everything was different. To my mind, those two stories were alike, so I had enough to go on. (If the stories had been in conflict, I would have asked him for as many as seven stories.)

## Values Exercise

"Scott, tell me the things that are important to you." He replied, "Money is important, and independence."

## Interests Exercise

"Scott, what are your interests?" Languages were very important to him; he had command of a few. The international area was central to his interests. Scott's exercise results will serve as a template. He can make sure that his next job will allow him to be independent, to earn the money he wants, to enjoy the international area, and so on. Or he can start his own business.

## Forty-Year Vision

Then I guided him through an abbreviated version of the Forty-Year Vision. I don't know how to help people unless I know where they are heading. If all I know is their past, their future

will be more of the same. We spent only five minutes on this exercise.

I start with the present to get people grounded in the present. If I simply ask: "What do you want to be?" it doesn't work. They have nothing to base it on.

"Tell me what your life is like right now. What is your relationship with your family, however you define family? Where do you live? What is it physically like? What are your hobbies and interests?

How is your health? What do you do for exercise? How would you describe the job you have right now? And tell me anything else you want to about your life today."

Next, I asked Scott to tell me about his life at age 43. Then I asked about his life at age 53. In part, he said: "I am living in the suburbs. I have a wife and four kids. The oldest is sixteen; the youngest is nine. (It is helpful to put down how old your kids are at each stage so you feel yourself getting older.) I have a small consulting firm, with perhaps four employees who do research and support me in what I am doing. I do a lot of business in Europe. Whatever I am doing is 'at the center of the world'—I feel I'm on top of the important things that are happening."

From my point of view, there were no conflicts in the results of his exercises. They all showed him in an independent situation.

Scott seemed to me to be the stereotypical entrepreneur. I do think he should have his own business, but not right now. Having people work for him sounded right because he seemed disorganized. As he himself suggested, one person could keep him in line and clean up after him. His business might have to do with international business, and also with high-tech. He wants to be at the center of what's happening.

Scott needs to *focus* on something that is a growth area and also satisfies his other needs. There are lots of areas that could fulfill him. The danger is that he may spend 20 years never selecting something to focus on. If a person like Scott is always exploring, it may be best to just arbitrarily pick something, because there is no one correct answer. Other people who are in a rut may need to spend more time exploring.

Scott happens to have contacts in the telecommunications industry. If he can get into the telecommunications field, he should try to learn what he can, and develop a business plan while he is there.

Scott now has a vision. He can follow the vision, or not. If he continues to try out every field he comes across, he will be in constant turmoil. He will simply go from job to job, wind up in his sixties with a lot of experiences but no career, and never reach his dream.

It's the same for you. Figure out the things you enjoy doing and also do well. Do your Forty-Year Vision. These exercises will serve as your anchor as well as your guide. You won't get as irritated in your next job, because you'll know what you're getting out of it. You will keep up your research and your knowledge of the field. You will gain the skills you need to go forward.

· · · · · · · · · · · · · · · · · · · · · · · · · · · · · ·

*When I examined myself and my methods of thought, I came to the conclusion that the gift of fantasy has meant more to me than my talent for absorbing positive knowledge.*

Albert Einstein

## The Result of Assessment Is Targets

If you go through an assessment with a career coach or vocational testing center, and do not wind up with a career direction or tentative business possibilities, the assessment has not helped you very much. You must go one more step, and decide what to *do* with this information.

## The Result of Assessment Is Power

The more you know about yourself, the more power you have to envision a career that will suit you. The exercises give you power. People find it hard to believe that I went through a period of about 30 years when I was painfully shy. In graduate school, I was afraid when they took roll because I obsessed about whether I should answer "here" or "present."

When I had to give a presentation, the best I could do was read the key words from my index cards. (Today, my throat is actually hoarse from all the public speaking I do.) I will be forever grateful for the kindness of strangers who told me I did well when I knew I was awful.

The only thing that ultimately saved me was doing the Seven Stories Exercise. When I was little, I led groups of kids in the neighborhood, and I did it well. It gave me strength to know that I was inherently a group leader regardless of how I was behaving now. (I was in my thirties at the time.)

The Seven Stories Exercise grounds you, and the Forty-Year Vision guides you. When people said: "Would you like to lead groups?" I said to myself, "Well, I led groups when I was 10. Maybe I can do it again." The transition was painful, and took many years, but my Seven Stories Exercise kept me going. And my Forty-Year Vision let me know there was plenty of time in which to do it.

· · · · · · · · · · · · · · · · · · · · · · · · · · · · · ·

*I was going to buy a copy of* The Power of Positive Thinking, *and then I thought: What the hell good would that do?*

Ronnie Shakes

# Part Two

. . . . . . . . . . . . . . . . . . . . . . . . . . . . . . . . . . . . . . . . . . . . . . . . . . . . . . . . . .

# Deciding the Kind of Business You Want: Start by Understanding Yourself

# How to Choose Your Business

*If you don't do it excellently, don't do it at all. Because if it's not excellent, it won't be profitable or fun, and if you're not in business for fun or profit, what the hell are you doing there?*

Robert Townsend

This section contains exercises to help you understand yourself better—your strengths and weaknesses, what you enjoy doing and also do well, and how you would like to live your life in the future. Later, you will read case studies showing how others decided whether or not to have a business and what kind of business they should have. You are on the path to coming up with tentative businesses ideas to explore.

Don't expect a business idea to just pop into your head, and don't settle on anything just yet. Selecting the right business is too big a decision to make impulsively, and will require still more thought. As you complete these exercises and read the later chapters, think about the possibilities that might be right for you. Then, compare the various possibilities and decide which you would like to do.

When you both understand yourself better and also begin to have an idea of the world out there, you will start to process new information very differently. Items in the news that you never noticed in the past will now seem to be relevant and ubiquitous.

There are three *basic* choices (there are more) when thinking about having your own business:

- Buy an existing business (including a franchise)
- Start a business, including one that's high growth
- Become a consultant in your own field

And remember, within each category, such as "buying an existing business," there are many industries—from a chemicals business to boat building. Chances are neither chemicals nor boat building is right for you. But knowing what you *don't* want is just as important as knowing what you *do* want.

Don't pick an industry just because it's in a fast-growth area. That thinking didn't help the dot.comers, did it? They all jumped on the bandwagon and were pushed off again a few years later. Pick the business that's right for you for the *long-term*. Yes, there are those who buy businesses for the short-term, build them and sell them at a profit. But that's not the typical small business owner.

Select an industry that **_has room for you_**. Some markets are already over-saturated, such as fast-food chains. Yes, you can make it, but it may be better to pick something where there is less competition.

Pick something that **_suits your style and experience_**. We've had quite a few Club members start their own pharmaceutical companies, but they had already been in that industry for decades. My brother's nano-technology business would not be for me, even if I understood the field. I prefer something more steady and more people-oriented.

Can you **_get passionate about_** the industry? Later, when you read Yadira's story about starting a growth business, you'll see that her first choice would have been a mistake. You have to believe in what you are selling so others will believe in it too.

Still later in this book, after you have selected a tentative business, you will start to develop your business plan. You may be surprised to know that it is worthwhile to develop a rudimentary plan even if you don't actually start that particular business. The process of developing the plan—using our quickie one-hour approach—can help you make up your mind about that business and give you some skill in thinking through a business so you'll be ready to assess the next one more quickly.

In fact, some elements of your first plan may inspire your second plan and make the business you choose even more worthwhile. That's because some of your best ideas will come from *outside* the industry you are targeting. Conduct your research. You'll find that no research is lost.

Now, let's get started understanding *you* better!

......................................

*All truths are easy to understand once they are discovered; the point is to discover them.*

Galileo Galilei

# Exercises to Analyze Your Past and Present: The Seven Stories Exercise

*The direction of change to seek is not in our four dimensions: it is getting deeper into what you are, where you are, like turning up the volume on the amplifier.*

Thaddeus Golas, *Lazy Man's Guide to Enlightenment*

In this exercise, you will examine your accomplishments, looking at your strongest and most enjoyable skills. The core of most coaching exercises is some version of the Seven Stories exercise. A coach may give you lots of tests and exercises, but this one requires *work* on your part and will yield the most important results. An interest or personality test is not enough. There is no easy way. Remember, busy executives take the time to complete this exercise—if it's good enough for them, it's good enough for you.

*Do not skip the Seven Stories Exercise.* It will provide you with important information about yourself for running your business successfully. After you do the exercise, brainstorm about a number of possible businesses. Then research each one to find out what the possibilities are for someone like you.

If you're like most people, you have never taken the time to sort out the things you're good at and also are motivated to accomplish. As a result, you probably don't use these talents as completely or as effectively as you could. Too often, we do things to please someone else or to survive in a job. Then we get stuck in a rut—that is, we're *always* trying to please someone else or *always* trying to survive in a job. We lose sight of what could satisfy us, and work becomes drudgery rather than fun. When we become so enmeshed in survival or in trying to please others, it may be difficult to figure out what we would rather be doing.

When you uncover your motivated skills, you'll be better able to identify jobs that allow you to use them, and recognize other jobs that don't quite fit the bill. *Motivated skills* are patterns that run through our lives. Since they are skills from which we get satisfaction, we'll find ways to do them even if we don't get to do them at work. We still might not know what these skills are—for us, they're just something we do, and we take them for granted.

Tracking down these patterns takes some thought. The payoff is that our motivated skills do not change. They run throughout our lives and indicate what will keep us motivated for the rest of our lives.

Look at Donald Trump. He knows that he enjoys—and is good at—real estate and self-promotion, and that's what he concentrates on. You can identify commonalities in your accomplishments—aspects that you must have that will make you happier and more successful. In my case, for example, whether I was a computer programmer, a chief financial officer or a career coach, I've always found a way to teach others and often ran small groups—even in my childhood!

· · · · · · · · · · · · · · · · · · · · · · · · · · · · · ·

*One's prime is elusive. . . . You must be on the alert to recognize your prime at whatever time of life it may occur.*

Muriel Spark, *The Prime of Miss Jean Brodie*

## The Seven Stories Approach: Background

This technique for identifying what people do well and enjoy doing has its roots in the work of Bernard Haldane, who, in his job with the U.S. government in the 1940s, helped military personnel transition their skills to civilian life. Its overwhelming success in this area won the attention of Harvard Business School where it went on to become a significant part of its Manual for Alumni Placement. Haldane's work is being carried on today all over the world through DependableStrengths.org. They have brought Haldane's method to places as diverse as South Africa and China, to colleges and universities and in their work with young people.

The Seven Stories (or enjoyable accomplishments) approach, now quite common, was taught to me by George Hafner, who used to work for Bernard Haldane.

The exercise is this: Make a list of all the enjoyable accomplishments of your life, those things you enjoyed doing *and also* did well. List at least 25 enjoyable accomplishments from all

parts of your life: work, from your youth, your school years, your early career up to the present. Don't forget volunteer work, your hobbies and your personal life. Other people may have gotten credit or under-appreciated what you did. Or the result may not have been a roaring success. For example, perhaps you were assigned to develop a new product and take it to market. Let's say you worked on a project for two years, loved every minute of it, but it failed in the market. It doesn't matter. What matters is that you enjoyed doing it and did it well.

Examine those episodes that gave you a sense of accomplishment. You are asked to name 25 accomplishments so you will not be too judgmental—just list anything that occurs to you. Don't expect to sit down and think of everything. Expect to think of enjoyable accomplishments over the course of four or five days. Be sure to ask others to help you think of your accomplishments. Most people carry around a piece of paper so they can jot ideas down as they occur to them. When you have 25, select the seven that are most important to you by however you define important. Then rank them: List the most important first, and so on.

Starting with your first story, write a paragraph about each accomplishment. Then find out what your accomplishments have in common. If you are having trouble doing the exercises, ask a friend to help you talk them through. Friends tend to be more objective and will probably point out strengths you never realized.

You will probably be surprised. For example, you may be especially good interacting with people, but it's something you've always done and therefore take for granted. This may be a thread that runs through your life and may be one of your motivated skills. It *may* be that you'll be unhappy in a career that doesn't allow you to deal with people.

When I did the Seven Stories Exercise, one of the first stories I listed was from when I was 10 years old, when I wrote a play to be put on by the kids in the neighborhood. I rehearsed everyone, sold tickets to the adults for two cents apiece, and served cookies and milk with the proceeds. You might say that my direction as a *general manager*—running the whole show, thinking things up, getting everybody working together—was set in the fourth grade. I saw these traits over and over again in each of my stories.

After I saw those threads running through my life, it became easy for me to see the elements I must have in a career to be satisfied. When I would think of business ideas for myself (or when other people made suggestions), I could find out in short order whether the business would address my motivated skills (running small groups, writing books, public speaking, and so on). If it didn't, I wouldn't be as happy as I could be, even though I *may decide to take certain positions as an interim step toward a long-term goal.* The fact is, people won't do as well in the long run in positions that don't satisfy their motivated skills.

Sometimes I don't pay attention to my own motivated skills, and I wind up doing things I regret. For example, in high school I scored the highest in the state in math. I was as surprised as everyone else, but I felt I finally had some direction in my life. I felt I had to use it to do something constructive. When I went to college, I majored in math. I almost flunked because I was bored with it. The fact is that I didn't enjoy math, I was simply good at it.

There are lots of things we're good at, but they may not be the same things we really enjoy. The trick is to find those things we are good at, enjoy doing, and feel a sense of accomplishment from doing.

To sum up: Discovering your motivated skills is the first step in career planning. I was a general manager when I was 10, but I didn't realize it. I'm a general manager now, and I love it. In between, I've done some things that have helped me toward my long-range goals, and other things that have not helped at all.

It is important to realize that the Seven Stories Exercise will *not* tell you exactly which career you should have, but the *elements* to look for in a career that you will find satisfying. You'll have a range to consider, and you'll know the elements you must have to keep you happy. Once you've selected a few business possibilities that might satisfy you, talk to people in those fields to find out if a particular field or industry is really what you want, and the business possibilities for someone with your experience. That's one way to test if your aspirations are realistic.

After you have narrowed your choices down to a few fields with some business possibilities that will satisfy your motivated skills, the next step is to figure out how to get there. That topic will be covered later in this book.

∙∙∙∙∙∙∙∙∙∙∙∙∙∙∙∙∙∙∙∙∙∙∙∙∙∙∙∙∙∙∙∙∙∙∙∙∙∙∙∙∙∙

*. . . be patient toward all that is unsolved in your heart and try to love the questions themselves like locked rooms and like books that are written in a foreign tongue.*

Rainer Maria Rilke, *Letters to a Young Poet*

## A Demonstration of the Seven Stories Exercise

To get clients started, I sometimes walk them through two or three of their achievement stories, and tell them the patterns I see. They can then go off and think of the seven or eight accomplishments they enjoyed the most and also performed well. This final list is ranked and analyzed in depth to get a more accurate picture of the person's motivated skills. I spend the most time analyzing those accomplishments a client sees as most important. Some accomplishments are more obvious than others. But all stories can be analyzed.

Here is Suzanne, as an example: "When I was nine years old, I was living with my three sisters. There was a fire in our house and our cat had hidden under the bed. We were all outside, but I decided to run back in and save the cat. And I did it."

No matter what the story is, I probe a little by asking questions: What was the accomplishment for you? and What about that made you proud? These questions give me a quick fix on the person.

The full exercise is a little more involved than this. Suzanne said at first: "I was proud because I did what I thought was right." I probed a little, and she added: "I had a sense of accomplishment because I was able to make an instant decision under pressure. I was proud because I overcame my fear."

I asked Suzanne for a second story; I wanted to see what patterns might emerge when we put the two together:

"Ten years ago, I was laid off from a large company where I had worked for nine years.

I soon got a job as a secretary in a Wall Street company. I loved the excitement and loved that job. Six weeks later, a position opened up on the trading floor, but I didn't get it at first. I eventually was one of three finalists, and they tried to discourage me from taking the job. I wanted to be given a chance. So I sold myself because I was determined to get that job. I went back for three interviews, said all the right things, and eventually got it."

What was the accomplishment?
What made her proud?

- "I fought to win."
- "I was able to sell myself. I was able to overcome their objections."
- "I was interviewed by three people at once. I amazed myself by saying, 'I know I can do this job.'"
- "I determined who the real decision maker was, and said things that would make him want to hire me."
- "I loved that job—loved the energy, the upness, the fun."

Here it was, 10 years later, and that job still stood out as a highlight in her life. Since then she'd been miserable and bored, and that's why she came to me. Normally after a client tells two stories, we can quickly name the patterns we see in both stories. What were Suzanne's patterns?

Suzanne showed that she was good at making decisions in tense situations—both when saving

the cat and when interviewing for that job. She showed a good intuitive sense (such as when she determined who the decision maker was and how to win him over). She's decisive and likes fast-paced, energetic situations. She likes it when she overcomes her own fears as well as the objections of others.

We needed more than two stories to see if these patterns ran throughout Suzanne's life and to see what other patterns might emerge. After the full exercise, Suzanne felt for sure that she wanted excitement in her career, a sense of urgency—that she wanted to be in a position where she had a chance to be decisive and operate intuitively. Those are the conditions she enjoys and under which she operates the best.

Armed with this information, Suzanne can confidently say that she thrives on excitement, high pressure, and quick decision-making. And, she'll probably make more money than she would in *safe* environments. She can move her life in a different direction—whenever she is ready.

Pay attention to those stories that were most important to you. The elements in these stories may be worth repeating. If none of your enjoyable accomplishments were work related, it may take great courage to eventually move into a field where you will be happier.

People have to be ready to change. Fifteen years ago, when I first examined my own motivated skills, I saw possibilities I was not ready to handle. Although I suffered from extreme shyness, my stories—especially those that occurred when I was young—gave me hope. As I emerged from my shyness, I was eventually able to act on what my stories said was true about me.

People sometimes take immediate steps after learning what their motivated skills are. Or sometimes this new knowledge can work inside them until they are ready to take action—maybe 10 years later. All the while internal changes can be happening, and people can eventually blossom.

*If one advances confidently in the direction
of his dreams, and endeavors to live the life
which he has imagined, he will meet with
success unexpected in common hours.*

Henry David Thoreau

## Motivated Skills—Your Anchor in a Changing World

Your motivated skills are your anchor in a world of uncertainty. The world will change, but your motivated skills remain constant.

Write them down. Save the list. Over the years, refer to them to make sure you are still on target—doing things that you do well and are motivated to do. As you refer to them, they will influence your life. Five years from now, an opportunity may present itself. In reviewing your list, you will have every confidence that this opportunity is right for you. After all, you have been doing these things since you were a child, you know that you enjoy them, and you do them well!

Knowing our patterns gives us a sense of stability and helps us understand what we have done so far. It also gives us the freedom to try new things regardless of risk or of what others may say, because we can be absolutely sure that this is the way we are. Knowing your patterns gives you both security and flexibility—and you need both to cope in this changing world.

Now think about your own stories. Write down everything that occurs to you.

• • • • • • • • • • • • • • • • • • • • • • • • • • • • • •

*The Ugly Duckling was so happy and in some way he was glad that he had experienced so much hardship and misery; for now he could fully appreciate his tremendous luck and the great beauty that greeted him. . . . And he rustled his feathers, held his long neck high, and with deep emotion he said: "I never dreamt of so much happiness, when I was the Ugly Duckling!"*

Hans Christian Andersen, *The Ugly Duckling*

# The Seven Stories Exercise® Worksheet

This exercise is an opportunity to examine the most satisfying experiences of your life and to discover those skills you will want to use as you go forward. You will be looking at the times when you feel you did something particularly well that you also enjoyed doing. Compete this sentence: "There was a time when I . . ." List enjoyable accomplishments from all parts of your life: from your youth, your school years, your early career up to the present. Don't forget volunteer work, your hobbies and your personal life. Other people may have gotten credit or under-appreciated what you did. Or the result may not have been a roaring success. None of that matters. What matters is that you enjoyed doing it and did it well.

List anything that occurs to you, however insignificant. When I did my own Seven Stories Exercise, I remembered the time when I was 10 years old and led a group of kids in the neighborhood, enjoyed it, and did it well.

When you have 25, select the seven that are most important to you by however you define important. Then rank them: List the most important first, and so on. Starting with your first story, write a paragraph about each accomplishment. Then find out what your accomplishments have in common. If you are having trouble doing the exercises, ask a friend to help you talk them through. Friends tend to be more objective and will probably point out strengths you never realized.

## Section I

Briefly outline below *all* the work/personal/life experiences that meet the above definition. Come up with at least 20. We ask for 20 stories so you won't be too selective. Just write down anything that occurs to you, no matter how insignificant it may seem. Complete this sentence, "There was a time when I . . ." You may start with, for example, "Threw a fiftieth birthday party for my father," "Wrote a press release that resulted in extensive media coverage," and "Came in third in the Nassau bike race."

_Don't just write that you enjoy "cooking." That's an activity, not an accomplishment. An accomplishment occurs at a specific time._ You may wind up with *many* cooking accomplishments, for example. But if you simply write "cooking," "writing" or "managing," you will have a hard time thinking of 20 enjoyable accomplishments.

Complete this sentence, "There was a time when I . . ."

1._____

2._____

3._____

4._____

5._____

6._____

7._____

8._____

9._____

10._____

11._____

12. _____

13._____

14._____

15._____

16._____

17._____

18._____

19._____

20._____

21._____

22. _____

23._____

24._____

25._____

## Section II

*Choose the seven experiences from the above* that you enjoyed the most and felt the most sense of accomplishment about. (Be sure to include non-job-related experiences also.) Then *rank them*. Then, for each accomplishment, describe what *you* did. Be specific, listing each step in detail. Use a separate sheet of paper for each.

Here's how you might begin:

Experience #1: Planned product launch that resulted in 450 letters of intent from 1,500 participants.

    a. Worked with president and product managers to discuss product potential and details.

    b. Developed promotional plan.

    c. Conducted five-week direct-mail campaign prior to conference to create aura of excitement about product.

d. Trained all product demonstrators to make sure they each presented product in same way.

e. Had great product booth built; rented best suite to entertain prospects; conducted campaign at conference by having teasers put under everyone's door every day of conference. Most people wanted to come to our booth.

—and so on—

## Analyzing Your Seven Stories

Now it is time to analyze your stories. You are trying to look for the patterns that run through them so that you will know the things you do well that also give you satisfaction. Some of the questions below sound similar. That's okay. They are a catalyst to make you think more deeply about the experience. The questions don't have any hidden psychological significance.

For now, simply go through each story without trying to force it to come out any particular way. Just think hard about yourself. And be as honest as you can.

## Story #1. _____

What was the *accomplishment?* _____

_____

What about it did you *enjoy most?* _____

_____

What did you *do best?* _____

_____

What *motivated you to do this?* _____

_____

What about it *made you proud?* _____

_____

What *prompted you to do this?* _____

_____

What *enjoyable skills did you demonstrate?* _____

_____

## Story #2. _____

The accomplishment? _____

Enjoyed most? _____

Did best? _____

A motivator? _____

Made you proud? _____

Prompted you to do this? _____

Enjoyable skills demonstrated? _____

## Story #3. _____
The accomplishment? _____
Enjoyed most? _____
Did best? _____
A motivator? _____
Made you proud? _____
Prompted you to do this? _____
Enjoyable skills demonstrated? _____

## Story #4. _____
The accomplishment? _____
Enjoyed most? _____
Did best? _____
A motivator? _____
Made you proud? _____
Prompted you to do this? _____
Enjoyable skills demonstrated? _____

## Story #5. _____
The accomplishment? _____
Enjoyed most? _____
Did best? _____
A motivator? _____
Made you proud? _____
Prompted you to do this? _____
Enjoyable skills demonstrated? _____

## Story #6. _____
The accomplishment? _____
Enjoyed most? _____
Did best? _____
A motivator? _____
Made you proud? _____
Prompted you to do this? _____
Enjoyable skills demonstrated? _____

## Story #7. _____
The accomplishment? _____
Enjoyed most? _____
Did best? _____
A motivator? _____
Made you proud? _____
Prompted you to do this? _____
Enjoyable skills demonstrated? _____

*We are here to be excited from youth to old age, to have an insatiable curiosity about the world. . . . We are also here to help others by practicing a friendly attitude. And every person is born for a purpose. Everyone has a God-given potential, in essence, built into them. And if we are to live life to its fullest, we must realize that potential.*

Norman Vincent Peale

## Homework:

Do the Seven Stories Exercise and think about the elements you must have to be happy in your own business.

# Your Current
# Work-Related Values

What is important to you? Your values change as you grow and change, so they need to be reassessed continually. At various stages in your career, you may value money, or leisure time, or independence on the job, or working for something you believe in. See what is important to you *now*. This will help you not be upset if, for instance, a situation provides you with the freedom you wanted, but not the kind of money your friends are making.

Sometimes we are not aware of our own values. It may be that, at this stage of your life, time with your family is most important to you. For some people, money or power is most important, but they may be reluctant to admit it—even to themselves.

Values are the driving force behind what we do. It is important to truthfully understand what we value in order to increase our chances of getting what we want.

Look at the list of values below. Think of each in terms of your overall career objectives. Rate the degree of importance you would assign to each for yourself, using this scale:

1—Not at all important in my choice of job     2—Not very but somewhat important
3—Reasonably important     4—Very important

Add other values that don't appear on the list or substitute wording you're more comfortable with.

| | |
|---|---|
| ____ chance to advance | ____ artistic or other creativity |
| ____ work on frontiers of knowledge | ____ learning |
| ____ have authority (responsibility) | ____ location of workplace |
| ____ help society | ____ tranquility |
| ____ help others | ____ money earned |
| ____ meet challenges | ____ change and variety |
| ____ work for something I believe in | ____ have time for personal life |
| ____ public contact | ____ fast pace |
| ____ enjoyable colleagues | ____ power |
| ____ competition | ____ adventure/risk taking |
| ____ ease (freedom from worry) | ____ prestige |
| ____ influence people | ____ moral fulfillment |
| ____ enjoyable work tasks | ____ recognition from superiors, society, peers |
| ____ work alone | ____ security (stability) |
| ____ be an expert | ____ physical work environment |
| ____ personal growth and development | ____ chance to make impact |
| ____ independence | ____ clear expectations and procedures |

Of those you marked "4," circle the five *most* important to you today:

If forced to compromise on any of these, which one would you give up?

Which one would you be most reluctant to give up?

Describe in 10 or 20 words what you want most in your life and/or career.

*Your health is bound to be affected if, day after day, you say the opposite of what you feel, if you grovel before what you dislike and rejoice at what brings you nothing but misfortune.*

Boris Pasternak, *Dr. Zhivago*

# Other Exercises: Interests, Satisfiers, and Bosses

## Case Study: Laura
## Using Her Special Interests

For many people, interests should stay as interests—things they do on the side. For others, their interests may be a clue to the kind of businesses they should run. Laura had food as her special interest. She had spent her life as a marketing manager in cosmetics, but she assured me that food was very important to her.

We redid her résumé to downplay the cosmetics background. Next, Laura visited a well-known specialty food store. She spoke to the store manager, a junior person, asked about the way the company was organized, and found that there were three partners, one of whom was the president. Laura said to the store manager, "Please give my résumé to the president, and I will call him in a few days." We prepared for her meeting with the president, in which she would find out the company's long-term plans, and so on. At the meeting, he said he wanted to increase revenues from $4 million to $40 million. Laura and I met again to decide how she could help the business grow through her marketing efforts, and to decide what kind of compensation she would want, including equity in the company. She met with the president again, and got the job!

It was the Interests exercise that prompted her to get into that field. Remember, all you need to do is make a list of your interests. Laura simply wrote food. Other people list 20 things. Here is the exercise:

## Interests Exercise

List all the things you really like to do. List anything that makes you feel good and gives you satisfaction. List those areas where you have developed a relatively in-depth knowledge or expertise. For ideas, think back over your day, your week, the seasons of the year, places, people, work, courses, roles, leisure time, family, etc. These areas need not be work related. Think of how you spend your discretionary time.

If you cannot think of what your interests may be, think about the books you read, the magazines you subscribe to, the section of the newspaper you turn to first. Think about the knowledge you've built up simply because you're interested in a particular subject. Think about the volunteer work you do—what are the recurring assignments you tend to get and enjoy? Think about your hobbies—are there one or two you have become so involved in that you have built up a lot of expertise/information in those areas? What are the things you find yourself doing—and enjoying—all the time, things you don't *have* to do?

Your interests may be a clue to what you would like in a business. Rob was a partner in a law firm, but loved everything about wine. He left the law firm to become a partner in a wine company. Most people's interests should stay as interests, but you never know until you think about it.

## Satisfiers and Dissatisfiers Exercise

You have to learn how to *take* orders before you can *give* orders. Simply list every job you have ever had. List what was satisfying and dissatisfying about each job. Some people are surprised to find that they were sometimes most satisfied by the vacation, pay, title, and other perks, but were not satisfied with the job itself.

## Bosses Exercise

Simply examine those bosses you have had a good relationship with and those you have not, and determine what you need in your future relationship with bosses. If you have had a lot of problems with bosses, discuss this with your counselor.

*My illness helped me to see that what was missing in a society is what was missing in me: a little heart, a lot of brotherhood. The 80s were about acquiring wealth, power, prestige. I acquired more . . . than most. But you can acquire all you want and still feel empty. . . . I don't know who will lead us through the 90s, but they must be made to speak to this spiritual vacuum at the heart of American society, this tumor of the soul.*

Lee Atwater, formerly of the Republican National Committee, shortly before he died, *Life* magazine, February 1991

# Your Special Interests

For many people, interests should stay as interests—things they do on the side. For others, their interests may be a clue to the kinds of businesses they should have. Only you can decide whether your interests should become part of your work life.

List all the things you really like to do—anything that makes you feel good and gives you satisfaction. List those areas in which you have developed a relatively in-depth knowledge or expertise. For ideas, think of your day, your week, the seasons of the year, places, people, work, courses, roles, leisure time, friends, family, etc. Think of how you spend your discretionary time.

- Think about the books and magazines you read, the section of the newspaper you turn to first.
- Think about knowledge you've built up simply because you're interested in it.
- Think about the volunteer work you do—what are the recurring assignments you tend to get and enjoy?
- Think about your hobbies—are there one or two you have become so involved in that you have built up a lot of expertise/information in those areas?
- What are the things you find yourself doing all the time and enjoying, even though you don't have to do them?

# Satisfiers and Dissatisfiers in Past Jobs

*Wherever I went, I couldn't help noticing, the place fell apart. Not that I was ever a big enough wheel in the machine to precipitate its destruction on my own. But that they let me—and other drifters like me—in the door at all was an early warning signal. Alarm bells should have rung.*

Michael Lewis, *Liar's Poker*

For each job you have held in the past, describe as fully as possible the factors that made the job especially exciting or rewarding (satisfiers) and those that made the job especially boring or frustrating (dissatisfiers). **_Be as specific as possible_** (See the example below, which shows that sometimes the satisfiers can be the perks, while the dissatisfiers can be the job itself.)

| JOB | SATISFIERS | DISSATISFIERS |
|-----|-----------|---------------|
| VP of Mfg., ABC Co | 1. Status—large office, staff of 23, exec. dining room<br>2. Fringes—four weeks' vacation, travel allowance, time for outside activities. | 1. Manager—cold and aloof, too little structure and feedback, no organizational credibility.<br>2. Limited promotional opportunities—none laterally, only straight line |
| JOB | SATISFIERS | DISSATISFIERS |
|  |  |  |

50

# Your Relationship with Bosses

1. You have to learn how to *take* orders before you can *give* orders. Make a list of all the *bosses* you have ever had in work situations. Use a very broad definition. They don't have to have been *bosses* in the strictest sense of the word. Include bosses from part-time jobs, summer jobs, and even professors with whom you worked closely in your student days.

   _____     _____
   _____     _____
   _____     _____
   _____     _____
   _____     _____

2. Divide the names from above into three lists: those people with whom you had no problems, those with whom you had some problems, and those with whom you had severe problems.

   | NO PROBLEMS | SOME PROBLEMS | SEVERE PROBLEMS |
   |---|---|---|
   | _____ | _____ | _____ |
   | _____ | _____ | _____ |
   | _____ | _____ | _____ |

3. Look for factors that might help explain why you had some problems or severe problems with some bosses and not with others (or why you have never had problems). For example, consider:

   - the type of people involved: age, sex, personality, etc.
   - the structure of your relationship with the people: how much and what type of power they had over you.
   - the broader contexts: the kind of work involved, the type of organizations involved, etc.

   Think about it. Do you see any patterns . . .
   . . . regarding the type of people?

   _____
   _____

   . . . regarding the structure of the relationship?

   _____
   _____

   . . . regarding the contexts?

   _____
   _____

This exercise is based on lectures given by John P. Kotter in his classes in power dynamics at the Harvard Business School.

*Natural talent, intelligence, a wonderful education—none of these guarantees success. Something else is needed: the sensitivity to understand what other people want and the willingness to give it to them. Worldly success depends on pleasing others. No one is going to win fame, recognition, or advancement just because he or she thinks it's deserved. Someone else has to think so too.*

John Luther

# Looking into Your Future

Your motivated abilities tell you the *elements* you need to make you happy, your Values exercise tells you the values that are important to you right now, and the Interests exercise may give you a clue to other fields or industries to explore. But none of them gives you a feel for the *scope* of what may lie ahead.

Dreams and goals can be great driving forces in our lives. We feel satisfied when we are working toward them—even if we never reach them. People who have dreams or goals do better than people who don't.

Setting goals will make a difference in your life, and this makes sense. Every day we make dozens of choices. People with dreams make choices that advance them in the right direction. People without dreams also make choices—but their choices are strictly present oriented, with little thought of the future. When you are aware of your current situation, and you also know where you want to go, a natural tension leads you forward faster.

When you find a believable dream that excites you, don't forget it. In the heat of our day-to-day living, our dreams slip out of our minds. Happy people keep an eye on the future as well as the present.

## Freeing-Up Exercises

Here are a few exercises to inspire you and move you forward, add meaning to your everyday life, and give it some long-term purpose.

It's okay if you never reach your dreams. In fact, it can be better to have some dreams that you will probably never reach, so long as you enjoy the *process* of trying to reach them. For example, a real estate developer may dream of owning all the real estate in Phoenix. He may wind up owning much more than if he did not have that dream. If he enjoys the *process* of acquiring real estate, that's all that matters.

## Exercise #1—Write Your Obituary

*Every now and then I think about my own death, and I think about my own funeral. . . . I ask myself, "What is it that I would want said?" Say I was a drum major for justice; say that I was a drum major for peace; say that I was a drum major for righteousness. All of the other shallow things will not matter . . . I just want to leave a committed life behind.*

Rev. Martin Luther King, Jr.

Rev. Martin Luther King, Jr. knew how he wanted to be remembered. He had a dream, and it drove his life. Write out what you would want the newspapers to say about *you* when you die. Alfred Nobel had a chance to *rewrite* his obituary. The story goes that his cousin, who was also named Alfred, died. The newspapers, hearing of the death of Alfred Nobel, printed the prepared obituary—for the wrong man. Alfred read it the day after his cousin's death. He was upset by what the obituary said because it starkly showed him how he would be remembered: as the well-known inventor of a cheap explosive called dynamite.

Alfred resolved to change his life. Today, he's remembered as the Swedish chemist and inventor who provided for the Nobel Prizes.

Write your obituary as you want to be remembered after your death. Include parts that are *not* related to your job. If you don't like the way your life seems to be headed, change it—just as Alfred Nobel did. Write your own obituary, and *then make a list of the things you need to do to get there.*

## Exercise #2—Invent a Business

If you could have any business in the world, what would it be? Don't worry about the possibility of ever making it happen—make it up! Invent it. Write it out. It may spark you to think of how to create that situation in real life, step by step.

## Exercise #3—If You Had a Million

If you had a million dollars (or maybe 10 million) but still had to work, what would you do?

When I asked myself this question some time ago, I decided I'd like to continue doing what I was doing at work, but would like to write a book on job hunting because I felt I had something to say. I did write that book—and I've gone on to write others!

People often erroneously see a lack of money as a stumbling block to their goals. Think about it: Is there some way you could do what you want without a million dollars? Then do it!

## Exercise #4—Your Fifteen-Year and Forty-Year Visions

Take a look at this very important exercise, which starts on the next page.

# Your Fifteen-Year Vision® and Your Forty-Year Vision®

*In my practice as a psychiatrist, I have found that helping people to develop personal goals has proved to be the most effective way to help them cope with problems.*

Ari Kiev, M.D., *A Strategy for Daily Living*

If you could imagine your ideal life five years from now, what would it be like? How would it be different from the way it is now? If you made new friends during the next five years, what would they be like? Where would you be living? What would your hobbies and interests be? How about 10 years from now? Twenty? Thirty? Forty? Think about it!

Some people feel locked in by their present circumstances. Many say it is too late for them. But a lot can happen in five, 10, 20, 30, or 40 years. Reverend King had a dream. His dream helped all of us, but his dream helped him too. He was living according to a vision (which he thought was God's plan for him). *It gave him a purpose in life.* Most successful people have a vision.

A lot can happen to you over the next few decades—and most of what happens is up to you. If you see the rest of your life as boring, I'm sure you will be right. Some people pick the "sensible" route or the one that fits in with how others see them, rather than the one that is best for them.

On the other hand, you can come up with a few scenarios of how your life could unfold. In that case, you will have to do a lot of thinking and a lot of research to figure out which path makes most sense for you and will make you happiest.

When a person finds a vision that is right, the most common reaction is fear. It is often safer to *wish* a better life than to actually go after it.

I know what that's like. It took me two years of thinking and research to figure out the right path for myself—one that included my motivated abilities (Seven Stories Exercise) as well as the sketchy vision I had for myself. Then it took *10 more years* to finally take the plunge and commit to that path—running The Five O'Clock Club. I was 40 years old when I finally took a baby step in the right direction, and I was terrified.

You may be lucky and find it easy to write out your vision of your future. Or you may be more like me: It may take a while and a lot of hard work. You can speed up the process by reviewing your assessment results with a Five O'Clock Club career coach. He or she will guide you along. Remember, when I was struggling, the country didn't *have* Five O'Clock Club coaches or even these exercises to guide us.

Test your vision and see if that path seems right for you. Plunge in by researching it and meeting with people in the field. If it is what you want, chances are you will find some way to make it happen. If it is not exactly right, you can modify it later—after you have gathered more information and perhaps gotten more experience.

## Start with the Present

Write down, in the present tense, the way your life is right now, and the way you see yourself at each of the time frames listed. *This exercise should take no more than one hour.* Allow your unconscious to tell you what you will be doing in the future. Just quickly comment on each of the questions listed on the following page, and then move on to the next. If you kill yourself off too early (say, at age 60), push it 10 more years to see what would have happened if you had lived. Then push it another 10, just for fun.

When you have finished the exercise, ask yourself how you feel about your entire life as you laid it out in your vision. Some people feel depressed when they see on paper how their lives are going, and they cannot think of a way out. But they feel better when a good friend or a Five O'Clock Club coach helps them think of a better future to work toward. If you don't like your vision, you are allowed to change it—it's your life. Do what you want with it. Pick the kind of life you want.

Start the exercise with the way things are now so you will be realistic about your future.

Now, relax and have a good time going through the years. Don't think too hard. Let's see where you wind up. You have plenty of time to get things done.

●●●●●●●●●●●●●●●●●●●●●●●●●●●●●●●●●●●●●

*There are more things in heaven and earth, Horatio, than are dreamt of in your philosophy.*

William Shakespeare, *Hamlet*

> **The 15-year mark proves to be the most important for most people. It's far enough away from the present to allow you to dream.**

# Your Fifteen- and Forty-Year-Vision Worksheet

1. The year is _____ (current year).
   You are _____ years old right now.

- Tell me what your life is like right now. (Say anything you want about your life as it is now.)
- Who are your friends? What do they do for a living?
- What is your relationship with your family, however you define "family"?
- Are you married? Single? Children? (List ages.)
- Where are you living? What does it look like?
- What are your hobbies and interests?
- What do you do for exercise?
- How is your health?
- How do you take care of your spiritual needs?
- What kind of work are you doing?
- What else would you like to note about your life right now?

Year _____ Your Age _____

_____
_____
_____
_____
_____
_____
_____
_____
_____
_____
_____
_____
_____
_____
_____
_____
_____

Don't worry if you don't like everything about your life right now. Most people do this exercise because they want to improve themselves. They want to *change* something. What do *you* want to change? **Please continue.**

2. The year is _____ (current year + 5). You are _____ years old. (Add 5 to present age.) **Things are going well for you.**

- What is your life like now at this age? (Say anything you want about your life as it is now.)
- Who are your friends? What do they do for a living?
- What is your relationship with your "family"?
- Married? Single? Children? (List their ages now.)
- Where are you living? What does it look like?
- What are your hobbies and interests?
- What do you do for exercise?
- How is your health?
- How do you take care of your spiritual needs?
- What kind of work are you doing?
- What else would you like to note about your life right now?

Year _____ Your Age _____

_____
_____
_____
_____
_____
_____
_____
_____
_____
_____
_____
_____
_____
_____
_____
_____
_____
_____
_____

3. The year is **xxxx** (current year + 15). You are _____ years old. (Current age plus 15.)

- Tell me what your life is like right now. (Say anything you want about your life as it is now.)
- Who are your friends? What do they do for a living?
- What is your relationship with your family, however you define "family"?
- Are you married? Single? Children? (List ages.)
- Where are you living? What does it look like?
- What are your hobbies and interests?
- What do you do for exercise?
- How is your health?
- How do you take care of your spiritual needs?
- What kind of work are you doing?
- What else would you like to note about your life right now?

Year _____ Your Age _____

_____
_____
_____
_____
_____
_____
_____
_____
_____
_____
_____
_____
_____
_____
_____
_____

The 15-year mark is an especially important one. This age is far enough away from the present that people often loosen up a bit. It's so far away that it's not threatening. Imagine *your* ideal life. What is it like? Why were you put here on this earth? What were you meant to do here? What kind of life were you meant to live? Give it a try and see what you come up with. If you can't think of anything now, try it again in a week or so. On the other hand, if you got to the 15-year mark, why not keep going?

4. The year is _____ (current year + **25**). You are _____ years old! (Current age plus 25.)

Year _____ Your Age _____
Using a blank piece of paper, answer all of the questions for this stage of your life.

5. The year is _____ (current year + **35**). You are _____ years old! (Current age plus 35.)

Repeat.

6. The year is _____ (current year + **45**). You are _____ years old! (Current age plus 45.)

Repeat.

7. The year is _____ (current year + **55**). You are _____ years old! (Current age plus 55.) (Keep going—don't die until you are past 80!)

Keep going. How do you feel about your life? You are allowed to change the parts you don't like.

You have plenty of time to get done everything you want to do. Imagine wonderful things for yourself. You have plenty of time. Get rid of any "negative programming." For example, if you imagine yourself having poor health because your parents suffered from poor health, see what you can do about that. If you imagine yourself dying early because that runs in your family, see what would have happened had you lived longer. It's your life—your only one. As they say, "This is the real thing. It's not a dress rehearsal."

# Your Forty-Year Vision® . . . Fifteen Years Is a Good Start

## How to Create Your Future One Step at a Time

*by David Madison, Ph.D.*

When my daughter was a month old, I started writing a daily diary to preserve memories of her growing up. She's now 36 and I haven't missed a day since. Now well past the 13,000-page mark—and with my daughter living in California with her husband and daughter—I sometimes wonder why I continue writing it. But someone once sent me a 10-year-old photo of friends and I was able to find the occasion, the day, and even the hour in the diary. What a triumph! An even bigger triumph: I was able to tell my daughter what she was doing (building a snowman with me) on the day her husband was born.

Whenever I go digging in the old diaries, I am usually astounded: This happened 15 years ago! The clichés turn out to be so true: "It seems like only yesterday," or "Where did the years go?" It's only when we *look ahead* that we feel that the future is so far away. Ten or 15 years out seems impossibly far away, but September 2010 and April 2020 will one day be a reality.

And it is so depressing to find out that people coast along for years—in jobs that they don't *really* like—because they fail to *imagine* in concrete terms: What can my life be like in 2010 or 2020? On a consulting assignment a few years ago, I worked with 17 people who had been downsized by a small bank. As a way of getting them to see the value of the Forty-Year Vision, I asked them what their *dream* careers were. Did they simply want to move to other banks and continue processing financial transactions? Most were emphatic: No! And their aspirations were across

the board: One wanted to get into filmmaking; another, physical therapy; another, the hospitality industry; and yet another wanted to teach ballroom dancing.

But guess what: No one had seriously considered trying to make such career moves because it was easier and safer to drift along in their current jobs, month after month, year after year. Their aspirations were just unfocused dreams that never moved beyond the wouldn't-it-be-nice stage, precisely because they had never made any attempt to *structure* the dream. They had never thought of making serious and realistic plans, and wishing upon a star won't make it happen!

But how is a 15- or 40-year strategy *manageable*? This won't seem nearly so intimidating or scary if you bear five things in mind:

1. Don't start with the most distant point on the calendar! We're the first to admit that possibilities a few decades from now would be too much to wrap your mind around—at first. The initial notch in the Forty-Year Vision is the five-year mark. And that's totally realistic: What do you want your life and career to be like in five short years? That's only 60 months out. And 10 years out won't seem so farfetched or daunting if the five-year mark has been given some form and content.

On the way to your Forty-Year Vision, make the Fifteen-Year Vision your primary stopping point. This benchmark allows you to do some really creative thinking and wondering. You can develop scenarios that are especially meaningful. Try this test: think *back* 15 years. In other words, were there steps you could have taken in the 1990s that would have shaped your life and career for the better today? The answer is probably "yes." There's a lesson here about your future!

2. Don't be fooled by the simple wisdom that *we can't predict the future*. Of course we can't—but that really doesn't have any bearing on *trying* to make the future turn out on your terms. Not being able to predict the future doesn't stop you from having kids, buying a 20-year CD to pay for college, or committing to a mortgage. Why let it stop you from seriously plotting your career? Five O'Clock Club career coaches try to overcome the skepticism or even ridicule that some people express when they hear about the Forty-Year Vision. We commonly hear, "I have trouble planning next week. Forty years? Give me a break!" But we're not asking you to predict 40 years out, much less *guess* the distant future: This is not supposed to be an exercise in crystal-ball gazing. The career coach who urges you to do the Forty-Year Vision is asking you to imagine, fantasize, strategize, as the first steps in trying to create the future on your terms.

There once was a commercial for public television that included the words "If it can be imagined, it can be done." Of course that's TV hype, because it's very true that not *everything* that can be imagined *can* be done. But it's also a fact that nothing will be done *unless* it is imagined. Goals are born in the imagination, and a Fifteen- or Forty-Year Vision is a tool to help get the imagination firing at maximum capacity—and to give you the motivation to do the necessary planning and strategizing.

Don't despair because you're *too old*. Sitting down at the kitchen table on your 50th birthday to write a Forty-Year Vision may strike most people as silly. But don't forget the lament of one senior citizen: "If I had known I was going to live so long, I would have taken better care of myself." Precisely because we *can't* predict the future, the Forty-Year Vision is a good idea. If you do make it to 85 or 90 or beyond, don't you want those years to be fruitful, exciting, and purposeful? We're living longer, and the age-65 cutoff for productive years has become meaningless! So the 50th or even 60th birthday is as good a time as any to let yourself imagine and plan for a long future—at least give the Fifteen-Year Vision a try!

3. Remember that the Forty-Year Vision is always subject to change. You're not chained down to anything; you're the one in charge. Your vision for the future is a pact you make with yourself. Your career coach will be the first to remind you that it is never written in stone—although having it *in writing* can be a very powerful tool and guide. As you grow and learn more about yourself and the realistic options you face, the Forty-Year Vision evolves too. Course corrections or even radical changes are part of the process.

4. The Forty-Year Vision is meant to be fun: It's not a term paper; it's not a test. Sure, it's serious business, but let your mind go and imagine all the possibilities you can create. As time goes by and events unfold, you'll need to do reality checks, but try to catch the excitement of imagining all the things you can accomplish.

Whether you choose to walk down memory lane with a diary or home movies, photo albums or scrap books, you know that nothing you do now can change what happened 10 years ago. But your daily routine in 10 or 15 years does depend largely on the visions and strategies you develop now. So give the Forty-Year Vision the benefit of the doubt. It could change your life.

*Steve Jobs,* the legendary founder of Apple Computer, has had his share of ups and downs, but he is known for staying the course. After he was ousted from Apple (by John Sculley, whom he brought in to head the company), Jobs labored for seven years on his new company, NeXT Computers, and then founded Pixar, which made him a billionaire. Later, he sold NeXT to Apple, while serving as a consultant to that company. What is the secret of his success?

· · · · · · · · · · · · · · · · · · · · · · · · · · · · · · ·

*There are very few people who have a vision and stick to it. Steve (Jobs) does.*

Keith Benjamin, quoted in *Success*, July/August, 1996

*You need a lot more than vision—you need stubbornness, tenacity, belief, and patience to stay the course.*

Edwin Pixar, cofounder of Pixar, on Steve Jobs as quoted in *The New York Times Magazine,* January 12,1997

*Asked what he wants to pass on to his children, Jobs answers: "Just to try to be as good a father to them as my father was to me. I think about that every day of my life."*

Steve Lohr, "Creating Jobs," *The New York Times Magazine,* ibid. (Steve Jobs was adopted)

David Madison is the Director of The Five O'Clock Club Guild of Career Coaches.

# The Ideal Scene

*Every great personal victory was preceded
by a personal goal or dream.*

Dennis R. Webb

This is another exercise to help you imagine your future. Relax for a while. Arrange a time when you will not be distracted. Set aside about an hour. Sit by yourself, have a cup of tea, take out a pad of paper, and imagine yourself 5, 10, 15, or 20 years from now—at a phase in your life when all is going well. Just pick one of these time frames.

Imagine in very general terms the kind of life you were meant to have. Start writing—it's important to write it down, rather than just thinking about it.

What is your ideal life like? Describe a typical day. What do you do when you get up in the morning? Where are you living? Who are your friends?

If you are working, what is it like there? What kind of people do you work with? How do they dress? What kind of work are they doing? What is the atmosphere (relaxed? frantic?)? What is your role in all of this? Describe it in greater and greater detail.

In addition to describing your work situation, think about the other parts of your life. Remember: we each have 24 hours a day. How do you want to spend your 24 hours? Where are you living? What do you do for exercise? How is your health? What is your social life like? Your family life? What are your hobbies and interests? What do you do for spiritual nourishment? What are you contributing to the world? Describe all of these in as much detail as possible. But don't worry if you are not able to identify seemingly important things, such as the city in which you are living, and the field in which you are working.

Keep on writing—include as many details as you can—and develop a good feel for that life. Work on your Ideal Scene for a while, take a break, and then go back and write some more. Change the parts you don't like, and include all the things you really enjoy doing or see yourself doing at this imaginary time in the future.

........................................

*For whatever we do, even whatever we do not do prevents us from doing the opposite. Acts demolish their alternatives, that is the paradox. So that life is a matter of choices, each one final and of little consequence, like dropping stones into the sea. We had children, he thought; we can never be childless. We were moderate, we will never know what it is to spill out our lives . . .*

James Salter, *Light Years*

## Case Study: Max
## Identifying His Future Career

Max, age 40, is a lawyer. A temporary placement firm sends him on assignments to various organizations. He imagined working in a suburban office of six casually dressed people who were on the phone all day talking excitedly to people all over the world. He had a partner in this business. His own role was one of making contacts with prospective customers. He also saw himself writing about the topic they were engaged in, and becoming relatively well-known within their small segment of the industry.

Max's Ideal Scene may seem general, but it contains a lot of information. It appears that he would like to be in his own small but hectic business, operating on an international level. It would be a niche business where he could develop an expertise and become known to his small marketplace.

The international element was strong in this exercise. It was also evident in his Seven Stories Exercise and his Forty-Year Vision. It was clear that an international focus had to be central in his future.

## You Can Develop Multiple Scenarios for Your Future

If you simply do the exercise up to this point, you will have done more than most people. You will have developed one scenario for your future. Some people develop multiple scenarios and think about the various possible futures they could have. Then they decide which they would like best, and which they think is doable.

It all starts with describing an Ideal Scene, but it takes a lot more than that. Writing down the scene makes it more serious, and is the start of a more concrete vision. The written vision and the plan are a lot of work, so you can see why most people do not develop visions—and therefore may tend to drift. But those who write down their visions usually find that they have a lot of fun doing it, and those who keep going realize that their future is, in large part, up to them.

Some people become less self-conscious and braver when they think not of what *they* would like to do, but what they think God has in mind for them. They try to discern God's plan for them, and it is this that motivates and inspires them. Whatever technique or inspiration you use to develop your vision, you will be better off for having done it.

•••••••••••••••••••••••••••••••

*Difficulty need not foreshadow despair or defeat. Rather achievement can be all the more satisfying because of obstacles surmounted.*

William Hastie, *Grace under Pressure*

## The Next Step: Define It Better and Research It

Some people are more ambitious, and want to go on to the next step: They want to flesh out their vision and then test it against reality. In Max's case, he had to figure out what kind of international business he could go into that would rely on his skills and support his values. He came up with a few ideas that excited him. Now he needs to investigate the potential for the various ideas, come up with a plan, develop new skills in the areas where he may be lacking, and take other steps toward fulfilling that vision.

You too will need to flesh out your bare-bones idea and then check it against reality. But be aware that other people will almost always tell you that it's not doable. Conduct enough research so that you can decide for yourself.

Then, if you are serious about achieving the kind of life that you have envisioned, think of what you need to do to succeed. Take a few little steps immediately to help you advance toward your goal.

•••••••••••••••••••••••••••••••

*. . . [I]n my foolishness and crude want of learning, everything I didn't know seemed like a promise.*

Ethan Canin, *Emperor of the Air*

## Encountering Roadblocks

Remember that this is not a sprint; it is a long-distance run. Do not become discouraged the first time you venture out. You will come up against lots of roadblocks along the way. That's life. Say to yourself, "Isn't this interesting? Another roadblock. I'll take a short breather (and perhaps even allow myself to feel a tingle of discouragement for a little while) and then I'll think of how I can get around this barrier."

Ask yourself what you have learned from the experience, because these experiences are here to teach us something. "What is the lesson for me in this setback?" And then get moving again.

*What we do is nothing but a drop in the ocean; but if we didn't do it, the ocean would be one drop less.*

Mother Teresa

---

From ***The Art of the Long View*** by Peter Schwartz

In order to make effective decisions, you must articulate them to begin with. Consider, for example, the choice of a career in biotechnology. A scenario-planner would tackle the decision differently. It depends, he or she might argue, on another set of questions: What is the future of the biotechnology industry? (That in turn depends on:) What is the path of development in the biotech industry? (Moreover:) What skills will have enduring value? (And:) Where will be a good place to begin? The hardest questions will be the most important. What is it that interests you about biotechnology in the first place? What sorts of things about yourself might lead you to make a decision with poor results? What could lead you to change your mind? Scenarios are not predictions. It is simply not possible to predict the future with certainty. For individuals and small businesses, scenarios are a way to help develop their own gut feeling and assure that they have been comprehensive, both realistic and imaginative, in covering all important bases. If you look at yourself on the level of historical time, as a tiny but influential part of a century-long process, then at least you can begin to know your own address. You can begin to sense the greater pattern, and feel where you are within it, and your acts take on meaning.

Michael Ventura, quoted by P. Schwartz

## My Forty-Year Vision

My own Ideal Scene evolved from the Forty-Year Vision I did 20 years ago. I imagined myself at age 80 in a beautiful living space with a housekeeper. I had a strong visual image of someone from the community coming to the door to ask my advice. What this *vision* meant to me was that I had lived my life in such a way that I had had a great impact on the community—people were asking my advice even when I was old. However, I wasn't poverty stricken because of my devotion to the community.

In my Forty-Year Vision I hadn't yet thought of The Five O'Clock Club or even considered a life in career coaching. But the image that came to me, and which I later developed, served as a template for my ideas and my research. My Seven Stories Exercise told me I had better be working with groups, and perhaps writing and lecturing. My Forty-Year Vision eliminated other interests of mine that would not have helped the community as much as career coaching.

It took many years to develop the concept and the focus of The Five O'Clock Club. For years, I continually used the Seven Stories Exercise and the Forty-Year Vision as my template. If an idea fit in with my vision and abilities, I considered it. If an idea didn't fit, I rejected it. I spent many long hours doing library and other research to select the field I wanted to be in. All of this finally evolved into the concept of The Five O'Clock Club.

As you can see, the Forty-Year Vision is simply a vision of your future. By studying it, along with the Ideal Scene, you can get at unconscious desires you may have. Making your desires conscious increases your chances of being able to do something about them.

First, write out your Ideal Scene. Then in the next section, follow Yadira step by step as she uncovers her dream.

*He was, after all, a good father—that is to say, an ineffective man. Real goodness was different, it was irresistible, murderous, it had victims like any other aggression; in short, it conquered.*

James Salter, *Light Years*

# The Ideal Scene Worksheet

Imagine yourself 5,10,15, or 20 years from now—at a phase in your life when all is going well. Just pick one of these time frames. Imagine in very general terms the kind of life you were meant to have. Start writing—it's important to write it down, rather than just think about it.

What is your ideal life like? Describe a typical day. _____
_____
_____
_____
_____
_____

What do you do when you get up in the morning? Where are you living? _____
_____
_____
_____
_____

Who are your friends? _____
_____
_____

If you are working, what is it like there? _____
_____
_____

What kind of people do you work with? How do they dress? _____
_____

What kind of work are they doing? _____
_____

What is the atmosphere (relaxed or frantic)? _____
_____
_____

What is your role in all of this? _____
_____
_____

Use another sheet of paper to describe it in greater and greater detail.

In addition to describing your work situation, think about the other parts of your life. How do you want to spend your 24 hours?

Where are you living? _____
_____

What do you do for exercise? _____
_____

How is your health? _____
_____

What is your social life like? _____
_____

Your family life? _____
_____

What are your hobbies and interests? _____
_____

What do you do for spiritual nourishment? _____
_____

What are you contributing to the world? _____
_____

Describe all of these in as much detail as possible. But don't worry if you are not able to identify seemingly important things, such as the city in which you are living, and the field in which you are working.

Keep on writing—include as many details as you can—and develop a good feel for that life. Work on your Ideal Scene for a while, take a break, and then go back and write some more. Change the parts you don't like, and include all the things you really enjoy doing or see yourself doing at this imaginary time in the future. _____
_____
_____
_____
_____
_____

# My Ideal Business

*Human . . . life is a succession of choices, which every conscious human being has to make every moment. At times these choices are of decisive importance; and the very quality of these choices will often reveal that person's character and decide his fate. But that fate is by no means prescribed: for he may go beyond his inclinations, inherited as well as acquired ones. The decision and the responsibility is his: for he is a free moral agent, responsible for his actions.*

John Lukacs, *A History of the Cold War*

Throughout this book, you have been actively planning, identifying action steps, determining good-fit work environments, and analyzing the appropriateness of career decisions. Your ultimate goal is to develop a rudimentary business plan on which you can begin taking action immediately.

Right now, you will do a simple exercise that will help you picture yourself in your Ideal Business. Then you will be able to identify some of the strategies you can use to get there.

. . . . . . . . . . . . . . . . . . . . . . . . . . . . . . . . . .

*Choose a job you love, and you will never have to work a day in your life.*

Confucius

## Describing Your Ideal Business

A visualization exercise will help you define your ideal business in specific detail. It only requires you to use your thinking and visualizing skills to complete it. This can be a business in its ideal state in its ideal state, or a fictitious business. At this point, you should not be concerned about whether or not this business appears to be realistic or feasible.

Creative visualization is a technique many people use to visualize clearly and specifically the results they want. Research has shown that the more clarity you have around what you are trying to achieve, the more likely you are to achieve it.

In sports, for example, many star athletes have used this technique with great success. Before and during the match, a tennis player pictures himself or herself successfully executing each stroke. Before the race, a slalom skier pictures every twist and turn in the course and exactly how he or she will negotiate each one. Previewing the action in detail, like running a movie in their minds, helps these athletes to achieve far better results than they would be able to achieve otherwise.

But sports is only one area where this technique is effective. You can use it in any context to set yourself up for success.

For example, what if you will soon be attending a meeting, and you feel a little uncomfortable about it. You can preview the meeting in your mind. Imagine the room that you will be in. Think of the people who will be sitting around the table. Who will be there? What are they likely to say? What do you think their key issues will be that have anything to do with you? What is your opinion of those issues?

How are you dressed for this meeting? How do you sit? Perhaps someone brings up a project that you have been working on. What would you say about your project in this meeting? Imagine yourself talking about your project.

If you didn't like the way you spoke about your project in your own mind, replay it and try again. Perhaps you need to informally meet with some of the attendees ahead of time to get a better feel for what may happen in the meeting, and then you can visualize the meeting again—but with more information.

You can use visualization for everything that may come up. You can visualize the next step you plan to take in your project, and the informal meetings you may have. If you have been reluctant to tackle a certain problem, such as working at a computer, you can visualize yourself using certain computer software.

You can use visualization now to start to imagine your own future. There are a couple of ways you can go about this.

You can work with your Career Buddy. Your Career Buddy can slowly read the questions to you while you imagine your Ideal Business, and then you can do the same for your Career Buddy.

Or you can imagine your future all by yourself. You can't rush this exercise. Instead, arrange a time when you will not be distracted. Set aside about half an hour. Relax for a while. First, you'll want to sit comfortably by yourself, and eliminate distractions. Take out your notebook.

You'll think about a series of questions. Let the answers come to you and picture the results silently as opposed to giving your responses aloud. At the end of the exercise, you can jot down your answers in this manual. When you are ready, start by getting very comfortable. Now imagine the following:

You see yourself one or two years from now—or further if you want. Some people find it more comfortable to imagine themselves 5 or even 15 years from now because they may want to imagine something very different from what they are doing now. Making big changes takes time, and you want to give yourself the time it really takes to make progress in your career. Very little that is significant happens quickly.

So here you are—1, 2, 5, 10, or even 15 years from now. You are in your ideal business. Everything is going very well. You've managed your business in ways that have brought you personal and professional satisfaction, in terms of what you are doing, with whom, where, and how.

Take a long time to imagine your ideal business, and take a long time to answer the questions below. Do not rush. Make the image as realistic as possible for yourself.

- What do you see?
- How do you feel?
- What are you saying?
- How do you talk about yourself in this ideal business?
- What has happened in your business?
- What are the signs that you are successful?
- In achieving this, what was the first thing you did?
- Who did you use as resources in achieving your goal?
- When did you contact these resources?
- What was the hardest lesson you learned?
- What was the best lesson you learned?

Now, without speaking to anyone, fill in the worksheet Describing Your Ideal Business. Jot down your answers to the questions asked above in as much detail as you can remember. Write and write in your notebook. The greater the detail of your description, the more firmly the scene can remain implanted in your mind.

........................................

*Life is an end in itself, and the only question as to whether it is worth living is whether you have had enough of it.*

Oliver Wendell Holmes

# Describing Your Ideal Business Worksheet

Thinking back over what you just visualized, answer the following questions as specifically as possible in order to describe your ideal work outcomes. Your answers will help you determine how you will know when you have achieved your goals.

What has happened in your business? _____
_____

What are the signs that you are successful? _____
_____

Looking around you, what do you see? _____
_____

What are you saying? _____
_____

How do you feel? _____
_____

How do you talk about yourself? _____
_____

What was the first step you took? _____
_____

Who did you use as resources in achieving this goal? _____
_____

When did you contact them? _____
_____

What was the hardest lesson you learned in achieving your outcome? _____
_____

What was the best lesson you learned? _____
_____

Even if you did not work with your Career Buddy on this, the two of you may want to discuss these results. Spend some time describing your ideal business and how you got there.

If you are not satisfied right now with your description of your ideal business, that's okay. Some people feel locked in by their present circumstances. Others simply have a hard time using visualization. Try it again in a few days, and see what you come up with. Or ask your Career Buddy to help you. If that still doesn't work, you may have to meet with a career coach.

Visualization can be a highly effective technique for creating a picture of what you want in your business. Once you have begun to see it in your mind's eye, a goal becomes much easier to realize. Knowing what you want sets the stage for achieving it.

......................................

*Life can only be understood backwards; but it must be lived forwards.*

Kierkegaard

# Your Ideal Business Environment

*Dear sir, be patient toward all that is unsolved in your heart and try to love the **questions themselves** like locked rooms and like books that are written in a very foreign tongue. Do not now seek the answers, which cannot be given you because you would not be able to live them. And the point is, to live everything. Live the questions now. Perhaps you will then gradually, without noticing it, live along some distant day into the answer. Perhaps you do carry within yourself the possibility of shaping and forming as a particularly happy and pure way of living; train yourself to it—but take whatever comes with trust, and if only it comes out of your own will, out of some need of your inmost being, take it upon yourself and hate nothing.*

Rainer Maria Rilke

Most of us occasionally think about what would be ideal for us in terms of lifestyle and work environment. The problem is, we may dream about that environment and do nothing to create it!

A motivating work environment can contribute greatly to business effectiveness and career satisfaction. So your next step will be to focus on identifying the work environment where you will be most productive and satisfied. That means getting even more specific about the situation that is ideal for you. Below are some elements you would need to consider in creating your ideal work environment. You will be asked to consider these elements as you complete the worksheet starting on the next page.

*Physical surroundings/location*—What does this environment look and feel like? Are you in an office or moving from place to place? Is it busy or quiet? Are you working primarily alone or surrounded by people?

*People*—What kinds of people are you working with? Are they energetic, quiet, creative, highly structured? Do you interact with many people or a few?

*Activities*—What kinds of activities are you engaged in? Are you working primarily with other people, with equipment, or with information? Are you a manager or an individual contributor?

*Style*—What type of work, communications, and management styles are prevalent? Are people formal or informal? How do they communicate with each other? How do they dress?

*Recognition and rewards*—What types of recognition do you receive? Do you get frequent recognition/acknowledgment from customers/peers? How are you rewarded for good performance?

A little while ago, you pictured yourself in your ideal business. Now, once again, imagine yourself in your ideal business some time in the future. See how many specifics you can come up with about the environment of that business. Complete the My Ideal Work Environment worksheet on the following pages, which looks at the five elements just presented.

Then talk to your Career Buddy. Take five minutes apiece to describe your ideal work environments to each other. Use the notes you took in this workbook, but elaborate even further. Your objective is to make your description as real as possible for your Buddy. Your Buddy, when listening to you, should ask you questions to help you make the picture clear for yourself. And you should do the same for your partner. When working with your Buddy, make sure each of you is focusing on your ideal environment and not your current environment. You should each be as specific as you can.

Assess what is needed to change your present work environment to make it an ideal work environment. If this change is within your control, what can you do about it? If the change is not within your control, remember that your response to the situation is always within your control.

Don't forget what we said earlier about visualizing the results you want to create. The more specific you are about the results you want, the more you are setting yourself up to achieve them.

# My Ideal Business Environment Worksheet

Now that you have identified your ideal business, the next step is to think about the specific elements that make up your ideal work environment. Review the list of questions in each category and jot down your thoughts in the spaces provided.

## Physical Surroundings/Location:

- Are you in an office or are you moving from one place to another?
- If you are in an office, describe its appearance. How is it furnished?
- Is it a formal or an informal environment?
- Are there distractions or is it quiet?
- Do you have a place you can go to relax, do necessary paperwork, talk with your coworkers?
- Are the processes computerized for control?
- Are you isolated or surrounded by people
- How do you get to work—bus, train, car, bicycle, car pool, walk?

## People:

- What kind of people do you work with (e.g., creative, energetic, technical, or mechanical)?
- Do you prefer to work with many people or a few?
- Do you socialize with your colleagues outside the work environment?

## Activities:

- Are you working with other people, with equipment, or with information?
- How many people are you managing or directing?
- Are you reading reports?
- Do you attend meetings regularly?
- Are you communicating with others?
- Are you responsible for complete tasks? Or are you responsible for a piece of a task?
- What kinds of activities are most rewarding? Least rewarding?
- Do you attend meetings of external professional organizations?
- How much do you travel?
- Are you a decision maker?
- How much freedom do you have to carry out your responsibilities?

## Style:

- Are people formal or informal in how they relate to each other?
- What type of management style is typical?
- Do people prefer to communicate mainly through talking or through written communication?
- What are people wearing?

## Recognition/Rewards:

- What types of recognition do you receive?
- How are you rewarded?
- Are monetary rewards based on individual or team performance?
- What are your working hours?
- Do you have flexible working hours?

*We live in an age when art and the things of the spirit come last. The truth still holds, however, that through dedication and devotion one achieves another kind of victory. I mean the ability to overcome one's problems and meet them head on. "Serve life and you will be sustained." That is a truth which reveals itself at every turn in the road. I speak with inner conviction because I have been through the struggle. What I am trying to emphasize is that, whatever the nature of the problem, it can only be tackled creatively. There is no book of "openings," as in chess lore, to be studied. To find an opening one has to make a breach in the wall—and the wall is almost always in one's own mind. If you have the vision and the urge to undertake great tasks, then you will discover in yourself the virtues and the capabilities required for their accomplishment. When everything fails, pray! Perhaps only when you have come to the end of your resources will the light dawn. It is only when we admit our limitations that we find there are no limitations.*

Henry Miller, *Big Sur and the Oranges of Hieronymous Bosch*

# Brainstorming Possible Businesses

*But when the family continued to struggle, and when Steve Ross was a teenager, he was summoned to his father's deathbed to learn that his sole inheritance consisted of this advice: There are those who work all day, those who dream all day, and those who spend an hour dreaming before setting to work to fulfill those dreams. "Go into the third category," his father said, "because there's virtually no competition."*

Obituary of Steven J. Ross, creator of Time Warner, *The New York Times*, December 21, 1992

Use the Brainstorming Possible Businesses worksheet to help you brainstorm possible businesses that you can then explore.

1. **_Across the top of the page_**, list the following elements as they apply to you. Use as many columns as you need for each category.

   - Your basic personality
   - Interests
   - Values
   - Specialized skills
   - From the Seven Stories Exercise:
   - the role you played
   - the environment in which you worked
   - the various subject matters in your stories
   - Long-range goals
   - Education
   - Work experience
   - Areas of expertise

Here is one person's list of column headings across the top:

- Personality: *outgoing*
- Interests: *environment, computers, world travel* (three different interests—takes three columns)
- Values: *decent earnings* so I can support a family
- Specialized Skills: *use of PC* From the Seven Stories Exercise:
- being *part of a research group*
- enjoy Third World countries (takes two columns)
- Goals from the Forty-Year Vision: *head up not-for-profit organization*
- Education: *masters in public policy*
- Work Experience: *seven years' marketing experience.*

This takes a total of 11 columns across the top.

*CHARLEY: Yeah. He was a happy man with a batch of cement.*
*LINDA: He was so wonderful with his hands.*
*BIFF: He had the wrong dreams. All, all, wrong.*
*HAPPY (almost ready to fight Biff): Don't say that!*
*BIFF: He never knew who he was.*

Arthur Miller, Death of a Salesman

2. **_Down the side of the page_**, *list possible businesses, fields, or functions* that rely on one or more of these elements. For example, combine marketing with environment, or computers with research and Third World countries.

At this point, do not eliminate anything. Write down whatever ideas occur to you. Ask your friends and family. Do library research and talk to lots of people. Open your eyes and your mind when you read or walk down the street. Be observant and generate lots of ideas. Write down whatever anyone suggests. A particular suggestion may not be exactly right for you, but may help you think of other things that *are* right.

3. *Analyze each business possibility.* Check off across the page the elements that apply to the first business. For example, if the business fits your basic personality, put a checkmark in that column. If it uses your education or relies on your work experience, put checkmarks in those columns. If it fits in with your long-range goals, put a checkmark there.

Do the same for every business listed in the left column.

· · · · · · · · · · · · · · · · · · · · · · · · · · · · · · ·

*It is never too late to be what you might have been.*

George Eliot

4. *Add up the checkmarks for each business, and write the total in the right-hand column.* Any business that relies on only one or two elements is likely to take many years of learning and preparation. Pay attention to the ones with the most check-marks. Certain elements are more important to you than others, so you must weight those more heavily. In fact, some elements probably must be present so you will be satisfied, such as a business that meshes with your values.

Those businesses that seem to satisfy your most important elements are the ones you will list as some of the targets to explore on the Preliminary Business Investigation worksheet. Also list positions and/or businesses that would be logical next steps for you in light of your background.

*You must have long-range goals to keep you from being frustrated by short-range failures.*

Charles C. Noble, major general

## *Case Study: Agnes* Broadening Her Targets

Agnes has been a marketing/merchandising/promotion executive in the fashion, retail, and banking industries. Her only love was retail, and her dream job was working for one specific, famous fashion house. Perhaps she could actually get a job with that fashion house, but what kind of business could she have after that? The retail and fashion industries were both retrenching at the time of her search, although she could probably get a job in one of them. She needed more targets, and preferably some targets in growing industries so she would have a more reasonable business concept.

In addition to the retail and fashion industries, what other industries could Agnes consider? In the banking industry, where she had been for only three years, some of the products she promoted had been computerized. In combining *computers* with *retail,* we came up with *computerized shopping,* a new field that was threatening the retail industry. Computerized shopping and related areas were good fields for Agnes to investigate. What about something having to do with debit cards and credit cards or Prodigy—all computer-based systems aimed at retail? Or what about selling herself as a consultant to banks that were handling the bankrupt retail companies that she was so familiar with? We came up with 20 areas to explore. Agnes's next step is to conduct a Preliminary Business Investigation (which you will read about soon) to determine which fields may be worth pursuing in that they hold some interest for her and there is some possibility of having a successful business. At this point she has exciting possibilities lined up—with lots to explore.

· · · · · · · · · · · · · · · · · · · · · · · · · · · · · · ·

*I've got peace like a river ina my soul.*

African-American spiritual

# Brainstorming Possible
# Businesses Worksheet

| Assessment Results ⟶ | | | | | | | | | | | | | | | | Total Check-marks Across |
|---|---|---|---|---|---|---|---|---|---|---|---|---|---|---|---|---|
| Possible Businesses | | | | | | | | | | | | | | | | |
| | | | | | | | | | | | | | | | | |
| | | | | | | | | | | | | | | | | |
| | | | | | | | | | | | | | | | | |
| | | | | | | | | | | | | | | | | |
| | | | | | | | | | | | | | | | | |
| | | | | | | | | | | | | | | | | |
| | | | | | | | | | | | | | | | | |
| | | | | | | | | | | | | | | | | |
| | | | | | | | | | | | | | | | | |
| | | | | | | | | | | | | | | | | |
| | | | | | | | | | | | | | | | | |
| | | | | | | | | | | | | | | | | |
| | | | | | | | | | | | | | | | | |
| | | | | | | | | | | | | | | | | |
| | | | | | | | | | | | | | | | | |
| | | | | | | | | | | | | | | | | |
| | | | | | | | | | | | | | | | | |
| | | | | | | | | | | | | | | | | |
| | | | | | | | | | | | | | | | | |

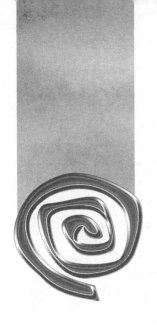

# Case Study: Chiron Finding a Future

*Growing up means eliminating what doesn't work for you.*

Jan Halper, Ph.D., *Quiet Desperation—The Truth about Successful Men*

Chiron is worn out. He is 45 years old, and has had lots of different jobs in his life. Getting jobs has never been a problem. He has just gotten another one, and is afraid that it, too, will go nowhere. His wife is in her early 30s, and they would like to have children, but feel they cannot afford them on Chiron's income, which is approximately $60,000 a year.

In addition to his day job, where he works 30 hours a week, Chiron still has the small business he started on the side—keeping the books for a small company—just in case. He earns very little at this business, which is why he answered the ad for the job he just landed: director of development for a small not-for-profit in the medical field.

## My Role as a Coach

Chiron came to see me because his career path had caused him so much stress. He couldn't take the instability. My job was to help him uncover the central things that may be holding him back in his career—the things that may cause him not to live up to his abilities.

To save him money and time in the career-coaching session, I asked Chiron to complete the exercises in this book before we met. I told him that if he could not complete all of them, he should at least complete the Seven Stories.

Chiron was very serious when he came for his session. He hoped he could turn his life around. I will give you some highlights from our sessions.

Every client is different, and every coach is different. But most coaches have similar goals. The purpose of the exercises is to get a sense of the person's career-related issues in an organized, methodical way. The exercises simply help a person talk about those issues. In addition, I try to teach the client the process we are going through so that he or she can think more deeply about the issues and do more self-analysis when I am not around.

## Our Initial Session

We reviewed Chiron's Seven Stories Exercise. I will show you how the discussion went. First, I asked him to rank his Seven Stories so that we could work first on the one he ranked number one.

## The First Story

Kate: "Chiron, tell me your first accomplishment."

Chiron: "I planned and organized a free folk concert."

Kate: "When did this happen, or how old were you?"

Chiron: "It happened in 1972. I was 23 or 24."

Kate: "Tell me about it."

Chiron: "I came up with the idea and organized the event. This was back when people were still upset about the war in Vietnam, and there had been a lot of protests. I wanted to turn that discontent into something good."

Kate: "So exactly what did you do? What was involved?"

Chiron: "I coordinated with various government offices to get permission for the concert. The government folks liked the idea because it was peaceful. It wasn't a political protest. Everything was donated, and everyone performed for free."

Kate: "How successful was it? For example, how many people attended?"

Chiron: "Twenty to thirty thousand people attended."

Kate: "Good grief! That's a lot of people! What prompted you to do this event? What led up to it?"

Chiron: "I wanted to make a difference. I wanted to do the community a favor."

Kate: "This was your number-one accomplishment. What about it made it number one for you?"

Chiron: "I picked this experience as number one because I was doing good and also having fun."

Kate: "What kind of time frame was involved? How long did the whole project take?"

Chiron: "Two months from start to finish."

Kate: "Even if you've already told me, what about it was most enjoyable for you? What was the most fun?"

Chiron: "Coordinating the folk groups and the other performers and all of the govern-ment offices. I also loved working with the press."

Kate: "What about it gave you a sense of accomplishment?"

Chiron: "Creating something out of nothing and having it be a success."

......................................

*Yet when most companies are confronted with problems, they try simply to fix them. They fail to use a problem or crisis as an opportunity to explore a new way to do business.*

John Sculley

## The Second Story

Kate: "That was great. Let's look at your next ac-complishment. What was it?"

Chiron: "I taught myself journalism and got hired as a reporter."

Kate: "When did this happen and how old were you?"

Chiron: "Around 1978. I was 29."

Kate: "So tell me about it."

Chiron: "I went after a job creatively. I targeted one newspaper where I knew there was a job opening. The other people going after the job were all journalism majors. But I figured out how to write a story by study-ing books on my own. Then I covered some news events as if I were actually writing for the newspaper. I sent the editor the stories and said, 'This is how I would have covered the story if I had been writing for you.' I did this with a few stories, and actually had a lot of fun doing it. After each one, I would call him. I got the job and beat out all those people who had better qualifications."

Kate: "That's a great accomplishment. What led up to your doing it?"

Chiron: "I had spent two sessions working with the Connecticut legislature, and that's what got me interested in being a journalist."

Kate: "You mentioned as your success the fact that you got hired; what about the job itself?

You didn't mention that as a success."
Chiron: "I loved the job."
Kate: "What about it did you love?"
Chiron: "I covered a diverse range of subjects: kids and skateboards; arson. Each time, I had to teach myself the subject area."
Kate: "What did you enjoy the most?"
Chiron: "Teaching myself and getting hired and covering a wide range of subjects. I enjoyed doing the research required."
Kate: "Is there anything else you'd like to tell me about this experience?"
Chiron: "Yes. I loved meeting new people."
Kate: "How long did you have this job?"
Chiron: "Only two months. My wife got transferred to a new job in another city. We weighed it and decided to move."

## Analysis of the First Two Stories

After I have heard two stories, I give the client some feedback so he or she will see the process I use. Later, the client should be able to do a better job analyzing the stories than I could. After all, he or she was there; I wasn't.

In this case, I gave Chiron my initial impressions, based solely on what he had told me:

"Chiron, it may be that your other stories show things very differently from these first two, but I'll tell you what I've noticed so far, for what it's worth.

"Both of these happened a long time ago—15 to 20 years ago. Part of our quest in going through the assessment process is to come up with goals for you so that your next experience has a better chance of winding up as one of your top seven stories.

"A second thing I noticed is that they were both of short duration. In addition, a lot of the jobs on your résumé were also of relatively short duration.

"This is not necessarily bad. A person can choose to work on short-term things forever, such as people who get involved in fads—like the 'pet rocks' people. They don't expect these fads to last. They expect them to be short-lived. Then they move on to the next thing. Planning fads is

their focus, and they become expert at it.

"Other examples are people who run events, or head up special projects. Some people can be very successful working on short-term projects—but they tend to have a specific area of expertise and they tend to intend to have project-oriented work.

"On the other hand, a person can decide to hunker down and remain in something more long-term so that he or she can become somewhat expert at it. That's another way to go.

"So, a person can choose to have a short-term project orientation, or a longer-term orientation. One is not better than the other. The important point is planning. An opportunistic approach of doing whatever happens to present itself rarely works. It's gets very tiring to constantly learn new things and not to build on your previous experiences.

"Other threads that appear in both stories are:

"You came up with an idea and did it. You had to be convincing. There was a lot of creativity and coordination. You showed initiative in both stories.

"I'm struggling to find a subject matter that appears in both. This may have no significance at all, but politics appears in both. In one story, you had to deal with the government, and in the other, you watched the state legislature for two sessions.

"Another possible thread having to do with subject matter is 'the press.' In the first story, you dealt with the press. In the second story, you were the press."

As I showed Chiron my thought patterns, he could decide whether or not what I was saying had any significance. He could think more about his own experiences. Then he could decide what was important about them and come up with conclusions of his own.

## The Third Story

Kate: "Tell me your third accomplishment."
Chiron: "Last year, I started my own bookkeeping business for a grocery store."

Kate: "Tell me about this one."

Chiron: "I needed something to do. I had lost my job. Friends and I brainstormed ideas. I liked the idea of performing a service that people would appreciate. I also like food, and I have an M.B.A., so doing bookkeeping for a food business seemed logical."

Kate: "What for you was the real accomplishment?"

Chiron: "I started the business from nothing. I built it myself. And now it's successful. When I collect the money every week, it tells me that I made this thing work."

Kate: "Even if you've already told me, what about this did you enjoy the most?"

Chiron: "It was 'my thing,' and I made money from it."

## Other Accomplishments

Chiron then went on to tell four additional stories. For example, the fourth was when he ran a successful political campaign for someone who was running for city council. At this time, Chiron was only about 26 years old.

After we reviewed all seven stories, I told Chiron that I noticed that three had government or politics or power in them. They all showed his ability to convince and required creativity, organization, and initiative.

In the bookkeeping business, he did not mention any interaction with the people—the people he did the bookkeeping for or even the bookkeepers he had hired to help him. In all of the other stories, he had mentioned enjoying the people: meeting new people through journalism, working with the legislature and the folk groups, or recruiting and organizing volunteers in the political campaign. This people orientation was an important element missing in the bookkeeping business. My impression was that he did not like the business. What he liked was the idea that he had started it and made it work well enough.

Other strong threads appeared to be:

- running a campaign,
- being a natural leader,
- being a major influencer,
- developing strategies, and
- doing his own thing.

What did Chiron have to say about this? He was solemn and intense: "Yes. I see myself as the General. In the army, there's a platoon leader who deals with day-to-day tactics. I'm the General who sees the overall picture. I'm making only $60,000 a year, but I really feel that I should be making double this."

I replied, "Based on what you've told me, I too see you as the General. You seem to be the type of person who has to lead, to develop strategies, to influence people. It may be that the subject matter doesn't matter much—as long as you feel you're contributing to the public good—providing a service."

That's it for his Seven Stories Exercise. The other assessment results were also important, although I won't go into them here. I did find it significant that he has an M.B.A.

As I review the results, I look to make sure all of the results are in agreement. For example, if a person says he or she does not value money, but imagines living in a palatial house, I would want to know how he or she planned to afford such a place. Most often, people's results are in sync. That is, there is usually some correlation among the various exercises.

Unresolved conflicts can hold a person back. In Chiron's case, there were a number of conflicts. The most important showed up in his Values exercise. Chiron places a very high value on his lifestyle. In fact, he and his wife go away just about every weekend to the cabin they have in the woods. They are able to do this because it doesn't cost much, and Chiron essentially works only 36 hours a week in both of his jobs combined. He leaves work early every Friday so they can go to the country. In addition, he takes French horn lessons and goes to the gym once a week. Traveling is another interest of his. At present, his lifestyle is important, and he is not willing to give it up. Yet he also wants to make $120,000 a year.

That's a lot of money. People who make that

much—even far less than that—work very hard and tend to work long hours. Chiron would have to resolve this conflict of wanting to maintain his lifestyle, work a 36-hour week, and yet make a large amount of money. This rarely happens unless a person develops some highly valued expertise.

> *When all is said and done, you have just*
> *one irreplaceable resource: this particular,*
> *unique, unrepeatable lifetime of yours.*
> *What were you meant to do with it?*
>
> William Bridges, JobShift: *How to Prosper*
> *in a Workplace without Jobs*

## It Is Not Easy to Find Out What Is Holding a Person Back

Chiron's conflict may seem obvious to you: How could he not see the problem? You can see Chiron's problem because I'm spelling it out for you. However, I may be wrong. It may be that the real problem is not apparent to me. Chiron is the only one who can know for sure why he is not reaching the level to which he aspires.

Perhaps you too have something that is holding you back. It may not be obvious to you or to anyone else. Our conflicts and beliefs are subtle and often rigid. Most people do not recognize their own conflicts. Even when a conflict is pointed out to them, it is difficult to take the steps necessary to correct it. People usually continue to do what they have been doing. Changing one's beliefs takes a great deal of insight and courage.

It would take some time for Chiron to resolve this conflict in his values. So we moved on to the next part of the process. We worked on Chiron's Forty-Year Vision. He came up with a number of possibilities. It's best if you too come up with a number of scenarios for yourself. Then you can match them against your requirements. To be thorough, Chiron also filled out the Brainstorming Possible Businesses worksheet. Across the top of the worksheet, I noted his assessment results: his Seven Stories,

his interests, values, education, and so on. That worksheet is shown on page 85.

Down the left-hand side of the worksheet, Chiron brainstormed possible careers, and also asked his friends to think of career possibilities for him. Those suggestions helped him think of still others. Then he put checkmarks wherever a career possibility fit in with a characteristic. This helped him get rid of possibilities that would not fit most of his requirements.

## The Three Scenarios

After all of this, Chiron came up with three possibilities that he thought he would find satisfying. He also thought that all three of these could happen within the next five years—when he would be 50 years old. The three possibilities were:

- be president of my own company
- be political director of a large national organization
- be COO of the medical not-for-profit for which he now worked.

We examined each of these so he could realistically see what would be involved—at least at the start. Then he could research each further, and think more about the direction he really wanted his life to take.

• • • • • • • • • • • • • • • • • • • • • • • • • • • • • • • •

> *Not everything that is faced can be changed;*
> *But nothing can be changed until it is faced.*
>
> James Baldwin

## Analyzing the Possibilities

Let's take a look at each possibility. Chiron and I had a preliminary discussion so he could get a feel for how long it would take for him to move to the level he described in each of the three scenarios. In real life, a person has to do a Preliminary Business Investigation by talking to people in those fields and assessing the likelihood of being able to make such a transition.

## Scenario 1: "Be president of my own company"

I asked Chiron what kind of company he could see himself heading up. He thought a publishing company sounded good. What size staff would he have? He thought 10 to 20 people. What kind of publishing company? He thought a magazine, such as in the health, cooking, or travel area. He imagined it as being a few monthly publications, subscription only (as opposed to street sales).

It takes most people about two years from the time they decide to start their own small business until the time they actually start it. They have a lot of research and planning to do: Who else is in that market? How are they doing? What are they doing? How much will it cost? Where will I get the money? Even if a person works 15 hours a week on the new business while working full-time doing something else, it still takes two years.

Therefore, by the time Chiron is 47, he will be able to start the business—probably on the side while continuing to work at his day job. He could run it for a few years part-time until it is far enough along that he could tackle it full-time. Then he would be 49 or so. It is unlikely that he would have a staff of 10 to 20 at that time. It is more likely that it would be five or so employees—if he is lucky.

Even if Chiron opted to raise the money instead of trying to finance the enterprise himself, that still takes lots of time.

The question is whether Chiron has the discipline to investigate this idea objectively, plan it, and carry it out. If not, he should not go impulsively into this business just because it sounds like a fine idea to him. He will only repeat past mistakes where he tackled something without being properly prepared.

## Scenario 2: "Be political director of a large national organization"

Chiron imagined himself in an organization that has a corporate staff of 12 or so. He would be the chief lobbyist with a staff of four to six. I asked him to pick an organization—any organization—just to make this example more real. He selected the National Association of Manufacturers, which is headquartered in Washington, D.C. Let's brainstorm this scenario.

Of course, Chiron would have to be willing to live in Washington at some point. After removing that barrier in his own mind, one scenario for moving ahead with this vision would be to get a job as a junior lobbyist in an area that would be of interest to the organization he eventually targeted. It would not be good enough to get lobbying experience, for example, in the utilities or tobacco field. He would need relevant experience because his future employers would want to capitalize on the contacts he had made. Then he could become a more powerful lobbyist, and he would be desirable to organizations such as the one he mentioned.

Chiron would have no trouble getting his first lobbying job. After all, it would not be that high level, and Chiron is very convincing in interviews. But since it would require a geographic move, that step could take a year. Then he would have to do extremely well in that field so he would have a few things to brag about. That would take two or three years, for sure. Then he would have to get into the right organization, and move up within it. That would be a few more years. I guessed that Chiron would be in his ideal job, making the kind of money he wanted in nine years, at age 54.

I think it's doable, and he has plenty of time, since most of us are living longer. The question, again, is one of commitment.

The third scenario will take the same length of time to achieve and require the same commitment. Life takes time. Making good money takes most people a lot of time and commitment. Chiron needed to decide what his priorities were.

# Brainstorming Possible Businesses Worksheet

Assessment Results ⟶

| Possible Jobs | Driving force: idealism | Service orientation | Artistic | Enterprising | Writer/journalist | Sales/influencing | Leader/the "General" | Strategist | Meet with leaders | "Business Owner" | Advisor | Politics/government | Food/health | Nonbureaucratic | M.B.A. | Earn $100,000/yr. | Mark large impact | Complex problems | | Total Check-marks Across |
|---|---|---|---|---|---|---|---|---|---|---|---|---|---|---|---|---|---|---|---|---|
| Lobbyist | ✔ | | | | ✔ | ✔ | ✔ | ✔ | | | ✔ | ✔ | | | | | | | | 7 |
| Bookkeeping business | | ✔ | | ✔ | | | | | | ✔ | ✔ | | | | | | | | | 4 |
| Political campaign mgr. | ✔ | ✔ | | ✔ | ✔ | ✔ | | ✔ | ✔ | | ✔ | ✔ | | | | | | | | 9 |
| Executive, present co. | ✔ | ✔ | ✔ | ✔ | ✔ | ✔ | ✔ | ✔ | ✔ | ✔ | ✔ | ✔ | | | ✔ | ? | ✔ | ✔ | | 15 |
| Development director | ✔ | ✔ | | ✔ | ✔ | ✔ | | ✔ | ✔ | | ✔ | | | | | | | ✔ | | 9 |
| Journalist | ✔ | | | | ✔ | ✔ | | ✔ | ✔ | | | ✔ | | | | | | | | 6 |
| Political activist | ✔ | ✔ | | | ✔ | ✔ | ✔ | ✔ | ✔ | | ✔ | ✔ | | | | | | | | 9 |
| Union organizer | ✔ | ✔ | | | ✔ | ✔ | ✔ | ✔ | ✔ | | ✔ | ✔ | | | | | | | | 9 |
| Arts organization | ✔ | ✔ | ✔ | | ✔ | ✔ | ✔ | ✔ | ✔ | | ✔ | ✔ | | | | | | | | 10 |
| Fund-raiser: music | ✔ | ✔ | | | ✔ | ✔ | | ✔ | ✔ | | ✔ | ✔ | | | | | | | | 8 |
| Pres. of my own co. | ✔ | ✔ | | ✔ | ✔ | ✔ | ✔ | ✔ | ✔ | ✔ | | | ✔ | ✔ | ✔ | ? | ✔ | | | 13 |
| State senator | ✔ | ✔ | | | ✔ | ✔ | ✔ | ✔ | | | ✔ | ✔ | | | | | | | | 8 |
| Pol. director, large org. | ✔ | ✔ | | ✔ | ✔ | ✔ | ✔ | ✔ | ✔ | | ✔ | ✔ | | | | ? | ✔ | | | 11 |
| . . . and so on | | | | | | | | | | | | | | | | | | | | |
| | | | | | | | | | | | | | | | | | | | | |
| | | | | | | | | | | | | | | | | | | | | |
| | | | | | | | | | | | | | | | | | | | | |
| | | | | | | | | | | | | | | | | | | | | |
| | | | | | | | | | | | | | | | | | | | | |

That also would take time.

Chiron had always prided himself on his ability to learn things quickly. However, at a certain age, those areas that were our greatest strengths can become our greatest weaknesses if we don't watch out. Chiron tends to not learn any area in depth, keeping him stuck at $60,000 or so a year.

There is no end to this story yet. We will all have to wait and see what Chiron decides to do with his life.

........................................

*In a fight between you and the world, bet on the world.*

Franz Kafka

## Chiron's Options

Lucky Chiron has many options. Many people would envy the life he and his wife have created for themselves. Chiron and his wife do not work long hours, earn decent money, go to the country every weekend, and have time to pursue other interests. Sometimes people are unhappy with their lives until they complete the assessment and discover they don't have it so bad after all. In Chiron's case, he and his wife can keep their lives—and their income—essentially as is. To gain the career stability Chiron wants, all he needs to do is stick with something long enough to become expert. Then he will have the kind of life many Americans want.

On the other hand, he could join the rat race with the rest of us. He may choose to do that because, for example, he thinks he needs the money to have and raise children (although people do raise children on what Chiron makes, and most wives work today).

If he wants to make a good deal more than he does now, he will have to work a good deal harder. Those who have spent years becoming expert in a marketable area can work less hard. But Chiron still has to develop marketable skills to command more money. Within that, he has many choices.

He has energy and brains and talent. He needs direction and hard work. That's not so bad.

For each of the three scenarios he targeted, he could develop a plan similar to the one Walter did in Developing a Detailed Plan, a few chapters back. That would help him to chart a course that he could then stick to if he is committed enough. The sooner he makes a commitment to a clear direction, the more likely he is to achieve that direction. If he keeps on hedging, his energies will continue to be dispersed. In his present job, he could develop a skill that he feels sure would also help him later.

If the direction he selects later proves to be wrong, Chiron will still be better off for having chosen something and for developing a marketable skill. Then he can build on his new marketable experience.

As far as the bookkeeping business is concerned, I think Chiron should keep at it until he has made a commitment to a new path. Otherwise, he may continue his pattern of jumping from one thing to another without properly researching it. Although the bookkeeping business is not the right career path for him, the more important lesson he needs to learn is commitment. Then the future will look bright for Chiron. You too have many options. And you too have plenty of time in which to achieve them. But you too must investigate them, and make a commitment. And give yourself a break. Remember that life takes time.

........................................

*BIFF: And suddenly I stopped, you hear me? And in the middle of that office building, do you hear this? I stopped in the middle of that building and I saw—the sky. I saw the things that I love in this world. The work and the food and time to sit and smoke. And I looked at the pen and said to myself, what the hell am I grabbing this for? Why am I trying to become what I don't want to be? What am I doing in an office, making a contemptuous, begging fool of myself, when all I want is out there, waiting for me the minute I say I know who I am!*

Arthur Miller, *Death of a Salesman*

*The most difficult thing—but an essential one—is to love Life, to love it even while one suffers, because Life is all. Life is God, and to love Life means to love God.*

Leo Tolstoy, *War and Peace*

. . . . . . . . . . . . . . . . . . . . . . . . . . . . . .

*It is often said that accomplishment makes [dying] easier, that those who have achieved what they set out to do in life die more contentedly than those who have not.*

Judith Viorst, Necessary Losses

*Great ideas come into the world as gently as doves. Perhaps then, if we listen attentively, we shall hear, amid the uproar of empires and nations, a faint flutter of wings, the gentle stirrings of life and hope.*

Albert Camus

# Preliminary Business Investigation: Businesses Worth Exploring

*Until you know that life is interesting—and find it so—you haven't found your soul.*

Geoffrey Fisher, Archbishop of Canterbury

Although it takes up only a few paragraphs in this book, Preliminary Business Investigation is essential.

Your Preliminary Business Investigation could take only a few weeks if you are high in energy and can devote full time to it. You have to test your ideas to see which ones are worth pursuing. As you research at the library, on the web, and by meeting with people in your fields of choice, you will refine those targets and perhaps develop others. Then you will know where to focus your efforts, and your business planning will be completed much more quickly than if you had skipped this important step.

People who conduct a Preliminary Business Investigation while employed sometimes take a year to explore various fields while they continue in their old jobs. If you are not at all familiar with some of the businesses you have selected, do some Preliminary Businesses Investigation *now* through the web, library research, and networking. You will find that some businesses are not right for you—once you find out a little about them. Eliminate them and conduct full research in those areas that seem right for you and that offer some reasonable hope of success.

Whether you are employed or between jobs, Preliminary Business Investigation is well worth your time and a lot of fun. It is the difference between blindly thinking you can do something and failing later, and finding out what is really happening in the world so you can latch on to an idea that may carry you forward for many, many years—even the rest of your life. This is a wonderful time to explore—to find out what the world offers. Most people narrow their targets down too quickly, and wind up later with nothing. It is better for you emotionally as well as practically to develop more possibilities than you need *now* so you will have them when you are actively researching.

Most people come up with only one idea and may take a very long time to find out that this concept is not workable, get discouraged, try to think of other business possibilities, research that one, and start all over again. That's another way to go about it. However, if you have brainstormed a number of possibilities, your research into one may overlap with some of the others and will save you time.

• • • • • • • • • • • • • • • • • • • • • • • • • • • • • • • • • •

*Life is God's novel. Let him write it.*

Isaac Bashevis Singer

It's better to brainstorm as many possibilities as possible *before you begin your research*.

1. List below all of the business possibilities that interest you at this point.
2. If you are not at all familiar with some of the businesses you have selected, do some Preliminary Business Investigation *now* through library research or networking. Eliminate the businesses that are not right for you, and conduct full research in those areas that *do* seem right for you and seem

to offer you some reasonable hope of success.

As you find out what is happening in the world, new possibilities will open up for you. Spend some time exploring. Don't narrow your possibilities down too quickly; you will wind up later with not much to go after. It is better for you emotionally, as well as practically, to develop more possibilities than you need *now* so you will have them when you are actively researching.

## Preliminary Business Investigation Worksheet
### Business Possibilities That Interest Me at This Point:

(Conduct a Preliminary Business Investigation to determine what is really going on in each of them.)

|  |
| --- |
|  |
|  |
|  |
|  |
|  |
|  |
|  |
|  |
|  |
|  |
|  |
|  |
|  |
|  |
|  |
|  |
|  |
|  |
|  |
|  |

*Counterbalance sources of stress in your life with sources of harmony. Develop closer ties to the people you love. Set up dependable routines in your schedule to which you can look forward during times of stress: a few moments each evening in a hot bath, regular nights to eat out, one day per month in bed, seasonal vacations. Create environments around you that are physically and emotionally restorative: a peaceful workspace, a blossom-filled window box you can see from where you eat, a permanent exercise nook. Regularly perform simple tasks that you can be certain will give you a sense of accomplishment.*

Jack Maguire, *Care and Feeding of the Brain*

# Part Three

. . . . . . . . . . . . . . . . . . . . . . . . . . . .

# Getting Yourself Ready

# Ambition, Courage, Follow-Through and Other Entrepreneurial Virtues

*Creativity requires the courage to let go of certainties.*

Erich Fromm

## Taking Steps Now

It is often said that, on their deathbeds, people express the regret that they didn't spend more time with their families. That may be especially true for *famous* people who were consumed with work and excelled professionally. Others on their deathbeds wish they had had the guts to do something more satisfying with their *professional* lives. Herbert Rappaport, Ph.D., author of *Marking Time,* says that one of the common themes he sees among depressed adults—well before they get to their deathbeds—is the deep sense of regret for not having *stretched* themselves. To be satisfied, there has to be a blend: we need healthy personal and family relationships as well as healthy work lives.

Life takes time. Having your own business takes knowledge as well as courage. It took me ten years from the time I knew I wanted to have my own business until I actually did it. Initially, I had three possible small business ideas: one hav-ing to do with art, one focused on horticulture and—the one I actually implemented—career management. I spent about two years taking courses and talking with people before I eliminated the first two ideas.

However, even after I *settled* on career management as my focus, it took me eight more years before I had a real business. During that time, I ran small job-search groups at night in my apartment, researched and refined career-development techniques, gave many speeches on the subject, and had fun endlessly improving and tweaking the business plan.

I was afraid to give up the money and the prestige of my day job where I had a staff of ninety in a computer services firm. However, I knew that if I were really committed to having a successful career development business, I needed to take a job in the *career development* field for a few years.

I delayed making such a move for so long that I disgusted myself. I repeatedly thought, "You're paralyzed by fear! What a pathetic life you will have lived if you don't *make* something of this." I had to stop planning and start doing!

Finally I took a step back in my old career path and became the chief financial officer of a 200-person outplacement firm, the ideal job from which to learn the inside of the careers business. I reminded myself that I was at the outplacement firm not to *stay* there but to learn enough to make The Five O'Clock Club into a real, full-time business. My new mantra became, "What a pathetic life you will have lived if you don't make this Five O'Clock Club work!" As I often told my clients: "If you have a dream and don't follow it, *no one will care*—no one but you."

About three months after joining the out-placement firm, I moved the Club out of my apartment and into rented space, and wrote a book to document The Five O'Clock Club methodology. That was in 1986. The rest, as they say, is history.

......................................

*The important thing is this: To be able at any moment to sacrifice what we are for what we could become.*

Charles Dubois

## Take a Job That is on the Right Path for Your Future Business

If you already have many years' experience in the field in which you want to start your own business, you may have already thought about the key issues you will face. So you can start now to develop your research and your business plan. But if you *don't* have experience, find a job or consulting work that is closely related to the kind of business you want to have. If you want to be a caterer, work for a caterer. But don't just cook. You probably already know how to do that. Learn the *business* side of the business.

When I went to work for an outplacement firm, I didn't work as a career coach. I already knew how to do that. I took a job on the business side of the business—first, as its chief financial officer, and then as the head of research, technology and administration.

When you *do* take a job to learn the *business*—there's lots to pay attention to:

- how they get customers,
- how much they charge,
- how they cross-sell other products to customers and get customers to come back,
- how they set up the next appointments,
- where they buy their products,
- who keeps their books,
- how many hours a week each person works,
- how much they pay the staff.

Do your best to *expand* your involvement on the *business* side. Help with the books. Write checks. Place orders. Help with purchasing or procurement. Call people who owe money.

In addition:

- Study books on starting your own business.
- Develop the personal habits you will need to succeed.
- Keep working on your business plan.

You can do *all* of these regardless of your present situation.

When I teach the class "How to Start Your Own Business" to those who are incarcerated, I tell my students: If you want your own beauty business, get started now—even if you are incarcerated! For example, they can work in the prison beauty salon, give hair advice to other women who are incarcerated and read beauty magazines. They can take surveys of the other women asking, "What do you look for in a beauty shop?" If you want your own business cutting hair, you can learn how to cut hair *now*—wherever you are. If you think you want to have your own gym, start *now* to teach people how to build their bodies.

But also learn the business side. If you want to have your own house-cleaning business, for example, you will not learn much if you just clean houses in someone else's business, *unless* you position yourself correctly: "I'm the best house cleaner in the world and some day I want to have my own house-cleaning business. It won't compete with your business because I'll be in another area of town. If you hire me, you'll have the best, most dependable housecleaner, but I also want to do other work for you as well. I can also help you *grow* your business and can make sales calls for you. I can collect some of your bad debts. Send out bills. Order supplies."

Even if you're not looking to be hired, interview owners and ask how they charge people, how they get new customers, how they keep good people, what kind of people they hire.

Make the most of *every* situation. If you are forced to work at McDonald's, to name a sad example, don't just fry the potatoes. Learn every aspect of the business. Notice *everything* and ask the manager business-related questions. Ask if you can help with the numbers, manage people, schedule workers. Do whatever you can to help run the business.

Be sure to keep a small-business notebook—one that is bound—and jot down things endlessly. Don't think that the notebook is so special that you don't want to clutter it up with trivia. Instead, put *everything* you learn into your notebook—even crazy ideas. It will help you to think of better ideas later.

The bottom line: Try to find a job or consulting work that fits with *what you want to do* in your own business.

· · · · · · · · · · · · · · · · · · · · · · · · · · · · · · ·

*I had to make my own living and my own opportunity! But I made it! Don't sit down and wait for the opportunities to come. Get up and make them!*

Madam C. J. Walker, creator of a popular line
of African-American hair care products and
America's first black female millionaire

## Develop Your Character

*Moral excellence comes about as a result of habit. We become just by doing just acts, temperate by doing temperate acts, brave by doing brave acts.*

Aristotle

Think right now of the skills and character traits you need to run your own business. Develop a plan for building all those skills and traits now. Are you organized? Do you get up on time or earlier? Do you *make yourself* do the things you don't want to do? Do you make yourself perform as well as you can out of *pride*, even though you may not *like* what you have to do?

Can you keep your eye on the prize and not be distracted? If you are focused on your goal, you will not be bothered (too much) by the people and the normal irritations of your everyday environment. Think ahead to what you want to do with your life and focus on that. Spend hours with relevant books and websites. Learn everything you can about running your own business.

Fill up your notebook with ideas of how you want to run your business, such as how to market your product or service. Develop a plan that's *at least* as detailed as the plans you see in this and other books. Pick up ideas from other people's businesses and plans. Business is business. You can get ideas from almost *any* kind of business. In fact, you'll get more creative marketing ideas by examining how people market *other* kinds of businesses. Think of how those ideas might fit into your business.

Do not give up. You may allow yourself to become depressed for a little while. Enjoy your discouragement, and then *get over it*. Pick yourself up and keep on going.

You have another 20, 30, 40, 50, 60 years to live. You can get a lot done during that time—one step at a time. Make progress every single week of your life—starting right now.

· · · · · · · · · · · · · · · · · · · · · · · · · · · · · · ·

*Once you fully apprehend the vacuity of a life without struggle, you are equipped with the basic means of salvation.*

Tennessee Williams

## How Do You React When You Are Faced with Life's Setbacks?

*Getting along with men isn't what's truly
important. The vital knowledge is how
to get along with a man, one man.*

Phyllis McGinley

When other people bother you, when you are faced with problems, a usually reliable solution is to talk it out with other people—those who have good heads on their shoulders, have a good sense of humor and stay calm. Here are a few others ideas mentioned in one of my favorite books, *Adaptation to Life* by George Vaillant.

### Sublimation:

The redirection of impulses to a higher purpose. In an odd 1989 movie titled, *New York Stories*, one segment directed by Martin Scorsese is about an artist (played by Nick Nolte) who uses his hypersuccess to lure beautiful young aspiring artists to serve as his assistant/lovers. He found that when he was happy, he was motivated to paint. But when he was depressed—such as when a girlfriend dropped him—he was also motivated to paint. No matter what happened to him, he was productive! You can do that too. When you face setbacks, you *can* choose to sublimate the bad things you may *feel* like doing (drinking, shopping, cursing, banging on the wall) and instead *focus on your goal*, and do something productive—something that will move you ahead towards your dream.

### Anticipation

When you are aware that someone bugs you, you can discuss with your friends how to handle that person the next time. When you know problems are coming up, you can prepare how you are going to handle them. Imagine yourself in that situation and imagine how you will handle the situation to come out the winner. Athletes envision hitting the ball over the net or over the fence, which can help make it happen! You too

can envision yourself handling future problems successfully.

......................................

*Every obnoxious act is a cry for help.*

Zig Ziglar

### Sense of Humor

Humor can help you to *observe* what's happening instead of being wounded or taking everything so seriously. From time to time, I lose my sense of humor and get slighted at the least little thing. I can be very thin-skinned. Then I'm vulnerable. When John Kennedy was running for president in 1960, during a news conference a reporter asked him if it was true that his father planned to buy the election for him. The other reporters in the room gasped. With a twinkle in his eye—and the faint hint of a smile, Kennedy replied, "Well, my father told me he couldn't afford a landslide." Humor deflected the arrow. See what you can do to take a humorous approach to your setbacks, but don't use humor that hurts yourself or others.

### Altruism

Helping others can take the focus off yourself. There are always people worse off than you are. When you help others, you feel more positive and powerful about yourself.

### Count Your Blessings

This is not mentioned in the George Vaillant book, but much research supports the notion that even those in the worst situations benefit from gratitude for what they *do* have: health, friends, resources, people who come into their lives, the nice weather, the Van Gogh print hanging on the wall, the lessons life teaches—*something*!!! Those who don't count their blessings are less happy and less productive. At every level in business, those who are happy, and *try to get along,* tend to be the ones who get promoted and recognized.

*When I started counting my blessings,
my whole life turned around.*

Willie Nelson

When my business failed in the early years, I counted my blessings because I had experienced a *clear* failure, not some ambiguous situation that may have resulted in a slow, more painful business death. One way to count your blessings is to do your Seven Stories Exercise! Understand the great things you've done! And once you've written your Forty-Year Vision you'll see that your blessings are enough to propel you forward. Identify your *strengths* as well as your weaknesses. Identify your dreams and what you need to do to get there, such as the skills and character traits you need. Develop a plan for improving yourself and make progress against that plan.

Keep at it. Never give up.

. . . . . . . . . . . . . . . . . . . . . . . . . . . . . .

*During our lives we're faced with so many elements,
we experience so many setbacks, and fight such
a hand-to-hand battle with failure, head down
in the rain, just trying to stay upright and have a
little hope. The Tour isn't just a bike race, it tests
you mentally, physically, and even morally.*

Lance Armstrong

## Follow Through

To be successful, you need not only the initiative and ambition to get started, but also the ability to follow through and bring each project to completion. Many people have great, marketable ideas, but don't execute them. If you can't bring the project to completion, the idea is useless.

On the other hand, your chance of success is good if you work hard at a *doable* idea—and stick with it.

Most entrepreneurs fail at first, and learn from those mistakes. Steven Jobs, founder of Apple computers, started NeXT, Inc. after he was fired from Apple. NeXT didn't do well. But Jobs'

Pixar animation has been a roaring success.

Walt Disney had many failures. For example, he formed his first animation company in Kansas City in 1921. He made a deal with a distribution company in New York to ship his cartoons and get paid six months later. The distributor went bankrupt, Walt was forced to dissolve his company and at one point could not pay his rent and survived by eating dog food.

My brother's nanotechnology company may fail with its first product, and maybe even its first dozen. That's the nature of business. But when they *do* hit on a successful product, it will be very big.

And, as I've mentioned before, The Five O'Clock Club completely failed—closed—three times early on. But each time we learned and did better.

. . . . . . . . . . . . . . . . . . . . . . . . . . . . . .

*Success is going from failure to failure
without a loss of enthusiasm.*

Winston Churchill

## Ambition

*You have to remember that about seventy percent of the horses running don't want to win. Horses are like people. Everybody doesn't have the aggressiveness or ambition to knock himself out to become a success.*

Eddie Arcaro, Hall of Fame jockey

I've coached people about their careers for almost thirty years. One mistake I made early on was mistaking potential for ambition. I could see a person's potential and we could talk about all the possibilities. Sometimes I would help people get into positions they were not ambitious enough to handle. If a person wants to work nine to five, go home, kick off his shoes and have a beer every night, there's nothing wrong with that. But he wouldn't go far in his own business. Nothing replaces ambition. Brains, education and financial resources are no substitute. Give me an ambitions person any day over one with a

Harvard education. The ambitious, determined person is the one who never gives up, figures out what's wrong and tries again.

..........................................

*Intelligence without ambition is a bird without wings.*

C. Archie Danielson

How can you tell whether you are ambitious? If you say, "I want to make millions," that is not a sign of ambition. That's a wish, a fantasy! My response is, "I'll watch where your feet go." Are you *doing* something about it or just talking? The truly ambitious are people of action.

On the other hand, unbridled ambition doesn't make sense either. How much money do you *need*? Read the next chapter to plan your wealth goal.

..........................................

*If the power to do hard work is not talent, it is the best possible substitute for it. Ambition by itself never gets anywhere until it forms a partnership with work.*

James Garfield, 20th US president

## Homework:

List the entrepreneurial character traits you already have and list those you would like to develop more.

*I've learned how much self-discipline I have. I've played 358 rounds of golf in the 2 weeks I've been self-employed*

# Your Wealth Goal

*We probably wouldn't worry about what people think about us if we knew how seldom they do.*

Olin Miller

When I lived in Philadelphia in my thirties, I was very involved with art, doing a lot of volunteer work for the Philadelphia Museum of Art as well as the Walnut Street Theatre Art Gallery. From time to time I was invited to events to thank the volunteers and contributors. At one such very small event, I was the only person in the room who was not rich. I was probably also the happiest person in the room.

For example, there was Ben, an elderly man, who had started out poor with a push cart, probably during the recession, and grew his business until it became a well-known local moving company. He was worth about $13 million. Also at the party was a sweet woman I'll call Mrs. Rich. Her family was one of the wealthiest in Philadelphia. Ben remarked to me how flattered he was that Mrs. Rich even spoke to him given her high status and his *low standing*. I reassured him that she was very sweet and he was likeable too.

Ben's comment struck me as odd because, only a few weeks earlier, I overheard a member of the Rich family speaking about the *Getty* family wealth and how the Rich's would never *catch up!* Ben was in awe of the Rich family. The Rich family was in awe of the Getty's. I was envious of none of them. As a career coach, I've heard enough behind-the-scenes stories from the rich and famous to know they have insecurities and even problems with alcoholism or drugs. They can be hobbled by weirdness and in-fighting.

........................................

*Envy is the art of counting the other fellow's blessings instead of your own.*

Harold Coffin

Luckily, I was *born* happy and satisfied, though I *am* somewhat ambitious. I don't want a boat or a mansion. One car is enough. Give me health, good relationships and a stable business. I remember meeting one successful entrepreneur in the early days of the Five O'Clock Club. He said, "God help me to grow, but help me to grow slowly." My sentiments exactly. Enough is enough.

Many people would be glad to have a business that provided them with $60,000 in income per year. Others want to put away a few million for retirement. Both of those are fine goals. But do you need Donald Trump's palatial homes or the clothes of a movie star? You need only so much to be comfortable and then you should spend the rest of your energy paying attention to your relationships. Howard Hughes became the richest man in the world but ended up as an eccentric recluse. Your business may take you away from your family for a few years while you get it going, but you need their support. Your quality of life hinges on this. Recognize when you have enough and focus on your relationships. Then give back to society. If you are simply using your money for yourself and your family, you are selfish. Remember that you thrive and survive in a community—be sure to *give back*—it's what you *owe* to society.

*If the grass is greener on the other side of the fence, you can bet the water bill is higher.*

Unknown

A genuinely good person is a person of moral excellence, but not in a vacuum. A good person is good for the community. In an obituary, a newspaper described a certain wealthy man as a good person. He did well for himself, made a nice living, and often took his daughter sailing on his boat. But whom had he cared for outside of his immediate family? No one. The obituary wasn't about a good person after all. It was about a selfish one.

*"Since you're a new client, I thought I'd take you somewhere nice. But my credit card is almost maxed out, so I may have to borrow a few bucks.*

*There is a loftier ambition than merely to stand high in the world. It is to stoop down and lift mankind a little higher.*

Henry van Dyke, American clergyman & writer

## How to Get "Enough"

If you are too concerned about what others think of you, you are likely to spend every penny you make to impress them. You will *never* become wealthy.

Many people confuse income with retained wealth. If you spend what you make, you have nothing left. You have *things*, but you are not wealthy and you are not financially secure. When you retire, you will require a large income to keep up with your standard of living. But if you could start now to live well *beneath* your means and sock some real money away, you are much more likley to end up wealthy.

........................................

*He who does not economize will have to agonize.*

Confucius

## Compound Growth

If you could put money away in a medium-growth investment account (mutual fund, annuity, etc.), your money is likely to double approximately every seven to ten years. That's what financial advisors tell *me*!

That's the beauty of compound growth. Growth at a constant rate over more than one year compounds from year to year. This can produce some surprises. For example, if you put away $10,000 in 2008, and your $10,000 grows at 7% in 2009 and again at 7% in 2010, then accumulation at the beginning of 2011 is 1.07 times 1.07 = 1.1449 times as great as it was at the end of 2008. If it continues growing at a steady 7%, production would be 96% greater after 10 years, 387% greater after 20 years, and so on. The surprising power of compound growth increases

as the period gets longer, and, of course, as the rate of growth gets larger. _**So your $10,000 investment will be worth $20,136 in just ten years. And $40,547 after 20 years. $81,645 after 30 years.**_

Now, if you put away $10,000 a year *every* year for ten years, you would wind up with $256,444 from the $100,000 you saved. If you saved *nothing else* and kept that money in moderate investments, you'd have $½ million by year 20, and $1 million by year 30.

But if you spend your extra $10,000 a year on bigger houses, new cars and fancy clothes, your neighbors will *think* you're rich, but you won't be. If you're like most Americans, you will have *plenty of debt* and no wealth.

In the early days of your business, be sure to reinvest the profits in the business to help it to grow. Make sure you *are investing* and not just spending. Spend for items that will bring you a *return* on investment. Buying artwork for your office will not bring you a return unless you are in the art business or must have an office that looks very fancy. Buying additional space may not even give you a return on investment. "Investment spending" often includes outlay for labor (people who can produce more for you to sell or who can actually do the selling), perhaps better marketing or more appropriate product literature—if that will make a difference in your business. You are looking for a *return* on your investment. Will buying better furniture bring in more revenue? If not, it's an expense and not investment spending. Your money is not growing. You might as well burn it.

The reinvestment of earnings is how real growth businesses get most of their financing. When your business starts to be profitable, don't reward yourself with a new car or house. Instead, continue to live as frugally as you can and stash the money away in a moderate-return investment.

Let's take another example. Let's say your business did not make much money for you for a long time. Now you're ten years away from retirement, have only $100,000 in a retirement account, but things have improved to the point that you are now able to contribute $40,000 a year every year towards your retirement account.

After 10 years, you would have $1,000,000 (because of compounding), not $400,000 ($40,000 × 10) PLUS $200,000 from what you now have in retirement from your previous savings (that $100,000 would become approximately $200,000 compounded after 10 years). These are not exact numbers. I am not a financial planner. But the concept is correct.

You could retire with $1.2 million minimum. Now, _**if you never touched the principal**_, (the $1.2 million), and had invested the money in something that gives a 7% return _with no additional fees from your investment company,_ you will be in good shape for retirement.

Don't ever touch the principal and you will have $84,000 per year every year until you die (plus social security payments) and _still_ end up with the $1.2 million!!!!!

Some rich people live extravagantly—even beyond their means! They too carry too much debt. But smart rich people:

- Never invade the principal!!! (Just live off the interest.)
- Rely on compounding (which means you must put the money away regularly).
- Pay yourself first. Decide how much you want to save and put that money away _before_ making a budget and asking yourself what else you might need/want. This creates a feeling of scarcity. You pretend

the money isn't there. It doesn't count. You can't spend it. You've already paid yourself first (by putting the money into savings) and now have to live on what's left. Except for real emergencies, the money you've socked away should be untouchable. It should be as inviolable as your 401K.

Of course, make sure your investment company is charging you a flat fee for its advice (akin to an hourly fee) and _not_ a percentage of your investments. Otherwise, it gets a percentage of everything you've worked so hard to save.

I'm simply passing on to you what our financial advisors have told us. You absolutely need a financial advisor—probably your accountant rather than a firm that stands to gain from your investments. You want objective advice.

•••••••••••••••••••••••••••••••••••••

_By sowing frugality we reap liberty, a golden harvest._

Agesilaus

•••••••••••••••••••••••••••••••••••••

_Without frugality none can be rich, and with it very few would be poor._

Samuel Johnson

## Homework:

Write a paragraph describing your intention to spend money versus save.

# Forming the Right Character for Entrepreneurship

## Sacrifice Now; Get Rewarded Later

*The ability to discipline yourself to delay gratification in the short term in order to enjoy greater rewards in the long term, is the indispensable prerequisite for success.*

Brian Tracy

..........................................

*Instant gratification takes too long.*

Carrie Fisher

If you have adopted the *credit-dependent* life style as most Americans have, the best advice I have to offer is this: Start *now* to cut back on your spending, get out of debt, and get used to living *beneath* your means. Having your own business means getting your financial house in order. You can't spend time sailing or going on cruises until you have made enough money to support those activities. For now, it's poverty time. This means investing in yourself, emotionally and financially.

Run your business frugally and live frugally. Remember: the best things in life are free. Find them and enjoy them. Do you want new furniture for your office? Buy *used* furniture instead. You can get gorgeous repossessed furniture from

companies that went bankrupt because they spent money on new furniture! Furniture doesn't generate revenue in most businesses. People do. Invest in revenue-producing items, such as talented people, better promotional material, and so on.

In the beginning, you will have debt—maybe even credit card debt—to finance your business. But you don't want to pile on the debt for vacations and luxury items. Your goal is to get out of debt and build your cash reserves, which will reduce your stress. When this happens, it is harder for the business to fail.

## Hard Work

*Do not wait; the time will never be "just right". Start where you stand, and work with whatever tools you may have at your command, and better tools will be found as you go along.*

Napoleon Hill

When your business is mature, you may have more flexible hours. But when it is young, it takes all of your attention, energy and money. There are endless chores and details.

I had a long-term plan, which of course changed in light of real-life circumstances. There was always work to do towards that plan, even in the early days when we had virtually no business. Working on the new business was a lot like one of my early hobbies, petit point—needlepoint done with a small stitch. It could take me three to five years to complete a 2-foot by 3-foot piece! One month I'd stitch flowers in my petit point, and another month I'd stitch an animal. It didn't much matter what I worked on, so long as I kept filling in the pattern. I worked on my petit point every spare minute—when visiting relatives, while watching television, even while riding in the car. In the end, I had a beautiful handmade wall hanging—a future heirloom.

In some respects, I approached my business as I would another large needlepoint. There were lots of details. Some things had to be done today no matter how I felt. But I could simply chip away at the other tasks, writing a book, getting trademark and copyright protection, developing marketing literature, delivering speeches, recruiting coaches, and completing all the pieces that make it a whole business.

In the early days of my business, the trick was to make myself work when there were no pressing tasks and no stimulation. No phones were ringing. I worked primarily by myself for many years. When I was totally bored, I knew what I had to do and I had to *make myself* do it. I developed techniques to get myself moving. For example, I would break down a project into *very* baby steps: Just *turn* on the computer. Get a drink of water. Now, open up the file and write a few sentences. Soon, I was into it and couldn't stop. I completed another piece in the "needlepoint" of my business.

## Integrity

*To give real service you must add something which cannot be bought or measured with money, and that is sincerity and integrity.*

Douglas Adams

WorldCom. Enron. Arthur Anderson. Adelphia. The corporate scandals have been all around us. Yes, people cheat in small businesses too. But the continued growth of your customer base depends on *your good name*. Are your customers saying good things about you? Do your vendors trust that you will pay? If you lose customers and alienate vendors, your business is doomed. As a small business, you are only as good as your word.

In our small business, our mantra is that we always do what is in the best interests of the job hunter or the person seeking help for career development. This means that we pass up lucrative corporate business when a company is trying to use us to hurt rather than help their employees, and we pass up important media interviews, if we suspect the resulting article or program may damage employees.

Don't forget that it's a small world. You can assume that your customers and vendors will talk to each other and exchange information. Whatever you do, the word will spread.

## Excel at Your Trade

*Quality is never an accident; it is always the result of high intention, sincere effort, intelligent direction and skillful execution; it represents the wise choice of many alternatives.*

Willa A. Foster

You must become focused and expert in what you do. Pick something you can become passionate about but also something in which you can excel and can compete in. Your whole life will revolve around your chosen specialty. It is also vital to understand your *limitations* as well as your strengths, develop your strategy for relying on your strengths and correcting your weaknesses.

I needed a field in which I thought I could make a unique contribution. The career coaching field was (and still is) very soft, relying on very little research and almost no methodology. I knew I could contribute something significant and make this field more rigorous. Pick a field in which *you* can excel.

## Develop Your People Skills

*He who wished to secure the good of others, has already secured his own.*

Confucius

"Business would be great if you didn't have to deal with people!" That's the joke. The fact is that everything you do has to do with people, primarily your employees and your customers. If they don't like you, you won't do well. If you don't like *them*, it will be hard to succeed.

So work hard at listening well and being flexible to maximize your chances that you'll be able to give your customers what they need. After all, you do have competitors.

## Develop a Thick Skin

You will be criticized and second-guessed. There are geniuses who stand on the side and take pot-shots. They have a new idea every day but never implement anything! Over the years, total strangers have given me suggestions, most of which are off-the-wall. Or fellow businessmen sometimes try to rattle me. "You have a unique business model, Kate, but someday someone will come along and sideswipe you. They'll have a better business model and you won't even see it coming." Well, *thank you* for the advice! These people enjoy seeing others fail.

Some critics are correct so you *do* have to pay attention and judge for yourself. But discount ninety percent of what you hear—even from your own family and friends. Notice what's happening and keep plowing ahead.

• • • • • • • • • • • • • • • • • • • • • • • • • • • • • •

*It is not the critic who counts, not the man who points out how the strong man stumbled, or where the doer of deeds could have done better. The credit belongs to the man who is actually in the arena, whose face is marred by dust and sweat and blood,*

*who strives valiantly, who errs and comes short again and again, who knows the great enthusiasms, the great devotions, and spends himself in a worthy cause, who at best knows achievement and who at the worst if he fails at least fails while daring greatly so that his place shall never be with those cold and timid souls who know neither victory nor defeat.*

Theodore Roosevelt

## Be Disciplined

*The critical ingredient is getting off your butt and doing something. It's as simple as that. A lot of people have ideas, but there are few who decide to do something about them now. Not tomorrow. Not next week. But today. The true entrepreneur is a doer, not a dreamer.*

Nolan Bushnell, founder of Atari and Chuck E. Cheese's

Do what you have to do. Don't ask yourself whether you *feel* like it. If you're asking yourself that question, the answer is probably "no." How you feel is irrelevant. Get it done anyway. Finish what you start. If you are not like this now, you must learn how to force yourself. You'll need to—if you want your business to succeed.

And keep yourself in shape physically. I do a lot of public speaking, so I have to get a minimal amount of exercise to make my lungs strong. As a business owner, you have responsibilities. You can't call out sick and you can't come in with a hangover. I don't know any small business owners who drink. Drinking is for people who hate their jobs and want to blot out their lives. You have a lot going for you. Drinking will destroy your ability to respond and your energy to get things done.

Learn to pace yourself. You can't be exhausted. If you work long hours, take naps. I don't know about those people who get only four hours of sleep a night. I'm not one of them: I need 8½ hours. If I don't get that amount a few nights in a row, I pay the price.

Figure out what *you* need to do to keep your health. Others can call out sick if they twist an ankle or "feel" a cold coming on. But not you.

No one is driving you but you and your desire to succeed.

## Long-Term Planning Coupled With a Focus on Today

*However beautiful the strategy, you should occasionally look at the results.*

Sir Winston Churchill

Some people are amused because my mind is often far in the future—many years out—developing strategies along several lines. Such planning keeps me calm. If there is any slippage in the timetables, or if I am overburdened in one area of our business, at least I am ahead in other areas and not caught by surprise. That's the good side of it.

However, in the old days, I had so much fun planning that my focus was entirely on what we would do in the *long-term* and not much on getting people to attend the Club right *now*. When I finally noticed what I was doing, I forced myself to focus on the short term. I repeated to myself, "How many people do you expect to attend this week? Next week? Why? What can you do about it?"

Entrepreneurs have to make quick decisions about many things. I still do long-term (and one-year) planning. But in my day-to-day work life, I'm a "let's get it done now" kind of person. Let's wrap it up and move on. Settle issues as soon as possible. If there's an important problem, or even a small problem—don't put off working on it.

But what's going on *today* must be understood as a part of the bigger scheme. That is, those who focus too much on the present can be blind-sided by competitors or market changes in general. All that matters to them is that they have business *now*, and they never give a thought to what might happen in the future. They are totally surprised when business drops off. They never figured out *where* the business was coming from or planned what to do if those sources dried up.

To make your business succeed, you need a balance between planning for the future and doing what has to be done today.

••••••••••••••••••••••••••••••••••••••••

*First say to yourself what you would be; and then do what you have to do.*

Epictetus

## Keep Panic at Bay

*Fear cannot be banished, but it can be calm and without panic; it can be mitigated by reason and evaluation.*

Vannevar Bush

Yes, there's always a chance you'll go bankrupt. Running your own business has its risks. But major companies go bankrupt too. As of this writing, Ford Motor Company just laid off 30,000 workers. Working for someone else also has its risks. And when you work for someone else, all of your eggs are in one basket. When you have your own business, the risk is spread in the sense that *many* customers are your source of income.

How can you keep panic at bay? Working hard is one way. If you take the afternoon off to play golf, that won't help. Getting good counsel is another way. Over those early years, I solicited feedback from wise people—at the SBA, SCORE, the local college MBA program, friends whose judgment I trusted, potential investors, successful entrepreneurs.

When I asked them to review my business plan, they were delighted. Our business plan was a little complicated and unusual because we had to do so much with very little capital. But that made it fascinating for those who gave me help. And their feedback and guidance helped me refine or support what I was doing, and kept me calm and assured.

Do your research and be observant to find out who gives good advice and who doesn't. It's not hard to find advisors, but you must be selective about whose judgment you trust. And don't judge them just by how high they've climbed. Sometimes you can get good advice from those who are not at a very senior level. Consider the source and keep going back to those good sources.

......................................

*We all admire the wisdom of people who come to us for advice.*

Jack Herbert

......................................

*Anxiety is a thin stream of fear trickling through the mind. If encouraged, it cuts a channel into which all other thoughts are drained.*

Robert Albert Bloch

## Develop Systems

*The five essential entrepreneurial skills for success are concentration, discrimination, organization, innovation and communication.*

Michael Faraday

If you want your business to grow, you must have systems that are one or two levels more sophisticated than your business needs. Sure, you can do your accounting in a notebook, but that works only right now. Instead, use an accounting system that will work for a business the size you expect to be a few years from now.

A corollary to that is: "If it isn't documented, it isn't done." When someone at our company does develop a system, I'm not impressed until that system is documented. For example, say someone does an analysis of our shipping costs and decides which vendor we should use for certain size packages. Unless that information is documented in a central administrative manual, that information is useful only as long as the person remembers it. If that person leaves or can't remember what they decided, it was all a waste.

If it's not documented, the job is not done. I want things documented so well that when a new person starts, he or she could simply be handed the manual and understand the process from

what's written there. The information is not for that person who wrote it, but for the company.

Even if you're a one-man shop, document your own procedures and you will save a lot of time and prevent errors. Otherwise, you are unlikely to remember what you have done in the past, you may be reinventing the wheel every few months wasting a lot of time, and too many decisions will be by the seat of your pants. Develop systems and follow them yourself. Keep your procedures updated. If you ever need others to help you, they have something to follow.

......................................

*Make everything as simple as possible, but not simpler.*

Albert Einstein

## Keep a Positive Attitude

*One of the things I learned the hard way was that it doesn't pay to get discouraged. Keeping busy and making optimism a way of life can restore your faith in yourself.*

Lucille Ball

Entrepreneurs as a breed are optimists. Otherwise, how could they keep pushing forward when the pragmatists would tell them it's not worth it? You do need to plan and research, but then you simply have to act and learn from real-life experiences.

If you're not an optimist, maybe you're not an entrepreneur. Train yourself to think optimistically. When faced with problems, don't think, "I'm Doomed!" Instead, think, "How can I get around this?" You *must* be confident in your own ability. Those who have been through hard times and *survived,* do better than those who have had smooth sailing all along and have no experience with setbacks. Stay away from people who try to make you afraid. Stay away from negative people. Even your own employees may try to put their own fears on to you. You are the leader. Be strong. Have faith and impart it to others.

## Focus

*I learned that we can do anything, but we can't do everything . . . at least not at the same time. So think of your priorities not in terms of what activities you do, but when you do them. Timing is everything.*

Dan Millman

You must prioritize. Since I have had my own business, I have developed the habit of asking myself, "What's the most important thing for me to work on today?" And "What are the two or three most important things to accomplish this year?" And then I let nothing get in my way. Those things *will* get done.

Every key employee has two or three goals that must be accomplished in the coming year. That way, the business moves ahead and is not side-tracked by the everyday problems that arise. Handle those problems, but keep your eye on the ball.

In the early days of my business, I kept my Seven-Stage Plan taped to the wall right next to my computer screen. (See Walter's story in a later chapter.) I couldn't ignore it if I tried. Then when "targets of opportunity" would come along— those 'brilliant' ideas that come your way and *get you off track*, I would ask myself, "Does it fit in with my Fifteen- or Forty-Year Vision? Does it fit in with my Seven-Stage Plan for the business?" If not, I didn't do it. I kept focused. Otherwise it's very easy to *be busy* all the time, working endless hours, but working on the wrong things.

. . . . . . . . . . . . . . . . . . . . . . . . . . . . . . . .

*Don't be a time manager, be a priority manager. Cut your major goals into bite-sized pieces. Each small priority or requirement on the way to the ultimate goal becomes a mini goal in itself.*

Denis Waitley

## Outwork and Outthink the Competition

*Effort only fully releases its reward after a person refuses to quit.*

Napoleon Hill

I remember reading the obituary of a famous film editor (whose name I don't remember). He said he was not educated and claimed that he wasn't brilliant, but he spent endless hours editing and reediting everything he did. He said it was the *time* he put in that made the difference.

Some time ago, a major corporation asked me if our company had a certain career development program for employees. I said that we didn't have one but could develop one. They would need it in 8 weeks, but didn't know whether or not they could get the funding. I said, "We'll develop it anyway. It's something we should have in our portfolio." If they can pay us, fine. If not, then at least we'll have it. I came into work at 6:00 AM and worked on that project until other employees showed up. I worked on weekends. I loved doing it and I knew my efforts would not be wasted. Later, other companies asked if we had that same career development program, and we did!

That's how I wrote books. No one asked me to write books. I just kept on writing because I knew they were necessary for the business. My efforts were not wasted.

Your efforts will not be wasted either. If you're not spending a certain amount of time on your craft (whatever your business is: whether it's scientific research or graphic design), you are not developing your craft. That's the discipline. Even if you have no assignment from someone else and no one is asking for something specific, give *yourself* an assignment and do it anyway. Just keep plugging ahead. That way, you're running the business rather than having the business run you!

. . . . . . . . . . . . . . . . . . . . . . . . . . . . . . . .

*Folks who never do any more than they get paid for, never get paid for any more than they do.*

Elbert Hubbard

Let's say you're working on your business part time. How many hours per week should you spend on your craft if you hope it will turn into your life's work? Nothing gets done in three hours. And it's hard to remember week to week to put those three hours in. If you plan to put in three hours, chances are you'll put in far less, and weeks will go by without any progress. What about 8 hours? Well, that's getting serious and eight hours a week, consistently week after week, *could* do it. You just keep track of your time. That way, if you put in less than eight hours one week, you have to make up the time the next week. Over the course of a year, you will have put in 416 hours—or about 10 weeks' worth of effort. That's not bad.

Usually, we say you have to put in 15 hours a week to get momentum going. After all, it's not only the time you spend on actual scientific research or graphic design or whatever your business is, but also the time you spend doing business research, contacting people, talking to them about your business and asking about the possibility of doing some work for them, getting feedback from them and developing your portfolio more. Everything you do relating to your business counts in your fifteen hours—even phone calls you make to set up appointments.

It's a good idea to carefully track the time you actually spend, so you are honest with yourself about the effort you are putting in. If you want to fulfill this dream, don't just let time pass. Fill it up and make progress.

Okay, you can take some time off for holidays. We can't all be like Jay Leno, who never takes a vacation. He says he loves it when he reads that fellow comedians are vacationing. It makes him work even harder because he feels as if he has a chance of getting ahead of them. That's what most successful people do. But you don't have to be like Leno—take some time off.

......................................

*Don't judge each day by the harvest you reap, but by the seeds you plant.*

Robert Louis Stevenson

## Pray

*"For I know the plans I have for you," declares the Lord, "plans to prosper you and not to harm you, plans to give you hope and a future. Then you will call upon me and come and pray to me, and I will listen to you."*

Jeremiah 29:11-13

For those of us who believe in a higher power, renewing the relationship is a great way to calm down. Just ask for guidance and strength. Ask your loving God what he wants for you. "God's will be done" helps you to accept whatever happens. And counting your blessings is the great stabilizer, no matter what you believe in. Those who feel a lack, feel stress. Those who feel grateful, feel happy and calm and can focus on what needs to be done.

......................................

*Reflect upon your present blessings, of which everyone has many; not on your past misfortunes of which all people have some.*

Charles Dickens

## Pick the Right Horse to Ride

*Wisdom is knowing what to do next, skill is knowing how to do it, and virtue is doing it.*

David Starr Jordan

It's so much easier if you've picked a business you know something about. Many people pick businesses they know nothing about because they think, "How hard can it be?" Businesses look *easy* from the outside. It will take you many years more to get your business going if you don't have first-hand experience. That's why we tell people to work for a few years in the field they are targeting and learn on someone else's nickel.

If you work as an employee in that industry, you will get ideas about how you could do things better, and you will also see whether you really like the area and the kinds of people who work in it.

## Weigh the Pros and Cons

*The fewer data needed, the better the information. And an overload of information, that is, anything much beyond what is truly needed, leads to information blackout. It does not enrich, but impoverishes.*

Peter F. Drucker

Yes, you must act quickly as an entrepreneur. But don't be impulsive. Whatever the idea, think it through. List the pluses and minuses and also list competing ideas. Is this how you should be spending your time and other resources? As Abraham Lincoln said, "If I had eight hours to chop down a tree, I'd spend six hours sharpening my ax."

## Too scared to take a step

*To fight fear, act. To increase fear—wait, put off, postpone.*

David Joseph Schwartz

Once I met a 65-year-old woman who said she had never been married, wanted to get married, but was waiting for the right person. That's obviously sad. It is also sad to hear someone, over the course of a decade, repeat the same dream, "I want to be an actress. "But she is not taking courses, going on auditions, or taking any steps towards what she says is her dream. Her fear is that if she actively tries to become an actress, she will find out that she is not very good at it.

Joseph, a Five O'Clock Clubber, told me that he knew that psychotherapy was the right field for him. "I know I would be great at it." When I mentioned that the industry has changed a lot, he didn't want any information. He simply wanted to keep his dream in tact.

If Yadira, who you will read about later, decides she wants a pastry business, it's a fiction until she starts to check it out. That means she's serious about change. It's very scary to take responsibility for your life, identify what you think you want to do, and do your research. This amounts to a reality check! When you're researching your idea, talking to people and check-

ing it out, do you still *like* the business idea? Yadira said she *loved* talking to people in the food world, and she said that with passion. She said, "I love it. I just can't believe I'm doing this. I feel guilty about spending my time talking about recipes!" She's on the right path. Now she needs the courage to keep at it! I think she is going to have an immensely successful business.

·······················

*Do not believe in anything simply because you have heard it. Do not believe in anything simply because it is spoken and rumored by many. Do not believe in anything simply because it is found written in your religious books. Do not believe in anything merely on the authority of your teachers and elders. Do not believe in traditions because they have been handed down for many generations. But after observation and analysis, when you find that anything agrees with reason and is conducive to the good and benefit of one and all, then accept it and live up to it.*

Buddha (Hindu Prince Gautama Siddharta, the founder of Buddhism)

## What Does Your Life Partner Say?

*A happy home is one in which each spouse grants the possibility that the other may be right, though neither believes it.*

Don Fraser

When a person is starting his or her own business, I ask what the spouse thinks of the idea. I'm looking for some objective information beyond what the client says or what I observe. I always ask, "What does your family think of this?" For one thing, you will need tremendous support. You will not have a regular paycheck. Or, if you keep your day job, your new venture will take time away from your loved ones. This can be wrenching for your family. It can make them feel insecure financially as well.

Yadira's husband is supportive in the extreme. He says that she needs to sell her product to major supermarkets. Yadira had not even spent one week in her food course, and her husband was talking about taking the company public!

That's actually not a bad response. I don't mean to generalize here, but various articles I've read say that women tend to succeed in their small businesses more often than men do. But men tend to make their businesses *bigger*. Men may be more likely to say "Let's go public!" while women may be content with something smaller. They may be satisfied with being profitable, but don't have the desire—or the time—to grow the business beyond something small.

Consider what your spouse has to say. He or she knows you better than I do and may point out personality flaws that I am not aware of. And your husband or wife will need reassurance that the time you spend away from home will not last forever.

........................................

*All serious daring starts from within.*

Harriet Beecher Stowe

## Homework:

List your three strongest entrepreneurial characteristics, your three weakest, and the specific steps you will take to shore up your weaknesses.

# Life Takes Time

*Great ideas come into the world as gently as doves. Perhaps then, if we listen attentively, we shall hear, amid the uproar of empires and nations, a faint flutter of wings, the gentle stirrings of life and hope.*

Albert Camus

To sum up, here is the process:

Step 1: Understand yourself: your values, interests, skills, and so on. The better you understand yourself, and the more honest you are about it, the better you will be able to assess the opportunities that will come your way.

Step 2: Figure out what you want. What on this earth would you be best served doing? What should your future be like?

Step 3: Figure out how to get there. Later on, we will show you how to develop a business plan for yourself.

Step 4: Identify your own character traits that might stand in your way. Some of your values may be in conflict. You may have a tendency to avoid commitment to unpleasant but necessary tasks. If you can resolve these issues, nothing can stand in your way.

## Internal Issues

Here are some common examples of internal issues that hold people back:

- Conflict in values. "I want to earn $300,000 a year, work a two-day week, and do as much good as Mother Teresa." The first value is at odds with the other two!
- Lack of self-esteem. People rise to their level of self-esteem. If you have low self-esteem, stop thinking just about yourself. Take the big picture approach and think of *what you were put on this planet to do*. Do what you were *meant* to do. God did not mean for you to bury your talents, but to use them and make them multiply.
- Inability to imagine a more fulfilling future. Get some help with your Forty-Year Vision. Be sure to write it down. Think about meeting with a Five O'Clock Club career coach.
- Depression can be clinical or situational, but it needs to be addressed. Get help! Jack Nicholson said to Greg Kineer in "As Good as It Gets," "You're giving depression a bad

name!" That's you if you don't tackle the depression and get on with your life and your business.

- Lack of focus. Some people see too many possibilities and cannot decide what to do. They flit from one thing to another and do not become an expert at anything.
- Failing to identify options. Other people imagine doing the same thing for 30 years, which is a *failure* to imagine! They need to explore more and *see what's out there*.
- Too many skills; master of none.
- Too few skills or need to bring them up to date.
- Too tense; don't have enough fun.
- Too much fun; don't buckle under and work.

Add your own thoughts to this list. There are plenty of things that hold people back.

## External Issues

In addition, you may be held back by a lack of financing, an unsupportive spouse, the competition, the lack of talented employees in your geographic area, and any number of other issues.

You will have to address these as you go along, but first let's look at some small business models.

• • • • • • • • • • • • • • • • • • • • • • • • • • • •

*A competitive world has two possibilities for you. You can lose. Or, if you want to win, you can change.*

Lester C. Thurow, Dean, Sloan School
of Management, M.I.T.

• • • • • • • • • • • • • • • • • • • • • • • • • • • •

*Monitor how you're thinking and behaving, and try to stop negative thoughts and behaviors in their tracks. Ask yourself: Why am I thinking or behaving this way? What's the positive alternative? What might make it easier for me—now and in the future—to think or act positively in this type of situation?*

Jack Maguire, *Care and Feeding of the Brain*

## Homework:

List the internal and external factors that may hold you back and how you plan to overcome them.

# Part Four

· · · · · · · · · · · · · · · · · · · · · · · · · · · · · · · · · · · · ·

# Buying an Existing Business (including a Franchise)

# Buying an Existing Business

*Profit is an illusion; cashflow is fact.*

Unknown

## Build or Buy?

The failure rate is twice as high for starting a business as compared to buying one. But most good businesses are not on the market. A family member or an employee buys them, or an insider finds out about them before they hit the market. You have to find the good businesses yourself, and we'll show you how. But you only want to buy a *good* business, not any old business. It takes experience to recognize a good business when you see one, and that experience is something you can get.

If you do buy a good business, instead of starting one yourself, you won't have to worry about finding a location, developing your initial base of customers or marketing materials, preparing operations manuals, developing sources for your raw materials, hiring employees, and all of the other issues involved in the first few years of a start up. As I've always said, "start-ups are hard." It sure would be nice to skip that stage.

But buying the *wrong* business can be a disaster. The seller will make his business look better than it is. You have to develop some skill to be able to see through that. What's more, it usually costs more to buy a business than it would to start your own. After all, the seller has to get something for all the time and effort he or she has put into it.

People who start their own businesses—and are successful at it—tend to make more money than those who buy a business. It could take you years to get a good return on your initial investment into someone else's business (although sometimes it takes no upfront cash at all—they may be able to take back the loan). In addition, a person who has started her own business has put more energy and imagination into it and therefore understands the business better.

## Be Able to Take the Business to the Next Level

Most business owners are not able to tell you what you should do next to grow their business, beyond the obvious idea of increasing your customer base. You will need some imagination—in addition to looking over a lot of businesses—to find a business that is ripe for expansion. You'll have to decide how you can add value to make this business worth more than you paid for it. If you are not experienced in valuing businesses, hire someone to value the business for you so you don't over-pay. The CPA you hire should be able to tell you the business's cash flow, analyze the receivables, value the inventory, and so on.

## Get the Experience and Training You Need

Just because the business is there and running doesn't mean *you'll* be able to run it. How much do you know about sales, accounting, and small-business management? If you are not well versed, the starting point for you is lots of courses, and most of these are free or inexpensive from the SBA, local colleges, and associations. You could also learn about the business by working for the person you want to purchase the business from or working for a competitor. Learn what you need to know before you plunk down the money. You may think: How hard can it be to run a deli? Well, it's pretty hard if you've never run anything before. Finally, read plenty of books on small business management, marketing, accounting, and so on. As I've said before, this is not "the only book you'll need" for starting your own small business.

## Developing a Business Plan

You may think that you are saved from doing a business plan if you simply buy a business. Au contraire! Ongoing businesses develop a yearly plan so they can analyze their competition, pricing structure, marketing, financials, and so on, and so must you! If you don't know enough about the business to develop a solid plan, that should be a warning to you that you don't know enough to buy it. We'll tell you how to do a quickie business plan in this book.

## Case Study: Mark
## Conducting Your Research

Advice is cheap. Mark, age 50, had been in the printing industry his whole life, and he wanted to get out because it's a shrinking field. His sister had an idea for him to work in the mortgage business, and he spent 1.5 years in that—earning almost nothing, working endless hours—and eventually lost his job. Now Mark's sister is encouraging him to buy a seasonal business at the seashore—a chicken wings restaurant. This sounds great to Mark because he doesn't want to work from 6 am until midnight and people don't eat wings for breakfast. Summer's coming. What should he do?

Mark should do nothing. It's all happening too fast. The urgency is artificial, and he doesn't have enough information. I went into Yahoo "maps," keyed in the name of the city and state Mark named, and the words "wings," and found a restaurant that serves wings. I don't know that area, but from the map, it looks like an excellent location. These people would be Mark's competitors, and he would be operating just four blocks away from them. The most important question is this: how much traffic do *they* get? Is there room for Mark?

Mark could easily get this information, and he would NOT have to ask the sellers. He should ask anybody *except* them. Mark could walk along their block and ask the neighbors. Is it a bustling place or is there very little traffic? Ask the neighbors where *they* buy chicken wings. Do they buy them from their neighbor or do they buy their wings from the people in the next town over (the next closest chicken wings place)? Mark can also ask the Chamber of Commerce. In fact, he should get to know them anyway—if he is sincerely interested in having a business in that town.

Since it is a "summers only" kind of town, what is Mark planning to do the rest of the year? Why does he want a summers-only business (which adds to his pressure)? Even if he now decides he doesn't want to have a wings business, if he is interested in this town, he should go there and do research anyway—just to see how the research works.

The research process is an unpredictable one: you have no idea what information will turn up. We tell our clients that the answer is not in here—in your brain. The answer is out there—in the marketplace. Mark's sister means well, and we all need some rah-rah, but her advice is far less helpful than it may appear. She sounds encouraging: "You can do it. I know you can do it. . . . Oh my gosh, I thought you *could* do it. I'm so surprised it didn't work." That's the sequence of events. It's like asking advice from people at the corner tap-room. You don't want to act on that kind of advice. If they're sure it's such a good idea, ask them to put in half the money as an investment. You soon find out how much they really believe in the idea. They mean well. They just want you to get over your anguish and move on so you can have fun again. But they aren't a good source of business advice. In fact, their advice is usually damaging.

Instead, ask the market. When we work with clients who want to buy an existing business, we ask them to first select the city where they think they'd like to run a business. Then, investigate that city. Meet with small business owners there. Tell them you'd like to have a business there and why. Ask them what they think. Get to know people at the local Chamber of Commerce. Ask them about your competition for the chicken wings business. Is it likely that the guy has a lot of traffic? What kinds of businesses tend to do well there? Talk to people on the mainland as well (where the businesses are more year-round rather than summers only) and ask what they think.

Later on, when Mark actually *has* a business and he needs people to talk to, he'll talk to those people he met during his research phase. They will be his source and may even become his friends. They'll tell him, "Oh, that weekend is always bad here because the annual pipe bending contest draws people away." Mark's sister wouldn't know that and her guess is as good as Mark's—actually, not nearly as good as his.

There's another reason for talking to all those locals—including the Better Business Bureau, the Chamber of Commerce and local businesses and banks. They are a source of information for businesses to buy. Brokers are not the only source, or even necessarily the best source. Local folks will know, for example, that "Joe ran his business for 25 years, but he's been tired since his wife died and the business has not been doing well. He's been talking about selling, but has not formally put the business up for sale. He'll probably take a mortgage back and continue to work with you a few days a week for a year—to show you the ropes while you get settled in—for very little pay."

Before you buy, conduct thorough research. Don't trust your gut.

## Case Study: The Dimitris Developed Their List of Prospective Businesses

One couple I worked with wanted to buy a manufacturing business in North Carolina. They didn't know anyone there, but the area they were interested in had a huge Greek community and he was of Greek descent. In addition to getting to know members of the local Chamber of Commerce, they joined the Greek organization there and also the Church. They told everyone they met about their desire to live and work there. They got excellent information from members of the community, better information than they would have gotten from brokers alone. They talked to local bankers, lawyers, you name it, told everyone their plans, and investigated businesses—from a spiral staircase manufacturing company to a chemical manufacturer. In each case, they had to "value" the company—decide what it was really worth, find out the price—including the seller's assumption of a mortgage, negotiate keeping the seller on for a while, and so on.

In addition, they made a list of all the local manufacturing businesses of a certain size. Their local library was able to help them. They came up with a list of 400 companies and wrote to all of them, saying: "Perhaps you know of someone who may want to sell their business to us. We are planning to live and work in this area." You can expect about a 4 percent response rate of people who are willing to talk to you—some just out of curiosity.

You'll probably have to look at the books of 20 businesses before you buy one. You'll find, for example, that the inventory is old and has to be thrown out, or the buildings are not up to code. Or the $35,000 you're thinking of as the purchase price is actually $50,000 when you include the repairs you'll have to make. You have to "run the numbers" to see how much money you are actually likely to make and how long it will take you to make it. If you ask the seller of a cash business how much they take in, they may tell you that the books don't really reflect the volume because they pocketed some of the cash. Isn't that convenient? They're saying, "This business is a money maker, but I can't prove that to you. You'll just have to trust me." It's in their best interests to inflate the money they made. That's why you have to check them out in the neighborhood. It's a reasonableness test.

- *What do the neighbors think?* Was the business doing well or not? Was Joe complaining about his lack of traffic? Why does Joe *really* want to sell? Be sure to build a strong network so somebody in the neighborhood can tell you what is going on with the business. Certainly people in the community will want you to be successful because they will be working with you in the future and you are going to resent them if they knew something and didn't tell you. People can give you information, even if they don't do it overtly, to let you know the kinds of problems this person had.

- *What do his key customers think of him?* Yes, you must speak to customers to find

out how well the business is doing. Ask the owner for a list of the top ten customers, and ask them what they think of the company, its products and services, its ability to deliver, its integrity, what it needs to do better (and assure them that you will indeed take care of these problems if you do buy the business). These people may be *your* customers someday, so although you are checking on the current business, you are also trying to solidify relationships so you can keep them as customers if you take over.

- *Talk to key employees*—if they know about the sale. Talk to them as if you were going to be their future boss. If you treat them roughly, they may convince the owner not to sell to you, or they may start looking for a new job the minute you take over. You want their loyalty and as little turnover as possible. Ask them if they are likely to stay. What do they think could be done better? What problems are they having now that they would like to see changed? Be sure to ask general questions, such as, "What's it like to work here?" That will tell you more than all of the targeted questions you can ask. For example, someone may say, "Well, it's difficult putting off the creditors, but other than that, it's fine."

Senior people tend to be savvier. I know. I was the "employee" potential investors asked about the company because I was the chief financial officer. You're likely to get more straightforward information from the more junior people, and you may notice a pattern. Employees may be your best source of information not only in deciding whether to buy the business, but in figuring out how to run it once you get there.

- Many times, my clients who were interested in purchasing a business have done *consulting work for the company* for a short time so they were on-site working with the owner. If you hang around there, you pick up a lot of information. You are there in the office, you hear people on the phone. That's another way to check things out.

- *Check with the company's banker, attorney and accountant*. These consultants will not necessarily tell you the straight-out truth. They should have some loyalty to their client. But the owner will not be able to sell the business unless he has an open-door policy for those who are serious buyers. The consultants are not going to give away trade secrets. In fact, you will probably be asked to sign a non-disclosure agreement and jump through other hoops. Then you examine the books and value the business, and you have to meet with their accountants, attorneys and bankers.

## The Company Culture

One problem with buying an existing business is that you're buying an existing culture. Perhaps the current owner is paternalistic and gives employees large gift certificates to Best Buy, or has a monthly luncheon, or pays their dental bills when they can't. You want the company to reflect *your* personality, but you can't make changes too quickly.

If, in the past, you've ever taken a job as the new head of a department or division in a company, you know what I mean. You can't change the culture overnight. You want to keep the culture the same for a while so people don't abandon ship. To some extent, you court employees so they stay on, and only after three or four months or more can you decide which changes to make.

If the company is in such bad shape that you think you need to immediately cut out half the staff, you probably should not have bought the company anyway—unless you are a business turnaround expert.

## Why Is The Owner Selling?

Selling a business is the same as selling a house. The realtor tells you a good story. But the owners want out because they can't stand the neighbors, a gang of bad kids moved in recently, the taxes have skyrocketed, or the energy bill is out of sight and there's no way to fix the problem. You're not going to hear the truth from the broker or the seller.

If the business owner wants to retire, that's one thing. But if the owner simply cannot take the employees, the expenses, or the customers anymore, that's another thing. That's why you need strong relationships with people in the community, others in the same industry, the company's vendors, as well as the owner's key advisors. Find out why the owner *really* wants to sell.

## The Reluctant Seller

The owner *says* he wants to sell, but when it gets down to it, does not want to part with his baby. José, recently unemployed and with a year's severance, had his heart set on a specific business in Vermont. The seller strung him along for over two years, finding reasons not to close the deal "for another few months." Unfortunately, no one could convince José to hedge his bets. He looked at nothing else while his savings and his energy drained away. Eventually he had to take a job back in his old field.

After you have looked at a good number of businesses, you will be better able to recognize a motivated seller—one who really wants to sell. She's the one who has been getting the business ready for sale. Just as a homeowner fixes up the place, cleans the basement and throws out a lot of junk, small business owners who have thought about it for a while do the same.

## Find Lots of Prospective Sellers

Remember that entrepreneurs can sell their companies to firms up or down the supply chain, or cut in one or two key employees and gradually step aside. So that leaves on the market companies that don't have strong relationships with suppliers or customers, or without employees who are candidates for succession. Either way, it only emphasizes the buyer's nightmare question: What does the owner know that you don't?

Here's the conundrum: If the owner is eager to sell, you have to worry; and if the owner isn't eager to sell, you have to overpay. And that's why you should look at a lot of places and also consider starting-up a business.

Either way, you will need a market niche. So why not research both at once? As usual, it comes down to networking—in this case, with the Chamber of Commerce, CPAs, consultants and lawyers. These are people in a position to hear of entrepreneurs who might be considering retirement.

Then, when meeting with such owners, if they don't want to sell, you can ask them what business they would start if starting over. You might get some wonderful suggestions, and perhaps even find your first investor or first customer.

So, generally you have to review quite a few businesses—concurrently—to find one that's suitable. It does take the average person I've worked with two years from the time they thought they'd like to have their own business until they actually got started. This time is spent getting to know the local market, digging up businesses to check out, then checking them out, negotiating, and developing your business plan.

## Continue to Work While Searching?

How do people make this transition from working for others to working for themselves? If possible, most try to get a job back in their old field or the field they want to be in while they work like crazy researching to buy or start a new business. The problem that most people face with this is the thought—the incorrect thought—that working back in their old field is forever. They're trying to get *out* of their old field. They want to move on. They don't want to work for anyone else. In fact, the big motivator for having your own business is the loathing some feel about working for someone else.

Therefore, you must NOT say to yourself, "So, this is what my life has come to. Here I am back in the same old grind." Instead, say to yourself, "I need to buy a little time for myself. If a job in my old field comes up—even if it's not exactly right for me, that's okay. I won't be there long. I'll do an honest day's work for an honest day's pay, and I'll have the time I need to research this business idea, check out the community, find lots of businesses and think this whole thing through."

In summary, you can get leads about businesses to buy from:

- Networking in the community with Chambers of Commerce, CPAs, consultants and lawyers, and
- Contacting existing companies directly.
- Business brokers
- Ads in magazines, newspapers and on-line

Remember, Americans are an impulsive bunch and that's why so many small business start-ups fail. Model yourself after your local Korean grocer or Indian motel owner who is more likely to succeed because they essentially did their research and started out with a business plan from others in their community. After the business is up and running, they have like-minded people to talk to for advice. You too need to develop a group of advisors because actually *buying* the business is the beginning of the journey, not the end.

## Case Study: Alicia
## Start Out, Then Grow

Alicia, age 30, wants to buy a Laundromat in Florida. Her parents are in that business and she's dreamed of owning her own business with thirty washers and thirty dryers.

Alicia may or may not be able to start out with thirty washers and dryers, but she *can* start out with something smaller, get something going, build it up, sell it and build bigger (or build on to what she has). Still, a business could cost her tens of thousands of dollars, which she doesn't have. She may know how to *run* Laundromats, but buying one will probably be her main stumbling block.

Alicia should certainly talk to the SBA about financing. That's always an important first step and will give her a feel for how the business works. She will probably have to ask her family to co-sign for her and the reference checks will be done on *them*. But then she must do more homework: Find all of the Laundromats in her targeted geographic area of Florida. She will need many to choose from. The better her research, the better her chances of finding someone who has a decent business that perhaps has not done as well as it should have during the past few years because the owner has lost interest, has gone through a divorce and can't keep it up, is ready to retire, or whatever. She can find a bargain.

You want a business you can breathe some life into, but you want to make sure that the business is not dead—that it *can* be revived. If you're really lucky, you may find someone who is willing to "take the mortgage back"—maybe someone who doesn't even require that much down but wants to see his business in good hands and needs steady income going forward. You would pay for the business as you go. This is the best-case scenario, of course, but it still can happen.

No matter how the financing works out, if Alicia simply finds one Laundromat and tries to buy it, she is in a very weak negotiating position, and increases her chances of winding up with no business at all or overpaying.

Therefore, she needs to look at 10 to 15 businesses at the same time. That's a lot of work, even if she already had a list of businesses to look at. But she doesn't. How can she get a list together?

- The Yellow Pages may be her best bet to start.
- Or try Internet research. Just go to Google and key in "Laundromat Sale Florida" and she'll get back loads of businesses for sale and probably their asking price.
- That's not enough. She needs to find people who do not yet have their businesses on the market, but would be willing or even eager to sell if someone came along. She can take the list of businesses she's found in the Yellow Pages (or wherever), call each one to say that she wants to write to them, and ask for their proper name and address. She'll write to each one saying that her family is in the Laundromat business in Florida and she wants to be in it too. "If you happen to know anyone who may be near retirement or otherwise be interested in selling a Laundromat, please let me know. I'll call you in a few days to follow up."
- She should also talk to her local Chambers of Commerce, local banks, local churches and other organizations and associations to ask them if they know of anyone who wants to sell. She needs to uncover those who have not yet advertised.
- While she's at it, she could also go to a business broker and tell them what she's looking for—but not until after she has developed her own list of laudromats. Otherwise, they'll come up with businesses for her and those will be the only businesses she would be considering. She is far less likely to get a good deal.

You never know which of these techniques will uncover the business of your dreams, so you must try them all.

## Examining the Business

Before the owner turns over the financials to you, you will be asked to sign a non-disclosure promising that you will not reveal confidential information to anyone. Read it carefully and make sure it does not restrict you in any other way, such as not allowing you to look at the books of competitors.

Then, if you're unfamiliar with financial statements—balance sheet, income statement, cash flow, and so on, hire someone to review the books for you, probably a CPA. Business owners are notorious for fixing the books. Business valuation is a tough problem and there are people who devote their lives to this issue. I love numbers and could happily study them for days, but I wouldn't trust myself to value a business I was buying. At the very least, I would need a second opinion. If it all looks like Greek to you, find someone who can understand what he or she is looking at.

On the surface, you can examine the business revenue and see how it has done over time in the company's most important products and services. Has there been a reduction in revenue for the company's most important line? Read the company's key contracts to see whether the owner priced them properly. Determine the profit margins on every major product and service, as well as every major account. Perhaps they're doing more and more business with XYZ company, but losing money every time they ship product to them because they have under-priced their products. Maybe they are making a profit on smaller accounts, which are now disappearing. Perhaps the owner wants to unload before this time-bomb explodes.

Let's take a look at two businesses. Business A has 3 percent profit, a little below the standard for that industry, and the revenue comes from sixty accounts. Business B has 10 percent profit, 80 percent of the revenue comes from one account, there are six accounts in total. Just based on those facts alone, which company would you buy? Business A with only three percent profit is by far the stronger company. The owner of business A is doing a lot of things right—he's attracted sixty accounts! To make this company more profitable, he probably needs to raise prices just a tad, perhaps reduce some expenses in a few

categories, and he's on his way. But business B could go out of business at any time—if they lost that one major account.

The rule of thumb is this: If more than 15 percent of the revenue is coming from one account, that is risky. If that account goes away, the business could fold.

The profit picture may not be what it seems to be for another reason. If the owner has under-paid himself, the profit picture will look rosier than it should. And if he has overpaid himself—taken the profits out of the company (which he is allowed to do), the bottom line will look bleaker than it should, but that may be the company *you* would prefer to own. The excess profit he is taking needs to be added back to the profit line to give you a true picture of the company's profits. In this scenario, I'd go with the second company and reinvest those excess profits to make the company grow.

Assess the expense categories. How are each of them doing over time relative to revenue? Later on in this book, we will step you through an income statement for a number of companies and you can try your hand at comparing them.

## Hedging Your Bets

Depending on the complexity of the business, you may want to try to get the owner to stay on with the business for two or more years. The former owner earns a salary or other compensation while you take over the management and grow the business.

Buyers are often looking for businesses that have languished in the last year because the owner is getting old or disinterested and now it is time to move on, but you want a business that is revivable, not dead. If the business has languished for three or four years, it is probably dead. You'd have to start from scratch to build up a client base, throw out worthless inventory, and so on.

Another variation on the theme is not buying somebody else's business outright, but getting equity in an existing business. For example, a company has ten employees, three of whom have serious equity. They want you to come in and head up marketing. They really want the company to grow from $12 million to $60 million and so you want equity in the business to make it happen. If you are looking at an equity deal, do the same kind of due diligence you would do if you were buying the entire business because, in fact, you *are* buying the business. You will be part owner.

## Analyzing the Business

Be sure to read the chapter "Analyzing the Business" later on in this book. You will need to understand the metrics of the business you are buying, and this chapter is an introduction to that important subject.

## What About the Business *You* Want to Buy?

Can you write up a page or more about the business you want and how it works, or are you going on your gut? Is it a mature business with lots of competitors? Is it a new, untested industry? How are the margins for a typical company in this industry? How is your prospective company doing versus the industry in general? Do the present owners know what they're doing? Have they kept good numbers? Will you be able to measure how well you're doing and be able to predict revenue? Or will you have to wait to see how the revenue comes out before you know you have a problem?

No matter what kind of business you want to buy (or start), do your research. Get to know the industry. That's why so many successful people buy businesses that are in a field in which they already have experience. Otherwise, you are looking at it from the outside saying to yourself, "How hard can it be?" How hard? Very hard. You could lose your shirt. Spend two years on research.

Often, the most important aspect a seller brings to the party is a brand name and a steady stream of customers. In the case of the Five O'Clock Club, we also have considerable trademarks, copyrights and other intellectual capital, as well as our databases that have taken decades to build. Those kinds of things are the most difficult to replace and that's where the value comes in. However, intellectual capital is difficult to value.

## Get Help

Hire someone, such as a CPA, to help you. Valuation experts routinely value companies, but you're doing it only a few times as you look at various businesses. After all, you would hire a housing inspector before you actually purchase a house. Why wouldn't you do the same thing when you're making what may be an even more life-altering purchase?

# Buying a Franchise

When you purchase a franchise, you buy the local rights within a specified geographic area to sell the company's products or services under the company's name and to use the company's system of operations. Buying a franchise has the advantage of being handed an operating system and basically being told what to do. It has the disadvantage of being told what to do—and not allowing you to be very creative.

So you have the advantage of having guidance and not having to think of everything yourself. The International Franchise Association cites the following as advantages of franchising:

1. The ability to rely on the experience of the franchiser and its operating system
2. Training
3. Advertising efficiencies
4. Buying efficiencies
5. Continuing support

Some franchises help you a great deal and you can earn a decent living. Others can result in disaster. Like anything else in life, you must do your research first. Talk to other franchisees, but not only the ones the company suggests you

speak to. Chances are, they will be glad to tell you their revenues, how many hours they have to put in, how much support they get from corporate. You can lose a lot of money buying a franchise, so buyer beware. Krispy Kreme donuts, for example, has been in the paper a lot because they over-expanded their franchise operations, getting lots of money from franchisees who could not make money. Baskin-Robbins, on the other hand, has a very good reputation as of this writing. They provide substantial guidance—even after they have your money. But then you have to adhere to their operating system, as is true with virtually all franchises. You're part-way between being an employee and being on your own.

Here are a few questions to ask yourself:

- Would you rather buy a Baskin-Robbins franchise and get their guidance and obey their rules or start your own ice cream store and be a little more creative? Do you want to sell someone else's brand or your own? If you long to do it yourself, then don't buy a franchise.
- Will they require you to continually buy

overpriced supplies that cut into your margins?
- Have you spoken to a lot of other owners of this same franchise and heard good things?
- How much will you earn per year—your take-home pay? How does that sound to you?

I spoke to a Mailboxes Etc. franchise owner who worked endless hours and earned $40,000 a year. However, on his own, he may have made nothing. Corporate headquarters will tell you how to set rates, bring in business, set up your shop, and so on. But then you can't do it any other way. Ask other franchisees how responsive the parent is when you have questions.

What kind of training do they provide? For example, you may get a week at their headquarters and then they'll have someone come to your location for a few days—or not. Is the training included in the franchise fee or is it additional? Can you shadow a current franchise owner to see and learn? If you were on your own, you would probably find training that cost less than the franchiser charges you. Ask existing trainees what they thought of the training and its cost.

Look for yourself (even Google search) what national branding is out there to help the franchisees profit. And before buying, visit or contact as many stores as you possibly can!

Every business requires the same basic analysis, whether you are buying it or starting your own:

- Take a look at the products and services delivered through this franchise operation. What do you think of them?
- Thoroughly analyze the market. Is the location desirable? Who are your competitors? How is the pricing compared with the competition? If the franchise owner has only bad locations to offer you, for example, having his good brand name won't save you from failure.
- Can it be a successful, profitable business? What benefits can a franchisee gain in

running his business under the franchise system that would be too hard to develop on his own? How effective is the franchiser's marketing research and materials and how applicable are those materials to the market near your franchise. How much money does the average franchisee make in your geographic area? How many hours does the owner put in? What are the hidden expenses?

## Starting Up With a Franchise

You can buy someone's existing franchise, or—most likely—you will be starting a new location for the company. They'll give you some ideas about marketing, but *you* have to bring the customers in. You're starting from scratch. However, if they are an established franchise, they have a recognized brand name, and that will help you a lot in your marketing efforts. After all, everyone knows Holiday Inn, but not everyone knows Joe's Stop and Sleep Motel.

Now ask yourself: "Do I really want to buy this business?" and "How much is this business worth?" Figure out how much this business would cost if you were to do it from scratch. This is difficult to do, but you should at least take a crack at it and do a reasonableness test. List the components of the business and figure out what it would cost if you did it on your own. How easily could you replace the employees, the inventory, the methods they use? How important is the location really? If it's a retail walk-in store, that's one thing, but if it's a consulting business where clients never come to that location, then the location is not as critical.

## Homework:

Write in your bound notebook any ideas from this chapter that are relevant to your business.

# Part Five

Starting Your Own Business
(including a high-growth business)

# Starting a Growth Business

*When you reach an obstacle, turn it into an opportunity. You have the choice. You can overcome and be a winner, or you can allow it to overcome you and be a loser. The choice is yours and yours alone. Refuse to throw in the towel. Go that extra mile that failures refuse to travel. It is far better to be exhausted from success than to be rested from failure.*

Mary Kay Ash, founder of Mary Kay Cosmetics

Yours is a growth business if you plan to go from working part-time on your business to full-time, or if you plan to grow the business beyond yourself and an assistant or two. For example, if you decide to start your own consulting business where you eventually want to have four other people working for you, then you are starting a growth business rather than planning to be an independent consultant in your own field. (Having a consulting business is covered in extensive detail later in this book.)

You can create a future for yourself that builds on your past or is very different from your past. You decide the kind of business you want to have and how you want to live your life. Here are a few examples.

## Case Study: Gwen
### Making a Future For Herself

Here's an extreme example. Gwen, age 36, has been incarcerated for eight years and is about a year away from parole. She wants a different life for herself and has been getting ready for release for some time. She has gotten rid of some bad character traits, and she took a Five O'Clock Club course (offered in the prison) on how to start her own small business.

The first time she came to class, she thought she would like to create an action toy figure named Tattoo, a samurai sword carrying tough guy. The next week, when I brought in a list of all the business ideas from the class, she thought her action figure looked pretty good on paper.

I then asked the class to complete the Seven Stories Exercise, and list everything they did that they were proud of, enjoyed doing and also did well. Gwen remembered a baby shower her cousin gave, and Gwen made chocolate favors for the event as a favor to her cousin. The guests were thrilled about the favors, and Gwen went on to make favors for other parties given by friends, including favors for a bachelor party, a wedding and a Sweet Sixteen party. Each time, the guests loved the favors.

That accomplishment happened almost ten years ago, but is something Gwen remembered fondly. She became enthusiastic about developing the plan for a different kind of business: selling chocolate favors to party planners as well as to people she knew at her Church, in her neighborhood, through PTA meetings, family and friends.

Gwen makes chocolates in just about any color and all orders are made fresh. She was a good student in my class, completing all of the exercises, reading the small business books The Five O'Clock Club donated to the library, and keeping meticulous notes in her notebook. She's developed her marketing and financial plans, and will be ready to go when she is released.

However, as it got closer to the time of her release, Gwen started to get cold feet, as can be expected. She started to name other business ideas (maybe I should run an Internet café), none of which had anything to do with her background or her Seven Stories Exercise. Yes, it's easier to have a dream than to pursue it. Having your own business takes courage—and research—and faith in yourself.

Here's hoping that Gwen follows through on her dream. She could be very successful, and we'd love to help her.

## More Common Examples

Jules, a 27-year-sales-veteran of the financial services industry started his own search firm. He knew everyone in the field and the needs of various companies. He met with five or six people who had search firms, but were not competitors of his. They took him under their wing, taught him the ins and outs, the business metrics, the computer systems that would be needed. Ten years later, he is still operating his business.

Earl had run the insurance division of a major bank that was getting out of the insurance business. The bank had spent millions developing the business and was now ditching it. Earl

knew the business thoroughly and got permission to take the insurance business elsewhere. However, it was far too large for him to run independently. He contacted over 100 insurance companies by direct mail, told them about this opportunity and spoke to those who were interested. Earl and his partner landed a deal with a major company: he and Earl got to keep 51% ownership and each also got paid a base salary of $200,000 a year!

Victoria worked in the events planning department of a major corporation and started her own events planning and concierge business.

A CPA with 25 years' experience in corporate America, Bob started a management and financial consulting business with his brother Ken. They serve as the part-time CFOs for both public and private companies.

Reuther, an attorney by profession who developed an interest in art, started his own arts advisory business that sets up exhibitions of famous artists sponsored by large corporations.

All of these people started with the Seven Stories Exercise and ended up with their own businesses in fields that were a natural outgrowth of their experience and interests. They all developed a business plan. Because many people are intimidated by the prospect of developing a business plan, The Five O'Clock Club developed a quickie version that gets people over that initial hump.

## The One-Hour Business Plan

You need a business plan not just to get financing, but—more importantly—to guide you and help you to think through every aspect of the business. When you are up to your neck in alligators, it's difficult to make so many decisions every day. It's better to have thought through a certain number of issues before you have to make an on-the-spot decision.

Just take an 8½" × 11" piece of paper (see page 134). Across the top, briefly identify your business idea. For example: "Hand-made chocolates for party favors."

Divide the rest of the page into three sections horizontally. In the first third, describe everything you can about *marketing* your product or service: your target markets, how you will market to them, your tentative brand name (which should encompass all future businesses that you might come up with. If Gwen thinks she will move beyond chocolates, her brand name should not restrict her to chocolates.), how your price compares with the competition, a description of your marketing brochure, and so on.

In the second third, describe everything about the *product or service itself*, such as the kinds of chocolate you will use, the wrapping for your products, the pieces you expect will be most popular, and so on.

In the third third, describe everything about the *dollars*: Will this business be profitable?

How much will it cost you to make them? How much time will it take to make a certain number of chocolates? To package them? To market them? What will you be able to charge? Figure out whether this venture is worth your while financially.

Now, if you can write these three parts down on one piece of paper—or on a page in your notebook—you will have the start of your business plan. It becomes real before your eyes. Then you can expand on each part. Keep researching, refining and writing. If you take this easy approach to business planning, you are more likely to at least write down something. *The worksheet is shown on the next page and is described in far more detail in the chapter, "The One-Hour Business Plan."*

# The One-Hour Business Plan Worksheet

**The Business Idea:**

**The Market** (everything about the market for your product or service)

**The Product or Service** (everything about your product or service)

**The Proof of Profitability** (everything about the dollars)

## You May Become Afraid

Peter had a lot of experience in the bagel business and he loves it. All of his Seven Stories and his Forty-Year Vision indicate that this is what he should do. But as he was leaving my office he said, "There are lots of other things I could do. I could always run a bicycle repair shop." I said, "Yes, you probably could. Do you own a bicycle?"

Peter said, "No, I don't own a bicycle."

Me: "Have you ever *repaired* a bicycle?"

Peter: "No, I've never repaired a bicycle."

Me: "A bicycle repair shop is a great idea, but it has nothing to do with you. You don't love bicycles. Bicycles are not in any of your Seven Stories accomplishments or your Forty-Year Vision. Let me name some other businesses that have nothing to do with you. You could sell chairs. You could even sell clothing. You could be a hairdresser. Peter, you could walk down the street and come up with a hundred business ideas, but none of them have anything to do with you."

When people come close to an idea that may suit them perfectly, they tend to get scared. They name business ideas that have nothing to do with them, such as Gwen's Internet café. It frightens people to actually commit to something sensible and then go forward with it. It happened to me and it may happen to you. Having your own business takes research and courage.

## Or Stay Dumb and Keep Dreaming

Earlier I mentioned Joseph, in his mid-forties, who is in the cable and satellite industry in sales and marketing. At a Five O'Clock Club meeting, he said he wanted to be a psychotherapist in his own private practice. Someone in our small group asked him if he had taken any classwork related to psychotherapy. He answered "no." Someone else asked if he read any psychotherapy magazines. He said "no." A third person asked if he has spoken to any psychotherapists to find out about their business. He said, "no, but being a psychotherapist is still a life-long dream."

Maybe Joseph will someday be a psychotherapist, but it is very unusual for a person to be so clear about a dream, and yet have done nothing towards it. A person who takes no action—not even to find out whether the dream is realistic—is simply wasting his or her time.

We want you to take action, even though the action may not be very clear. Read the case studies that follow and see how people have muddled through to find the businesses that would be right for them.

# Case Study: Yadira
## *Determining the Kind of Business She Wants*

*Unless a variety of opinions are laid before us, we have no opportunity of selection, but are bound of necessity to adopt the particular view which may have been brought forward.*

Herodotus, 5th century BC, Greek Historian

When a Five O'Clock Clubber wants to start a growth business, we typically work with the client for a year or more. As coaches, we do not breathe a sigh of relief when a business is finally up and running and the person makes his or her first sale. Making that first dollar does not make it a business; *stable revenue* makes it a business. The coach and client continue to work together until the business is stable.

After many years in corporate America, Yadira knew she wanted to have her own business. In this chapter, we will show you everything she went through to make this decision. Most people don't wake up one day knowing the kind of business they want to have. It can take a very long time of exploration—exploring yourself as well as the market.

Yadira, 36 years old, had worked as a senior mortgage manager for a bank. She and I started working together when she was told she would lose her job in three months and would get a one-year severance package. She didn't want to wait for her job to end; she wanted to start the coaching the minute she heard the news.

Yadira did her Seven Stories Exercise as well as her Fifteen- and Forty-Year Visions. At first, she thought she simply wanted another job. We came up with various job targets for her. For example, she could work in real estate, since she had experience in the mortgage area. She vaguely mentioned that she might want her own business, perhaps food related, maybe catering. Or she could have her own business as a residential mortgage broker.

Since she had fifteen months' grace (three months' notice and one year of severance), we agreed to explore first the possibility of starting her own business. If it did not go well, she would have plenty of time to conduct a job search. We met twice that first week and then once a week after that for a few months.

••••••••••••••••••••••••••••••••••••••••

*The processes used to arrive at the total strategy are typically fragmented, evolutionary, and largely intuitive.*

James Quinn, *Strategic Change: Logical Incrementalism*, 1978

## Her Decision-Making Style

Yadira told me each of her Seven Stories in an extremely detailed, tortured, negative manner. For example, one of her Seven Stories involved volunteering to be a Brownies leader. She developed the organizational structure in her neighborhood after the leader had resigned. Yadira said she had written up ideas about what the Brownies should do and how the organization should work—all this sounds pretty straightforward. But when she described that Brownies accomplishment, she was full of such angst and hand-wringing that I would have thought she was describing a mistake—a failure.

It turns out that hand-wringing was Yadira's style. I had to get used to it and be prepared for it. Later, when she would wring her hands about something, it did not necessarily mean that we were on the wrong path; it simply meant that this is *how* Yadira thought about things. It was her decision-making style. Every time Yadira recounted an accomplishment, she told the story with anguish and ambivalence. And these were her *enjoyable* accomplishments!

I pointed this out to her because I knew it would help her to be aware of it. That's one benefit of working with a coach. Your coach can hold up a mirror to you so you can see who you are and how you react to life. Although Yadira experiences a huge amount of anxiety, she eventually makes a decision and does the right thing.

Are you aware of *your* normal decision-making style? Self-awareness will help you when you face problems in your business. It will keep you calmer to know that your emotional response has more to do with your style than it has to do with the business itself. This self-awareness can make you more relaxed when you are struggling to make a decision or handle a problem. You will learn that this is simply how you react to stress.

. . . . . . . . . . . . . . . . . . . . . . . . . . . . .

*To boldly go where no one has gone before.*

Opening phrase of *Star Trek: The Next Generation*

## A Leap Into the Future

Then we reviewed Yadira's Forty-Year Vision. You may remember that with the Fifteen- or Forty-Year Vision, you start with yourself in the present, and then imagine yourself five years and then 15 years into the future. The results at the five-year point are often unimaginative and simply straight-line the present. At the five-year point, Yadira imagined herself working for a small company in her neighborhood or perhaps for herself. However, at the 15-year point, when she would be 51, she did not even mention the possibility of working for someone else. Instead, she imagined having a business that had expanded to two or three locations, had much larger quarters and had 10 to 20 employees. In fact, she had a partner and together they planned an acquisition! That's pretty specific even though we don't yet know what *kind* of business it might be.

. . . . . . . . . . . . . . . . . . . . . . . . . . . . .

*Imagination is more important than knowledge.*

Albert Einstein

## Define the Environment First

When I help a person imagine his or her Fifteen or Forty-Year Visions, I *tease* or *squeeze* as much as I can out of them. Often, people don't know the *kind* of business they want—i.e., the exact product or service. But we need *something* as the starting point. That something is often the kind of *environment* they see themselves working in. People are usually aware of the environments they prefer.

So I probed, "Yadira, tell me about the environment. What are people doing all day? Are they scurrying in and out of the office or are they on phones all day talking to people? Is it chaotic or is it calm? Are some of them researchers, working on the computer? How are they dressed? Are they dressed in business clothes so they can go out and meet with customers?" I focus primarily on the *other* people in the business, the 10 to 20 employees. What are *they* doing?

For example, I was working with Jorge at the same time as Yadira. When I asked him this question, he imagined having a staff of seven; one was doing research; three were out making sales calls; the rest were involved in the core of the business, whatever that was. It may not sound like much information, but Jorge's scenario is very different from a person who says that he or she is working alone, or one who says that there are fifty people assembling something at workstations, or someone who imagines working outdoors. These are all different *environments* and the description narrows down the kinds of business the person may want.

A person may protest, "But I don't *know* what I'll be doing." I say, "That's okay. Just hang in there and imagine. Tell me anything. You can change your mind later." And then I probe again: "What is the atmosphere? Is it fast paced, crazy and wild? Or is it calm, where people are just thinking and researching? Do your employees work indoors or outdoors?" This is very important information.

.............................................

*No great thing is created suddenly, any more than a bunch of grapes or a fig. If you tell me that you desire a fig, I answer that there must be time. Let it first blossom, then bear fruit, then ripen.*

Epictetus

## Imagine Your Ideal Scene

Yadira was able to imagine even more about herself at age 51, 15 years from now. She said, "One of my hobbies is breeding Norwich Terriers and I want to bring them into the office." Well, when you have your own business you can do anything you want. Yadira was getting the hang of it.

Likewise if you are contemplating your own business, push yourself further, even though you don't really know the answers. You can always change your mind later. But getting *something* down on paper is much better than ending up with a blank sheet because you don't want to "commit." This early self-brainstorming isn't a commitment. This is an exploration.

Imagine your ideal scene—fifteen years out. Imagine what your everyday life will be like ideally. If you have children, how does your business affect them? Or your spouse? Really *feel* the business environment even though you still don't know the subject matter. Actually, the subject matter is *not* the most important decision at this point. That may take a month to a year or more of research. But if you know the lifestyle you want, you'll select a business that gives you that lifestyle. For now, you want to understand *what you value*.

So that was one of my early sessions with Yadira. You probably thought we could select a business in just one session, didn't you? But we *still* don't know the kind of business it is!

I remember the old days when I wrote down *my* Ideal Scene. I sat on my sofa with a cup of tea, and thought I would write a page or two. Once I got into it, I wrote for six hours! I just couldn't stop. I imagined how I would run the business, the kind of people who would work there, the impact I would have on the community, the lifestyle I would have (which included taking occasional naps!), writing books and giving lectures, and running small groups. I wrote and wrote about the environment and the business, but still did not know what the business would be about! That would take research and a lot of time. But at least I knew the kind of life I wanted to live.

.............................................

*Do not repeat the tactics which have gained you one victory, but let your methods be regulated by the infinite variety of circumstances.*

Sun Tzu c. 490 BC, Chinese military strategist

## The Exploration Begins

At first, Yadira decided to investigate interior design. She was interested in creative outlets and had a lot of exposure to interior design because of her mortgage brokerage background. So Yadira made a list of mortgage brokers in her neighborhood and set up appointments to talk to them about interior design. After these meetings, she changed her mind: She thought she might want to have a mortgage brokerage business instead. So she started to find out what it would be like to be a mortgage broker.

If she did want her own mortgage brokerage business, first she would work for a mortgage broker who would not be a competitor of hers when she started her business, such as one in a different geographic location. That's the correct strategy: work for somebody else so you can learn on his or her nickel, but don't work for someone who may be a direct competitor in the future.

But Yadira lacked passion when she talked about mortgage brokerage and even interior design. She sounded intellectual and logical. This doesn't necessarily mean that her targets were wrong, but a lack of passion is unusual for someone who will devote his or her life to an endeavor. Small business owners must be passionate and knowledgeable about their businesses or they will not be successful.

If I thought for sure that she was on the wrong track, I would have said something. But I had met with her for only a few hours total, so I didn't know how she operated. Perhaps the lack of passion would be her style while she conducted research and the passion would emerge as she got more involved.

I also recommended that she read a lot of books and magazines on running a small business and being an entrepreneur. I often give would-be business owners a one-inch thick stack of reading material and ask him to read it before our next weekly meeting. If he has not read the material by the second meeting, I doubt his interest in having his own business. Most would-be entrepreneurs devour the material and ask for more. If a potential small business owner does not want to *study* the field of small business ownership, that's a pretty sure sign that he or she should *not* have a small business. I'm looking for eagerness and passion.

I'm also looking for staying power. Yadira got frustrated when she could not get in to see a specific mortgage broker. This did not bode well for her having her own mortgage brokerage business. She was stumped during the investigation stage! How would she tolerate the ups and downs later?

Passion helps an entrepreneur ride through the real setbacks. Most entrepreneurs have failed a number of times. They become devastated, but they bounce back. I told her stories about my own business, and the number of times I failed. I told her I was concerned about whether she would be able stay the course in her own business. But despite her lack of passion about the specific businesses she was investigating, she continued to read hordes of entrepreneurial books, which was a good sign.

Because she became frustrated easily, it was unlikely that Yadira would last more than three weeks in the wrong business. She was starting to wonder whether mortgage brokerage was the right field for her. I didn't know the answer to that, but there were signs that she should continue exploring having her own business—of some kind.

Then Yadira thought of a few business ideas that were more suited to her creative nature, and not just a logical extension of her banking background. For example, she could do wedding planning with her sister-in-law, or make "Depot Dinners" for people who could grab them as they got off the train returning from their jobs in the city. So we played around with these ideas while she continued to investigate the mortgage brokerage business.

Yadira discovered she would have to get a license from the Board of Health before she could sell dinners at the train station. She could not *believe* this setback. But this was nothing compared with the setbacks she would face later. People expect a business to be *easy* to run *because* they know nothing about the business.

...............................................

*Running a company is easy when you don't know how, but very difficult when you do.*

Price Pritchett

So I broke the news to her, "I don't know if you should have your own business. This information you've gathered would never qualify as a *setback*. You are simply finding out what it takes to run a specific business. You have nothing invested except a very small amount of time." I pointed out that there are plenty of people with far fewer resources who have food-vending trucks. She could ask them how they do it. This was not difficult. I told her even *I* could find out in one day. But she turned the obstacle of needing a food license into an even bigger obstacle: to get the licensing, she would need a new $25,000 kitchen. Obviously, she had no real passion for this idea; otherwise, she would have been *excited* about the research rather than frustrated by it. She would have seen the "obstacles" as things she could add to her "to do" list, rather than seeing them as insurmountable barriers.

...............................................

*A mediocre idea that generates enthusiasm will go further than a great idea that inspires no one.*

Mary Kay Ash

## Finally—Some Passion

We had worked together four or five weeks when Yadira switched from her "I want it quickly, easily frustrated" mindset and started putting real effort into her future. She signed up for classes at Peter Kumps Cooking School. She loved cooking and felt that if she was going to do something with food, she needed to learn more about cooking.

Yadira pursued her cooking with real pas-

sion while she also kept mortgage brokerage as a fallback. We brainstormed the different places she could work to learn something about the food industry. For example, she could work for a caterer, a restaurant, or a food store on the buying side so she could learn about food costs.

Yadira immediately started talking to people in these areas, and when she reported back to me the following week, she made light of any "setbacks." She was now committed to making something work. In addition to taking courses at Peter Kumps Cooking School, she started to work as an assistant there, which means that she washed dishes. That was great because she got to hang around the school more. And her brain kept working on her food idea.

That's what happens once you get committed. The obstacles seem like nothing and the ideas start popping. For example, she could imagine herself doing a cooking class for kids in her upscale neighborhood. She talked to people at Zabar's, a "gourmet Epicurean emporium," and she imagined making something that she would sell to them. As she explored, she found that desserts were her passion, especially pastries.

If you are researching an area you love, it won't feel like work. It's interesting and fun and keeps you moving forward. But it takes time. You can see how it can take two years from the time a person says, "I want to have my own business," until the business can be started. (Consulting businesses take far less time to start.) That's why most people keep their day jobs while they do the research. Money was not the issue for Yadira at the moment because she still had her severance and her husband had a good job and was very supportive of her exploration. So she could work at this full time.

...............................................

*I found that the men and women who got to the top were those who did the jobs they had in hand, with everything they had of energy and enthusiasm and hard work.*

Harry S. Truman

## Keep Your Notebook Religiously and Start Your Hanging Files

If Yadira really loves the food business, the research she was doing would be a benefit later. However, she was having so much fun that she felt like she was playing and being a little flighty and it was hard to get her to take her research seriously. Yadira probably felt a little guilty doing something she enjoyed so much. How could she call this work?

So every week, I insisted she write her ideas in the notebook she had purchased expressly for that purpose. For example, when she re-searched the food-cart business, she attended a food-equipment exposition. I made sure she took notes in her notebook, but she ended up with enough information to fill a *file* on food carts and such items. She needed to make a file *now*. If she later need to buy a foodcart for any food-re-lated business, she would never remember what she had learned at that exposition. She said she could barely remember it *now*! So in addition to keeping her notebook of ideas and thoughts, she grudgingly started making her hanging files of the information she was gathering.

I could press this point with Yadira because of my own experience. I spent years doing research before I started my business (I had a day job), and I kept the files of that early research. When we got to the point in our business where we needed that information, I simply pulled out the file. I was amazed by how in-depth it was. I told Yadira she would feel that way as well.

Yadira refined her vision as she went along. One week she announced that she'd like to make fruit tarts as well as pastries. To show her how resolved she had become, I teased her, "How about mortgage brokerage, are you interested in that?" "NO! I'm not interested in mortgage bro-kerage" "Well, how about the "Depot Dinners" business? Do you want to do that right now?" "No, of course I don't want to deliver dinners at the train station." I said, "Fine, so you want to have a dessert business. For the past two months,

you have talked about nothing but pastries and desserts."

......................................

*A deliberate search for a plan of action that will develop a business's competitive advantage and compound it. For any company the search is an iterative process that begins with a recognition of where you are and what you have now. Your most dangerous competitors are those that are most like you. The differences between you and your competitors are the basis of your advantage. If you are in business and self-supporting you already have some kind of competitive advantage no matter how small or subtle. Otherwise you would have gradually lost customers faster than you gained them. The objective is to enlarge the scope of your advantage, which can only happen at someone else's expense.*

Bruce Henderson, Founder, Boston Consulting Group, Harvard Business Review, 1989

## The Momentum Builds

Yadira's whole life was now desserts. She subscribed to *Gourmet News, Nations Restaurant News* and *Griffin News*. When we had our weekly meeting, she brought in half-a-dozen food-related magazines. She entered the pastry program at the French Culinary Institute—a six-month program that costs $20,000—just for pastry! She used the education grant she got from her former employer to pay for part of the culinary institute tuition and some government money to pay for another part of it. She was still working for the Peter Kumps School, and she volunteered one day a week for about 2½ months to help test recipes for a person who was writing a recipe book. Over time, she also worked at a couple of other places. Each of these was short term, and took just a little time, but added to her knowledge of the industry. Luckily, Yadira had that year of severance.

As you can see, Yadira was determined to be a trained expert in her field. Other people make desserts and feel no need to go to the French

Culinary Institute and spend $20,000. They just cook. But Yadira imagined herself selling her pastry to upscale shops and restaurants, even providing the pastry shells to chefs who did not want to make the shells themselves. She imagined mass producing them, perhaps employing local housewives, teaching them to cook and prepare these foods. That way, she could work with the kind of people she liked and have fun while doing what she loved. What a difference from the Yadira I first met!

. . . . . . . . . . . . . . . . . . . . . . . . . . . . . . . . .

*The world is all gates, all opportunities, strings of tension waiting to be struck.*

Ralph Waldo Emerson

## Stage One, Stage Two, Stage Three, . . . SEVEN Altogether

Now that Yadira is starting to formulate a business, she needs to outline the stages of her business so she will be able to see how far she has come. The outcome will enable her to have a focus and a clear direction. Not surprisingly, she did not want to write anything down, but I insisted!

### Stage One:

This stage includes whatever *you're doing right now* or what you have done in the past to prepare for this business. In Yadira's case, it included the following:

- Attend Peter Kumps Cooking School.
- Assist in a test kitchen at the International Cooking School of Italian Food and Wine.
- Enroll at the French Culinary Institute's Classic Pastry Arts Program.
- Take classes at the New York Baking and Cake Company, and Alliance Française.
- Get on-the-job training at a restaurant.
- Work at a hotel pastry shop or caterer (which she plans to do next).

- Subscribe to and read food-related magazines, especially trade magazines.
- Attend a trade conference on the restaurant and food delivery business.
- Check out equipment and supplies stores and pastry shops.
- Network with the National Association of Confection Brokers.

Wow! In retrospect, you can see that Yadira was on her way.

So if a small business is your dream, write out your *own* Stages document and keep it permanently in your notebook for easy reference. In the early days of my business, I kept my Seven Stages taped to the wall right next to my computer. That vision kept me on track. I was forced to look at it every day. It's easy to get distracted. If I wanted to do something that was not on the list or did not lead up to something on the list, I did not do it. You must stay focused. You have only so much time, energy and money to spend on your business.

Below are the *highlights* of Yadira's other stages, each of which contained much more detail.

### Stage Two

- Develop both a wholesale and a retail product line.
- Develop a list of target markets.
- Determine equipment needs.
- Finalize selection of a business name.

Yadira is going to make pastry for desserts, but she could also make pastry that other chefs would use for main courses and appetizers. So Stage 2 for Yadira is deciding what her product line will be. If she makes crêpes, she could have dessert crêpes, dinner crêpes or other kinds of crêpes. Then she needs to define her target markets. To whom will she sell her wholesale product line? For example, she could target pastry chefs, as well as kitchens that have no pastry chefs. Her retail product line? She could target party planners, individuals who are giving parties, or small retail stores who could carry her line.

## Stage Three:

The opening and the day that she actually starts her business

## Stage Four:

Stabilization of the business (developing business processes, and so on).

## Stage Five:

Expansion number one (for example, in addition to pastries, she could make soups, savories or related items)

## Stage Six:

Expansion number two

## Stage Seven:

Maintenance. Keep the business going.

The stages of your plan are important, but none of the stages have dates on them. Implement each stage as fast as you can, but accept the fact that everything takes time. You don't know what's going to stand in your way. Putting dates on each stage may make you rush through a stage prematurely rather than doing it well, and that will set you back. Or you may get discouraged when you didn't hit those arbitrary dates. Real life takes longer.

Yadira is still researching and developing her initial thoughts. So she has plenty of other issues to research. For example, she needs to decide what she wants to do about refrigeration and location, develop her marketing and staffing strategies. But as she goes along, Yadira will find out that some of her ideas are unrealistic or unprofitable. She will have to amend her stages and her plans until she has a concept that is fairly well thought out.

At this point, she simply needs to have an outline to follow and develop her plan a little

more. But it would be counter-productive to over-analyze and over-plan and never get started. Some things you can only learn by doing, so at a certain point you just have to say that you have researched enough. You know that the business concept is worth trying. It's time to get started on the simplified business plan.

Yadira is well on her way to having a growth business. The business she'll end up with is certainly not anything that we could have known from day one. In her case, it was a grueling intellectual process, but we got through it. I will probably work with her for about nine months to a year. There's no need to meet with her every week, now that she has some momentum going. Once a month should do it. She is now selling quantities of pastries to a local bakery shop and also selling boxed desserts to a gift store. I expect to see her through this initial phase. Once the business is somewhat stable, she can go out on her own.

By the way, Helen, another client of mine, decided on her own to start a version of "Depot Dinners," and has run that business successfully for two years now!

· · · · · · · · · · · · · · · · · · · · · · · · · · · · · ·

*We act as though comfort and luxury were the chief requirements of life, when all that we need to make us happy is something to be enthusiastic about.*

Charles Kingsley

## Most People Have a Job and a Dream

Most people don't have the financial freedom to explore full time and also take a $20,000 course. Most have to work while they explore. I urge them if at all possible to take a job that fits in with their long-term plan, so they are learning on someone else's nickel. But they'll earn more than that nickel. If your day job has nothing to do with your dream, you are just earning money but getting no momentum. But if your job has something to do with your dream, you earn experience as *well* as money in your new field. When Yadira took those low-paying jobs, she was not just getting a few bucks, she was getting experience and contacts.

It takes two years to be able to start your business because during that time you are not only doing research; you are also making the mental adjustment from being an employee to being the owner and boss. You also have to make a *financial* adjustment and develop your business plan. Then you can get started.

•••••••••••••••••••••••••••••••••••••••

*Twenty years from now you will be more disappointed by the things that you didn't do than by the ones you did do. So throw off the bowlines. Sail away from the safe harbor. Catch the trade winds in your sails. Explore. Dream. Discover.*

Mark Twain

## And Then You Get Scared!

Well, actually, you don't get started. The opposite happens. You get scared. Take a look at Yadira. She was having so much fun, she felt guilty reading pastry magazines and helping a woman with recipes. Something was not right about this. So I said to her, "Did you ever hear people say, "I'm so happy I can't believe I get *paid* to do this?" The ideal is to love something so much that you cannot believe you are getting paid. That's how I feel about my job. A lot of entrepreneurs feel that way.

But as a person gets closer to implementing his or her dream, panic can set in. It's safer to dream than to take steps to make something happen. At least you have your dreams. But if you try and fail, you have nothing. As Billy Joel says in his song, "Piano Man," "Well, I'm sure that I could be a movie star if I could get out of this place."

A guy at the bar dreams of being a movie star, and he's sure he would be successful. It's safer to just keep drinking and dreaming that you *could* be a movie star, than to take steps to make it happen and run the risk of finding out you were wrong. It's safer to dream than to *find out* you don't have the talent or the drive or the fortitude to fulfill that dream. Being an entrepreneur takes courage—the courage to *act on* your dreams and *make them happen.*

# Case Study: Robert
## *First, Thirteen Years of Research*

*Leaders establish the vision for the future and set the strategy for getting there; they cause change. They motivate and inspire others to go in the right direction and they, along with everyone else, sacrifice to get there.*

John Kotter

Over the years, when I visited my brother, Robert Dobbs, and his family, he would ask me to peer into his microscope to see his latest development—beautifully round titanium dioxide particles. For thirteen years, after coming home from his day job, Robert conducted his own research and perfected his materials. At just the right time, he met another materials scientist and Five O'Clock Clubber, and they started Primet Precision Materials, Inc., a nanotechnology business.

Here are some of the things Robert told me about their business—not something you read about everyday in the newspaper.

Over the last 3 years there have been about 5,000 articles in the popular press (including business) about the promised wonders of nano-materials or the nano-revolution. (A nanometer is one billionth of a meter—about 8 to 12 atoms in diameter.) However, these wonders did not find their way to the market place. They are now about to materialize through Primet.

Hundreds of millions of dollars have been spent in the pursuit of advanced technologies based on nanomaterials. Do a search on nano and the Internet will flood you with links describing many exciting applications.

A short listing of these wonders include:

- fuel cells that enable lap-top computers to run for months,
- coatings that are so wear-resistant as to make products last seemingly for ever,
- plastics that are stronger than steel,
- automobile tires that last the life of the car,
- engines made with slippery materials so no oil is needed,
- transparent photocatalytic paint that is applied to highway sound barriers that clean up pollutants as they are created by cars and trucks,
- machines that are so small they are hard to see with the naked eye.

As universities forged ahead in developing these wonders, so did industrial and government researchers. Much of this effort was provided by funding support by national governments. But, as with many glamorous and exciting things, there is a dull side. Where would companies get the raw materials to make all of these wonderful devices? For nanomaterials to be used widely, someone has to be able to supply millions of tons of particles. They require materials that are smaller than the devices themselves. Often they require particles that are measured in billionths of a meter. Researchers have produced these small particles at an extremely high cost, sometimes still exceeding $15,000 per gram. Some nanomaterials companies now produce materials at lower costs in production but are either still too expensive for broad usage or they have processes that can only produce a small amount of material per machine. What good are wonderful devices if no one could afford to manufacture them because the materials are too expensive? As in all things wonderful, there was one last barrier that had to fall before the impossible became real.

Enter Robert and Primet Precision Materials. They have the technology to produce nanometer particles in large tonnage capacities, from hundreds of thousands to millions of tons per year, at price points attractive to manufacturers of competitive products. More importantly, Primet technology enables even further advances in the nano-revolution.

They've produced nano-particles of compositions no one else has ever succeeded in making and that are critically needed in some of the most exciting advancements in consumer products.

One of Primet Precision Materials' active collaborations is in the conversion of coal to jet aviation fuel. They can disassemble coal at the molecular level and harvest special molecules used in the preparation of new medicines. Coal has rare molecules that were millions of years in the making, possessing amazing properties. Once the coal is gone, it's gone. Once it's burned to make heat, it's gone forever. But for those who

still want to burn coal, Primet can remove all of the pollutants prior to its being burned, at a very low cost. Acid rain from coal plants could easily and quickly be a long gone concern.

Primet is also active in making improved sunscreen materials. In this effort, they made materials that were only a dozen atoms in diameter. This breakthrough is of particular interest to those working on photonic devices where photons of light are used instead of electrons in ultrahigh speed computers and other microelectronic devices.

Where do you begin when you have the solution to the most pressing materials problem in the nano-revolution? Primet is being pulled in many directions by companies with a crying need for nanomaterials so these companies can bring their discoveries to market in new products. Primet is strategically placing their efforts in three categories: very large scale production application, very high value materials and the making of finished products.

The very large scale application requires hundreds of thousands of tons of material that will improve most of the products we use daily such as: improved coverage wall paint, brighter fabrics, nicer paper, won't-fade-in-the-sun wood varnish, and many more.

In the very high value materials category Primet is active in advanced microelectronic materials allowing for smaller circuitry, the elimination of more expensive materials and new manufacturing routes for making circuits that more efficiently remove heat, eliminating an expensive component called a heat sink. Lap tops being too hot will be a thing of the past. In this same category, Primet provides materials that enable the creation of new properties in polymers, making them stronger, harder, more wear resistant, impact resistant and more UV resistant than traditional plastics.

Then there are some areas where it makes more sense to forward integrate and produce the high value product itself rather than selling materials to someone else to produce the

same product. These are Primet's most exciting endeavors, although they can't tell us what
they are. Well, it's not nice to tease, so Robert
described one exciting area. Billions of dollars
of machines are used in the manufacture of
computer chips. Many of these machines are
made of exotic alloys and in specialized shapes
that are very expensive to process. Eliminate
most of that expense while providing the same
exotic alloy components, and you have a major
business. In this area, Robert will help lower the
cost of chip making facilities and also lower the
operating cost of producing chips.

Robert believes that Primet technology
is about to drive a very interesting period of
technological advance. Many of the wonderful
inventions we've been hearing about for years
can begin to march forward to the market. For
most of these products the only missing ingredient was a supply of material at a reasonable cost
and, in some cases, available in millions of tons
per year.

These two supply barriers have been de-
molished by Primet. By now, they have relationships with major research universities, dozens
of scientists who clamor to get in on the action
and want to be part of this development, and
large companies testing various samples to see
which ones will change their industries. Primet
will go through dozens of products that "don't
work." That's the nature of the scientific research
business. And then something will hit and it will
be huge.

Primet now employs a few dozen scientists,
are at the commercialization phase in the development of their business, and are looking for
global penetration. They have targeted companies that would be most likely to purchase their
nano-particles or hire them for co-development
roles. Primet Precision Material's nano-particles
will enable other people's inventions to be com-
mercialized. Theirs is the only process that can
be scaled to the production quantities that will
be necessary for wide-scale use of new inven-

tions that require nano-particles.

They are using the standard Five O'Clock
Club targeting approach in their business development. They are targeting:

- Titanium dioxide manufacturers. Titanium
  dioxide alone is an $8 billion industry,
  mostly large companies with over $500
  million in sales, but also several specialty
  niche producers.
- The semiconductor and electronics manufacturing industry.
- The fuel cell industry, which will grow
  phenomenally if they can get the platinum
  out. GM, Exxon, and many, many other
  companies are working on fuel cells—but
  they need nano-particles. That's where
  Primet comes in.

The nano-revolution is ready to roll because
Primet Precision Materials has figured out how
to make these materials cost-effectively, and in
large quantities, both of which are necessary to
supply new materials to the world's leading companies. Primet is now partnering with Cornell
University on various projects and the company
attracts scientists from all over the world.

But it can take years of development before
they know whether something works. The first
dozen developments may fail. But that's the
courage of an entrepreneur: to keep investors
satisfied that you are on the right path, while
keeping your employees passionate, productive
and focused.

Most businesses evolve over time. You learn
as you go along. Opportunities appear and disappear. But the head of the venture has to stay
focused and keep this ship on track.

Robert Dobbs and his colleagues may be
reached through his website, www.primetpreci-
sion.com.

.........................................

*Whoever said anybody has a right to give up?*

Marian Wright Edelman

*Leadership is a potent combination of strategy and character. But if you must be without one, be without the strategy.*

Norman Schwarzkopf, commander
of Operation Desert Storm

Now you've read a few small business case studies—ranging from a pastry business to a nanotechnology company. Later, you'll read about others. I hope you can now see why it can take years of research before you can actually start a business. You have to understand yourself as well as the kind of business you want.

# Part Six:

Becoming a Consultant in Your Own Field

# On Your Own: Becoming a Consultant

*He profits most who serves best.*

Arthur F. Sheldon

A new business, even a consulting business, is like a little baby. You need to nurse it along, watch it every second, know that it's going to burp and cry. You have to figure out what's wrong and take care of it.

Fifteen percent of those who attend the Five O'Clock Club are consultants in their own field and want help with their "babies." Some want to consult temporarily, but others would like to give up the corporate life ("It gave me a false sense of security. I've lost three jobs in a row.") and try the consulting route.

The Five O'Clock Club method of developing leads and interviewing is exactly the same for those looking for full-time employment and for those who want consulting assignments. However, there are a few differences for those who want to run a consulting business rather than simply landing one or two assignments.

Just like those who are looking for full-time work, consultants should define their target markets, segment them, and develop a marketing strategy aimed at each one. However, it's hard work for any firm to develop strong relationships and become well known in its target markets. Therefore, it's better to identify and develop your markets and offer them a number of services, rather than offer a narrow service to all of the markets in your geographic area. Focused marketing is key. Here are other hints:

- Remember that the business is ⅓ marketing; ⅓ administration; ⅓ delivery of your consulting services.
- Develop written plans for each market, study what your competitors are doing, determine how to differentiate yourself from your competitors and how to keep future competitors from entering your market.
- One-on-one marketing means getting to know each customer and getting repeat business and referrals from each customer.
- Mail quarterly to at least 500 names— depending on the business you're in.
- Keep track of your costs for each job or project. Then calculate the hourly rate you are actually making rather than what you think you're making. Most consultants over-service their accounts.

- It's okay to lose money when you're starting up but know whether you're making money or losing it and how much.
- Keep track of your revenue by category. Do your clients say they want one kind of service but actually purchase another? For example, many Five O'Clock Clubbers have *said* they're interested in Executive Coaching to help them do well in their jobs, but most actually purchase only our job-search advice.

- What profit margin are you aiming for? Rule of thumb: If you operate solo, charge two times your direct labor expense (see the table in the chapter, *Negotiating a Freelance or Consulting Assignment*) and then keep your other expenses in line.

The following chapters contain a lot more detail on having your own consulting business.

# How to Start Your Own Consulting Business

Five O'Clock Clubbers who are interested in actually having their own consulting businesses often take consulting assignments on the side while they keep their day jobs. They get consulting experience while staying secure financially. Sometimes people will move their main job from a five-day week to a four-day and then a three-day week while getting their consulting business going.

If you think you want to launch a consulting business, your mindset must be different from those who are trying to land temporary consulting work.

Having your own ongoing consulting business is like being on a continual job hunt, requiring marketing and administration, not just actually doing the consulting work. To assure continued business, a rule-of-thumb is to devote $1/3$ of your time to marketing, $1/3$ to administration and $1/3$ to actually delivering the service. In addition, your marketing literature is more likely to be a brochure rather than a résumé.

## Consulting Options

Many people who start their own consulting businesses do only that. They land three assignments and then no more. That's because they knew three people who had promised to use their services, but they had no marketing plan beyond those three people. They thought no further ahead than "getting started."

Other consultants land one assignment with one client company, essentially working on that account full-time. Or they may have a list of clients, and one client starts to dominate the business. Pretty soon, the consultant is dependent on that one client. The assignment may last for years, but this is not the same as having your own consulting business. You are now simply working for one employer and getting paid as a

155

consultant rather than being on payroll. The rule of thumb: do not have more than fifteen percent of your revenue from one client.

A third category of consultant is continually on a roller-coaster. These consultants land an assignment or two and spend all of their time "delivering" the service. When those assignments end, they have no business, perhaps for weeks or months—and are forced to market again. It is a very stressful way to live.

> The rule of thumb: do not have more than fifteen percent of your revenue from one client.

Finally, there are consultants who land two concurrent in-house assignments, working two days a week for one employer and two or three days a week for another, usually for companies that could not afford the consultant full time. Jim, a Five O'Clock Clubber, worked two days a week as the head of marketing for a restaurant chain and two days a week as the head of marketing for a telecom company, earning more money than he had ever earned full time.

This arrangement gives consultants the stability of having continual employment while hedging their bets. For example, if one assignment ends, Jim still has income while looking for another assignment. However, if the assignments come and go, this too can be a more stressful life than the consultant had hoped for.

> These are not businesses:
> • Landing a few accounts
> • Working as a consultant for one employer
> • Working on one assignment and then marketing

## The Starting Point: What is Your Vision?

*The more I've thought about it over the years, the more I've concluded that what really leads to outstanding consultants, and I think then outstanding performance in almost anything you can think of, is the willingness to really take risks, take risks with your thinking, to take risks in how far you're trying to push the client, and not to be conservative and too cautious. I had a conversation with a colleague recently who was learning how to ski, and he said that, in the course of his ski week, he concluded that, if you weren't falling, you weren't learning, and I think that's, you know, a general rule of life. You've got to take risks and be willing to fail.*

Fred Gluck, Managing Director, McKinsey & Co, *Pinnacle*, June 19, 1994.

Even if you've done your Forty-Year Vision before, it's time to re-do it if you're considering having your own consulting business. How do you imagine yourself five years and fifteen years from now? Answer all of the questions in the Forty-Year Vision exercise. Then think about your business itself five and fifteen years from now:

### Your Product and Service

• What kind of service will you be offering? (That is, what will you be doing for clients?) You can't do everything. Be specific.

### Marketing Issues

• Who is your target market? Which industries and which people within those industries?
• How will your company distinguish itself from other consulting firms that offer the same service? What will be your competitive advantage?
• How will your target audience find out about you? What is your marketing plan?
• How will you juggle multiple clients so you will not become too dependent on one client for the bulk of your revenue?

### Money Issues

• How will you price your services? (The pricing for the first few clients may be different than what you can charge later.)

- How will you keep records? How will you track the profitability of each account so you can tell which accounts are profitable and which are not?

## Running the Business

- How many employees do you imagine having (or would you like to remain solo)?
- If you plan to run solo, how will you assure that you spend approximately ⅓ of your time on marketing, ⅓ on administration and ⅓ on delivery?
- If you want to have other employees, what would those employees do? Five and fifteen years from now, how many will be in administration, sales, service delivery, whatever?
- What will the atmosphere be like within your firm? (Aggressive? Competitive? Collegial? Laid-back?)
- What are the values you want to instill in your firm? (Competitive, aggressive and profit-driven? Do-good and reasonably priced? Highest quality? Low cost?)
- What kind of lifestyle do you want to have? Work 80-hour weeks or not? Live close to work or not? Attend lots of conventions and trade shows or not? Be able to nap in the afternoon or not?

It's your life and your business. You can create it. Start writing, and write as much as you can about the kind of business you want to have.

Don't ignore the financials. Some people believe that once they get clients, the money will follow. But many consultants and small business owners undercharge. Sonya specialized in making formals and wedding dresses and wanted to grow her business. I asked her to keep an index card on each order she received, and write on that card what she would be paid, the cost of all materials and other expenses related to that "job," and the amount of time she spent on that project. This simple record-keeping allowed her to look at her business objectively. When she included time spent on trips looking for the perfect buttons and conducting many fittings, Sonya was amazed to find out that she was earning about 10 cents an hour! Sonya would have to raise her prices or reduce her expenses.

Unless you track your business by project, you may find—as even many large consulting firms do—that some of your "best" accounts are money losers! When big firms find out—because someone on staff does a client or project profitability analysis—they usually resign those accounts. You must do the same after your business is up and running.

..........................................

*What do you want to achieve or avoid? The answers to this question are objectives. How will you go about achieving your desire results? The answer to this you can call strategy.*

William E Rothschild

## Marketing Your Business Through Direct and Targeted Mailings

*Failure is not the worst thing in the world. The very worst is not to try.*

Anonymous

If you want to have a real consulting business (as opposed to a temporary assignment or working as a consultant for one firm), you will need methods for developing new business while you are delivering services to current customers. There are some standard practices you can follow, and they resemble to a large extent the normal Five O'Clock Club job search:

1. Develop a list of your target markets (industries by company size; fields).
2. Research the names of the organizations and the people you would like to contact at each organization.
3. Develop your cover letter and brochure and send them to those organizations.
4. Do follow-up phone calls to at least 50 of those organizations. Ask for a meeting.
5. Keep records

6. Mail to your list at least quarterly. (Email more frequently.)

Janet started her own public relations business. She specialized in small, unusual companies, such as those who made Venetian blinds or roof-top water towers, and she got excellent media coverage for them. But, as would be expected, she worked so hard on these accounts that no new business came in. To drum up new business, Janet conducted a quarterly mailing to 300 names (with no follow-up phone calls.) She described her latest assignments in the cover letter, and included her brochure as well as a value-added piece (which I will explain later). Routinely, Janet got 4 or 5 new clients every time she did a mailing, and her business grew from $30,000 the first year to $70,000 by the third year. Since Janet was operating out of her home, and since most of her expenses were tax-deductible, that revenue was fine for her.

Gary, a Five O'Clock Clubber, was a 45-year-old former actor who specialized in presentation coaching for executives. When he came to the Club, he had a brochure, a small amount of work and a lot of talent. The group encouraged him to conduct thorough research in his target areas, which consisted of public relations firms and senior executives at companies. Gary attended the Club every week so he would stay focused on making his follow-up phone calls to ask for meetings.

Within just a few weeks, he landed new business with executives at two major corporations and with two on-air anchors at a television network. He came to the Club a few more sessions to make sure that he had the routine down—the routine you should follow: make your lists; do your mailing at least quarterly; conduct follow-up phone calls. During the next nine months, Gary earned significant money. What's more, he had a real consulting business, balancing marketing with delivery and administration.

As his firm grew, networking and referrals became his primary source of leads. But direct contact got the business off the ground. [For more about Gary's experience, see his story a few pages back.]

When you become very busy servicing your clients, you must still do your quarterly mailings—perhaps with no follow-up phone calls. Do not stop marketing. Certainly, ask your current clients for the names of people who may be able to use your services, but that is not enough to get—and keep—most businesses off the ground. When you are well established, referrals alone may carry you forward. However, will those referrals be enough in a down-market? It's best to have a solid marketing plan in place so you have control over your business and are not so dependent on others, or the vagaries of the market.

For much more information on developing your target list, please refer to our book, *Short-cut Your Search: The Best Ways to Get Meetings.* Remember that having a consulting business is exactly like a job search, but a *continual* job search where you have to keep on marketing.

## What to Include in Your Mailings

Basic mailings include:

- a cover letter,
- your brochure, and
- a value-added piece.

You could use a "status-report" cover letter, letting readers know the kinds of projects you've been working on and reminding them to keep you in mind if they need similar help. If you are at the beginning of building your business, do follow-up phone calls to get to see people to introduce yourself. Your goal, like that of a Five O'Clock Club job hunter, is to find out "if they would consider using someone like you when they have a need." If they say "yes," then you ask, "Do you mind if I stay in touch with you?"

> When your firm is solid, networking and referrals may be your primary source of leads. But direct contact is often what's needed to get the business off the ground and give it a kick-start when things slow down.

If you have plenty of business to keep you busy, you are not likely to have the time to follow up with phone calls, but would expect prospective clients to call you if they have a need. If they do call you, and you do not have time to service them yourself, refer them to someone who can. Be seen as a "source." If your long-term plan is to have a number of employees, line up sub-contractors who can help you on an "as needed" basis.

In addition to the cover letter and your brochure, enclose a value-added piece. This could be an article about you from a newspaper or magazine, an example of your work, an original piece on your subject matter (such as: "How to Make Presentations" from the presentation coach), or simply the reprint of an article that you think would be of interest to your target audience ("Perhaps you've already seen this, but I thought it might be of interest to you.") Writing your own articles can be time-consuming, but they do give you credibility in your field.

## Naming Your Firm

Many would-be consultants think the name they select is the make-or-break step in the development of their consulting firm. However, it is far less important than you may think. Many consultants choose names that do not differentiate them at all. Names that are descriptions of what you do or generic to your field are almost useless in distinguishing you from others offering a similar service. Who will remember whether your consulting firm is called "Risk Management Resources" or "Risk Management Solutions?" That's why using your own name (such as, "J.D. Placer Consulting" or "David Pandozzi and Associates") may be superior to using company names that are merely descriptive of your services. Your own name is distinctive. Therefore, the most simple approach to naming your firm is to use your own name, followed by a one- or two-line description of your services, such as "specializing in risk management solutions." The name of your consulting firm is far less important than the "specializing in" line.

## Your Brochure

Let's not go crazy here. Sure, your marketing materials are important, but making those calls and following up is much more important. You may spend a small fortune on a glossy brochure only to find that you'd like to change it after you've used it a short while.

Here's a handy formula approach to your brochure. If you want to do something more extensive, be my guest. But remember, keep your eye on the bottom line.

Place an $8\frac{1}{2} \times 11$ sheet sideways (with the 11″ side across the top). Fold it in thirds so it is $8\frac{1}{2}$ inches high. [See our example in this chapter.] On the front fold, center, write the name of your firm: "David Pandozzi Associates." On the next line, write your positioning statement: what it is your firm focuses on, such as "specializing in risk management solutions" or whatever your specialty is. David wrote "entertainment and information through technology."

Now, open up the sheet to develop the inside of your brochure. On the left third, state the situation your prospective clients may be facing. For example, "Today, the risk management area is. . . ."

Across the second and third folds, list what your firm offers. You can simply say, "J.D. Placer and Associates offers:" followed by bullet points of what you want to offer. List first the service that is likely to be of most interest to your target audience.

Then, close your brochure. On the back center-fold, have your bio and perhaps your photo. At the very bottom of that fold, list your firm name, address, phone, fax and email. Then, take it to Kinko's to have it copied on decent paper and folded, and you're set.

David Pandozzi's brochure was developed a decade ago. The content is out-of-date, but you can see that this is a simple and effective brochure that is based on our formula approach. Chances are, you too will have to update your brochure from time to time as the market changes, and as you revise what you want to offer.

Even though this brochure was developed a decade ago, you can see here the elements of good brochure development. You need not stick to the "formula" described in the article, but you will probably need to address every *aspect* of that formula. Develop your own brochure, focusing on the issues and trends that would be of interest to your target market.

| This is his bio. | This is the very back of the brochure. | This is the front of the brochure, which people will see first. |
|---|---|---|

### Background

David Pandozzi is recognized as a leading expert in applying information systems to business problems. For MajorBank, Mr. Pandozzi:

+ *Built their widely advertised, powerful international ATM network to deliver uniform worldwide service,*

+ *Managed their system for delivering banking services to the home,*

+ *Managed extensive partnerships with major suppliers including IBM, DEC, Stratus, Olivetti, etc.,*

+ *Defined and installed an integrated banking system in 45 countries, and*

+ *Developed the MajorBank US retail banking system strategy.*

Mr. Pandozzi also worked on personal computer technology at the Xerox Palo Alto Research Center and at TRW Systems on digital satellite communication systems.

Throughout his career, Mr. Pandozzi has concentrated on integrated marketing, financial and technical input to produce systems that provide *important business and market* impact.

David
Pandozzi
Associates

*Entertainment and Information Through Technology*

200 East Pittsburgh Avenue
Chicago IL 55532
Phone: (703) 555-3819
Fax: (703) 555-3278

David
Pandozzi
Associates

*Entertainment and Information Through Technology*

The type size used in the sample below and on the preceding page is smaller than actual so that we could fit the brochure in this newsletter without having you turn the page sideways. This page is approximately 8.5 inches across, Your brochure will probably be on paper that is 11 inches across.

## The Business Challenge

Many companies, perhaps even your own, are facing the challenge of applying leading-edge technologies that are poorly understood and not tested in the marketplace, yet are destined for global implementation.

The new challenges include:
- Developing effective, marketable combinations of entertainment and information media with the new high-tech consumer terminals and delivery systems;
- Selecting partners and negotiating teaming arrangements with companies that stretch from Wall Street to Silicon Valley; Hollywood to Tokyo;
- Managing high tech projects, often international in scope and involving a broad range of corporate cultures;
- Managing a continual, rapid cycle of consumer testing and product redesign;
- Developing strategic technology plans that allow both effective near term testing and avoid early obsolescence.

You have imbedded value in your company today that these new distribution methods can tap for you. Many of your competitors are already hard at work at realizing these values.

DPA will help you meet the challenge.

## Consumer Entertainment and Information

The **delivery of entertainment** through:
- Film,
- Television,
- Magazines,
- Book publishing, and
- Music

Is merging with the **delivery of information** in:
- Travel,
- Financial quotations,
- TV listings,
- Computer software, and
- Sports, general news and MORE!

Using **new technologies** including:
- Personal computers with facsimile and video,
- Two-way interactive digital TV sets,
- Hand-held interactive digital terminals,
- Portable CD readers,
- Digital CD "books" with text, music and video, Screen-based telephones, and MORE!

Over **telecommunication systems** such as:
- Interactive cable,
- Video over phone lines,
- Conventional phone lines and cellular systems,
- Direct broadcast satellites, and
- Digital "cellular" radio systems,

**In new and unexpected combination of techniques.**

## David Pandozzi Associates

Serving as an objective "third party" member of your development team, DPA acts as a senior management "insurance policy" and "early warning system" to insure that your venture is proceeding as you have planned.

When a problem does arise, DPA is there to make appropriate remedial recommendations and work with the team to formulate and carry out alternate plans.

DPA provides:
- An introductory program of meetings and management consulting on the technology and partnering aspects of electronic distribution tailored to your company's media,
- The technical capabilities needed to reach business decisions on new delivery opportunities,
- Assessment and evaluation of technology proposals as either a first or "second opinion,"
- Management advice on partnership and teaming arrangements,
- Expert assistance in the management of technologically intense ventures,
- Development of project plans and management review processes, and
- Technical and business expertise on the payment and fulfillment aspects of electronic distribution.

> Speeches build your credibility: they are a way for your target audience to actually experience your service.

# The Personal Touch: Giving Speeches

*I'm not afraid of storms for I'm learning how to sail my ship.*

Louisa May Alcott

Delivering speeches is a common lead generator for those in their own consulting businesses. Think about it. It's a chance for your target market to actually experience your service. The American Management Association offers courses delivered primarily by independent consultants who are trying to grow their businesses.

There are plenty of places where you can deliver speeches that are aimed at your target audience. Again, start with research. Look in the Encyclopedia of Associations (at the library or on the Web), and research all of the organizations that you think would be appropriate for you. Call the headquarters and ask for the name of associations in your geographic area. Then do a mailing to those associations about the possibility of speaking to their group. Don't expect to be paid for your speeches until you have quite a name for yourself—your goal at the outset is exposure.

Think creatively about where you can speak. Five O'Clock Club counselors, for example, speak at industry and professional associations, alumni associations, and organizations such as the Junior League. It all depends on the kind of service you are offering and who would use your service or influence those who would use your service.

Have handouts at your speech, such as articles you have written or that have been written about you. These give you valuable credibility. Also hand out your brochure and other information. It is helpful—and professional—to put all of your information in a manila-type folder with a label on the tab that reads, for example, "Public Relations for Small Businesses," and your phone number, or "Risk Management Advice" and your phone number.

At the speech, capture the names, addresses, phone numbers, email addresses and job titles of those in the audience. Simply pass around a sheet or ask for business cards. Add these names to your leads database, and mail to them quarterly.

# Your Leads Database

A leads database with fewer than 200 to 500 names is not a leads database. If, for example, you have a database of 200 to 500 good names, and you get a 2% to 5% response rate on a mailing, you can expect 4 to 25 calls. These calls are leads—prospects—and will not necessarily result in business. Therefore, if you have fewer than 200 good names on your database, you may get a zero response! That does not mean that the mailing "didn't work." The mailing was too small to be a valid test.

"Good names" means people who are likely to use your service or recommend you to others. Over time, you will cull your list, removing those you no longer consider appropriate and adding others.

> If your database has fewer than 200 to 500 good names, you will not get much of a return on your mailings.

## Building Your Leads Database For Future Business Success

Build your leads database by capturing the names of people who hear you at speeches. Also add to your list the names of those who have actually worked with you in the past. Eventually, those who have had the experience of working with you will be your best source of leads. When you mail to them, they are likely to refer others.

Note the source of every lead that you add to your database: how they heard about you. For example, note the association they are a part of or the reprint of the article you wrote that prompted them to call you. Over time, you will observe that some lead sources are better than others. It may be, for example, that your best leads came from two or three association meetings where you spoke. If so, you could put a special effort into contacting others from that same source.

On the other hand, you may notice over the course of a few years that no one from another association ever used your services. That association is NOT a good source of leads, and you may want to purge those names from your database after, say, two years. Or you may notice that those in certain industries or organization sizes are more responsive to what you are offering. Start focusing on organizations that are more like those, and get rid of organizations that do not seem to be your "target."

In addition, after a name has been on your database for a certain length of time, say four years, consider removing it. Don't purge a name too quickly, however. Someone may call after being on your leads database for a full year. Perhaps they heard you speak at a time when they were just exploring what options they wanted to use when they were ready to use a service such as yours. It may be a long while before they actually take a step.

When you have 500 good names in your database, you then have a critical mass and should get some mileage out of your mailings. If you don't have a consulting business now, but would like to have one someday, start building your leads database now so you will have it when you are ready. You will be so glad you planned ahead.

# Clients Want You to Work with Others Who are Just Like Them

*There is always a better strategy than the one you have; you just haven't thought of it yet.*

Sir Brian Pitman, former CEO of Lloyds TSB, *Harvard Business Review*, April 2003

You know your field. You have lots of credentials and maybe even lots of experience. In the eyes of your customer, that may not make you an expert unless you also understand how your customer sees you.

Henry started his own investment advisory business, managing the money for individuals who had $1 million or more to invest. What was his target market? "Anyone with more than $1 million to invest."

That's a *qualifier*. That's not a target market. That's like saying, "My target market is anyone who needs my services." If you already have a business, but do not know who your customers are—those people who are buying from you—then you are helpless when you have a downturn in your business.

Service businesses with target markets do better. Although it's true that Henry will be providing essentially the same service to all of his clients, and *he* doesn't care anything more about them except that they meet his $1 million qualifier, the *clients* care. Clients care that he is working with other clients just like them. Then they feel better understood and they think that Henry has some expertise beyond basic money management.

Those who select a few target markets do better in their speeches than those who simply want an assignment, any assignment. We are a nation of specialists.

At the same time you are targeting, you can stay open to other opportunities outside of the targeted markets, and may well land work with some of them.

So too with Henry. He can—and probably will—handle anyone. Those people may make up, for example, 20% of his business. But, ideally, the rest of his business will consist of specialty areas.

People like to deal with people who care about them and—even better—are just like them. Brainstorm as many targets as possible at the planning stage. Then conduct a preliminary target investigation of each segment. Then develop a marketing plan aimed at each segment, and implement it.

Keep in touch with likely prospects so that prospective clients will remember you when they have a need. This ongoing follow-up is crucial in generating multiple leads and multiple sources of revenue. New clients must be generated on an ongoing basis.

Remember that it is better to have a continual flow of clients—to be seen as the source for your kind of work. Schedule in those you can handle—perhaps putting some people on a waiting list if you have too much business—and refer out those people you would rather not work with. It's better to have too many clients and refer out the overflow.

Henry decided that physicians may be one good target market for him. Other preliminary targets were small business owners, former investment executives, and—very important—friends who associated with wealthy people.

The retired investment managers would need help managing their own portfolios because they were out of the information loop and found themselves handling their own investments more and more conservatively.

### Target #1 for Henry: Physicians.

A "campaign" implies doing more than one thing. Henry needed credibility in this target market. So he planned to write a financial advisory column for *Physician's Money Digest* or another appropriate magazine or newsletter. He decided to join a few trade associations for physicians and lecture at association meetings. He can reprint his article and hand it out at the meetings. He can also include his article in mailings to physicians.

It will be easier for him to capture this market when he can say, "I'm handling the portfolio for one physician where I . . ." It gives him credibility in this target market. Physicians—like everyone else—want to work with people who see their field as different and who deal with others in their field.

Later, Henry can say that he specializes in working with physicians. He may even be able to say to a cardiologist, "I'm handling the portfolio of another cardiologist . . ." and have more credibility with that sub-group. His target market is more likely to trust him and refer others to him.

In his quarterly mailings, he can enclose a copy of one of his articles and his cover letter can refer to how he is helping some of his physician clients.

### Testing Your Targets

You need multiple targets. Some may be good sources of business for you while others may not. Some may generate lots of leads, but no business. Some may simply expect free advice. Over time, you will be able to analyze which targets are working for you and which are not. Then you will delete from your database those names that are from your weakest targets and focus more on those targets that are working. For example, within target #1, Henry may find that he gets business from—and enjoys working with—cardiologists, for example—but finds that dermatologists are not responsive to him. He can drop the dermatologists and work with those who *are* responsive.

## Where Are You in the Growth of Your Business? It's a Little Like a Job Hunt

It's helpful to look at your business the way a job hunter looks at his job search:

<u>Stage 1</u>: You try anything to generate leads, to understand how things work. You talk to anyone who will listen. You want six to ten potential sources (such as associations) that will generate leads for you on an ongoing basis.

You refine what you consider good sources of leads. Some drop off your list because you realize that they are not worth your while, and you add others. You should have some contact on a regular basis (such as quarterly) with those who remain on your list.

*Stage 2*: You are in a full Stage 2 of your business when you have 6 to 10 sources per quarter that are generating high-quality leads (the right kind of people at the right organizations who actually come to you for consulting) on an ongoing basis. When you notice that certain techniques are working for you, you can try more of the same. Get rid of those techniques that generate inappropriate leads (such as firms that can't afford you, or bureaucracies that never come to a decision and require too much of your sales time). Learn to rely on the dependable sources of leads, rather than those one-time-shots that may or may not generate the kind and numbers of leads you want.

> **A simple two-sided brochure may be all you need in the beginning.**

*Stage 3*: You are now up and running with a smooth, predictable flow of new leads and new clients. While you continue to generate new sources of leads, people are now calling you to give speeches, make presentations to management at their offices, be interviewed for articles, and so on. You have a critical mass of clients you work with regularly and they refer their associates to you. In addition, you mail quarterly to your database of those who have not become clients (and perhaps monthly to those who have).

It will probably take a year before you are established and strong. Give yourself time to become known in your marketplace and you too can have your own, thriving consulting firm in your own field.

· · · · · · · · · · · · · · · · · · · · · · · · · · · · · ·

*The real competition out there isn't for clients, it's for people. And we look to hire people who are, first, very smart; second, insecure and thus driven by their insecurity; and third, competitive. Put together 3,000 of these egocentric, task-oriented, achievement-oriented people, and it produces an atmosphere of something less than humility. Yes, it's elitist. But don't you think there has to be room somewhere in this politically correct world for something like this?*

Ron Daniel, McKinsey & Co, *Fortune*, November 1, 1993

# Creating Your Own Job: Consultants Who Made It Work

*by David Madison, Ph.D.*

*As technology makes it easier for a business to find and collaborate with outside expertise, a huge and competitive market for consultants will arise.*

Bill Gates, The Road Ahead, Viking Books, 1995

## Deanna Dell, Health Care Consultant

"I wish I had connected with the Five O'Clock Club all along. I always thought about my organization and the people in it, more than I thought about what was happening to me. I never thought about: what's right for my career next?"

These reflections came after Deanna had spent 28 years working at a community hospital in Maryland. She had begun her career as a registered nurse, but her talents for management were soon recognized by the hospital administration. Over the years she was promoted many times: to supervisor of nurses, to head nurse of intensive care, to VP of nursing, and eventually to Chief Operating Officer of the hospital itself.

"I didn't even have a résumé," Deanna recalls, because she'd never even thought about moving elsewhere. But after 28 years with one organization—in the increasingly turbulent world of health care—Deanna realized that it was time to move on. To be fair to herself and her career, she needed to consider other options.

One of Deanna's obsessions throughout the years has been management by team-building and mentoring. So, after leaving the hospital, one of her first approaches to exploring a new career was an intensive self-study program on leadership. "I went to the library, and over the next few months I read about 35 books on leadership and excellent organizations. When I was at the hospital, I had always tried to bring improvements to the delivery of health care by looking at what good companies do."

It was at the library that Deanna discovered the Five O'Clock Club books. "I realized I needed help, and when I found out about the Club, I called the main office in New York and was referred to Harvey Kaplan's branch in Rockville, MD."

Deanna arranged for a private session with Harvey to help get a résumé put together, and she took his advice to do proper assessment. "I took the homework very seriously. I spent a lot of time on the Seven Stories—which helped me come to understand what it is about myself that gives me the greatest satisfaction: my passion for improving health care delivery—wanting things to be right for the patient."

Deanna attended weekly sessions of the Five O'Clock Club for well over a year, treating it as an ongoing support system as she went about forging her new career. Five O'Clock Club coach, Jim Dittbrenner, who assists Harvey at the Maryland branch, also worked with Deanna, and both coaches encouraged her to move in the direction of consulting, based on her wealth of knowledge of the health care world—and her own vision of the future. Deanna had also done the Forty-Year Vision: "I wanted more control of my life—I wanted to make a greater impact on the quality of health care, to align myself with professionals who share the same vision and goals, and still have some balance between career and personal goals."

Another attendee of the Five O'Clock Club actually played a key role in helping Deanna become an independent consultant. She knew that health care clinics in the region needed help with improving practices and implementing quality assurance, and made the introductions that helped Deanna land an assignment. But Deanna believes that a good lead has to be considered in the context of working the whole method: "I used every facet of the Five O'Clock Club process. I had already been identifying targets: I had targeted five major health care systems, and had been going on informational interviews." Deanna ended up helping public health care clinics develop tools for assessing the quality of their services, and she discovered how much she enjoyed her new role: "I found that I really liked being a consultant: I get the job done and I'm able to coach the team and see results—and then get to help the next client."

The next big step came when Deanna was contacted by a woman she'd known for years, who consulted for physicians in the process of setting up ambulatory surgical centers. She actually was looking for someone to partner with, in order to scale back her own role in the business. She was delighted to find that Deanna was on her own—and available.

The consulting practice now actually bears her name, Deanna Dell Associates, and she is doing what she loves, working toward the goal of excellence in health care delivery. "The doctors say to me, 'I don't have the time for the paperwork and detail it takes to get things up and running. I want to practice medicine.' From start to finish it takes about 14 months to two years. I'm doing all the things I love to do—hire the best talent, put the best practices in place in the best physical environment, get the centers operational, and ultimately affect the quality of healthcare for a lot of people."

Deanna's only regret, as she is well under way in her consulting practice? "I should have done career planning much earlier. I should have left the hospital about *five* years earlier!"

## Gary Stine, Executive Leadership Coach

"I wonder if you can imagine yourself the way I already see you?" This is one of the questions that Gary asks as a consultant to senior executives. "I watch executives interacting with people for five minutes and can see what kind of leaders they are. I ask them what they want their legacies to be."

Gary is now almost five years into his successful career as consultant to senior corporate leaders, and he acknowledges that the Five O'Clock Club played a pivotal role in getting his business off the ground. He has already made the decision to become a coach when he arrived at the Club. He had recently completed a degree in landscape architecture—after a twenty-year career as an actor, primarily in regional theatre. But he realized that his new degree would be taking him in the wrong direction.

"I knew I should be coaching people, and had had one big client, a PR firm, but that came to an end. I realized I really didn't know how to look for work. I didn't understand the process."

Gary's wife referred him to the Five O'Clock Club. "I was startled to see so many accomplished people who shared my plight—people who knew how to do their work, but didn't know how to *find* work, didn't know how to set themselves off from the pack."

He attended faithfully, learned the Five O'Clock Club process and benefited fully from the group. "I needed to have my energies channeled. The group is there to support and prod. You'll achieve the desired results if you do the work that the group suggests."

Gary benefited most from the Five O'Clock Club understanding of networking as the ongoing process of forming lifelong relationships. "The outcome was that I got work, lots of it, by knowing how to network. I learned how to ask for what I wanted. It was difficult for me, but I learned how. I got an introduction into a major firm, and that led to more and more referrals." Initially focused on coaching presentation skills, Gary worked with television anchor people to hone their skills, with executives who wanted to get better at seminar presentations—and with the Five O'Clock Club career coaches to improve their public speaking skills. His role has broadened considerably to include coaching on executive leadership skills.

As Gary was getting his new business off the ground, he attended seven Five O'Clock Club sessions. "I stopped coming because I was getting so much work."

## Helping U.S. Companies Survive in a Global Economy:
### The Consulting Practice of Robert Dobbs

While Robert was working along getting his growth business going, he did consulting work "on the side" to keep money coming in. Here is a description of his consulting business.

During the last forty years the U.S. has put hundreds of astronauts into space; this fall, in October 2003, China launched its first man into orbit, 38-year-old Yang Liwei. Do we need to worry that China is catching up? Four decades of accumulated experience on the part of the U.S.

might make such a question seem an absurdity to many people.

But are we as strong as we think we are? Years of corporate excellence are accompanied by entrenched patterns that can, in a changing world, cripple an organization. The flight of shuttle Columbia ended in disaster not simply because a piece of foam hit the wing, but also because NASA itself is plagued with systemic faults. According to the panel that investigated the agency, "NASA has conflicting goals of cost, schedule and safety. Unfortunately, safety lost out." Hence NASA is in crisis, while China's success will help it attract and retain top talent. Great, mature organizations have problems that young ones don't have—and, of course—vise versa.

This is perhaps a metaphor for what is happening in the global corporate world, and Robert Dobbs makes his living helping executives come to terms with the changes that are needed to rapidly bring new industrial products to market. He even teaches a course on "Commercializing New Industrial Products." Robert brings to his new venture a wealth of experience helping top executives make the fine adjustments to a changing world.

> The accounting system needs to fit the new industrial product you're taking to market. Often, the single most competitive weapon is the accounting system.

While many U.S. corporate failings can obviously be traced to our own blindspots, Robert points out that China, in fact, stands to gain as the U.S. yields ground willingly in the manufacturing arena; indeed China is aggressively on the initiative as American companies give up manufacturing for the glamour and profit of brand management. Not too many years ago we could rightly view China as a country that got by through sheer force of numbers—its strength derived from manual labor in a country of more than a billion people. But Robert notes that

China sent legions of its brightest and best to be educated in the United States, and has an excellent educational system of its own. It adopted the practice of importing whole U.S. factories, literally unbolting the machines and reassembling everything in China, thus establishing a very fast learning curve in how to make a wide range of products. Hence China was able to move from a manual labor to a manufacturing basis—condensing 150 years worth of progress into just a couple of decades. The next phase will be manufacturing on a high-tech level, on a very competitive basis globally. Launching a man into space can be seen, literally, as a warning shot.

> China imported whole U.S. factories, literally unbolting the machines and reassembling them in China, establishing a fast learning curve.

While U.S. industries run the risk of simply being outperformed by foreign manufacturers, Robert helps his clients make important course corrections and reverse negative trends, to regain the competitive edge. He points out that many managers and executives, as they try to adapt and explore new options, have been frustrated by simply not understanding the importance of their own corporate cultures very well. In some cases they have forged ahead trying to turn out new products that the rank and file of the workforce has no affinity for. He discovered this early in his career when a client whose workers prided themselves on high volume production were asked to create small quantities of a high value precision product that required attention to detail.

> While U.S. industries run the risk of being outperformed by foreign manufacturers, Robert helps his clients regain the competitive edge.

One of Robert's first steps when he is asked to analyze a company is to develop an appreciation for what they do well, not necessarily what they do most. "The overwhelming majority of new industrial products are not killed by the competitor," he points out. "For instance, it is rarely understood that the accounting system needs to be designed to fit the new industrial product you're taking to market. Often, the single most important competitive weapon is the accounting system. I've seen clients actually losing money on products they thought were highly profitable."

Robert has been impressed over the years with high quality of American managers and executives—but is amazed at the same time by their lack of "street savvy." For example, there may be high levels of competency in terms of command and control skills, but lack of shrewdness in terms of riding business cycles. It is extremely common for companies to take on more business than they should in boom times, hiring staff, putting bonuses and rewards into place—thereby establishing entitlement attitudes—only later to be plagued by layoffs when the boom time abates. The layoffs mean inefficiencies, disruptions and the collapse of morale. "There's no reason for a business to shrink because the economy shrinks," Robert says. "Down markets are perfect opportunities to increase your business. Up markets are perfect opportunities to improve your profitability."

# Part Seven

Marketing—Making Sure the
Right People Know About You

# Marketing Your Small Business

*Business has only two functions—*
*marketing and innovation.*

Milan Kundera, Czech Novelist

## To Be Successful, You Have to *Market* Your Product or Service

Most people who have developed an expertise in a product or service—including me—do not feel like marketing. They simply want to do their jobs. "Can't I just focus on doing what I love doing and what I'm good at?" Sure. If you can find someone else to market your business, that would work just fine. *But most small business owners have to do their own marketing, and we can make it easier for you.*

For many people who are just getting started, "marketing" is a negative word. They think that if they're good, the business is supposed to come in the door by itself. Many think that when they have to market themselves, it has a negative implication on the quality of their work.

However, those who have built a thriving business have somehow learned how to market— and probably very aggressively. But they may

not tell others what they have done to become successful because of the negative image that marketing can have. "I just did my job well, and my business grew," they say.

Others may say, "All of my business comes from referrals." That may be true now but it was not true when the person was starting out and had no business to speak of. They simply do not remember what it was like in the early days and this makes it difficult for you to learn start-up strategies.

## Building a Business Requires Continual Marketing

In every field, those who get ahead are not necessarily the most talented or the best at what they do, but those who have learned how to market themselves. The most successful actors, dentists, engineers and bus drivers are those who not only do their jobs well but are also good at promoting themselves.

So if you want to be successful as a business owner, you must develop your own marketing plan and figure out how best to let others know that you exist and how competent you are.

## Select the Methods That are Best for You and for Your Target Market

There is no one way to market your business. Choose techniques that suit your own personality as well as the markets you are targeting. What is appropriate in one field is not appropriate in another. And one small business owner may be more comfortable with certain promotional techniques, while another may choose something very different.

Those who are just starting out may need to take small steps, but they still need to move forward if they want to grow.

Whichever techniques you choose, you must pay attention to what is working for you and what is not, and modify your plans accordingly.

As you read these chapters on marketing and the case studies throughout the book, make a list of ideas that seem right for you. Later, you will use these ideas to build your marketing plan.

## What About Your Dentist?

When your dentist finished dental school, he or she needed to start a private practice. Obviously, he asked his family and friends to refer people, but that is not enough to build a practice. Even if your dentist graduated first in his class, he would have taken a very long time to build his private practice if few prospective patients knew that he existed. Spreading the word—letting lots of people know that you exist and how good you are—is called marketing. It is not taught at dental schools.

- When he was starting out, perhaps he _lectured_ at local schools and gave out printed information on good dental health—provided by an organization—with his name stamped on. The children could take the information home to their parents. He was marketing himself.

   You too should have a brochure or marketing piece.
- Or maybe your dentist gave presentations to the local hockey team to tell them how to protect their teeth during the game—and again handed out his literature. _Speeches (or demonstrations) can be a helpful and effective way to market, and we'll show you how._
- After a while, "marketing" becomes ongoing and second nature. For example, when your dentist has a slow day, I'll bet the hygienist gets on the phone and calls those people who have not had their teeth cleaned for a while. In addition, your dentist probably sends out _reminder notices_.

You—as a patient—do not see this as intrusive. You probably don't even think of it as "marketing," but it is.

- After the hygienist cleans your teeth, your dentist also checks them to see if there is anything else you need to have done. In business, this is called _"cross-selling"_—that is, offering additional products and services to the same customer. When your dentist does it, you don't find it an intrusion or offensive. It's what you need, so you don't even think of it as marketing. But it is.

We'll teach you how to offer _your_ customers professional, ongoing products and services in a way that they will not find offensive. In fact, they will appreciate you for taking good care of them. Just as your dentist keeps your teeth in order by encouraging you to have regular checkups, you will do the same with your customers. Every successful business person understands the importance of _building strong, long-term customer relationships_: working with the same customers over the years and providing them with additional services that are helpful to them.

- Your dentist has probably also formed _relationships with other professionals_, and they refer business to each other. For example, your dentist has relationships with dentists who are in specialty areas. And your dentist may have relationships with people in other professions who refer people to dentists, such as the *coaches* of sports teams.

- Finally, your start-up dentist may become involved with __unique forms of promotion__. For example, he may be featured in an ad for your local bank, which is promoting the services they provide small business owners. The ad promotes the bank's services as well as your dentist's.

Other offbeat opportunities may come your way—or you may wind up making them happen. We'll give you a few ideas.

## Marketing—Without It, You Don't Have a Business

Don't we all wish that customers would come our way so we could simply do our jobs and work at what we love? If you want to have a business, managing the business—however small it may be—*is your job*. A rule of thumb for a start-up is this: ⅓ of your time should be devoted to marketing; ⅓ to administration; ⅓ to production or delivery. You need all three for a healthy business. Eventually, even 75% of your business may come from current clients and referrals, but you will still need to nurture your present contacts and develop new ones to make your business grow. We'll tell you how.

### Honing Your Business Building Skills: My Own Example

Speeches are an important part of The Five O'Clock Club's marketing efforts, so we'll tell you later exactly how we go about it. In the beginning, I would become so nauseous before speeches that I would wonder why I had scheduled the thing. I had lectured almost every week at The Five O'Clock Club for many, many years, so I was comfortable in that setting. It was like being with family. But when I ventured outside, it not so easy. Still, I forced myself to keep practicing.

If you want to have a thriving business, you can't simply be good at your own field. You must also become good at marketing.

Since I had a business background and not a career coaching background, I needed credibility in the career coaching field—and differentiation from others in the field. My goal at that time was to make sure that I could have a thriving private practice when I wanted one and keep food on the table. To build my own credibility and my career coaching practice early on, I not only ran the Five O'Clock Club in the evenings and coached there, I also lectured outside twice a month or more, became knowledgeable about certain industries, and wrote a book, among other things. Think of what you should do to become more credible in your field or industry.

Building expertise and credibility takes years, and the process never ends. Once you have mastered one skill, you decide the next skill you need to advance your business, and go through the same long process with that one. You may need to improve your knowledge of your own field, presentation skills, business-building skills, your strategic partnership-building skills, or your knowledge of accounting. It takes patience and time to become an expert—and to become known as one.

For example, for quite a while I worked at building my TV-performance skills. I have been doing TV off and on since 1986, but never received formal training until 1997. Broadcast skills—like all skill building—takes constant practice. This is what I did to build this new skill:

- Went to a media coach once a week—faithfully.
- Practiced for hours every week.
- Got on as many TV shows as possible. Sometimes I would do three shows a week. Two were a waste (at 5:30 AM!) but that's what practice is all about. There's no return on investment except that I was improving my skills; I took the tape of the shows back to the media coach for a critique.
- Watched others do it. I taped and studied

parts of TV shows—for example, newscasters saying "good morning," and took the tape to the media coach for us to analyze together, and then practiced more. Over the course of a few weeks, I practiced saying "good morning" hundred of times: there's more to any skill development than meets the eye!

- I regularly appeared on two TV shows. This was still practice; few people in our target market watched these shows at 10:00 AM and 2:00 PM But I was developing my skills so I would be ready when I got on a show that has a good audience.

> You have to devise *your* strategies and manage *your* expectations about the work it takes to build your skills in new areas.

There is no quick solution for any of us. If you want to become good at something (public speaking, accounting, or sales calls, for example) you must do a lot of it. If you want to become a good public speaker, you should do much more speaking (to safe groups) when you are learning than you will have to do after you become an expert. Most of the time your early speeches won't have a monetary payoff because, after all, you may not be that good and you may not attract the kind of audiences that will result in a payoff for you.

Does this mean that delivering speeches is ineffective? Nay, as Shakespeare put it, "The fault is not in our stars, but in ourselves." Over time, you will get better at this—or any other skill you decide to develop—and it will eventually pay off. Then you will attract lots of customers. You will build relationships with organizations that like you.

## Lead Generation versus Image Building

Certain marketing efforts are primarily "lead generators"—they are meant to bring in new customers. Other marketing efforts are "image builders"—they are meant to make you look credible, but often do not bring in new business.

*Image builders* make you look good to your prospect base and may be necessary for your credibility, but may not *directly* result in sales. These could include:

- Writing an article for a trade magazine. You would then get permission to reprint the article (make copies) and distribute it to your sales leads. The purpose of print coverage is the reprint value. Copies of the article could be in your marketing materials for years to come. But it's unusual for the phone to ring off the hook just because you got mentioned in an article.
- Getting on radio or TV. Then you could say, "As seen on the Joey Campbell Show." Or "perhaps you have read about us in the *Wall Street Journal*." Again, don't expect the phone to ring. But you can now talk about your appearance everywhere, or post a sign in your store window.
- Developing a website. The website builds credibility. Getting people to go there is the trick to making it a lead generator, but most significant businesses need a website for credibility.

*Lead generators* help you to give your pitch to specific individuals or organizations, which may lead to sales.

- Getting in for a sales call may actually lead to a sale! This is lengthy process, which will be covered in much more detail later.
- Giving a speech, such as at an industry meeting. Be sure to capture the contact information of everyone there so you can

re-contact them later. Otherwise, it's in one ear and out the other.

- Direct marketing (or flyers under the door) to prospects.

....................................

*In marketing I've seen only one strategy that can't miss—and that is to market to your best customers first, your best prospects second and the rest of the world last.*

John Romero

## Some Common Marketing Techniques

"If you build it, they will come." Well, it worked for Kevin Costner in "Field of Dreams," but that's show biz. If you build it and don't *market* it, it will sit there. Only you and your closest friends will even know your business exists!

During the dot.com boom, many entrepreneurs who had already gotten millions of dollars in venture capital wanted to partner with The Five O'Clock Club because we had an established brand name. Some had great product ideas; others didn't. But the investment money they got did not save their businesses. Most of them had given very little thought—if any—to marketing! They were totally focused on developing their product or service, thinking that was all they would need and then "they will come."

People not only have to know about your business, the *right* people need to know about it—and they have to want what you're selling.

Marketing includes many things: the right product for your market, a price that attracts purchasers while allowing you to make a comfortable profit, promotion so the right people know about you, and distribution of the product so it gets into the right hands. You've got to get people to *try* your product and service and then keep using it.

Marketing is ongoing, and becomes foremost once you have a product idea. Then you must sell your product or service at a *profit*. After you start selling, *margins* are everything. A high volume

will not make up for losing money on every sale. So, here are some basic steps to follow:

- Find out something about your customer before you spend years developing your product and hoping all will turn out well. Conduct some informal market research. Simply talk to people you think are potential customers and ask them who they now purchase these products or services from, what they think of the supplier, the product or service, the price, the delivery, and so on.
- Find out about your competitors, what worked for them and what did not and how you will establish yourself as different and/or better. Keep a hanging file on each competitor and keep notes on what your potential customers say about your competitors.
- *Target* your markets. You can't serve everyone well. Decide who you want to target.

....................................

*There is more similarity in the marketing challenge of selling a precious painting by Degas and a frosted mug of root beer than you ever thought possible.*

A. Alfred Taubman

## To Whom Do You Want to Sell?

Basically, you can choose between selling to organizations (often referred to as a "corporate" sale) or to individuals (often referred to as a "retail" sale). The Five O'Clock Club sells to both, and we have two completely different marketing programs, two different databases of clients, two completely different approaches in talking about our service, and two completely different pricing structures. We started out in retail and much later moved to corporate sales: It's hard enough to sell to one market and do it well. Pick your first target market: organizations or individuals.

Be sure to read the sections, *How to Become a Consultant in Your Own Field* and *Selling to Organizations* for ideas on marketing in general and specifically to organizations.

Finally, read every chapter in this marketing section even if you think it doesn't pertain to your business. These chapters are full of ideas and advice that may pertain to your situation.

••••••••••••••••••••••••••••••••••

*If you want to build a ship, then don't drum up men to gather wood, give orders, and divide the work. Rather, teach them to yearn for the far and endless sea.*

Antoine de Saint-Exupery

<u>**Word of Mouth**</u>. Many new business owners say they'll use "word of mouth" to market their product or service. They say their product or service will be so great that people will tell others. "Word of mouth" generally doesn't work for start-ups. After you have a solid base of customers, however, you will get many new customers who heard about you from your present base.

<u>*Advertising*</u>. Advertising is the second most likely promotion technique named by new business owners, and is often a bad way to spend your money. People need to see your name continually, and advertising is so expensive you cannot afford to run it enough to make a difference. Furthermore, advertising is less credible than public relations (that is, unpaid coverage in the media) and public relations gives new businesses much better results than advertising. Advertising works best for *established* products and services—unless you're rich and can spend the money it would take.

Try advertising if you want—but plan to repeat the ad regularly for a real test to see if it works for you. Track what you spent versus the business you got in.

<u>*Publicity*</u>. Good press coverage ultimately works to your advantage because it builds your brand name and consequently your credibility when you are giving speeches or simply calling on prospects.

Generating publicity is a lot of work, and does not replace giving speeches or forming strategic partnerships—but it is worth it to get your name out there.

We'll tell you more about public relations (publicity) in another chapter.

••••••••••••••••••••••••••••••••••

*Tell me and I'll forget. Show me and I'll remember. Involve me and I'll understand.*

Confucius

<u>*Speeches or demonstrations*</u> are often a good idea. Your audience is getting a sample of your style or product and what you have to offer. Of course, the more people you speak to, the better. You can give them informative handouts, and your brochure as well as other support material.

When you are well-organized, you will capture the names of all the attendees for your leads data base. Your attendees were interested in your subject matter. Even if they are not ready to use your service now, the odds are that they *will* need you someday. They are the kind of person who is interested in your product or service (they actually attended a seminar, right?). Build your business by keeping a database—as most successful business owners do—and consider mailing to them quarterly just to remind them that you exist, and asking them to refer their friends too. After each mailing, you can expect a bunch of new referrals from people on your list.

Ten years ago, I had a facial and to this day I receive mailings from the business owner. If I ever decide to have another facial, I know where to go. Later on, we will tell you more about building your own leads database and managing your quarterly mailings, including purging from your list those people who are unlikely to ever buy.

<u>*Sales Calls*</u> are usually a requirement when marketing to organizations and making large sales to individuals. Please read the chapter, "Selling to Organizations."

*Most conversations are simply monologues delivered in the presence of a witness.*

Margaret Miller

<u>*Strategic Partnerships*</u>. A partnership can be as simple as giving your literature with your name on it to a business in a related field, and then putting *their* literature on a table at your office—or recommending them to your customers. They would recommend you in return. You refer customers to each other.

This is a powerful tool for building your business and regularly getting clients—even when you are not out promoting yourself.

. . . . . . . . . . . . . . . . . . . . . . . . . . . . . .

*In the business world, everyone is paid in two coins: cash and experience. Take the experience first; the cash will come later.*

Harold S. Geneen, chairman, ITT Corporation

<u>*Yellow Pages Advertising*</u>. Even if this technique was a good one in the old days, I don't know about its effectiveness now. Many people are not even keeping their yellow pages directories and now search for businesses on line. You'll have to think about this one.

<u>*Selling on eBay*</u>. I love eBay. I buy on it all the time. ebay is great for selling products (but generally not services), and there is plenty of information on eBay itself about how to sell effectively. Many people make their entire livelihoods from selling on eBay—everything from hand-made soap to automobiles. There are also middle-men who will do your selling for you.

Like anything, start-ups are hard—you have to get a good number of sales under your belt, and a good rating from your customers, before others will take a chance on buying from you on eBay. But that's not hard to do. In the early days, I used to go into a certain bookstore and buy my *own* self-published book just so they would keep on carrying it. I couldn't buy a lot because I didn't have the money, but it was important

for me to keep the book stocked in that one store. Later, of course, I wrote books through traditional publishers and didn't have that same worry.

<u>*The Web*</u>. These days, if you don't have a website, you look very small. Chances are, you'll need a website for credibility. (But your local Laundromat and deli probably don't have websites, so not every business needs one.) If you do build one, don't expect people to rush to your site just because you put it up. The only people who will go there are those you specifically tell to go there, and those who find you through search engines or through a link from someone else's site. Later, you can build web traffic through the use of traffic builders (there's no reason to spend more than a hundred dollars or so on this service). Publicity can also build traffic to your website.

. . . . . . . . . . . . . . . . . . . . . . . . . . . . . .

*Using "power copy" is the key to an effective digital communication. If your readers don't relate your words with your brand you don't stand a chance.*

Jeanniey Mullen

<u>*Emailing*</u>. We send thousands of emails a week to those who ask to be on our lists. Different kinds of emails go to human resources executives, employees and job hunters, and the media. In the old days, we used far more snail mail than we do now—and snail mail can be very effective in certain situations—but we do rely on email for our business. Of course, we offer an opt-out because we don't want to send the emails to those who don't want them. Recipients find them valuable: We usually send informative articles with our promotional message at the bottom, or invitations to free lectures. We are actually surprised when someone opts out!

Create your own email database of customers to whom you mail regularly. Put your email address on all of your marketing literature because many customers will want to contact you through email rather via telephone. Try to answer all emails the same day. At least scan them all to see which ones require your immediate attention. Eventually, you will need spam filters to get rid of the junk, and virus programs to warn you of danger in an incoming email.

When you are very small, you can have your email address at yahoo or aol. But to appear larger, you will need an email address that has your company name as the core. It's looks more professional if someone writes to Kate@FiveO-ClockClub.com rather than KateWendleton@aol.com.

The bottom of each email should have a signature that gives all of your contact information as well as a promotional tagline. It will include your name, title, address, phone, perhaps fax, and your website address followed by your slogan.

Be careful of wayward email. I have heard many a horror story of someone hitting the send button on something that should not have gone out. In our office, all email to a customer must be eyeballed by one other person before it is sent out (unless it is a standard, already approved message).

_Conducting Studies_. Another way of keeping in touch, and perhaps getting some publicity, is to conduct a survey, analyze the results, and let your target market know about it. We routinely survey job hunters as well as human resources executives and then analyze the results. Generally, we ask only a few questions on a specific topic.

_Writing Articles_. Writing an article for a trade publication will give you credibility. Then you can reprint the article (with permission) and hand it out with all of your marketing literature or every time you give a speech or demonstration.

_Trade Shows_. Have a booth (which we found not appropriate for us and too costly) or be a speaker at trade shows (which worked better for us).

_Premiums_. Pens, blankets, notebooks and key chains with your logo on it may be a help. On the other hand, we didn't spend money on items like this for many, many years, and then used them only for our customers and very important prospects.

_Flyers_. For local sales, distribute flyers to your church, schools, PTA, slip them under the windshield wipers of cars and under house and apartment doors. Enclose them with every order. Ask your doctor, dentist and others to distribute them. Depending on your service, you may want to target local banks, realtors, and so on. Give this some thought.

_Demonstration/Samplings_. This falls into the same category as speeches. Prospective customers have a chance to try before they buy. For example, you could give a free tasting of your catered food at a local fair.

_Discounts_. Do you need to do this? Don't think that giving your product or service away is the path to sales. If you want to give a discount, perhaps give it on the first purchase only.

_Co-Promotion_. Reduce your expenses by co-promoting with other vendors. If you are both selling to the same target market and are not competitors, this is something to consider.

• • • • • • • • • • • • • • • • • • • • • • • • • • • • •

*Vision without action is a daydream.*
*Action without vision is a nightmare.*

Japanese Proverb

## Measuring How Well You are Doing

*What we call results are beginnings.*

Ralph Waldo Emerson

Test your techniques in the market. At the Five O'Clock Club, we have tried everything. Many of our ideas failed—including advertising on the big screen in movie theaters! Don't be so married to your idea—so invested emotionally and financially—that you find it hard to give it up. Try something, give it enough time and effort to work, and then measure the results. Perhaps you need to tweak it to make it work. If it works, you can move it from the test stage to something wider.

Sometimes it is hard to tell what is going to work and what is not. Log all phone calls that come in and note how the person heard about you. In the old days, when we were religious about this, we found that someone made a purchase when they had heard about us from three different sources within the same general time frame. For example, they may have heard one of our coaches speak at a meeting, heard an interview on the radio, or read about us in the *Wall Street Journal. Then* they decided to pick up the phone.

Over time, you will find that certain marketing techniques are a waste of your time and you will discard those. On the other hand, you could give two speeches, for example, and one may result in a lot of business while the other—to the same kind of group—results in nothing. It's part of the law of averages.

We usually keep names on our retail leads database for two years. If they don't use our service within two years, we drop their names. And we also note the *source* of the lead on each person's record. So if we find that a certain marketing technique has been a waste, we can delete all records that came from that source.

We keep forever the names on our corporate database. A decision-maker at one company may not be allowed to use our service, but she moves to another company that does allow her to use our service and she already has a good impression of us.

There is a shelf-life gestation period. People will hear about you and they file it away. It sometimes takes a while—maybe years—for people to come around.

## Dissatisfied Customers

*Your most unhappy customers are your greatest source of learning.*

Bill Gates

You don't want dissatisfied customers. Either make them happy, or refund part or all of their money. (You don't have to say they were right if they were not. Just say, "We're sorry we were not able to live up to your expectations," and give them their money back if that is reasonable.)

Some people are impossible to deal with, so pass them on to your competitors ("You might consider calling Joe Doakes who also delivers this service. He may be a better match for you.").

Others have valid complaints, and you must do what you can to make them happy. We say, "We have no dissatisfied customers." The word spreads. Customers who are dissatisfied tell dozens of people about you. You cannot afford negative word of mouth.

Sometimes you can tell on the first call that this will be a problem customer. In our case, if we call on an organization where the human resources person says, "But we don't care what happens to the people we let go," that customer will not be a good match for us no matter how much they pay us. Our whole business is based on the premise that we care about the job hunters and see them through their search. We want to deal with employers who also care that their former employees are taken care of. Trust your gut.

## Following Up With Past Clients

At The Five O'Clock Club, we have to think of ways to stay in touch with customers and former customers, both retail and corporate. As far as our retail customers are concerned, we may send a postcard every year or two telling them about the upcoming meeting schedule and we include our website, www.FiveOClockClub.com. Most of them will not need our services when we happen to send the postcard, but every card says, "Be sure to tell your friends about us"—and they do. We get a surge of calls after each mailing, not from the people we sent it to, but from their friends.

On the corporate side, they too do not need our services on a regular basis—only when they may be letting someone go. So how do we stay in touch? Some business owners are great at stopping by to say hello to customers. I'm not one of them because I'm on the shy side (although I have no trouble speaking in front of a large audience).

We decided to do what we do best: inform and entertain. We hold seminars every two months especially for our corporate customers and others in the human resources community. For years, we partnered with other organizations who were also interested in this target market, and they provided the space while we invited the executives to attend and ran the meetings. We usually had 120 to 160 executives (customers and prospects) in the room, and no vendors are allowed. We put together panels of prestigious speakers on topics of current interest to this community. We also provide a directory of all attendees (a lot of work), but the attendees appreciate having a directory with the contact information for others in their field. Some of our coaches and staff attend to serve as hosts and introduce the human resource executives to each other.

Now, we have grown. We hold the same kinds of events, but we have no co-sponsors. This gives us more freedom (we don't have to worry about promoting another organization), but we do have to foot the entire bill ourselves. At this stage of our growth, this is just perfect.

These regular events help us keep in touch with our current customers, introduce ourselves to others, and do something worthwhile for the industry.

••••••••••••••••••••••••••••••••••••••

*If you make a product good enough even though you live in the depths of the forest, the public will make a path to your door, says the philosopher. But if you want the public in sufficient numbers, you would better construct a highway.*

William Randolph Hearst

## Homework:

Take out your bound notebook. List all of the techniques you could use to market your product or service.

# Researching Your Business Idea

*Natural talent, intelligence, a wonderful education—none of these guarantees success. Something else is needed: the sensitivity to understand what other people want and the willingness to give it to them. Worldly success depends on pleasing others. No one is going to win fame, recognition, or advancement just because he or she thinks it's deserved. Someone else has to think so too.*

John Luther

## How Long Will It Take?

Intensive research will be required regardless of the kind of business you want to start. Research will help you get to know your industry, size up your competition, identify your future customers, and test your product or service idea.

If you want to start a *consulting* business in a field in which you are already expert and which requires no office space, you could have your business up and running in six months. This research-based preparation would include:

- developing a list of all the people you want to target,

- preparing your marketing materials,
- acquiring in-depth knowledge of your competition and how you stack up against them, and
- testing a few trial balloons to make sure your concept is workable.
- Be sure to read the chapters on consulting businesses for more information on the research required for that and other kinds of businesses.

If you want to buy an *existing* business, expect to spend two years researching:

- the geographic area,
- the industry(ies) you are considering,
- the various owners of businesses you may think about purchasing,
- the neighbors,
- the chamber of commerce and other local organizations that can tell you about your market, or even the specific businesses you are targeting.

When you read that chapter, you'll see how a lack of research can hurt your decision-making process.

If you want to start a *growth* business—one that employs other people and earns money for you even when you are not working directly on revenue-producing activities, expect the research and set-up to take at *least* two years.

Much of this book is research-oriented. Read it all, even the sections that do not seem to apply to you. You will get ideas from every section. Carry around your bound notebook to jot down your ideas and the results of conversations you have along the way. And start your hanging files to organize the paper information you gather and the internet research you print out.

If you have not yet decided which kind of business to pursue, research is the only answer, as you can see in Yadira's case study.

•••••••••••••••••••••••••••••••••••••••

*Successful people often experience more failures than failures do. But they manage to press on. One good failure can teach you more about success than four years at the best university. Failure just might be the best thing that ever happens to you.*

Herb True, super-salesman, as quoted by
Robert Allen in *Creating Wealth*

## Why Is Research Important?

Research can help you decide which fields, industries and population segments are the best markets for your business. Knowing that you're entering a multi-billion dollar market is not helpful. Who are the competitors at your level? Which *segments* do you stand the best chance of competing in? Research those segments. In that process, you will eliminate some segments and add others. For example, in the process of researching the healthcare industry, you may decide that hospitals would be a good segment for you to target, or you may decide that they are not. You may decide to target hospitals of a certain size, or a certain specialty, or in certain geographic areas.

If your product or service is meant for the retail market, you may think that people in their early twenties are right for you. But in the process of your research, you may decide that those in their thirties and forties will better appreciate your service, and find that those in a certain salary range and geographic area are more likely to purchase it.

Eventually, you'll wind up with a detailed list of organizations, organization sizes or population segments to target and plans for how to contact them. But for right now, simply develop a list of *tentative* targets.

For example, if you want to sell to the corporate market, should you target the publishing industry? Investment banks? Which targets do you think would be most receptive? If your product or service is for the retail market, are you targeting the youth market? The parents? The elderly? Who?

Whether you are targeting corporate or retail, be more specific. Who are the purchasers (the ones who authorize the spending)? Who are the influencers (those who can encourage others to buy)? And who are the end users (those who the product or service is actually being purchased for)? You will need to market to all of them.

Explore the kinds of businesses and target markets that *may* be appropriate for you. At this point, it doesn't matter if you are correct. Just jot down the industries, geographic areas, and/or population segments you think may be best for your product or service, and start researching them.

Let's say you want to target the hospital industry, the HMO industry, and the medical research industry—all within a 100-mile radius of your home/office. During the course of your research, look for the following about each industry in your tentative target list:

1. trends and future prospects in each industry;
2. areas of growth and decline in each industry;
3. the kinds of challenges the industry faces

that could make them want your product or service;

4. the culture of the industry;
5. your major-league competitors selling to each industry, which may or may not affect you;
6. your future competitors—companies that are of the size you want to be—who sell to your target industries.

In the bibliography at the back of our book, *Shortcut Your Job Search*, you will find many sources for exploring these issues and concerns. Having a *lot* of information on an industry will help you determine whether or not you are in sync with a particular industry and whether or not there is a place for you. For now, you need only a small amount of information to decide that an industry should go on your *tentative* target list. You will continue to research throughout your business plan development because, as you will see, the entire business plan process is a *research* process. You will continue to refine your targets, your marketing, pricing, accounting systems, workforce needs, and so on as you go forward.

..........................................

*The will to persevere is often the difference between failure and success.*

David Sarnoff, *Wisdom of Sarnoff and the World of RCA*

## Competitive Research

Regardless of the kind of business you want to have, you will have competition. Research can help you figure out:

- who competitors are
- their strengths and weaknesses, and your competitive advantages
- niches that you might fill that they do not
- how you are different from them
- how they market themselves, position themselves and price their services
- how they actually *sell* their services and products

- their specific target markets and how they are perceived by their various target markets
- their revenue and their likely profitability.

## Read Books and Business Magazines

Learn to love business. I look at everything as a business. I see a hot dog vendor, watch his hours, what he serves, how quickly he can handle customers, his personality, what he does with his cart at night. You too need to become interested in business in general and not just the product you're selling. You won't be successful just because you have a great product. In the old days, Macintosh (Apple) had a far better product than Microsoft. But Microsoft knew how to run a business better and they beat the pants off Apple.

Look at the plans for businesses you're not even interested in: Paper recycling business, day care center, house cleaning services. Some of your best ideas will come from outside your industry. Use promotional and other ideas from these businesses to help you develop the plan for your own.

Read books by and about entrepreneurs. Read the biographies of those who have started businesses from scratch. Steve Jobs' story is more inspiring in many respects than Bill Gates. Steve was an adoptive child and had to make it on his own. Bill's parents were upper middle-class and gave him a leg up. Read what made McDonald's a success (real estate, not hamburgers). How did Mary Kay of Mary Kay Cosmetics do it? Business biographies help you get into the mind of an entrepreneur and understand which strategies worked and which didn't.

Read books about entrepreneurial thinking, marketing, accounting, and turnaround management—not textbooks, but real-life books that business people read. You'll find that they disagree with each other, and each author has a favorite way of doing things based on his or her own experiences. You'll pick up ideas for your bound notebook from all of these sources.

And read books about character development. You can be ethical as well as successful.

And, again, record every discovery and thought in your bound notebook and place all research in the appropriate hanging file.

. . . . . . . . . . . . . . . . . . . . . . . . . . . . . . .

*For what a business needs the most for its decisions—especially its strategic ones—are data about what goes on outside of it. It is only outside the business where there are results, opportunities and threats.*

Peter F. Drucker, "Be Data Literate—Know What to Know," *The Wall Street Journal,* December 1, 1992

## Library Research

Find a university or big-city library that's conveniently located and has an extensive business collection. The great thing about libraries is that you will not be on your own: Librarians are usually experts at helping people explore fields and industries, so plan to spend some time with the business reference librarian. Be specific. Tell the librarian what you want to accomplish. I

have always said, "The librarian is your friend." I personally love libraries (although I now do most of my research on the Internet).

Computer-aided research at the library and at home will make your work immeasurably faster, easier, and more accurate. Make it work for you. Don't play around. This is fun but it's also serious business.

. . . . . . . . . . . . . . . . . . . . . . . . . . . . . . .

*There are going to be no survivors. Only big winners and the dead. No one is going to just squeak by.*

Ronald Compton, CEO, Aetna Insurance Company

## Basic Research

If you are not sure of the business you want to pursue, you can spend two days just researching industries (or fields). One of my favorite tools is the *Encyclopedia of Business Information Sources.* It lists topics, such as *oil* or *clubs* or *finance* or *real estate.* Under each topic, it lists the most important sources of information on that

*"Its wise to build as close to your competition as possible.*
*That way you can keep a keen eye on them."*

topic: periodicals, books, and associations.

Using this resource, you can quickly research any field in depth. You also may want to read the U.S. Department of Labor's reports on various industries or professions (*www.bls.gov/emp* and *www.bls.gov*). They helped me considerably in the late 1970s when I needed to discover which fields may possibly grow. It was that research that helped me decide on the career development field.

Or perhaps someone will invite you to an association meeting, trade shows or lectures on the fields or industries in which you are interested. Yadira attended trade shows for the food industry and researched food carts among other things. When I was interested in horticulture as a business, I attended classes where the students were all full-time groundskeepers, loved every minute of it, but decided that field should stay as a hobby for me. Subscribe to newsletters and magazines. That way, some of the research material comes to you on a regular basis and you can read it without becoming overwhelmed.

You may need to spend time in the library to gather a list of organizations or trade shows. You may use an industry directory or local business publications that provide listings of organizations. If you think you can work in many industries, get a sense of those that are growing and also fit your needs.

•••••••••••••••••••••••••••••••••••

*Few executives yet know how to ask: What information do I need to do my job? When do I need it? And from whom should I be getting it?*

Peter F. Drucker, "Be Data Literate—Know What to Know," *The Wall Street Journal*, December 1, 1992

# Where Else Can You Find Information?

## Associations

Almost every industry and profession imaginable has an association—sometimes several—and these are important sources of information. If you don't know anything at all about an industry or field, these groups are often the place to start. They tend to be very helpful, and will assist you in mastering the jargon so you can use the language of the trade. *The Encyclopedia of Associations* is a massive list of professional groups. If you are interested in the rug business, there's a related association.

You may also try the Internet. To zero in on key associations, go to Google or Yahoo, key in the field or industry in which you are interested, and the word *association*. For example, key in the words *rug association* and you'll get a listing of a dozen or so! Or try www.business.com, which includes links to hundreds of associations (see below for more detail).

Just by their very nature, associations are welcoming—so call them. If they have lots of local chapters, chances are there's one near you, and it will be a great place to network. Contact the headquarters, and ask for information and the name of the person to contact in your area. Then call that person, and say you are interested in the association and would like to attend its next meeting. If there is no local chapter in your area, associations can still send you information.

Associations usually have **membership directories**, which you will have access to when you join. This directory can become the keystone of your research contact list. You can *contact members directly.*

You can write, "As a new member of the American Rug Association, I thought you could give me some information that would help me in my business development." Fellow members are a great source of information.

Associations often publish **trade magazines and newspapers** you can read to stay up-to-date on the business. By reading these, you'll learn about the important issues facing the industry and find out who's been hired and who's moving; you should try to talk to the people you read about. If an association is large enough, it may even have a library or research department, or a public relations person you can talk to. Associations often sell books related to the field.

An association's __annual convention__ is a very quick way to become educated about a field. These conventions are not cheap (they run from hundreds to thousands of dollars), but you will hear speakers on the urgent topics in the field, pick up literature, and meet lots of people. You can network at the conference and later. If you spend a couple of days at a conference, you'll know more about an industry than many people who are *in* the field right now. You can contact people in the industry (many of whom were *not* at the conference) and say, "Were you at the conference? No? Well, I was and maybe I can give you some of the information that I learned there." This is a chance for you to become an insider! The two of you can exchange information. So share the information you pick up.

Since the EOA is the most complete source of association information, we recommend you use it first. A few websites are also helpful. Associations on the Net (www.ipl.org/ref/aon/) lists more than 2000 associations. Simply key in a profession. If you put in "accounting," for instance, you'll find 22 organizations. Also try www.business.com; under each business category, there's a link to "associations."

Or, as I mentioned earlier, just go to Google, key in the word "association" and an industry or field name (e.g., "rug," or "accounting"), and you'll come up with leads. But as of this writing, nothing beats the EOA.

• • • • • • • • • • • • • • • • • • • • • • • • • • • •

*The choice of a career, a spouse, a place to live; we make them casually, at times, because we do not know how to articulate the choices . . . I believe that people often persuade themselves that their decisions do not matter, because they feel powerless to make the best decision. Some of us feel that, no matter what we do, our decisions won't matter much . . . But I believe that we know at heart that decisions do matter.*

Peter Schwartz, *The Art of the Long View*

## The Press

Read newspapers *with your target in mind,* and you will notice all kinds of things you would not otherwise have seen. Contact the author of an article in a trade magazine. Tell him or her how much you enjoyed the article and what you are trying to do, and ask to get together just to chat. I've made many friends this way.

• • • • • • • • • • • • • • • • • • • • • • • • • • • •

*The ability to learn faster than your competitors may be the only sustainable competitive advantage.*

Arie P. de Geus, *Harvard Business Review,* March/April 1988

## Chambers of Commerce

If you looking for a business out-of-town, call the chamber of commerce in your targeted area. Ask for a list of industries and organizations in their area.

• • • • • • • • • • • • • • • • • • • • • • • • • • • •

*In this high-risk society, each person's main asset will be his or her willingness and ability to take intelligent risks. Those people best able to cope with uncertainty—whether by temperament, by talent, or by initial endowment of wealth—will fare better in the long run than those who cling to security.*

Michael Mandel, *The High-Risk Society*

## Small Business Administration and SCORE

Drop by and find out what they have to offer in your area. Attend their classes, read their literature, make use of their experts. Use all of the help you can get—for free!

• • • • • • • • • • • • • • • • • • • • • • • • • • • •

*Research is the process of going up alleys to see if they are blind.*

Marston Bates, *American Zoologist*

## Case Study: Universities

Universities—especially MBA schools—often have advisory sections where students, under the guidance of a professor, will review your business plan or simply talk to you about your business. They'll spot problems or give you ideas. I was always open to getting feedback from various sources and had my business plan reviewed every few years just to hear what other professionals had to say.

In addition, universities have libraries or research centers on fields of interest. A professor may be an expert in a field you are interested in. Contact him or her.

## Networking

This is a great research tool. Network with others who have a business similar to the one you want to have. Find out how they did it, the problems they faced or still face. Probe and find out all you can so you can get started on the right foot.

......................................

*Avoid the crowd. Do your own thinking independently. Be the chess player, not the chess piece.*

Ralph Charell

# Get Sophisticated about Using Reference Materials

Research will result in your One-Hour Business Plan—and more! The more you research, the more your plan will develop. Don't forget the soft side of your business: how you want to manage others, where you can recruit employees, the lifestyle you want to lead, and so on.

......................................

*Wisdom is the principal thing; therefore get wisdom: and with all thy getting get understanding. Exalt*

*her, and she shall promote thee: she shall bring thee to honour, when thou dost embrace her.*

Proverbs 4: 7–8

## Two Kinds of Research

There are two kinds of research. *Primary* research means talking to people who are doing the kind of work you're interested in or people who *know* something about those industries or organizations. You can get in touch with such people through networking or by contacting them directly. *Primary research simply means talking to people. Secondary* research is reading materials in print, at the library, or online. In a sense, secondary research is *removed* from the source—it is information written by and about people and organizations.

It is vital to conduct *both* primary and secondary research and keep a balance between the two. Some people would rather spend their time talking. Others prefer to spend their time in the library or working at their computers. But whichever one you *prefer,* do more of the other. You need balanced sources of information in your research. So, if you like to stay at home or in the library, get out more and talk to people. If you're a person who *loves* the Internet, don't kid yourself that you'll get hired online! And don't *waste* time online and claim you've spent *hours* on job search! Be careful how you spend your time online. Or if you're the type who likes to meet people and press the flesh, spend some time at your computer or in the library so you will sound intelligent and well informed when you have meetings.

Primary research—talking to people— doesn't just happen in offices. You're researching when you're talking to people on a bus or a plane or at a coffee shop. You say, "I see you're wearing a Lois Lane sweater. I'm interested in the clothing business. I was wondering what made you buy that particular sweater." Market research happens when you talk to prospective customers and find out their interests.

You're researching when you go to an *association* meeting, talk to people there, and find out more about what is happening in the industry. You can research while you're at a *party*. These are all examples of primary research—talking to people.

*The greatest obstacle to discovery is not ignorance—it is the illusion of knowledge.*

Edward Bond, *Washington Post,* January 29, 1984

.........................................

*There is no knowledge that is not power.*

Ralph Waldo Emerson, *Old Age*

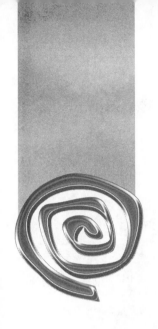

# Targeting: Becoming an Expert in a Niche

*An expert is someone who has succeeded in making decisions and judgements simpler through knowing what to pay attention to and what to ignore.*

Edward de Bono

Are you a member of an industry or trade association that has to do with your target areas? Do you read trade journals related to your target areas? Do you deliver speeches to your target areas?

If you are interested in the health care market, join a health care association and read health care industry trade journals. If you are interested in the technology market, join technology-related associations and read up on the technology market.

What you read in the newspaper is not enough. Clients expect you to recognize the names of some of the major organizations in their industry.

In addition, of course, you *can* sell to anybody, but you are not going to do as well in the future if you do not have a few niche markets. You will lack credibility. You will come across to prospects as unknowledgeable—and they will be right.

In the long run, specializing makes it easier for you to get new business. And when you experience competition, you will be in a better position to land the business.

Customers want someone who understands their industry. Period. They would rather work with a specialist. If you want to be seen as a specialist, select targets.

## Select Your Targets

Brainstorm as many targets (specialties) as possible. Select five to eight specialties in some of the following categories:

- industry-specific (such as health care, entertainment, the military, manufacturing, associations, Wall Street, electronics)
- profession or field-specific (such as nurses, flight attendants, attorneys, sales and marketing professionals, chief financial officers, CEO's)

Note: You may specialize in specific segments of the not-for-profit area. "Not-for-profit" is not a specialty itself because it is too broad.

*"Let's just say there's one less company we have to contend with."*

You may target specific demographic groups and develop those as a specialty, such as:

- age (recent college graduates; those over fifty)
- gender (women, men, gays)
- ethnicity (Italians, Asians, African-Americans)
- situations (homemakers, those with disabilities, those who are incarcerated, the in-college market, etc.)

Finally, to cast a wider net, you may add to your list general targets such as members of Rotary Clubs, Junior Leagues, etc.

· · · · · · · · · · · · · · · · · · · · · · · · · · · ·

*This may seem simple, but you need to give customers what they want, not what you think they want. And, if you do this, people will keep coming back.*

John Ilhan

## Select a Socioeconomic Level

Some small business owners only want to market to the wealthy. Some want to market to the masses. Select the socioeconomic level that is most appropriate for your business at this stage.

When we were starting out, I thought our target market was a professional earning $40,000 up to $70,000 a year. I was shocked when the first person walked in who earned over $100,000 a year. Now, those earning over $100,000 a year make up 30 to 40 percent of our customer base. And we get a surprising number of senior executives who earn well over $500,000 a year!

As they say, look at who buys from you and *that's* your market.

· · · · · · · · · · · · · · · · · · · · · · · · · · · ·

*Spend a lot of time talking to customers face to face. You'd be amazed how many companies don't listen to their customers.*

Ross Perot

## The Customer is Right

Targeting your market is not simply a marketing ploy. In fact, the customer *is* right. The better you understand his or her area, the better you will be at delivering service.

Ed had been marketing to the financial services industry and wanted to target the hospital market. Despite his excellent credentials and his conviction that he could serve hospitals just as well as he did the financial services market, Ed could not get a toehold in the hospital market. They saw him as an outsider, which he was.

Then he joined the hospital marketing association, read hospital marketing trade publications and talked to lots of executives in hospital marketing. Then when he had a meeting at one of the largest hospitals in the country, the manager asked him: "Are you *sure* you've never serviced a hospital before?" He had mastered his target market and increased his credibility. He landed the assignment and was then able to add a brand-name hospital to his list of customers. Getting more customers in the hospital market was relatively easy.

The hospitals were right. Why should they believe that Ed's service would work for them? They believed that hospitals were different—and they are correct.

Today, prospective customers rarely believe you when you say that "what I do works for everybody." They are correct in their expectations that you should broadly understand their field, industry or demographic group.

If you have already have a business, but do not know who your customers are—those people who are buying from you—then you are helpless when there is a downturn in your industry.

In bad times, if you know who your customers are, you can develop credibility—and contacts—in that niche and be better able to compete against those who are simply offering a generic service.

Remember that this works on the retail side as well. If you are a caterer who specializes in racy cakes for bachelor parties, knowing this will turn off those who may be interested in cakes for church affairs or Sweet Sixteen parties. Pick your niche(s) and be seen as an expert or specialist in that niche.

•••••••••••••••••••••••••••••••••••••••

*Statistics suggest that when customers complain, business owners and managers ought to get excited about it. The complaining customer represents a huge opportunity for more business.*

Zig Ziglar

## Build Your Credibility

Become a specialist: read the trade journals, attend the industry association meetings, speak at those meetings and write for their newsletters. Then make copies of your articles to hand out at your speeches, to include in your mailings and to refer to in your emailings.

If, for example, you decide to target Italians (you sell Italian food or organize trips to Italy or whatever), write articles for publications for the Italian community, address Italian groups, such as the Knights of Columbus and Italian professional associations. Form a strategic partnership with those organizations so they will promote you in their newsletter or magazine—and further build your client referrals. Capture for your database the names of those who hear you speak, but screen them to capture only likely prospects for you, such as by salary range, age, etc. (For example, by having attendees fill out cards where you ask them to check off this information.)

Research each target area. This is called a "Preliminary Target Investigation. (For research hints, see the chapter "Lining Up Speeches.") Develop a marketing plan for each area and implement it.

Finally, use your mailings to keep in touch with likely prospects (associations and other organizations as well as your individual customers) so that they will remember you when they have a need. ***This ongoing follow-up is crucial in generating customers on an ongoing basis***.

Be seen as the source for your kind of work. Take on the work you can handle. Put others on a waiting list. Refer to other vendors those prospects with whom you would rather not work. It's better to have too many customers and refer out the overflow.

As your business grows, more and more of your business will come from referrals. But you will still need to conduct ongoing marketing to keep your business thriving in market down-turns, to attract the kind of customers you enjoy working with in the best of times, and to grow your business.

........................................

*Authentic marketing is not the art of selling what you make but knowing what to make. It is the art of identifying and understanding customer needs and creating solutions that deliver satisfaction to the customers, profits to the producers and benefits for the stakeholders.*

Philip Kotler

## Test Your Targets

You need multiple targets. Some may be good sources of business for you while others may not. Some may generate lots of leads, but no sales. Some may just want to talk or expect free advice. Over time, you will be able to analyze which targets are working for you. Then delete from your database those names that are from your weakest targets and focus more on those targets that are working.

Remember to maintain an exploratory mind-set—assessing the targets you are pursuing, and being open to others.

Make an organized effort the basis for your marketing campaign. You may already know people in your specialty area and be able to line up speeches and partnerships easily or contact them in some other way. On the other hand, you may need to become known as an expert by writing articles, delivering speeches and forming partnerships.

You are now ready to begin an intensive campaign to make lots of contacts with organizations in each of the specialty areas (targets) you

have selected. The campaigns will overlap so you will be able to compare the performance of each and gain perspective. Notice which ones respond to you, which audiences buy from you or ask to meet with you. Do more with those targets that are responsive, and drop those that do not work for you.

........................................

*Marketing is not an event, but a process . . . It has a beginning, a middle, but never an end, for it is a process. You improve it, perfect it, change it, even pause it. But you never stop it completely.*

Jay Conrad Levinson

*Homework:* List your specific marketing niches and what you might need to do to build your credibility or experience in those target markets.

*"Even though I started my company 10 years ago, I still consider it a start-up. Because it hasn't made one penny and not a soul knows we exist."*

# Your Two-Minute Pitch: The Keystone of Your Marketing

*If I venture to displace, by even the billionth part of an inch, the microscopical speck of dust which lies now upon the point of my finger, what is the character of that act upon which I have adventured? I have done a deed which shakes the Moon in her path, which causes the Sun to be no longer the Sun, and which alters forever the destiny of the multitudinous myriads of stars that roll and glow in the majestic presence of their Creator.*

Edgar Allen Poe, *An Essay on the Material and Spiritual Universe*

## Navigating the Minefield

The *Two-Minute Pitch* is the answer to the request, "So, tell me about your company." With a great pitch, people are more likely to see your product or service as *appropriate* for them. However, as we say at The Five O'Clock Club, "If your pitch is wrong, everything is wrong." You may have a great product or service—the best in your industry—but if you don't know how to position it properly, you will not get business.

Even The Five O'Clock Club sales team did it wrong when we first started calling on prospective corporate clients. For fifteen years, we had sold to the retail market—to the job hunters themselves—and we saw ourselves as employee advocates, doing whatever was in the best interests of employees.

Pitching to the *corporate* market was different. Yes, employers who cared about their employees liked our interest in employee advocacy. They knew we would take good care of their employees. But employers primarily wanted to know how our services and prices were different from our competitors'. Our corporate values stayed the same, but we had to emphasize different qualities. *Then* the corporate sales came in.

In fact, our pitch got so good that we put it into a magazine-format brochure titled, "The *New* Outplacement Model: Giving Job Hunters What They Need Most," which you can find at the back of this book.

## The Same Message in All Materials

Your pitch has to be consistent throughout your marketing materials. The tagline on your brochure is your pitch. Ours is "America's Premier Career Coaching and Outplacement Service." That tagline is meant to appeal to both our retail and corporate customers, and it appears on the front of all of our books and our monthly magazine.

Our verbal pitch has to carry the same message: "We're a national career coaching and outplacement service." One of our most important marketing tools is a bi-monthly event, called the HR Network, a breakfast seminar for Human Resources executives. At each seminar, 120 to 160 human resources executives listen to experts on various HR-related topics. I open the meeting with a brief "pitch" about us before I introduce the panelists.

First I say something friendly about the audience, the weather, or the place where we are holding the event—just to get their attention. Then I may say the following with a few ad-libs thrown in:

It's good to see so many familiar faces. If this is your first time at an HR Network Seminar, it probably won't be your last! I'm Kate Wendleton, president of The Five O'Clock Club. The Five O'Clock Club is a national outplacement organization.

We hope you'll *think of us first* when you have outplacement needs. All Five O'Clock Club outplacement programs are *one year*, a great benefit to give to your employees. We have a superior outplacement coaching model based on *25 years of research*, making our programs more effective and far less expensive than traditional outplacement.

These breakfasts are meant to *make you HEROS in your companies* because of what you learn from the panelists and from each other, and also because we hope you'll become a hero by telling your employer about The Five O'Clock Club outplacement program.

In your handouts, you'll find a list of our customers—some pretty prestigious names. The human resources people at those companies were heroes when they introduced their employers to the Five O'Clock Club. You can be a HERO too by finding out about us.

You can see Five O'Clock Club *outplacement coaching in action*. It's a real eye opener. Almost any Monday, come to the Roosevelt Hotel near Grand Central, where we hold the sessions—at 5:30 pm to 7:30 or at 6:30 to 8:30—to suit your schedule. (Sign-up form).

Our next breakfast, on *Friday, July 7th will be on Hot Legal Issues That Affect HR*. It'll be a sell-out, so be sure to sign up now.

Look through your folder of handouts and get more involved with the Club. Thank you for coming and thank you for allowing us to be part of your professional lives.

And now on with the show. Our first speaker is . . .

Although this introduction is brief, it's very important. I have only a few minutes to pitch to the audience about the Club. It's the only time we sell during the entire program. Many of our current customers and important prospects are in the audience. These breakfasts are our way of giving back to our customers and to the human resources community in general. When we take reservations for these popular events, our current customers get priority—even at the last minute.

The above pitch evolved over a few years! Although I'm an experienced speaker, I practice the pitch with our staff a number of times before each event, polishing the content as well as the delivery. After all, I have only one shot at this every two months, and a brief one at that.

You may think it needs no polishing. For example, the pitch could be, "I'm Kate Wendleton, president of the Five O'Clock Club, a national outplacement organization." That's fine when written. But when *spoken*, it's stronger to break the thought up into two sentences and therefore say the company name twice.

And we designate an HR Hero of the Year

each year naming the HR person who stands out for handling employees with dignity and consideration. We make a big presentation at the breakfast, and include that person on the cover of our monthly magazine. It's quite an honor and in keeping with our theme. You too can decide on a theme and carry it through to other efforts.

## Track Your Leads

You will use your pitch continually. When you (or someone on your staff) answers the phone and the caller says, "Tell me about your service," the answer *must be scripted*. Just to give you an idea of how seriously you should take this, I have printed below the script we use with *individuals* who call our office. Our pitch (or description of our service) to human resources executives is different because the service they purchase is different.

You have to "qualify" your callers before you go into a pitch about your products or services. For example, if you run a cleaning service and someone calls to ask about it, first find out who is on the phone and how they heard about you. Record every call so you can analyze later how people hear about you.

You may say, for example, "I'd love to tell you about your service. May I first have your name and phone number in case we get cut off?" After you get that information ask, "Could you tell me how you heard about us?" And record this on your call log. And then say, "We have a lot of services. Are you calling about cleaning for a business or residence?" And then give the appropriate pitch.

Why is it important to capture contact information at the outset? This is a "lead," and you will want to follow up with the caller later. Leads are precious and you can track the percentage of leads that turn into sales. Then you can figure out what you're doing right—and what you're doing wrong—so you can increase your "conversion rate"—the percentage of leads that turn into sales.

## Develop Your Script Book

At The Five O'Clock Club, we have a book of scripts (pitches) that our staff uses. Whoever answers the phone can choose the right script, depending on what the call is about. It's great for getting new employees up to speed quickly and for making sure that each staff member covers all that should be covered. Here is the pitch to someone who asks about attending our small group job-search coaching sessions:

### PITCH FOR THE INSIDER PROGRAM

Caller/Customer: Do you have a group in (CITY)?

Five O'Clock Club: Yes we *do* have a group that serves the (CITY) area! May I get a little information about *you* first?

### FILL OUT THE INSIDER PHONE LOG

May I have your name? May I have your telephone number? What field are you in? What is your salary range? How did you hear about the Five O'Clock Club? Your location?

Here's how the small group career-coaching program works. We call it the Five O'Clock Club's *Insider Program. The Insider Program* is our **FASTEST GROWING AND MOST POPULAR SERVICE**. Many members find it much more convenient, and it is also much more affordable than our physical branches.

**The way it works is like this:**

You will receive a set of 16 audio lectures on CDs, which are all done by KATE WENDLETON, President, and author of the books! The content of the CDs is *truly excellent*! You listen to a lecture each week according to a schedule. Obviously, you can listen to the CDs as often as you want!

You will join a weekly teleconference of your peers in a small group headed by a senior Five O'clock Club career coach. You will meet with the same group every week, for example, on Tuesdays at 7 pm, or Thursdays at 7:30.

During your first week, you listen to the lecture, join your small group, and *listen* to how each person in your group is strategizing his or her search. You can learn a lot by simply listening to the others in your group.

By the second week that you come back, you will have read the materials. You will listen to the lecture, join your small group, and this week your group and counselor will help you strategize your search: they'll help you figure out how to **get more interviews in your target area, or turn those interviews into offers!**

The coach's job is to help you (say slowly) **move your search along**. They'll help you figure out how to get more interviews in your target area, or turn those interviews into offers!

The program is *so* effective that the average person who attends on a regular basis finds a new position within **just ten weeks** or is negotiating to close on an offer.

Those who attend are all professionals, managers, and executives who are generally in the $40,000 to $200,000 salary range—although we have people both below and above that range. You will be in a group of your **peers**—those who are at **your salary level**. Members of the Insider Program tend to exchange e-mail and sometimes telephone numbers. They bond together as a group remarkably well!

The Five O'Clock Club is a **members-only** organization. Membership is $49 a year and includes a Beginner's Kit to get you up to speed on your search. It also includes a subscription to our excellent magazine, *The Five O'Clock News,* and other benefits, such as discounted movie tickets. You can find hundreds of articles from back issues of our magazine and other benefits and discounts on our website.

The fee for the *small group* sessions—which is in addition to the Membership fee—is 10 sessions for *only* $360 if you earn less than $100,000 per year, or 10 sessions for *only* $540 if you earn over $100,000 per year or are appropriate for a senior-level group. Or you can sign up for 20 sessions at an even greater discount. If you get a job before you have used up your sessions, you may transfer unused sessions to anyone you like.

Richard Bayer oversees the *Insider* program and will be **more than happy** to speak with you. Would you like to speak with him now?

In your own small business, even if you are the *only* one answering the phone—develop a script and *write it down*. Don't try to wing it—you can refer to the written script to make sure all important points are covered. You can polish it over time and get it right.

## Positioning Your Business Correctly

People tend to pitch their businesses incorrectly unless they're thinking clearly about its positioning. Here's a typical example. I was chatting with Kathy before the start of a small business class. Here's the way the conversation went:

Kate: So, what kind of business are you planning, Kathy?

Kathy: Catering.

Kate (sensing her positioning was incorrect): Well, I doubt that. What kind of catering?

Kathy: Haalal food for Muslims. I would aim at Islamic women who prepare these foods. I can make everyday dishes and can also cater parties—from weddings to sweet sixteen parties.

Kathy was initially positioning herself incorrectly. Describing herself simply as a caterer was misleading. The caller could assume she does everything from ordinary parties to barbeques with chicken wings—which is not what she had in mind.

This doesn't matter so much when she's talking to *me*, but it does matter when she's trying to get a customer. Your pitch screens you out (lets customers know you are not right for them) as well as screens you in (lets them know you are just right for them).

Most businesses have to reposition themselves, if only to emphasize certain parts of their business offerings and downplay others. Figure out the needs of your prospect, and make sure that your pitch makes you look appropriate to that target market.

## Sugar, Sugar, Sugar: Use the Jargon of the Industry You Are Targeting

Cheryl had been selling in the *sugar* industry. In her small group, Cheryl talked about bulk sugar, liquid sugar, brown sugar, white sugar, sugar cubes, truckloads of sugar, and train-carloads of sugar. Everything was sugar, sugar, sugar!

Yet Cheryl wanted to sell in the bulk food industry. It's easy for an outsider to see that Cheryl simply needs to say *bulk food* instead of *sugar*. But when it's happening to you, it can be much more difficult to see that *you are positioning yourself incorrectly*.

Companies want to buy from vendors who have experience in their industry. Individuals want to buy from companies who have experience with the kind of help they need. If you offer cleaning services, to name an easy example, and you are trying to sell your services to small businesses, they will ask you about other small business you have serviced. Talking about all of the homes you clean will not be relevant to them.

*Use the jargon and the words of your new industry.* If you don't *know* the new jargon, then you must learn it—just as we had to learn to reposition ourselves for the corporate market. You cannot pass the translation responsibility on to the people who will be calling you.

Cheryl may think, "If our service is useful in the sugar industry, they should be able to *see* that it can work in the bulk food industry." But they think Cheryl's committed to the sugar industry. It is *her* responsibility to show them that she un-

derstands and can fit into the new target industry by using their jargon.

Eventually Cheryl learned to say *food* instead of *sugar*. She soon landed a terrific account in the food industry. A few years later, she repositioned the service again and got a terrific account in the computer software industry!

......................................

*Great minds have purposes, others have wishes.*

Washington Irving

## Where Your Pitch Is Used

Your Two-Minute Pitch is the backbone of your marketing. You'll use it in phone and in-person conversations and in all of your literature. The same theme will run throughout. You'll be ready when someone calls and says, "So tell me about your company." You'll use a 15-second version of it at parties and church events when people ask what you do. You are continually selling.

When developing your pitch, keep in mind

- to whom you are pitching
- what they are interested in
- who your likely competitors are
- and what you bring to the party that your competitors do not.

Think about your target audience and what you want to say to them. Examine your product features and benefits to find things that fit.

......................................

*All managers establish relationships over their careers . . . the unsavvy [managers] form fewer of those relationships. They are also more likely to let relationships fade when they move on to new positions. . . . The savvy managers . . . consistently seek to build relationships and then keep them up once they move on. It doesn't take much time, just a phone call now and then to ask, How are you doing?*

Joel M. DeLuca, Ph.D., *Political Savvy*

## Your Pitch in a Sales Meeting

Here is a format for a meeting, briefly, so you can see where your Pitch fits in:

1. Exchange pleasantries—so the manager will focus on you.
2. Tell the manager why you're there, such as, "Jane suggested I contact you because she thought you might be interested in hearing how we have solved the *c.difficile* problem in other hospitals."
3. Then the manager will say, "Fine. Tell me about it." Rather than launch into your pitch, say, "I do have a lot to tell you, but first I'd like to find out a little about you." You need to know to whom you are pitching.

- Are you currently having a problem with *c. difficile*?
- Have you tried other solutions in the past? What has your experience been?
- Are you interested in solving this problem now? Do you have the resources to address it?

And *then* you give your Pitch, depending on what they say.

When you have a sales meeting, you are likely to be asked, "So Jane, tell me a little bit about Prestige Catering." If you have not done your homework and you know nothing about the company, you will be in trouble. Find out something about them *before* you give your pitch. Otherwise, you will not know how to position yourself.

So, for example, you could say, "There are a lot of things I have to say about our company, but I'd like to keep it relevant to your situation. What do you see as your needs right now?" Or say, "I can tell you a lot about Prestige Catering, but first I'd like to know what it was about our brochure that made you call us."

Once they tell you something about what is going on with them, then you will be able to position yourself appropriately. Know something about them before you give your Two-Minute Pitch.

## Your Pitch in the Cover Letter

Your cover letters can be much more effective when you use The Five O'Clock Club format.

1. *Paragraph one* is your introduction. You might say, "I have been following Apex Chemicals for some time and admire your emphasis on tight controls. Arch Controls focuses on the close monitoring of business units. I would be glad to tell you the latest trends in the control industry and how other companies are benefiting from the advanced, inexpensive technology." Your opening paragraph is generally *specific to the company*.
2. *Paragraph two* contains your summary. *That is your pitch*. "Arch Controls has been helping companies such as yours since 1991." And so on.
3. *Paragraph three* contains the bulleted accomplishments, or features and benefits. For example, you may list some of the projects you have recently worked on—especially for companies that would be of interest to the one you are targeting. For example:

You may be interested in some of the specific things we've done in the chemical and pharmaceutical industries: (followed by bulleted examples)

- Reduced expenses in 4 units, saving the company over $200,000. And so on.

4. *Paragraph four* is the close, where you ask for a meeting, such as: "I will call you in a few days to set up a mutually convenient time to meet." Then you'll follow up with a few phone calls.

*Know how to ask. There is nothing more difficult
for some people. Nor for others, easier.*

Baltasar Gracian, *The Art of Worldly Wisdom*

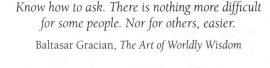

*The heights by great men reached and kept
Were not attained by sudden flight,
But they, while their companions slept,
Were toiling upward in the night.*

Henry Wadsworth Longfellow

## The Outline of Your Pitch

When developing your pitch, first ask yourself, "What is the most important thing that I want them to know about us?" No, it's not that you're all hard workers and dedicated. That doesn't separate you from your competition, and it's a useless thing to say. Your opening statement should be a *positioning* statement having to do with the field you're in or the one you're going after. For example, "Interrep is an international marketing firm." Or Beebee's Wash'n'Fold means you can get your laundry done in only four minutes: two minutes to drop it off and two minutes to pick it up."

Now what's the *second* most important thing you want them to know about you? This thought should separate you from all the other international marketing firms (or laundromats), such as "with expertise in international marketing systems." What is the third most important thing? This statement usually supports the first two and may be an overarching statement that introduces the *accomplishments* that will follow, such as "Our breadth of experience includes strategic planning, business generation, and people development. On the strategy side, we wrote the business plan for the Amerilite division, which encompassed . . ."

Here you would give concrete examples of your organization's accomplishments—but not *too* detailed because you can give the details later. For example, you could say, "We do the laundry

for dozens of people in your building. What's more, we overwinter clothing, mend and alter, and can do anything that has to be done with clothing." You don't have to cover everything your company does in one or two minutes. Give them an overview, and—if yours is a complicated business—you can interject, "I can tell you more about that later."

The final statement in your pitch could be something like, "I'm excited about talking to you today because of the strong international component of your business."

That is how you can think through the formulation of your pitch. It has an overarching statement with organized details to enable the listener to grasp the key points you are trying to make. Now, when you have tried your pitch on a few prospects, you will modify it to better suit your audience and you will probably end up NOT using the above formula at all.

When I am rehearsing small-business owners on their pitches, the most common comment I make is: "Make me want to buy! Sell to me!" For example, you can include sentences such as,

- "Our most popular request is for our cheesecake desserts, especially the amaretto which is like none you've ever had."
- "Our clients come to us for manicures and pedicures but they wind up getting our facials, which make them feel like they've been on vacation."
- "Our list of clients rival any in the international marketing industry. One client recently said to us, "You make me look like a genius because I selected your firm."

Don't just list your products and services. *Sell* them! Show enthusiasm. If you don't believe in what you do, why should they?

*Courage is doing what you are afraid to do.
There can be no courage unless you're scared.*

Eddie Rickenbacker

## Repositioning Yourself in Your Pitch

Remember, *most* organizations have to reposition themselves based on the kind of client they are targeting. For example, when we asked Janie to "tell us a little bit about your company," Janie said, "We've developed gift baskets for teens and mothers, babies and sweet sixteens."

If we were a retail customer, that positioning may have been okay. But we were pretending we were a potential corporate customer, and therefore her positioning was all wrong. Once Janie found out a little about us, she easily repositioned her firm: "We've done gift baskets for retirement parties and employee recognition campaigns. For one Fortune 500 company, we produced over 300 baskets recognizing employees in various departments for their outstanding accomplishments."

A very different pitch, isn't it? But it still would have been better for her to find out their needs *before* going into her pitch. Know something about your audience and its needs before you launch into a pitch.

The richness of a pitch is in the details—the examples.

## More Customization

In your pitch, do not tell your company's life story. Instead, say things that are relevant. Position your company, and tell accomplishments that would be of interest to the organization. *Memorize* your pitch, and then *modify* it depending on whom you are talking to.

Philip, for example, had been in marketing for years and specialized in developing new products. He decided to start his own consulting firm. He met with one company that already had dozens of new products. They wanted their products taken to market. Philip had to change his pitch. Instead of saying, "We develop new products," he said, "We're expert at taking products to market."

Be sensitive about your target market. Find out their needs, what they're missing, and their problem areas. Then position yourself accordingly.

## Practice Your Pitch

Most people write out their Two-Minute Pitch, or the key points, and rehearse it in front of a mirror, with their small group or with others in their companies.

There are a lot of surprises during the sales call or a conversation with a prospect, but some things are *certain*. You will have to tell them about your company. This is *not* a surprise. Even if they don't ask, you still have to give your pitch—your Two-Minute Pitch.

*I know you are asking today, "How long will it take?" I come to say to you this afternoon, however difficult the moment, however frustrating the hour, it will not be long, because truth pressed to earth will rise again. . . . How long? Not long, because you still reap what you sow. How long? Not long, because the arm of the moral universe is long but it bends towards justice.*

Reverend Martin Luther King, Jr., at the end of his march from Selma (last lines of his speech)

## What Point Are You Trying to Make?

When you rehearse your Two-Minute Pitch, ask yourself: What *point* am I trying to make? What impression do I hope people will get about me?

I was listening to a client's pitch, and could not understand the point this executive woman was trying to make. After she had finished:

Kate: I don't get it. What point are you trying to make?

Client: Look, I want them to know that I have 20 years' experience in capital markets, whether it's in aerospace or petroleum, metals and mining, or real estate. *My experience is in capital markets.*

Kate: That's a great pitch. Why don't you just tell them exactly that up front?

### They Won't "Get It" on Their Own, So Just Tell Them.

Most small business owners think: I'll just tell them what we do, and they'll see how it fits in with their needs. But they probably won't see. If you want them to see how all of your work has somehow been involved in international, say, "All of our work has somehow been involved in international." Isn't that easy?

> Don't expect the decision-making team to figure out something about your company. If you have a conclusion you'd like them to reach about you or your firm, tell them what it is.

If you want them to see that your staff has intensive product knowledge in the financial area, tell them that. Do you want them to know that one of your staff members is expert in FORTRAN, which this prospective customer happens to need? Then don't say, "Our staff has a broad range of expertise in various computer languages." That's not your point. Do you want them to know that you can promote their hotel and get hundreds of people to come? Tell them. Don't make them figure it out for themselves. They won't.

Don't think to yourself, "I thought that if I told them that we know virtually every programming language they would just understand that we also know how to manage project teams." No! *Tell* them what you want them to know and how your company's background fits in with their needs.

Make your message so clear that if someone says, "Tell me about CyberTeam," they will know what to tell the other decision-makers about your company.

### What Will They Say about You When You're Gone?

If they're looking for a paper supplier and you're a paper supplier, and you're talking to them about their paper needs, chances are good that everyone else they're talking to is also a paper supplier. When you leave, the purchasing manager is not going to say,

"Oh, my gosh! I just met a paper supplier."

Instead, you want them to say, "Oh, my gosh. I just met somebody who is an expert in monitoring paper usage and determining our re-order quantities. And they're working on a project in our industry doing exactly what we're trying to do."

What do you want them to say about *your company* when you're gone? *That's* your pitch. Repeat it enough during the meeting so that you know how they'll position you to *other* people after you leave.

## Communicating Your Pitch

Many people try to cram everything they can into their Two-Minute Pitch, but when your pitch is too densely packed, people won't hear what you want them to hear. Think about those who are considered the great communicators today. We judge communicators very differently from the way we did in the past, when the Winston Churchill type was ideal.

Today, our standards are based on the medium of TV. The best communicators speak on a personal level—the way people talk on TV. Whether you are addressing a big audience or are on a job interview, cultivate a TV style—a friendly, one-on-one conversational style, not a *listing of what I've done* style. Speak the way you would normally speak.

The decision-maker is assessing what it would be like to work with you. Make your pitch understandable. Before people go on TV, they decide the three major points they want to make—what they want the audience *to remembe*r.

Many people have pitches that are too heavy in content. Let's return to the woman executive we were discussing: "I have 20 years' experience in capital markets in airlines, real estate and petroleum, metals and mining—assessing customers' and prospects' financial requirements based on the industry's point within the business cycle as well as the specific company's. I assess client credit, etc."

People can't listen to that. It's too dense. It needs some filler around the important words to resemble the way people really talk: "I have 20 years' experience in capital markets—capital markets has always been my chief interest. I had this experience in three different areas, but the area where I spent the most time was in the airlines. I'd like to tell you more about that because it is a related industry."

The new pitch is more *conversational* than a list and will be more effective than simply getting all the facts out.

## Vary Your Pitch by Organization

Change your pitch for every organization with which you meet. If you're pitching yourself to a large organization, you will probably have a different pitch than if you are pitching to a small organization. When you know something about the organization that you're meeting with, you should be able to modify your pitch. Now, this does not contradict what I said earlier about having your pitch down pat. You *can* have it down pat, then you can ad lib a bit and modify it to suit this target market. Know your main point and your subordinate points, and modify those for each organization.

## Emphasis and Tempo

When you say something important, emphasize it by slowing down. For example, in the sentence "We worked on that project for over nine months," you could slow down on "nine months" to give it emphasis. Like this: "We worked on that project for over [slowly] *nine months*." That's what TV announcers do. They speed up back-

ground words and slow down on the important words. Then your listener will not miss what you consider important.

I speak quickly, but when I am on a sales call talking to someone who is laid back and casual, even *I* can change tempo and slow myself down a little bit so that I match their pace.

But if I were meeting with somebody who is more fast-paced and chop-chop, then I can operate at the fast-paced end of my spectrum. If you speak very slowly to someone who is fast-paced, they'll think you're slow and won't fit in with their needs.

## More about Filler Words and Pointer Words

As indicated earlier, filler words can be useful. They help *engage* your listener. Words can high-light important points that are coming up. You might say, for example, "One of the most interesting projects that we've ever worked on was . . ." Those are highlight words. They point to whatever you're going to tell them next. You're saying, "What I'm about to say will be important." And then you may name an accomplishment. You may want to follow that (or a different accomplishment) with "That was one of the most satisfying things we've ever done because [slowly] the client gave us carte blanche and we smoothly handled every problem they had ever encountered in the past on this kind of project." That phrase points *back* to what you just said, so they don't miss it.

## Smile

When I rehearse people who are giving their company pitches, I find that I commonly tell people to *smile* (as well as *sell*). When you smile, it has an impact on the viewer. Even if you're on the phone, when you are smiling, it impacts the listener.

When you smile, people see you as more competent and more self-confident. If you do not smile, then you look worried and you look less qualified than you really are.

When you smile, the other person has a *vis-*

*ceral reaction* to you. Their tendency, unless the person is a brick wall, is to smile back. A good healthy smile helps you during the interview, and the hiring manager is more likely to think that there is good chemistry between you.

Use your hands as you would in a normal conversation. Don't sit there like a rock. Pay attention to the hiring manager's style. Take a look at the things around their room. Is the person more formal or more laid back? You can adjust your presentation accordingly.

## Two Minutes Is a Long Time, So Show Enthusiasm

In this TV society, people are used to 15-second sound bites on the news. As the communicator, you have to engage the listener. Reinforce your main points. Don't say too many things.

Show *enthusiasm* during those two minutes. If you're an introvert and a low-key person, force yourself to sit *forward* in your chair. Sit almost on the edge of your seat. It will thrust your body forward and make you look more energetic. And using your hands a little will also give much more energy to your presentation. The interview process is an extroverted process, and low-key people are at a disadvantage. So, *act* a little extroverted on the interview; whether you're extroverted or not, you have to act that way more than you normally would. Otherwise, people may doubt that you have the energy to get work done.

The good news is that you do not have to act that way in your day-to-day job of managing projects!

I once did a magazine article on who got jobs and who got to keep them. I talked to the deans of business and engineering schools. I learned that the person most likely to get the job was the one who sounded enthusiastic. And the one who got to keep the job was the enthusiastic one—even more than people who were more qualified. Employers decided to keep someone who was willing to pitch in and do anything to help the company.

Even more interesting to me is that this same thing is true for senior executives. In my line of work, I sometimes have the opportunity to follow up with organizations when someone doesn't get a job or assignment. I am amazed by the number of times I am told (about people making from $150,000 to $600,000) that the applicant lacked enthusiasm: "He was managing 1,300 people, and I don't know how he did it. He just doesn't sound enthusiastic. How could he motivate his troops if he can't motivate me? Anyway, I don't know that he really wants the job. He didn't sound interested."

I know we have landed many an assignment because of our enthusiasm for our service and the people we are helping. Customers tell us, "We can see that you care and are not just in this for the money. We know you'll take good care of our people."

## Depend on Your Small Group

Your Five O'Clock Club group is terrific at giving feedback on the Two-Minute Pitch. Tell the other people in the group who they should pretend to be. That is, they should pretend that they are a homemaker, a purchasing agent for an electric company, a single male in a professional job—whoever your target market is. Then they say to you, "So tell us about your company." Then you say your pitch—you can refer to your notes—and ask them for their comments.

Your group can comment on both the delivery and the content. They can tell if your pitch is clear, if you're being too modest about your offerings, if your pitch is too general, or if you are not enthusiastic and convincing enough. Then refine your pitch and practice it again in your group the following week. Keep practicing it until you get it right. (Sometimes people use tape recorders to record the pitch.) It may take you three or four weeks to get it perfect, but that's what your small group is for.

Remember: The Two-Minute Pitch is one of the most important parts of your marketing efforts. Most successful Five O'Clock clubbers said that once they got their pitch down, things seemed to work out better in their search. So practice your Two-Minute Pitch in your small group and take it to the world!

......................................

*A very large amount of human suffering and frustration is caused by the fact that many men and women are not content to be the sort of beings that God had made them, but try to persuade themselves that they are really beings of some different kind.*

Eric Mascall, *The Importance of Being Human*

## Homework:

Develop both your written as well as your verbal pitch and practice your verbal pitch in your small group. Tell your small group to pretend they are part of a certain market segment, such as the purchasing agent for a film company, or a prospective customer who has called about party planning services. Then, give your pitch to that prospect and get feedback from the group. Perhaps you will need to qualify the prospect to find out why they called you or what they are really interested in.

Then ask your group:

- Was the product or service clear to them?
- Did you "sell" it, making them want to buy?
- Did you smile—even if you were pretending to be on the phone?

# Naming Your Business

"Pasta and Cheese" was the name of a successful restaurant in Manhattan. It became so successful that imitators decided they liked it, one of whom opened a restaurant called—guess what—"Pasta and Cheese!" The original company had not trademarked the name of their restaurant, nor could they have trademarked it because it was a generic name and was not trademarkable.

When you name your business, you have a lot to consider. Pick a name that:

- Represents what you stand for.
- Encompasses what you plan to do even fifteen years from now. Companies sometimes have to change their company name because they enter into additional products and services that their original name no longer reflects.
- Can be trademarked if you want to protect your name from being used by others.

When we selected the name "The Five O'Clock Club," we wanted a name that had a friendly tone and could accommodate a business that expanded beyond career coaching and perhaps into other training areas, such as art appreciation. "Five O'Clock" implies the time after work when you are free to think about other things, such as your career. It soon became apparent that focusing on careers was enough of a business to keep us occupied for many years. However, we would not have had to change the name if we had decided to get into other social activities.

When selecting a logo, the trend these days is towards a very modernistic style—such as a swoosh—which may or may not mean anything to the customer. We opted for a more old-fashioned, more complicated logo which connotes a certain feeling and allows us to use parts of the logo separately, such as the clock-face or the silhouette of the people.

Whatever your brand name, you will need a tagline and a pitch—both verbal and written. Your goal will be to build your brand name, even if your focus is just your immediate community. Over time, your brand name means what you want it to mean—so long as you repeat the same pitch over and over.

## The Naming Process

Decide what your business will be now and in the foreseeable future, and the target market your name is meant to appeal to. Then, make a list of the adjectives you want people to think of when they hear your business name. Is it aimed at working people or the very rich? Is it fast-paced or casual? Is it meant to convey comfort and warmth or toughness and durability?

"The Five O'Clock Club" was meant to convey sociability and caring, among other things. We developed a list of ten or so adjectives and it took quite a few years until we came across a suitable name.

We also have to think of book titles. One of our earlier books was titled *Through the Brick Wall,* a great title that lends itself well to graphics. We had a list of adjectives that we wanted that book title to convey, and then brainstormed a list of *700 possible titles!!* Naming something is a lot of work.

You can hire a naming professional, but it is very expensive. Decide whether this is an appropriate expense for your business. If you don't hire an expert, expect to spend a good deal of time coming up with potential names and then testing them in the market, however informal that testing may be. Then you'll want to sleep on it for a while. After all, you hope to live with this name for decades.

## The Brainstorming Session

This is how we brainstorm names at The Five O'Clock Club. We usually have 6 to 8 people in a brainstorming session. It's best if the session contains a diverse group of people—not just managers. You could even include friends and relatives. The person requesting the meeting describes the product or service that needs a name and gives the list of qualities a prospective customer should think of upon hearing the name. The person needing a name may have done some research ahead of time: the kinds of names that are typical in the industry, synonyms from the dictionary, and the like.

Then the participants name anything they want. No idea is a bad idea because a bad name may help someone else think of another name. All of the names are listed on a flip chart so everyone can see the names that have already been suggested. Even if someone in the group is pretty good at coming up with names, he or she may need to hear the ideas others have to get the thinking process going. You never know where the good names will come from, so don't judge a person's suggestions based on his or her likeability or seniority.

After the group has come up with a lot of names, they pick the names they like the best and try to imagine what an outsider would think of this name for this particular product, product line, service or business. People may say that a certain name makes them think of something negative. Others may have difficulty pronouncing the name or think it sounds too close to a competitor's name.

The Five O'Clock Club has competitors with names that sound like law firms: Lee, Hecht, Harrison and Drake Beam Morin. Their names are obviously meant to appeal to the corporate executives who would buy their services rather than the employee who would use the services. We took an approach that is the opposite of theirs and it has worked well for us. Even our name tells customers that our service is very different from our competitors'. Their name implies that their services model is out-of-date and that what they offer is a commodity—they all offer the same thing. Our service is different, and our name reflects that.

After you have come up with a few names you want to consider, it's time to make sure none of them have legal issues.

## Trademarks

We went through the trademark registration process not only on our business name, The

Five O'Clock Club, but for our various processes such as the Seven Stories Exercise, the Forty-Year Vision, and a program we ran for ten years called Workforce America. These are all registered trademarks of The Five O'Clock Club, and we have to keep them up-to-date and protect them. That is, we have to keep them registered and also go after anyone who may be using similar terms that may create confusion in the eyes of the public.

If you want to have your own consulting or service business, there's nothing wrong with a name such as Chapman Marketing Services or Dobson Advertising. Even if you grow and wind up with a staff of seventy or have multiple locations, the name will still work. What's more, you don't have to worry too much about trademark restrictions—unless there is another company in your same category with the same name.

By the same reasoning, if you want to have a corner deli, you can call it just about anything you want—such as A&J Deli—so long as it does not infringe on anyone else's trademark.

But if you want to expand to other geographic areas or grow the business into something bigger than a neighborhood store, think of a more marketable name—and one that can be trademarked.

Trademarks are registered for certain categories. Someone who was starting a coaching service or a training service of any kind cannot use the Five O'Clock Club name. However, if someone wanted to start a line of computers and for some reason wanted to call it The Five O'Clock Club, they would not be infringing on our present trademark. The court standard is whether a trademark causes a "likelihood of confusion." If the company is in a different industry and it's not a household name, then it's more likely you can use the name.

When we went through the trademark research process, sometimes the name we had in mind was already claimed by someone else in the same category. Then we had to go to another name on our list. (By the way, book titles cannot be trademarked, so we do not have to do a trademark search on book titles.)

You can check each name on the Trademark Electronic Search System, or TES, at www.uspto.gov, which also includes pending trademarks you should avoid. You can also contact the PTO at (800) 786-9199 for general information about trademark registration or to ask about the status of specific trademark applications and registrations.

Then search the web to see if anyone is using the name without having registered it. You can still register the name even if they're using it. Once you register it, no one may use it in the future for the category under which you register it. However, prior users may generally continue to use the name.

If your brand name is important to you, and you expect to be more than a Mom and Pop business, hire an intellectual-property attorney to do a thorough search and protect your business name.

As you go along, be sure to review all of your selected names against your criteria list. Sometimes you will get off track in your brainstorming and research and forget the kind of name you were looking for.

# Developing Your Marketing Literature

*In the factory we make cosmetics; in
the drugstore we sell hope.*

Charles Revson

Not every business needs marketing literature, but most do. Take a look at what your competitors are doing and judge for yourself. Marketing to corporations may require more sophisticated materials than literature for the retail market. Whatever you do, test it before you spend a lot of money. You'd be surprised by how much your literature will change over the first few months or years.

In our section on "Becoming a Consultant in Your Own Field," we have sample brochure for consultants. Brochures are easy to make. The samples below were all done in Word using clip art from the Internet. An administrator (not a graphic artist) in our office developed them for people who are incarcerated. They developed the wording and The Five O'Clock Club laid it out, giving them something to look forward to upon their release. When they get out, these brochures will give credibility to their small businesses.

Research shows that sales increase when prices are given rather than when you expect people to call to find out the price. In the brochures shown below, the inside of the brochure contained prices where appropriate.

· · · · · · · · · · · · · · · · · · · · · · · · · · · · · · ·

*Customers buy for their reasons, not yours.*

Orvel Ray Wilson

· · · · · · · · · · · · · · · · · · · · · · · · · · · · · · ·

*People don't want to be "marketed TO"; they
want to be "communicated WITH."*

Flint McGlaughlin

# Julie's Cleaning

## Prices:

- **STUDIO – $50**

- **One-bedroom – $60**

- **Two-bedroom – $70**

Price includes cleaning one kitchen, one bathroom, and one living room.
Additional rooms $10 (study room, dining room etc.)
We also organize clothing closets

## Tel: 212-222-1000

Cleaning Service by appointments only

# DEBBIE'S Designs

## Clothing with a Personal Touch

16 Riverdale, Dr
Destinytown, NC 28473
910.333.7777
www.deb.des.org

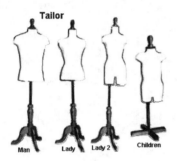

*Dresses*

## Suits

*Pants*

*Skirts*

*Knit or Crochet*

Accessories are available

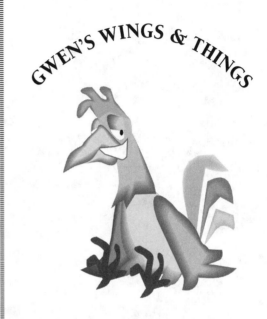

GWEN'S WINGS & THINGS

**555 Thrush Drive
Brentwood, NY 55555
Tel: 718 273-1867**

## Free Delivery

(Minimum order $10.00)

Log on www.gwen.deliver .com

for Catering & Special Orders

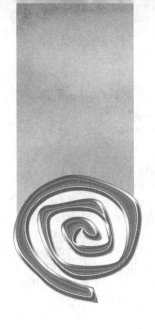

# Selling to Organizations (the Corporate Sale)

*The single most important thing to remember about any enterprise is that there are no results inside its walls. The result of a business is a satisfied customer.*

Peter Drucker

Often the only way to actually sell your product is to make a sales call. To make one sale, you are likely to have to call on quite a few organizations, and the ones you call on should be good prospects—that is, people who are likely to buy—or you are wasting your time.

Eventually, you will need to develop metrics—that is, measurements of how many sales calls you must make to land one sale. Making the call is the *start* of the process. The key is keeping in touch with the good prospects you have called on!

Here's one way to look at the process of marketing to organizations:

1. Develop your targets—the industries or organization size (small, medium or large organizations) where you want to sell your products or services, as well as the title of the person you want to sell to (such as, the president, the purchasing

department, the head of marketing).
2. Develop a brochure or marketing piece that makes you look appropriate to these targets.
3. Become known in your target markets. This is what most people mean by "marketing."
4. Measure how well you are doing in your marketing efforts.
5. Meet with prospects and "act like a consultant."
6. Follow up intelligently.
7. Have fun!!!

There are many ways you can get organizations to know about you and perhaps contact you themselves. But, in the end, you generally need to make a sales call—that is, have a meeting with the buyer or purchasing influencer.

We'll help you get plenty of *meetings* in your target markets. And, we'll show you how to measure how well you're doing in your marketing efforts, so you can determine whether or not you're meeting the right people and how well you're doing in those meetings. We'll teach you how to "interview like a consultant," which will keep you calm—and help you ask the right questions during the meeting. Then we'll show you how to follow up intelligently—so you can turn those meetings into sales and get the business you deserve. And, finally, we want you to have FUN in the process. If you're not having some fun in your life, you won't have good meetings, and you'll take longer to get a sale. After all, they can choose who they want to work with, and often—all things being equal—they choose people they like.

.......................................

*Every man is born into the world to do something unique and something distinctive and if he or she does not do it, it will never be done.*

Benjamin E. Mays, "I Knew Carter G. Woodson," *Negro History Bulletin,* January–March 1981

# What Is a Target?

Everything starts with your marketing targets. We say, "If your targets are wrong, everything is wrong."

Nothing in your marketing campaign is going to work out well if your targets are vague or ill-defined for long. Targets are the starting point, the basis for everything else you do in your marketing efforts.

> **If your targets are wrong, everything is wrong.**

A target consists of:

- an industry or company size you think would be interested in your product or service. Let's say for example, banking or health care. And/or you could target organizations of a certain size, such as those with 1000 to 8000 employees, or those in a certain revenue category;
- a specific department or division within those organizations, the area you think

would do the buying or be a major influencer, such as marketing;
- a certain geographic area, let's say St. Louis.

Those *three* elements make up a target. In the beginning of your marketing efforts, come up with as many targets as you possibly can in case you need more targets later on in your efforts. You'll conduct a Preliminary Target Investigation (through the Internet and networking) on your first list of targets. This will help you refine your Marketing Plan, which will guide your efforts. Of course, we'll show you how to do all of this.

## Case Study: Janie
## Her Targets No Longer Worked

Janie had been in business for over twenty years selling computer staffing to the hospital industry in the Southwest. She now has a staff of over 30 full-time employees and 200 computer consultants who she assigns to organizations when they need help in the information technology area. She had grown her business to over $5 million in revenue a year. But in the past few years, Janie's margins had been shrinking. Clients wanted bigger discounts. They wanted rebates if they hired someone for a month or more. It became a constant struggle.

Let's analyze Janie's targets. Her company was focused almost exclusively on large hospitals. The department or division was the Information Technology area. Janie's targets *had* been correct for years, but now they were not. She needed to think about things anew—test *new* targets and see how they compare with the way she is being treated in the hospital industry. Would the pharmaceutical industry or the publishing industry be just as stingy as hospitals now were? Would other heathcare-related industries be better for her and easy to expand into?

Janie could test her new-target theory simply by selecting a representative sample of companies in other industries and seeing how they compared. If she found that *all* industries were now stingy in the IT area, she may want to expand the *kind* of staffing she does and move out of strictly IT staffing. For example, she could move into accounting staffing with a focus on Sarbanes Oxley, a hot area as of this writing.

I don't mean to minimize this decision. It's basically reexamining the core of her business—the targets her company focuses on—and making a change there. She has only three choices: change the industry or organization size, change the function she services, or change the geographic area. Many problems have to do with incorrect targets.

...........................................

*The world fears a new experience more than it fears anything. Because a new experience displaces so many old experiences. . . . The world doesn't fear a new idea. It can pigeon-hole any idea. But it can't pigeon-hole a real new experience.*

D. H. Lawrence

# Prepare Your Brochure or Marketing Piece

When you have completed the exercises in this book, you will be in a better position to develop marketing materials that make you look appropriate to your targets. Then you will be desirable when you go in for a meeting. Remember, your marketing piece is likely to be looked at for only 10 seconds at first. So, it's vital that key ideas or words pop out. Can the reader *easily* figure out what you are offering, and how you are different from your competition? Make sure you have gathered competitive information and have a hanging file on each competitor. Research their websites to see what they say about themselves. Then test your marketing literature in the market. Listen carefully to what prospects say. Do they see how you are different? Does your verbal pitch about your product or service match your written pitch? Your message should be consistent.

*Duty largely consists of pretending that the trivial is critical.*

John Fowles, *The Magus*

# Developing Your Marketing Plan

Once you've thought of a few *tentative* targets, you are ready to work on your Marketing Plan. This Plan will guide you throughout your marketing efforts. In my small group, I often ask someone to name an industry or organization size that he or she is targeting and the group helps that person brainstorm how to go after that target.

### Case Study: Sidney
### Market to Small Organizations

Sidney wants to provide bookkeeping services to small businesses. He needs only five ongoing clients because he would like to work one day a week at each client's office. Of course, this means that he may have to learn various accounting and computer systems and master them all, but Sidney thinks he would enjoy that.

Sidney will need to brainstorm the various segments he could market to. Before he starts marketing, Sidney will need a tentative brochure that describes his services and would appeal to small business owners. In addition, he needs experience handling the bookkeeping for a small company or two. Even if he worked for a *low* fee for a little while, he would gain the credentials and credibility he needs:

- In exchange for working for a reduced fee, Sidney would ask his first clients to **serve as a reference for him**.
- Sidney could get a few **testimonials** from clients and put those on his literature or as a handout in his information packet.
- He could get a small business accounting or bookkeeping certificate from a community college, for example, to add to his credentials.

Sidney needs to brainstorm his target markets. He can market directly to the organization for which he wants to do work or he could market to an intermediary, an influencer. Here are a few ideas:

- Sidney could visit local banks and make his pitch to those who service small businesses. These people are "influencers." Sidney could provide them with his literature, including the testimonials that would give him credibility, and follow up with them regularly, emphasizing, for example, that he already has 3 clients and can handle only two more.
- He could also market to small accounting firms that would be too pricey for the account size that would be just right for Sidney.
- Sidney could target businesses in his local area, such as in a shopping center or office building and go door-to-door marketing his services. Chances are, no one will need his help right at that moment; He will have to follow-up later.
- He can get lists of 300 to 500 small businesses in his geographic area from the library or the Internet and send them his brochure along with a cover letter. Then, he could follow up with a phone call.
- Sidney should pick a geographic area that is under-serviced. Most small business growth has been occurring in the suburbs. And major metropolitan areas are full of competitors. For Sidney, the suburbs may be the place to go.

## Case Study: Byron
## Segmenting Your Targets

Byron wants to sell to the not-for-profit area. This is *not* a target because it's too broad. Not-for-profit could include associations, hospitals, universities, the government—and each of those subtargets is huge!

Breaking your targets into manageable subtargets is called *segmenting your targets*.

## "Not-for-profit" is too broad to be useful.

It could include:

- associations
- hospitals
- universities
- the government

—and all of those subtargets are huge!

Byron realizes now that not-for-profit is not a target any more than *for-profit* would be a target. So he thinks his product would be well received by the health care market and he'd like to focus on that. Oops. He's not there yet. Health care is unwieldy as a target! It could include, for example, hospitals, home health care, HMOs, pharmaceutical companies, nursing homes, hospice care, health insurance companies, crisis intervention programs, congregate care facilities, medical billing, health-care consulting firms, medical device manufacturers, and distributors. (Who makes the catheters? And who makes the beds?)

You could go on and on. Health care could also be anything having to do with the aging of America, for example. You could brainstorm lots of other job targets having to do with health care itself.

## Break Your Targets Down into Subtargets

Health care, for example, could include:
- hospitals
- home health care
- HMOs
- pharmaceutical companies
- nursing homes
- hospice care
- health insurance companies
- crisis intervention programs
- congregate care facilities
- medical billing
- health-care consulting firms
- medical device manufacturers
- distributors

**Health care could also include:**

- Anything having to do with the aging of America
- Vitamin companies
- Health-care publishing
- Lots of other subcategories, depending on your interests

## *Rank* Your Targets—To Organize Your Work

*The only joy in the world is to begin.*

Cesare Pavese, Italian writer

So Byron needs to rank his targets and decide which targets he wants to go after first, second, third, fourth. He could practice on targets that don't mean that much to him. Or he may want to focus first on targets where he thinks he is most likely to be well received. Still, his first step is to rank his targets.

Then he'll need to *measure* his targets. If the total number of organizations he's going after is fewer than 200, that's not good. When he adds up all of his targets, if he focuses on something that is just too small, his efforts will be doomed from the start.

As a separate but very relevant issue, he could think about the state of the market within each of those targets. Some markets are growing and some markets are retrenching. If some of his important target markets are retrenching, he'll need to go after even more potential purchasers.

On the other hand, if your target industry is very interested in your product or service, you may be able to get away with targeting fewer prospective buyers.

Remember Janie, who I had mentioned earlier. Both computer staffing and hospitals were less interested in her service than they had been in the previous ten years. In the past, she didn't have to target that many companies. Now, however, she needs to target additional hospitals and also target another industry or two to see which may be responsive.

*If you cannot catch a bird of paradise, better take a wet hen.*

Nikita S. Khrushchev, quoted in *Time,* January 6, 1958

## Developing Your A-List, B-List, C-List

Let's say Byron decides to target hospitals as well as medical equipment manufacturers. There are eighty hospitals in his geographic area, but he decides to stay away from the government-owned hospitals because he *thinks* the bidding process will be too time-consuming for his small company. Still, he wants to keep them on his database because he wants to know about him—just in case they're dying for what he has to offer. Those hospitals will go on his C-list—those he really doesn't care about.

The remaining hospitals can be divided into two groups, an A-list and a B-list. The A-list includes hospitals he would die to have on his client list. These could be the larger or most prestigious hospitals that are private. The remaining hospitals would go on his B-list. He'd love to get a sale from them, but they wouldn't be as great to brag about as the A-list hospitals.

All of the hospitals will go on his database and he will mail or email all of them regularly. But Byron will first contact by phone his B-list organizations to try to set up an appointment with someone there. In his case, it is the Head of Patient Safety. He can get his feet wet, use his B-list hospitals for practice, and maybe even get a sale. He can test his marketing materials and even practice the kind of proposal he will need to write to land a sale.

Because he does not care as much about his B-list as he does about his A-list, he will probably be more relaxed and confident and will get to practice his pitch. He is *practicing*. He will also be testing his market to see if he gets a good response from these B-list organizations. He doesn't want to go after the most prestigious hospitals first and give them a bad impression of him. After he has a few sales from B-list hospitals, he will appear more credible to A-list hospitals.

*Many are stubborn in pursuit of the path they have chosen, few in pursuit of the goal.*

Friedrich Nietzsche

If the companies on Byron's B-list are *not* interested in him, that's important for him to know. He needs to talk to the people in his small group to find out what he is doing wrong. However, if he is well received by the companies on his B-list, then Byron can contact the companies on his A-list. He could say something like, "I am already talking to a number of hospitals in our area, but we would like to work with you as well." This script is just one approach. Be sure to talk to your small group about the right things for you to say to those on your A-list.

- Your A-list: You'd love to have them on your client list.
- Your B-list: They're okay.
- Your C-list: They don't interest you, but you'd be glad to have a sale.

> **To get a sale within a reasonable time, target at least 200 buyers.**

Your marketing effort will have more impact if it is focused by targets and segments of targets. For example, if Byron is going after the health-care market, talking to all of the hospitals on his B-list within a certain period gives him credibility. He can say, "Oh, I talked to . . ." and name the hospital that he talked to yesterday, "and they are using the same system you're using. They've considered other options, but now they're considering us." It makes him sound credible.

Remember what we said above about segmenting your targets. The pitch that you use with one of these targets, say, hospitals, will be very different from the pitch you would use with a different target, say, health-care manufacturers.

Your approach cannot be casual—even in the initial stages of your marketing efforts. You might be tempted to say in a meeting, "I don't care

whether I sell to a hospital or a manufacturer, so long as I have some connection to health care. This product can work just about anywhere." *You* may not care, but your prospective buyers care. They want to know that you understand—and care about—*their* industry. They want specialists in their industry.

## *Case Study: The Five O'Clock Club* How We Get Meetings

We're not a start-up anymore, but our experience may still be helpful to you. We have researched and developed a database of thousands of decision-makers—human resources executives—within our targeted geographic areas. Each record in our database contains each person's contact information, of course, but we also note whether the person is the decision-maker or an influencer, whether they are a current client of ours, use a competitor instead, or don't use our kind of service at all.

Here's how we let the entire database know about us:

- Publish a monthly magazine—16 pages, glossy on career-related topics. This magazine goes to decision-makers and influencers. That way, our entire database hears about us monthly and this keeps up our brand-name recognition.
- Hold a breakfast seminar every two months that is open to human resource executives only. No vendors are allowed, which is a big deal since those who want to sell to human resources tend to go to every human resource association meeting. We start the seminar with a Two-Minute Pitch about the Five O'Clock Club and its services, and then it's on with the show! The panelists are prestigious people within the HR community or experts in issues that are of interest to human resources executives. The room holds 180 people, and our clients are given preference in case too many people make reservations, which

generally happens. Often, people have to go on the waiting list.

- Make phone calls to as many as we can of those we most want to attend the seminar urging them to register.
- Invite human resources executives to observe our "Coaching in Action" so they can see how well we will take care of their former employees.

- Ask for a meeting with those who have attended the most and do use outplacement services.
- But much business comes from people who have simply attended the breakfast and have gotten our magazine.

We do lots more to market to our targets, but all of our efforts are low key and, we hope, informative—not "salesy."

# Getting Lots of Meetings with Organizations

*If I try to use human influence strategies and tactics of how to get other people to do what I want, to work better, to be more motivated, to like me and each other—while my character is fundamentally flawed, marked by duplicity and insincerity—then, in the long run, I cannot be successful. My duplicity will breed distrust, and everything I do—even using so-called good human relations techniques—will be perceived as manipulative. . . . Only basic goodness gives life to technique.*

Stephen R. Covey, *The Seven Habits of Highly Effective People*

## Developing a Detailed Marketing Plan

It's best to focus on one target for a condensed period. For example, Byron can make a list of all of the hospitals within the geographic area he's interested in. This list will become his Marketing Plan. Let's say there are 80 hospitals that are appropriate for him; he would put those on his list. Then he would mount a campaign to get plenty of meetings with the Head of Patient Safety in B-list organizations and then the A-list organizations in that target area, hospitals. The C-list would simply get his marketing literature.

A second target could be health-care manufacturers. He would make a second list, this one containing manufacturers he considered appropriate in his geographic area. Again, he would rank them as A, B or C. And he needs to find the correct position to target. Health care manufacturers would not have a Head of Patient Safety. He would need to find an equivalent title, such as the Head of Product Quality.

> **Make a list of organizations within each target. Eighty hospitals in Byron's geographic area are appropriate for his product or service.**

Then, *stagger* your targets so you can focus on each target in turn. Byron will focus on the hospitals first, and when that's under way, he'll start on the health-care manufacturers. To get plenty of meetings, he'll consider lots of techniques for becoming known and landing meetings in his target markets. These could include:

- Networking—that is, using someone's name to get a meeting,

- Contacting the correct people directly by mail or email when you *don't* have a networking contact,
- Speaking before industry meetings, such as Hospital Patient Safety organizations,
- Writing articles in industry trade journals,
- Putting out a press release about his new product or service.

All of the above techniques are essentially free or relatively low cost. It's easy to spend money on trade shows, advertising, and so on, but you are a start-up and need to watch every penny.

If you try lots of techniques, you can see which techniques result in meetings and/or business for you. Use more of *those* techniques. Use mailings, for example, *if* they result in meetings for you. If they don't result in meetings, concentrate on other approaches.

> **Make sure every** *decision-maker and influencer* **in your target market knows that you exist.**

Byron has 80 hospitals in his first target. Remember that the Heads of Patient Safety in those hospitals don't even know that he *exists*. You want potential purchasers to hear about you within a reasonable time. Advertising is usually better for established companies, not start-ups. So consider the other techniques listed above. Your goal is to make sure that as many decision-makers and influencers as possible know about you within a reasonable time.

## Some Methods for Getting Known in Your Target Areas:

- Networking—that is, using someone's name to get a meeting,
- Contacting the correct people directly by mail or email when you *don't* have a networking contact (but you must find out their correct name first. The title alone is not enough),

- Speaking before industry meetings,
- Writing articles in industry trade journals, and
- Putting out a press release about your new product or service.

Let's reemphasize an important distinction here. *Networking* means using someone else's name to get a meeting ("Sue suggested I contact you."). *Direct contact* means pursuing people whom you may have known in the past, but especially people you have *never* met: association members, or the Heads of Patient Safety you identified on the Internet, through newspaper or magazine articles, or from library research.

By the way, when we say that you should "make sure everyone on your target list knows that you exist within a reasonable time," we mean *decision makers and influencers*. We don't mean purchasing, *unless* the other departments have nothing to do with the decision-making process. For example, when companies are purchasing copier paper, that item may be decided strictly by the purchasing department. In other cases, the department that uses the product or service (Patient Safety, in this case) may be the sole decision-maker, or purchasing may *oversee* the bidding process that is being conducted by the Patient Safety department.

You cannot *network* into 80 or 100 Patient Safety Heads within a reasonable time. The last thing you want is to find out you're too late! If you rely primarily on networking, you may get around to contacting an organization three months into your campaign and hear one of them say,

> **"We just hired a firm to do that. I wish we had met you before."**

So, if you have a list of 80 organizations you want to contact, divide up your list. Perhaps you can network into 5 or 6. If you know someone who can refer you in, use his or her name, contact the decision-maker, and say, "Jim Smith suggested I contact you."

That would leave 75 more organizations out of your list of 80. Select 20 of those that you really want to get in to see, even though you don't have a connection. It doesn't matter if they don't have a need or already use another vendor. You just want them to know about you and you want to introduce yourself to them. To these 20, you would send a *targeted mailing* and follow up with a phone call.

That would leave 55 organizations on your list. For the remaining 55, you could do a direct-mail campaign. That is, you would send your cover letter and brochure, but you would *not* follow up with a phone call. You're just letting them know that you exist, so *if* they have a need for someone like you, they'll give *you* a call. By combining these various techniques, you will be able to contact all of the organizations on your list within a reasonable time.

---

### Get Lots of Meetings

ABC company
Avrey
Allister Metal
Goopers
Haskell
Jesking
Fortunoff
Patricin
Costco
DiscCity
Oliphant

Divide up your list. If you have a list of 80 companies:

- Network into 5 or 6 if you can
- Send a targeted mailing to 20
- For the remaining 55, use a direct-mail campaign

---

*It's true that when God closes a door, He opens a window. But the hallways are hell.*

Sol Wachtler, Chief Judge, State of New York Court of Appeals, after serving time in jail

......................................

*I do not believe they are right who say that the defects of famous men should be ignored. I think it is better we should know them. Then, though we are conscious of having faults as glaring as theirs, we can believe that that is no hindrance to our achieving also something of their virtues.*

Somerset Maugham

Let's see where you are. So far:

1. You've brainstormed your targets. That is, you've thought about the industries, the size of the organizations you want to contact, and the kinds of people you want to contact (such as finance, human resources, IT, or whatever). And you've brainstormed as many targets as possible—with the help of your coach or your small group.
2. You've ranked your targets: *Hospitals* is your first target. *Health-care manufacturers* is your second.
3. You're aiming to have a focused, compact campaign. You've decided to go after all the B-list hospitals at the same time so you can say, "I'm talking to so-and-so at Presbyterian Hospital right now." This gives you credibility.

That's where you are in your marketing campaign.

......................................

*It is work, work that one delights in, that is the surest guarantor of happiness.*

Ashley Montagu, *The American Way of Life*

## Marketing Campaign Management

### Conduct a Campaign Aimed at Each Target (industry, function, geographic area)

You have a plan. Now you need to get meetings and do well in those meetings. What's more, you will have to follow-up after the meetings to turn those meetings into sales. You may get excited when you line up one meeting, but when that meeting falls apart, or the decision-making process takes a year—you may become discouraged.

Instead, schedule many meetings, get better at delivering your pitch in meetings and refine your marketing literature to fit with your target markets.

For each meeting, you will plan for the meeting, hold the meeting, and follow up.

## Planning for the Meeting

Don't just walk in to the meeting. Research the company. Think about their possible needs.

- <u>Develop what we call your Two-Minute Pitch</u>. That is, in the hospital market, how do you respond when people say, "Tell me about your organization." For example, your pitch to hospitals might be, "Our management team has thirty years combined experience in hospital patient safety. We specialize in patient quality control procedures and have been able to reduce patient deaths from *c. difficile* by 70% in each of the places where we worked previously. We've now developed a system that can be used by any hospital and we would like to tell you about it."

  Your pitch to (and your product for) hospitals might be very different from your pitch to manufacturing companies in the health-care field. For that target, you may want to emphasize the *materials* you use that will not allow *c. difficile* to grow or will kill off the bacteria.

- <u>Be sure your brochure or other marketing literature makes you look appropriate</u> to the hospital market.
- <u>Develop your plan for getting many meetings</u> in this target market. That is, identify the organizations you'll be able to network into, and directly contact the others. For more information about this technique, read our book, *Shortcut Your Search: The Best Ways to Get Meetings*.
- <u>Make a list of the key points you want to cover at the meeting</u>.
- <u>Develop your list of qualifying questions to ask them at the beginning of the meeting</u>.

· · · · · · · · · · · · · · · · · · · · · · · · · · · ·

*I found that values, for each person, were numerous. Therefore, I proposed to write my value names and to annex to each a short precept—which fully expressed the extent I gave to each meaning. I then arranged them in such a way as to facilitate acquisition of these virtues.*

Benjamin Franklin

### The *Two-Minute Pitch*

The way you position yourself is used throughout your campaign:

- in your brochure,
- in your meetings with decision-makers,
- in your networking meetings with influencers, and
- in your cover letters.

It is the response to "So, tell me about your organization." A great pitch helps people see your organization as appropriate for their needs. At The Five O'Clock Club we say, "If your pitch is wrong, everything is wrong." That is, if the way you are positioning yourself is wrong, you're derailed from the start and everything else about your marketing campaign will be wrong. It can't work.

Your brochure is your written positioning. The Two-Minute Pitch is your oral positioning. And they must correspond. Give your overview statement: "We specialize in getting rid of *c. difficile* in hospital settings" and then give examples of your accomplishments, which may correspond to some of the bulleted accomplishments in your brochure. Notice which points the decision-makers respond to and which points they do not. There may also be points that are a turn-off to your target market. Chances are good that you'll want to get rid of them. Refine your pitch. When your pitch is correct, you will use it throughout your entire campaign.

## The Meeting Itself

In the meeting itself:

- Get information (find out about them first: "How big is your *c. difficile* problem? How are you handling it now?") and then give information.
- *Don't* try to "close" too soon to get the offer.
- Get another meeting.

Most people think meetings result in sales. But there are usually a few intervening steps before a final sale is made. **Meetings should result in getting and giving information**.

- Did you learn the issues important to each person with whom you met?
- What did they think were your strongest positives?
- How can you overcome the decision makers' objections?

Most people try to close on a sale too early. Instead, try to get the next meeting or the next step ("May I meet with your head nurse to discuss this situation?") After all, most organizations need to see you more than once and may have you meet with more than one person before they can make a decision. Keep in the running. **Don't think like a used car salesman who is trying to coax people to "buy now." Think like**

**a consultant** trying to land a $5,000, $40,000, $90,000, or $150,000 consulting assignment. Be pro-active in the meeting, asking questions to better understand their situation. Have a pad and pen in hand for taking notes. Find out what's *going on* in the organization. Ask about their *needs*. How can you satisfy those needs? Who's doing what in this organization?

How might you help? What are the most important problems the organization faces right now? A consultant takes notes because a consultant knows he has to *analyze* what happened during the meeting and later make a proposal about how to handle the situation.

Here is the drill for consultants:

- Research the organization thoroughly.
- Dress and look the part.
- Know your key selling points for this organization. Know how you differ from your competition.

Find out:

- What is going on? What are their needs?
- How can I satisfy those needs?

Work to outclass your competition.

- Ask how you stack up against others.
- Make sure you have all the information you need.
- Find out when they hope to decide.
- Find out if they have any objections to you.

Plan your follow-up.

- Get and give information.
- Don't try to get a sale right now.
- Get the next meeting.
- Consultants write proposals. So will you!

*Think about your competition*. You do have competition, you know. And if you *think* you're the only one they're considering, you could come away dumb and happy—confident that you did a great job. Your competitor may be their present way of doing things. But you won't know how you stack up *against others* unless you ask! Say to the decision-maker:

- What vendors do you now use for this type of service? How satisfied are you with them?
- Where are you in the decision-making process? Are we the first you've met with? Second? Last?
- How many other companies are you talking to?
- And how do you see us compared with the other organizations you're talking to?
- Is there any reason you would not consider us in the mix?

Ask yourself:

- Have I gathered all the information I need to write a good proposal about what I would do for this organization?
- Do I know when they are likely to decide: Now? A few months from now? Three Years from now?

Do *all you can to keep in the running and to keep visible after the meeting* so they select *you* when they have a need.

Always have 6 to 10 possibilities going:

- Always try to get the sale—even at companies that are not on your A- or B-list. Otherwise, you'll never get 6 to 10 possibilities. *That's* what momentum is all about—having a lot of things going.
- However, you must make sure that each sale is profitable. In the very beginning of your business, you may have to take an assignment or two that is not profitable just so you have some credibility in your field. But very quickly, you must pass up even prestigious looking business that is not profitable. This has happened to us many times. Some huge, brand-name companies know every vendor would love to have their name on the client list. They force the vendors to take a loss on the business, and often vendors are willing to do that so they are able to brag about landing such prestigious accounts. But not only do you

lose money on this business, others will hear about your low prices and then expect the same of you.

When The Five O'Clock Club is in this situation, we walk away from the deal. We will not take business that is a loss. When our competitors "win" this business, we are happy for them because we know it will hurt their margins. As you will see later, margins are everything.

- Even when a big sale seems certain, keep the pressure up on your other marketing activities.

• • • • • • • • • • • • • • • • • • • • • • • • • • • • • •

*Chaos often breeds life, while order breeds habit.*

Henry Adams, American historian

In the meeting, you're also *planning* your follow-up. You're not sitting there thinking, "I hope we get a sale." Instead you're thinking, "I wonder what we should do to follow up after this meeting."

• • • • • • • • • • • • • • • • • • • • • • • • • • • • • •

*Great is the art of beginning, but greater the art of ending.*

Henry Wadsworth Longfellow

## The Follow-Up

After the meeting, you must follow up. This is the brainiest part of the process. In our book *Mastering the Job Interview and Winning the Salary Game,* you'll read lots of case studies to help you understand this part. But here are a few suggestions.

After every meeting, have a debriefing session with those who were on the sales call with you, with others in your office, or simply with yourself. The meeting you had with a prospect is the *beginning* of the sales process, not the end (unless they gave you the order on the spot!). Generally, they forget about you the minute you leave the room. After all, they have their jobs to get back to. So, here's an example:

By the time Jeffrey came to The Five O'Clock Club, he had been meeting with one telemarketing company for *four* months talking about their marketing systems. Yet he wasn't getting a sale. So his small group said to him, "Jeffrey, what do you think might be their *objection* to using your company?" He said, "They're afraid that we don't understand their industry."

Jeffrey's situation was easy for his small group: He needed to let his prospective customer know that he understood their industry. The group suggested he do some research, and find out more about the telemarketing industry. (That's why it's best to call on a number of companies in the same industry at the same time!) So after doing that, Jeffrey wrote the decision-making team a letter that essentially said, "Here are the marketing problems in the telemarketing industry. If you hire us, here's what we will do." He identified their competitors, how he saw this company stacking up against their competitors, and what Jeffrey's company would do to help market them more effectively. They hired Jeffrey's company immediately—*once* he had overcome their objections.

Actually, you'll be doing this intensive follow-up with 6 to 10 different prospective customers at the same time. It's a lot of hard work *and* brainpower. In fact, you should put as much time and energy into the follow-up phase as you did into the planning and meeting phases. You need to keep track of every prospect you're following up with, what you've done with them already, and what you should do next. Some products and services have a long sales cycle (ours is one year or more), and you can easily let slip away prospects you've already called on. Don't waste those calls. Keep track of your follow up.

Five O'Clock Clubbers know that they must put more effort into this part of the process—more than any of their competitors do. They want to make sure their follow-up is better than anyone else's. Then they have a better chance of turning their meetings into sales.

*The more I want to get something done, the less I call it work.*

Richard Bach, *Illusions*

It takes brainpower because the kind of follow-up you do depends on:

- the kind of organization you're meeting with,
- your personality,
- the number of times you've met with the prospective purchasers (Have you met with five people for one hour each, or have you met with just one person for half an hour?),
- the information you've gathered in those meetings, and
- who your competitors are.

..........................................

*The amount of money you receive will always be in direct proportion to the demand for what you do, your ability to do it, and the difficulty of replacing you.*

Dennis Kimbro, *Think and Grow Rich: A Black Choice*

> **Have 6 to 10 hot prospects in the works at all times. Five will fall away through no fault of your own.**

With 6 to 10 things going, you increase your chances of having three good assignments. Tell your small group what's going on and get their help to decide what you should do next.

Give every phase of your marketing the attention it requires, and do as well as you can in each area of your campaign: planning for the meeting, having the meeting, and following up after the meeting. Don't skip any step in the process.

..........................................

*Passion costs me too much to bestow it on every trifle.*

Thomas Adams

### Follow-Up after a Sales Call

- This is the brainiest part of the process.
- It takes as much time as lining up meetings and having meetings.
- Work to keep things alive with 6 to 10 organizations.
- Don't write a silly *thank-you* note after a meeting. Instead, write an *influence* letter or proposal.
- Tailor the follow-up to each situation.
- Build a relationship. If the organization says there won't be a decision until February, that's okay—just keep in touch.
- Whether to call, write, or e-mail is not the issue. Uncovering possible objections to you and *proving* you should be on their vendor list *are* the issues.
- Try to find out: Would *you* be the organization chosen when the purchasing decision is made?
- Your coach will want to know:
  - ∆ Who did you meet with?
  - ∆ What are each person's key issues?
  - ∆ Why would each want to use your product, service or organization?
  - ∆ What are each person's objections to your product, service or organization?
  - ∆ What can you offer vs. competition?
- Decide the next steps, such as:
  - ∆ another meeting; meeting with others,
  - ∆ an in-depth review of documents, procedures, requirements, etc.
  - ∆ developing a few ideas and then meeting again, and/or
  - ∆ drafting a proposal.
  - ∆ inviting them to visit you, sample your product or service, or talk to references.
- State the *next steps* in your follow-up letter. For example, "I'd like to get together with you to discuss our ideas on . . ."
- Influence the influencers.
- Be in sync with their timing, not yours. (If they will not open the process up for bids for a year, then you cannot make them do it sooner.)

### Fee Negotiation

- Starts with your first meeting: position yourself so they see you at an appropriate level.
- Mantra: "We can work something out."
- Manage the process to get the right price.

# The Stages of Your Corporate Sales Campaign

*The last thing one discovers in composing
a work is what to put first.*

Blaise Pascal

## Measure How Well You Are Doing in Your Sales Efforts

So, how can you tell whether you're doing well in your sales efforts? It's *not* good enough to say, "I'll know my efforts were effective when I get a sale or two." That's too late.

The first guidepost in evaluating your efforts is the Preliminary Target Investigation, which will help you check out your various targets and prevent you from wasting months going after targets that are inappropriate for you.

Then, we'll tell you how to measure the effectiveness of your efforts in terms of Stages 1, 2, and 3. It took us *four years of research* to develop this method for measuring the effectiveness of sales efforts.

You'll find that the sales and marketing process is a *research* process. As you go along in your marketing campaign, try to be objective about

your organization: Which targets are working for you? Which techniques are resulting in meetings for you? It's ongoing research.

........................................

*Dying is no big deal. The least of us will
manage that. Living is the trick.*

Walter ("Red") Smith, funeral eulogy for
golf impresario Fred Corcoran

---

### Measuring the Effectiveness of Your Marketing Efforts

During a five-month campaign, you sent 100 packages of marketing materials and met with 75 people. But was this *effective*? Measure where you are.

Stage 1 means *keeping in touch with* 6 to 10 people in your target area. These may or may not be the ultimate decision-makers. Get information on your targets (are these the right targets for you?) and feedback on your efforts.

---

Stage 2 is the core of your campaign. *Keep in touch* with 6 to 10 of the right *decision-makers* at the right *level* in the right *organizations*. When they say, "I wish I had a need right now—I'd love to use your product or service," you have a GREAT campaign. Now, aim for 10 to 20 ongoing Stage 2 contacts, and then even more. But if you're *not* getting this kind of positive feedback, your target is wrong, your positioning is wrong, or your offering is wrong. You have to fix something.

Stage 3 will happen naturally: 6 to 10 hot prospects—organizations that seem to need your product or service right now. Aim for three concurrent sales. Keep your marketing campaigns going. You *will* need more business.

## Stage 1: Your Preliminary Target Investigation

During Stage 1, network and make direct *contacts* in your target markets. As you gather information, analyze it: which markets seem worth pursuing and which do not? Don't waste months on targets that are unlikely to work out.

---

### Preliminary Target Investigation

- Networking or contacting people directly to gather information.
- Building contacts in your target market.
- Analyze your target markets: Which targets are working for you and which are not?

**All of the above will continue throughout the life of your company**

---

So it may be that at the beginning of your business, you've brainstormed plenty of targets—maybe you've come up with 3 to 10 targets.

Maybe you thought, "Gee, I think hospitals would be the most likely customers for our product or service." But in your Preliminary Target Investigation, you talked to managers at 4 hospitals—briefly—just to see what hospitals were actually doing in your specialty. And then you said to yourself, "Now that I have a feel for hospitals, I don't think hospitals are a good match for us. This is not a priority for them" (or "they will not be willing to spend the right money for this"). Because you've gathered some information, you can eliminate that target or move it down the list, or modify your product or service to better suit them.

If you did not talk to hospitals in a concentrated way, it would be more difficult to assess whether or not you'd want to do business with hospitals. You would be like all the other business owners out there who meet with prospects in a random manner and hope they make a sale. Instead, *assess* the hospital market:

- Is this a good target for us or not?
- Are they interested in what we have to offer?
- Can they pay what we need to charge?
- How can I make our product or service more appealing to hospitals?

With a *structured* marketing effort, you can say, "This hospital target does not work for us. I need to get rid of it!" Otherwise, you're just wasting your time—trying to set up meetings—and not even realizing that this target is not working for you.

So, eliminate inappropriate targets and decide which targets are worth a full campaign. Rank them: Target 1, Target 2, Target 3, and so on, depending on which ones you want to go after first, second, and third.

For example, you may see in the business news a list of the 100 fastest-growing companies in your geographic area and think they would be a great target for you. You can test this target—selecting 10 companies of various sizes, for example, and seeing how well received you are. If your test works, you can go after the other fastest-growing companies on the list. However, do not stop marketing to your present targets.

All of this happens during your Preliminary Target Investigation: brainstorm as many targets as you can, select the ones worth checking out, investigate them, eliminate some, rank the remaining ones, and mount your campaigns with overlapping targets.

You *must* stay in touch with a certain number of the people you've met during this investigative period. Those are your Stage 1 Contacts. For a good Stage 1, you need to have 6 to 10 people with whom you want to *stay in touch*. If you have *no* intention of staying in touch with some people you've contacted, they don't go on your Stage 1 List.

Stage 2 is the meat of your marketing efforts, and this is where you should put most of your effort. You're in a good, solid Stage 2 when you're talking to 6 to 10 of the right people at the right level at the right organizations. The *quality* of your contacts has changed and you're being well received. That is, they're saying to you, "I'm so sorry we don't have a need right now. We'd love to purchase your product or service."

That's a solid Stage 2, and it means that you've got a great campaign going.

You're talking to the *right* people, and they *like* you; they really like you. They'd love to use your product or service. It just so happens they don't have a need right now. But that's okay because the positive feedback means you're working the right targets with the right pitch.

---

### Stage 2–The Stage That Matters Most

**Get in to see the right people**

- at the right level,
- at the right organizations, and
- make sure you are being well received.

---

> **"I wish we had a need right now. We'd love to use your product or service."**

What should you do next? Work hard to get more quality meetings: Talk to *more* of the right people at the right level in the right organizations.

What *else* should you do? Stay in touch with all of them—because someday they're going to need your product or service—they already said they *want* to work with you!

This is the description of a terrific marketing campaign! You shouldn't expect that an organization would have a need just because you happened to talk to them at this moment. Stay in touch with them—with at least 6 to 10 organizations *on an ongoing basis*. But if you *don't* intend to talk to them again, *they don't count* as Stage 2 contacts.

Then develop *more* quality contacts. That's right: 6 to 10 are not enough, 6 to 10 was a minimum range to help you *test* your presentation to this marketplace. It worked. Now, increase that number, and *aim for 12 to 20 or even 40 or more*, and keep in touch with all of them. We're not suggesting the impossible! These recommended numbers are the result of solid research, which we are now passing on to you. Stage 2 is crucial: We know that Five O'Clock Clubbers who follow this methodology and generate these numbers end up with continual sales.

---

### This Is a Terrific Campaign!

- Although they don't have a need for your product or service right now . . .
- Talk with people and stay in touch with . . .
- At least 6 to 10 (and later 12 to 40) on an *ongoing basis*.
- Someday, they'll need you.

## Refining Your Campaign

Look at your Stage 2 contacts by target, and notice which targets are best for your organization. Become a researcher on your own behalf. You might notice, "Hospitals are being responsive to us. I think I need to contact more decision-makers and influencers in the hospital market. We also need to market to them in other ways (industry speeches, articles in trade journals, and so on) to keep our name in front of them." If you notice which targets are working and which are not, you'll have a better, faster sales cycle, and you'll feel calmer in your marketing efforts because you'll have more control.

If you can't get a healthy Stage 2 going—if you are not being well received—ask your small group and your coach to help you figure out what's wrong. But you have to bring them good information. For example, if you're in a meeting—even when the prospect is not considering a purchase right now—ask the decision-maker, "If you had a need right now, would you consider using our product or service?" If the decision-maker is candid and gives you reasons *why not*, tell this information to your group.

This is what I love about The Five O'Clock Club process: It's a research-based approach. There can be only two possible problems here: either your *target* is wrong (you're going after the wrong industries, positions, or geographic areas), or your *positioning* is wrong (your pitch is wrong, you don't look the part, your marketing materials position you incorrectly). Ask your coach and your small group for feedback. (The worst situation, however, is that *no one* needs your product or service. But you cannot conclude that until you have segmented your targets and gotten feedback by *target*!)

> Notice which targets are being most responsive to you. Instead of 6 to 10, aim for 12 to 20, or even 40 Stage-2 Contacts.

If you've done Stage 2 well, Stage 3 will take care of itself. Being in Stage 3 means you're talking to 6 to 10 organizations *on an ongoing basis* about a *sale*, or the *possibility* of a sale. Don't worry about Stage 3. Worry about Stage 2. In Stage 3, we want you to aim to have 6 to 10 *hot prospects*. Don't stop at 2 or 3! That's not enough. Out of 6 to 10, *5 will fall away through no fault of your own.* So you see that two or three hot prospects are not enough. Chances are they will disappear for reasons beyond your control: They decide to freeze purchases; There's been a change in management; and so on. As we say at the Club, "they fall away through no fault of your own."

To get more hot prospects who say they want to use your product or service, don't worry about Stage 3. Instead, develop more Stage 1 and Stage 2 contacts. Some Stage 1 contacts will bubble up and become Stage 2 contacts. Build up the number of Stage 2 contacts. Instead of 6 to 10, aim to have 20, 30, or even 40. A certain number of those will bubble up to become Stage 3 contacts—that is, where decision-makers are actually getting ready to purchase your product or service.

Keep that momentum going. Your small group is so helpful here. Just when you think, "There's no *way* I can get more meetings in this target area," your small group will tell you how to keep the momentum going in your marketing efforts.

> Out of 6 to 10 hot prospects, 5 will fall away through no fault of your own.

- If Stage 2 is working, do more of the same.
- If Stage 2 is *not* happening:
  - △ Your targets are wrong, or
  - △ Your positioning is wrong.
  - △ Ask your small group and your coach what is wrong.

*We're a society that's not about perfection, but about rectifying mistakes. We're about second chances.*

Harry Edwards, in "Hardline," *Detroit Free Press*

Remember, talk about your marketing campaign in terms of stages. If your small group asks how your campaign is going, don't say, "I don't have a sale from that target yet" or "I think I might get a sale from that target." Instead, *analyze* your campaign. Say, "My campaign is going great. I have 6 things in Stage 2; 12 in Stage 1; and one Stage 2 contact may become a Stage 3." If you use this mind-set and this shorthand, you will become better at analyzing how well you really are doing, and your small-group members will also be able to tell—and we can help you more.

Also tell your small group how you're *keeping in touch* with your contacts. It's okay if prospects don't have a need right now. In another month or two, some of the organizations you're keeping in touch with *may* have a need. So you must keep in touch with them *so they will think of you when something comes up.* Your coach and your small group can help you with this part as well.

---

To get more hot prospects going:

- Develop more Stage 1 and Stage 2 contacts.
- Some Stage 1 contacts will bubble up to Stage 2.
- Instead of 6 to 10, develop more.
- A certain number of Stage 2 contacts will bubble up to Stage 3.
- Keep your momentum going.

---

## Three Concurrent Sales

Yes, we want you to have three concurrent sales. It sounds like a lot, but often the first sales prospect you get is not the best. They may refuse to pay what you need to stay profitable. If you have nothing else going, it may be difficult to walk away from them. If you have three concur-

rent sales, you are in a better position to compare the prices, *and* you increase your chance of getting *more* profitable sales.

## Have Fun!

Finally, we want you to have three hours of fun a week—whether you like it or not. It's a little joke of ours, but the fact is, if you don't get three hours of fun a week, you are less likely to have good meetings and the support of your family. You'll be too stressed and come across like a drone, rather than seeming like a person who everyone wants to do business with.

And always remember how vital it is to take the initiative and follow up. When they say, "I'll call you on Tuesday," they really mean it. But they will *never* call you when they say they will. *The ball is always in your court.* It is always up to you to figure out what to do next—and your small group can help you do that.

---

- Get three hours of fun a week—whether you like it or not!!
- Attend The Five O'Clock Club consistently.
- Market continually.
- *They* never call when they say they will.

---

*Let the past drift away with the water.*

Japanese saying

Now you have an overview of The Five O'Clock Club approach to an organized corporate marketing campaign. You have a lot more ahead of you in other chapters. And you may want to look at our book, *Shortcut Your Search: The Best Ways to Get Meetings*, which goes into the direct marketing approach in more depth.

---

*The price one pays for pursuing any profession or calling is an intimate knowledge of its ugly side.*

James Baldwin, *Nobody Knows My Name*

*"Congratulations to Larry here, who actually picked up his phone and spoke with a customer. This might be a breakthrough for our company.*

# Speeches or Demonstrations: An Important Promotional Technique

*There are always three speeches for every one you actually gave. The one you practiced, the one you gave, and the one you wish you gave.*

Dale Carnegie

## Speeches Are Used to Promote Just About Everything

A few years ago there was a movie called *Mr. Holland's Opus* about a would-be composer who takes a teaching job to support himself and finds out, 30 years later, that teaching has become his life. A *New York Times* reviewer said, "The title is a dud. The film is probably 20 minutes too long. Its star has been stuck in the down cycle of an erratic career. The director is a virtual unknown. And even the movie's producer needs several paragraphs to explain what it's about."

Yet, the movie was a box-office leader for months—and made a hefty profit. How did that happen? The producers made a decision early on that the film could succeed only "through a national campaign that got people talking about the film before it opened." The company decided to market it in a grass-roots fashion, "targeting every audience that would have a reason to love this picture."

The company went to music groups, teachers' organizations, civic and political leaders, arranging special showings of the trailer of the film. The movie was shown to meetings of the American Symphony Orchestra League, the American Federation of Teachers and the National Association of Merchants. The trailer of the film was shown at the national marching band competitions at the Hoosierdome in Indianapolis and at Giants Stadium in East Rutherford, NJ.

## Advertising Alone Would Not Have Done It

Advertising is expensive. Publicity is fleeting. Speeches and demonstrations are the only medium where a prospective client gets to see what you are like up close and actually feels that he or she is "getting a sample" of what you are like.

In the old days, when we got 1100 leads from a string of radio shows, it cost a lot of money to send information to all of those people. Of those who received the information, about 30 signed up to attend the Club—once—to try it out. The majority of those did not come back until they felt they really needed the service. They were simply trying to find out what we were like so they would know whom to call when they needed help. We couldn't tell how serious they were, or if they were the kind of people who could benefit from our services.

But when you give a speech or put on a demonstration, you probably have a quality audience to begin with. The people who show up have made some effort to be there. They're listening to you or sampling your product, so they get an idea of what you're like. Chances are, they'll remember you for a long time. You can give them literature to take home—more literature than you can send in the mail.

They may use your services now, or they may keep the information and call you later. If you have captured their names and addresses—and perhaps some demographic information—you can add those names to your database. These leads are certainly better than TV-show folks who have heard a 20-second sound bite.

If they do decide to use you, they are already partially sold. After all, they have already sampled what you have to offer!

## Lining Up Speeches or Demonstrations

(Note: David Madison, the head of our Speakers Bureau, contributed heavily to this section on lining up speeches. Many of the concepts in this chapter may also be used for lining up sales calls. You should also read the chapter, "Selling to Organizations.")

Not every business will benefit from speeches, of course, but don't rule them out just yet. After all, we showed how your dentist may have given speeches in the early days of his or her business—to school groups or sports teams. Consultants and those providing services to high-net-worth individuals rely heavily on

speeches. If you provide custom-made clothing, you can put on a mini fashion show at a PTA or Junior League meeting. If you make pastries, you can give out small samples at a fair and tell people about your work. If you run a fishing excursion business, you can do a slide show at your church or synagogue or any local social organization. And in-home demonstrations are appropriate for other businesses.

Standing before a group of people eager to hear your words of wisdom or see your demonstration—can truly be a *golden opportunity*. Meeting people face-to-face is a crucial factor in generating business: it often works much better than print advertising. That is, listings in the Yellow Pages, local newspapers, professional journals or magazines do not bring steady streams of clients. *Print advertising is expensive*, and results are commonly disappointing. But getting out and meeting people usually doesn't cost very much, and brings the valuable connections that result in customers and customer referrals.

Public speaking or demonstrating at organizations may be an ideal way to present yourself and your product or service. You're looking for that *golden opportunity* to present live and in person before a sizeable group or even an appropriate small group. You become a known quantity: prospects see your style and get a feel for what it would be like to work with you. You obviously hope that this will have immediate and long-term impact for yourself, i.e., new business.

## Finding Organizations for Speeches and Partnerships

By "organizations" we mean the wide variety of associations and groups we are all familiar with: business, trade and professional, civic, alumni, religious and cultural. Most of these groups hold monthly (sometimes quarterly, even weekly) meetings to which outside speakers are invited. Most would welcome speakers. There are several ways to find out about organizations and identify those that would be of interest to you.

## The "Who Do I Know?" Approach

If you stop to think about it, you probably know a lot of people who are active in associations, and who would be willing to refer you to the program planner. So what you need to do is *really think about it*: write down names, lots of names . . . of friends, relatives, current and past associates and co-workers, of people you know through church or synagogue, PTA, Little League, bowling, charity work, etc.

Have you looked through your whole Rolodex lately? Is there an old address book in a bottom drawer that you couldn't quite bring yourself to throw away? Is there a stack of business cards you haven't looked at lately? How about the Holiday card list that you conscientiously compiled one year? Or a list of people you invited (once upon a time) to a wedding or graduation or shower? All of these can be resources to jog your memory.

You should be able to come up with dozens or even hundreds of names. All of the people on your list know you—or will at least remember you—even people you haven't been in touch with for a long time. So a telephone call from you won't be unwelcome.

## A Script You Can Use With Friends Who May Belong to Associations

Start with small talk. Then say:

"I'm calling because I'm trying to identify clubs and organizations in our area that welcome outside speakers to their monthly meetings. I'm trying to book speaking engagements to talk about fishing excursions.

"Do you belong to any clubs or organizations or associations?"

"Who is the president?" Or: "Who is in charge of arranging meetings?"

And: "Do you have any friends or associates who are really involved in organizations?"

This is a no-anxiety call since you're talking to folks you know, asking for information. A few dozen of these calls will result in a list of organizations to put on your targeting list.

And obviously there is nothing wrong with the "in person" approach; many small business owners prefer to spread the word about their business when they see friends at PTA meetings or church suppers. And don't hesitate to stand up in a local meeting and remind people about your service or product—if appropriate.

But whether you prefer the telephone or face-to-face method, it is important to be disciplined and proactive in making the "Who Do I Know?" approach work. Make the list, including the friends you know you'll be seeing at PTA—and don't put a check by their names until you've made the contact.

## There are Plenty of Non-Association Targets Too

While our focus in this chapter will be formal professional and alumni organizations, there are many other setting in which *speeches, workshops, seminars, demonstrations and panel discussions* can be used to promote your business. As you are networking and pursuing the "Who Do You Know?" approach, you will become aware of other venues that don't fall into the "organization" category:

- Churches & Synagogues
- Libraries
- Community Centers
- Adult or Continuing Education Programs
- Special Event or Theme Expos
- Social Groups

### Finding Associations by "Hitting the Books"

Sometimes we overlook the most obvious resources. Don't forget to Google in the word "Associations" or "Clubs" and your nearest big city to see what pops up. This can give you an idea of the most active organizations in your area: they have a website. So chances are they are well established *and they are in your neighborhood.*

Which is something you don't always know when you start digging in the massive **_Encyclopedia of Associations_**. How should you use this gigantic resource? Consult the Encyclopedia according to the industries, fields or businesses *that interest you,* e.g., bankers or designers or engineers . . . or by gender, race, age, ethic background, religion or sexual orientation. In the EOA you will find listings, e.g., for Women in International Trade, The Irish Business Organization, Black Journalists Association, the Gay Officers Action League, and the Association of Christian Social Workers. The EOA is a source of useful information on literally thousands of associations.

You should be speaking to as many groups in your chosen area as possible. You get better as you rub shoulders with and advise the people you've targeted as *your* specialty.

The EOA includes information to help you qualify organizations, e.g., number of members and local chapters and location of national headquarters. A specific organization may sound interesting to you, but if there are only 350 members nationwide in 6 chapters, with the home office a thousand miles away from you, it may not be worth your time and money to make an exploratory phone call; there probably isn't a chapter near you. But if an organization has 11,000 members in 175 local chapters, there's a fairly good chance that there will be a chapter near you.

In just one sitting with EOA you will be able to compile a list of several dozen organizations to target. The *Encyclopedia of Associations* can be found in libraries and it is also available on CD-ROM and On-Line.

## And Speaking of "On Line"

We all know how addictive the Internet can be: one link leads to another, to yet another . . . and we are amazed at what's "out there." So put

this resource to use in finding organizations to target! A few key words and a few clicks can yield mountains of information and leads, especially on industries, companies, *and associations*. On AOL, for example, start by clicking on the "Research & Learn" tab.

## Exploiting the Law of Large Numbers

We have suggested coming up with dozens or hundreds of target organizations, by networking with friends or researching at the library and on the Internet. Why so many? Now and then speeches may come your way through serendipity, but if you are serious about using public speaking for business development, you must *make the law of large numbers* work for you. You need dozens of leads (at least) to generate the number of speeches that will make a difference in your business.

And this process requires patience and persistence. If your first 20 contacts did not work, at the very least, we would suggest sending out 20 more—but we would also analyze the presentation and the pitch. Are you doing something wrong? How can you improve your approach? The law of large numbers *does* work . . . but you have to work it smartly. And you have to keep going.

# The Call to Find Out Who Is in Charge

Whether you have identified an organization through your network of friends, digging in the EOA or surfing the net, it's a good idea to put in an initial telephone call to find out who is in charge. At this point you are calling simply to verify information; perhaps a former associate has told you about an organization and even given you a name and number. Before sending a letter of introduction, you will want to be sure that you have the correct spelling of the name, address, etc. And especially if you are using information from the EOA, you will want to make the call to verify. In fact, using the EOA will probably yield information about the national headquarters only. If you have decided that the organization is large enough to warrant a call to national headquarters, you can say:

"Hello, I'm trying to find out if you have a chapter in the _____ area . . . Oh, you do, that's great; can you give me the name of the contact person for that chapter?

[**If they want to know why:**] "I'm a specialist in preventing the spread of *c. difficile* bacteria, something I think your members would be interested in learning about. I want to contact your chapter in my neighborhood." Or (perhaps to a woman's group), "I'm a specialist in making party favors out of chocolate, and I'd like to put on a demonstration for your group in my geographic area."

The association's headquarters is usually pleased to receive such inquiries, and will probably give you the name and work number of the chapter president.

Now you can call the local chapter contact; but again, not to make a presentation—so this is not a cold call—but just to verify information:

"Hello, I wish to address some correspondence to Ms. Phillips and I would just like to verify the spelling of her name, title and address."

Or: "Hello, I'd like to address some correspondence to your chapter president. Could you give me the person's name and address (or email address)?"

You have now identified organizations that interest you; you have secured correct names, titles, addresses, and phone numbers. Depending on your style and temperament, you may now choose to "break the ice" with an introductory letter or make cold calls to the individuals on your list. The former, the Targeted Mailing approach, is usually preferred by those who are uncomfortable calling strangers. Just send a letter followed by a phone call. There is nothing especially heroic about cold calling, and if it goes against your grain, don't try it. Move on to targeted mailing with full confidence that your marketing efforts will pay off.

## The Targeted Mailing Approach

You are writing to an organization with the intention of making a follow-up call in a few days. Since the purpose of your letter is actually to educate and build credibility—operate on the assumption that your target needs to be introduced to your organization—you will need to send several pieces of information with this letter. You want your mailing to have impact. All of the following items could be included in your mailing:

1. A flyer or literature describing your organization.
2. Copies of newspaper clippings about you.
3. Copies of articles you've written.
4. Your business card.

## Follow-up & Tracking Results

Select a tracking system of some kind. Computer programs such as FileMaker Pro or ACT are ideal for keeping track of follow-up activity. If you are inclined to do it the old-fashioned way (i.e., paper), you can just start with a blank book.

You can use a 5 × 8-inch loose-leaf binder with a page for each targeted association. Insert a new page alphabetically for each new target that you identify, and keep a running history of all your efforts (letters, emails and phone calls) on that one page. Even as the notebook grows to 50 or 60 pages, it is easy to flip through once or twice a week (glancing at the last entry on each page) to remind yourself of calls to make. And you can leave a couple of pages at the front of the binder to record the fruits of your labor: the list of speeches booked! It is very handy to have all of your speech marketing activity documented *in one place*, easy to reach for on your desktop.

However you choose to do it, be sure to document your efforts; if you have mailed to 10, 20 or 30 associations, you will need a system that works for you. You will be in chaos if you don't keep careful records . . . because what comes next *requires* that you become a detailed-oriented person if you're not one already.

## The Follow-up Phone Call

This can be the most difficult part of the process, especially for those of us who don't like the idea of making telephone calls to people we've never met.

But remember that, although you are calling someone you don't know, this is not a cold call: your mailing has helped "break the ice." You can even expect some people to say, "Oh yes, I got your mailing, I'm glad you called." And in this the age of voicemail, you probably won't be able to reach your target on the first try. Don't lament making 12 follow-up calls and getting voicemail 11 times. This very process actually works in your favor, smoothing your way: you are alerting your target to the nature of your call. You are reminding the busy person to look for the packet of information that has already become buried on his or her desk. And now you are no longer a total "stranger;" it won't be so hard to pick up the phone to call this person again (now you can't say "she doesn't know me from Adam and doesn't know what I want").

### A Script To Use When You Get Voicemail On Your First Call:

"Hi, this is _____ from_____; I'm calling to follow up on a packet of information I sent you. Chocolates Galore makes favors for parties and events and we put on demonstrations so your members can learn how to make their *own* favors. People love watching the process in action. I'd like to tell you about what we do. If the packet didn't reach you, I'd be glad to get another one to you; again, my name is _____; feel free to call me at _____. I'll try to get back to you another day." (The idea here is that you can recruit people to work for you in your business, or you can get audience members to decide to hire you rather than do it themselves.)

Here is how you can take that same approach and make it into a request for a sales call rather than a request to present before their organization:

"Hi, this is _____ from _____; I'm calling to follow up on a packet of information I sent you. Chocolates Galore makes favors for parties and events and we have done many events for organizations just like yours. Even if you don't have an event in mind at the moment, I'd like to tell you about our affordable events. If the packet didn't reach you, I'd be glad to get another one to you; again, my name is _____; feel free to call me at_____. I'll try to get back to you another day."

It's a good idea to repeat your name and phone number *slowly*. You have called a busy person who will not want to listen to voicemail 2 or 3 times to get a phone number.

### A Script to Use When You Get the Person on the Phone

Sometimes you may even get the person on the phone; you can say:

"Hi, this is _____. I'm calling from Chocolates Galore. I sent you some information about us and I wanted to find out if you have received it."

[If "Yes"] "As you can see, there are many benefits that Chocolates Galore offers to associations. For example, our cooks give hundreds of demonstrations to groups such as yours; We also provide favors for events you may have."

### How to Handle Objections

Occasionally you hear that you are simply too late: "Your topic really sounds great, but we already have our monthly programs planned through next spring." Next spring may sound an eternity away—and you get the sinking feeling that all your efforts have been for naught.

But don't give up! It is important to persist *because next spring will get here*: "Are you the person I should be talking to when the time comes to plan the next series of meeting? When would be a good time for me to call again—January or February?" And don't assume all is lost because you haven't been able to get on the schedule; remind your contact that you would be available in an emergency: "Please keep Chocolates Galore in mind if one of your scheduled speakers cancels." You may receive a panicked last-minute phone call from a meeting planner: "Would you be available for our meeting next Wednesday night? Our scheduled speaker has cancelled."

Remember too that our focus is not just speeches. Speeches are usually the first step in introducing an organization to your product or service, *but the process can go forward before a speech takes place*. Your contact may be very amenable to hearing about the other benefits available through Chocolates Galore. The packet you sent includes full details about your offerings; this broader subject can be pursued even if you were "too late" for getting included in the schedule of monthly meetings.

Another objection is really a non-issue and is easy to deal with: "We don't pay for speakers." Simply point out that you usually speak for free: "That's a pretty common situation.

Sometimes—depending perhaps on your positioning—your contact may have concerns that you will be hard-selling your products. Organizations have been burned by bait-and-switch speakers: a great-sounding topic turned out to be a pretext for blatant attempts to get people to open their wallets.

One approach in overcoming this objection is to point out that your presentations are commonly welcomed by groups because of the entertainment. "We like to take 5 minutes to explain what Chocolates Galore does, but then demonstrate how people can make their own chocolate favors. We speak to a lot of associations because they know that their members get value."

If there is still skepticism, you can offer to provide references: "I'd be happy to put you in touch with organizations that have heard me speak."

## They May Be Pleased You Called

Don't forget that, in most cases, you're calling *volunteers*: people who have been saddled with the responsibility of planning the monthly

meetings: they may be thrilled to hear from you. Obviously you want to be prepared to overcome objections, i.e., you need to anticipate resistance and know how to deal with it. But these calls can be fun because it's just as common for people to welcome your efforts.

## The Cold Call Approach

If you don't have telephone reluctance—if the thought of calling strangers doesn't upset you—then cold calling could work for you. You can skip the call to verify information. You're calling to get through to the right person. You're breaking the ice by breaking the ice.

### A Script to Use When Making The Cold Call:

"Hi, my name is _____; I'm from Chocolates Galore, a maker of party and event favors. I'm calling you in your capacity as President of the _____ organization. Are you free to talk?"

You ask this simple question out of courtesy and self-interest; you don't want the conversation to continue if the person is in a meeting, having a bad day or otherwise distracted. And the person will appreciate that you asked. If it is a bad time, ask when you could call again . . . and get off the line. Most people *will* suggest a better time to call.

Have you ever heard of Chocolates Galore?

["No."] We speak at meetings such as yours and demonstrate how your members can make their own chocolates. Do you have monthly or quarterly meetings to which you invite outside speakers?"

If the answer is "No," you have qualified the organization as a place not to speak; you can cross it off *that* list. But it may still be a viable target as a *customer*:

"We offer favors for events and meetings and also do event planning. I'd like to send you information describing our products and the benefits we provide to professional groups."

If the person is friendly and seems willing to

talk, you can ask for referrals for speeches: "Do you belong to any other organizations that do hold monthly meetings?"

## The Script to Use

*[If the answer is "Yes, we have monthly meetings."]:*

"We present frequently to organizations such as yours—learning how to make party favors is usually very popular. I would assume that your members are interested in being entertained."

Notice that the last sentence was *positive statement*, rather than a question, such as, "Would your group like to see a demonstration on making chocolate party favors?" Experienced sales people avoid asking questions that can be answered "No"—unless "No" would be helpful, e.g., "Do you have monthly or quarterly meetings to which you invite outside speakers?" helps you to qualify the organization.

But if you don't *want* a "No," make an observation or comment that is more likely to keep conversation going, "I assume that your members are interested in being entertained."

A brief Q&A session may follow, but you can be 100% confident that the person will not be in a position to book you for a speech or presentation during this initial cold call, even if he or she sounds interested and enthusiastic. And so you should anticipate the "send me your literature" response—and bring it up first.

## The Script to Use to End the Cold Call:

"Actually, what I'd like to do at this point is send you information about Chocolates Galore. That way you can really learn what we're about and I can call you again in a few days. What address should I use?"

What has happened? You have offered to end the conversation; the person has not had to find some way to get you off the line. You have not been a nuisance. People will appreciate that you have been courteous, and your relationship has gotten off on the right foot.

## End the conversation by reinforcing who you are:

"Thank you for taking the time to speak with me. Again, my name is _____ from Chocolates Galore. In case you want to reach me, my number is_____."

## The Cold Call Follow-up Letter

Dear XXXXXXX:

Thank you for your time and interest during our telephone conversation [**on October 2nd . . . or "this morning"**]. As promised, enclosed you will find information about Chocolates Galore or **however you position your company.**

[The balance of the letter lists the services you offer.]

The scripts for the follow-up call and for handling objections are the same as those above.

# The Value of Persistence

Whether you have approached organizations through targeted mailing or cold calls, you will now be in perhaps the most frustrating stage of the process: trying to reach the people you have written to.

As mentioned earlier, voice-mail can be an ally. But you may have left a few call-backs. What if the return phone call never comes? You should *not expect* return calls.

You may be ready to jump to the easiest conclusion. "They haven't called back because they're not really interested, right?"

Wrong!

But how do you account for 6 or 8 or 10 unreturned calls? Among other things, you must manage your expectations. Waiting for the phone to ring is not realistic.

Just remember that the person you're trying to reach is a probably a volunteer for the professional organization, and is genuinely very busy at work. The failure to call you back is not about disliking Chocolates Galore. People dislike the cold calls from salespeople pitching insurance or investments. Believe it or not, usually people have not called you back simply because of the tendency to procrastinate. "Yes, Chocolates Galore sounds interesting, but I can't worry now about scheduling meetings for our association six months from now. I'll do it later."

Follow-up in the age of voice-mail requires persistence and good record keeping. Whether you are using a computer or a paper tracking system, make a note of each attempt to reach the person. Did you leave a message on voice mail or with a secretary? It is helpful to know that. If possible, get the secretary's name; he or she can become your ally. As long as you are not being obnoxious or discourteous—betraying impatience or annoyance in your voice—there is no harm in leaving 6 or 8 or even 10 call-backs.

What usually happens?

Of course if the person is genuinely disinterested in Chocolates Galore, your call will never be returned. But when the person finally calls you back—or to your shock and surprise—actually answers the phone on your 7th attempt, the conversation usually begins with *their apology* for not getting back to you: "Gee, I'm really sorry I've been so hard to reach." It is rare for someone to be rude, resentful or on the attack. You will probably never hear, "Why have you being bothering me?" Usually a Q & A will ensue, the common objections may or may not be voiced, and you'll be moving along to getting your chance to appear at one of the monthly meetings of the association.

## Choosing a Topic

Be sure the topic you choose is beneficial to the members and not a sales pitch. You are trying to educate and entertain. At the end of your speech or demonstration, you may speak for a few minutes about your services ("We provide party planning and party favors, so keep us in mind if you have something you'd like help with.")

## Examples of topics our panelists have covered in selling to HR

When The Five O'Clock Club runs meetings for senior human resources executives every two months, some of our panelists are interested in selling their services to this audience. But an indirect sales approach is best. Each panelist provides handouts and we make sure their topic is value-added for the audience—something the audience will be glad they learned about. Here are a few examples that are appropriate for our target audience:

- *Executive Compensation Agreements:* Diane Lerner, senior executive compensation consultant, Watson Wyatt, will address "Negotiating Employment and Severance Contracts with Senior Executives." Diane will cover the dos and don'ts for executive employment contracts—how to avoid having the next Dick Grasso or Michael Ovitz situation.
- *Politics and Leadership:* Joel DeLuca, author of *Political Savvy* and a corporate consultant, will report on the latest academic research on the subject of company politics, tell you how you can use leadership development to deal effectively with organizational politics, and show how politics *blocks* innovation but *leadership* can accelerate the innovation process.
- *Electronic Communications Policies:* Claudia Cohen, Epstein Becker and Green, will tell you how you can monitor electronic communications. Employees may have camera phones and use blackberries and instant messaging. Do you have a policy on that? Courts require companies to keep their emails. Are you in compliance?

None of these topics have to do with our services. If the audience goes away only learning about your services and not learning about the subject, they will feel taken advantage of. Try to keep your presentation informative and entertaining. And provide handouts.

## At the Speech Itself:

### Being Your Own Stage Manager

There are some basic ground rules to bear in mind as you go forward arranging your speaking engagement. You have worked hard to get the booking and are pleased that a group has invited you to make your presentation or demonstration. But although you are a guest, don't forget that you need to maintain an element of control.

Actually, you have to act as your own stage manager; you will be giving a performance, and you don't want to be walking into a situation that will be working against you. Depending on your preferences, there are some things you need to find out.

- Do you like to work from a podium? Do you need a table? Ask if there is one.
- Do you prefer to use a microphone? Unless the room is very small, a lot of your energy will be wasted simply trying to make yourself heard if you don't have one. If your host asks ahead of time if you want a mike, always say "Yes." That way, you will at least have the option.
- Will your presentation be handicapped if you don't have a flip chart or black board? Ask if one will be available.
- Where are you positioned on the program? At the end? Before or after a meal? Before or after the business meeting? You may have little control over these factors, but you will be in a better frame of mind if you are not caught by surprise.

## When to Just Say "No"

And believe it or not, sometimes it's better to say "No." You may find out that the occasion or the setting are inappropriate. For example, beware of the invitation to speak at a "special" meeting of an association. David Madison, the head of our Speakers Bureau, happily accepted an invitation to speak to a "special meeting" of an organization with 3,000 members. 3,000 notices were mailed out—but only 2 people showed up! We know from experience that people are accustomed to attending regular monthly meetings of their organizations, but "special" meetings don't usually draw very well—unless the subject is really exciting. Although it may sound flattering that the program chairperson wants you to speak to a "special" meeting, try to be scheduled for one of the regular monthly or quarterly meetings.

If a meeting is scheduled at a restaurant (very common), make sure that it is a sit-down affair. Some of our career coaches have horror stories of being asked to speak to an organization, only to find out that the members were gathered for the happy hour. Who wants to try to make a presentation to people standing elbow-to-elbow at a bar?

## On-Site Sales

You could take a few samples of Chocolates Galore products with you—to sell after the speech. Mention that you just happen to have a few items with you and would be glad to sell them to anyone who is interested. They could just meet you after the speech. Have your items priced clearly. You will probably be there answering questions from the audience members who have gathered around you. Have change handy and price your items in a way that's easy to make change. And you may want to offer a discount just so they get sold.

For example, our books retail for $13 each, but at speeches our career coaches often sell a set of the four basic books for $40. That's a real bargain, and the coach who is selling the books doesn't have to spend a lot of time trying to figure out how to make change. We also accept checks and credit cards.

Put your items on display as soon as you arrive for the speech. Make an attractive display so people will want to see and examine them. To make sure that people don't assume that the items are "a free sample," you may want to have a little sign, "For Sale At Discount."

The display should be near the podium if possible. It is rare, by the way, that the room set-up makes this impossible. You want to be able to gesture toward the items or lay your hands on them, or pick them up, during your speech. There should be many occasions during your talk to make points about Chocolates Galore and how you made a specific item, and you will want to be able to reach for that item to illustrate your point.

This is an occasion to remember one of the cardinal rules of sales: Don't ask a question that can be answered "No." Thus it is not necessary to ask your host ahead of time if you may have a table near the podium to sell books. _**Do not ask the host ahead of time, "May I bring items to sell**_?" You may inadvertently be encouraging your host to say, "Oh no, we can't have you selling anything." But there will usually be no objection or resistance when you're there setting up the display. Your items will be displayed attractively, and most people, including the host, will be impressed.

A meeting planner once cautioned me that it was against policy for guest speakers to sell anything. So I left the books at home, right? Of course not. I brought the books and set up my display right beside the podium. The first person to buy a set of books was the meeting planner!

### Script to Use to Introduce Your Items for Sale:

"As you can see, I've brought along the some of the items we use as party favors. When I speak to organizations such as yours, I'm authorized by Chocolates Galore to sell the favors at discount. If you're interested, come up and look at them afterwards and talk to me."

If you feel comfortable mentioning price:

"At organizations, we offer a set of four chocolate rosebuds for $25—at stores they're $45."

Again, you're free to price the items however you wish, but our experience has been that you will sell more by offering a discount for a certain quantity.

## A Signup Sheet . . . or Cards . . . or a Raffle!

Remember that your appearance before an association is an ideal way of promoting your product or service; you are your own commercial: 30 or 40 or 100 potential customers are sitting in front of you. They have seen you in action, and that is invaluable (an ad or a Yellow Pages listing has so little impact because you are an _unknown_ quantity). So to take full advantage of this in-person edge, _it is important to capture names; failure to do so is a very costly oversight._ You want to be able to get in touch with the people who have already seen you face-to-face. You retain these names _for your own database_. To build your business, you should be trying to build a database of at least 500 names for quarterly mailings. You can capture names by:

- circulating a sign-up sheet
- handing out blank cards
- having a raffle (i.e., get people to fill out a sheet or put business cards in a bowl)

Raffle off your product if it is not expensive. Ask everyone in the audience to put a business card or a sheet with their contact information in a bowl—an excellent way to capture names and _business_ addresses, if that is what you want. However, you will probably want home addresses: not everyone has a business card, people don't change homes as often as they change jobs—and they may not want your information mailed to them at the office. So don't abandon the practice of sending around a signup sheet or blank cards.

As you watch your speeches accumulate—10, 20, 30 speeches given—you will also have the satisfaction of seeing your database of names growing. And you will really begin to see the impact of your mailings when you get beyond the 500-name level; the law of large numbers will work in your favor in the generation of clients.

## How'm I Doing? You Want to Know

One of the great fears of any presenter is the 'dead audience'—no rapport, no reaction . . . a sea of stone faces. You know what? *That almost never happens!* For the simple reason that—because of your topic—your audience wants you to succeed. They're on your side from the start.

But to improve your chances of success you want to be perceived as someone who can help each one of them. And there are things that you can do to build rapport with your audience . . . and get a reading.

- Offer something of value.

I like to say, e.g., "You may want to take notes, because I'm going to tell you the four parts of a good cover letter." That's valuable information. I sometimes say, "I have eight points to suggest for changing careers, please feel free to take notes." If people are no longer taking notes after my 3rd or 4th points, I know I'm probably not connecting.

- Connect by using real life examples.

A speech devoid of real life stories will be a dull speech. As much as possible move from one story to another to make your points: "One of my customers, Susan, had planned a Sweet Sixteen party for her daughter. For that party, I made . . . ." "For a bachelor party of 20 men, I made. . . ." Or, "for a mid-sized hospital in Oregon, we cut the *c. difficile* rate by 80% in just one year."

- Use your notes as little as possible!

By all means work from your notes, but use them to help you tell your stories. Use your notes as a guide as you "just talk" to your audience. If possible, break free from the podium!

- Hand out an evaluation form.

I don't do it myself because I don't want to hear the bad news!!! I'm a harsh self-critic anyway. But many speakers do it because it is a good way to get feedback, and can help in trying to make improvements.

## Practice Makes Perfect: It's Really True

If you are new to public speaking, the first phases of the process can be the most stressful—*so don't trust your own fears.* When I started out, I was nauseous when I got up to speak. But my stage fright diminished with each new speaking engagement. I became more comfortable with my material, I looked at my notes less and less, and I discovered which stories got the best response. So don't let your stage fright scare you away; grab every opportunity you can to step up to the podium.

## Why Does It Take So Long? Fine Tuning and Follow-up

With time and experience, the dud speeches become rare; usually the events are positive and productive, and you should work to keep relationships with organizations alive.

A few days after the speech you should call your contact. Reiterate what a good experience it was for you—and make the point that you would like to come back. "Please keep me in mind when you do your meeting planning for the spring." Your contact's name should go into your database (along with all the other names you captured at the event). Also make a notation in your tickler file to write your contact at a later date; in this letter you can suggest additional speech topics.

## Don't Forget To Talk About Strategic Partnerships

It may be possible at the time of your speech to bring up the subject of strategic partnerships where they refer members to you or where you provide chocolates for their future meetings; if you are speaking at a dinner meeting, for example, you may be seated next to the meeting planner or the president. It would be very appropriate to explain that Chocolates Galore has much more to offer organizations than speakers.

But even if you don't have an opportunity to mention strategic partnerships at the time of your speech, use the follow-up call or letter to suggest the broader relationship—such as supplying the favors for their annual event.

......................................

*Tomorrow is often the busiest day of the week.*

Spanish Proverb

......................................

*Don't duck the most difficult problems. That just insures that the hardest part will be left when you're most tired. Get the big one done—it's downhill from then on.*

Norman Vincent Peale

*O God, thy sea is so great, and my boat is so small.*

prayer of Breton fishermen

......................................

*When you cannot make up your mind which of two evenly balanced courses of action you should take—choose the bolder.*

W. J. Slim, general, British Army

......................................

*It isn't that they can't see the solution. It is that they can't see the problem.*

G. K. Chesterton

# Public Relations Tips for Your Small Business

*by Steve Bolerjack*

*It is not enough that a man has clearness of vision, and reliance on sincerity, he must also have the art of expression, or he will remain obscure.*

George H. Lewes

In working with the Five O'Clock Club on public relations issues, I've learned many members are associated with smaller businesses—either as owners, consultants or freelancers. As a small business owner myself with a background in corporate public relations, I'm always interested in helping such individuals learn to become their own best self-promoters, both for themselves and their businesses. I believe it's a good idea to learn good P.R. techniques whatever your career goals or job search level may be.

> It's a good idea to learn good P.R. techniques whatever your career goals or job search level may be.

## Why Public Relations for Small Businesses?

What comes to mind when you hear "public relations?" Most likely, your reaction is the same one I usually get from both large and small business clients. I have been a P.R. consultant for years, yet I'm always surprised that most clients think of public relations in the same outmoded way: merely old-fashioned publicity—"ink"—or worse, contrived sham productions—"stunts." I also hear the term misused as a fuzzy catch-all, meaning anything from marketing and advertising to surveys and free samples. And nearly everyone presumes a P.R. effort requires a big expensive agency.

None of these perceptions are remotely accurate anymore. Certainly, P.R. will always focus heavily on publicity, but today it includes community participation, bylined articles, public speaking, media commentary, relationships with local area reporters and development of good professional citizenship.

These elements of P.R. can be particularly effective at local and regional levels and therefore, especially useful to people in small business. Shopowners, freelancers, contractors, entrepreneurs, writers, consultants, homeworkers and others making a living at a more "grassroots" level actually have opportunities and forums beyond the usual advertising and networking options—and they can learn to be their own best promoters. However, good P.R. is still an art of sorts and requires some research, thought and planning (but not necessarily expense!) at any level.

> Surprisingly, even large corporations often fail to realize who their audiences actually are.

## A Modern Definition

It's always good to start with a good, clear definition: "public relations" is simply accurate, consistent and timely communications that convey the right message to the right audience. This is true across-the-board for businesses of any size.

## Creating a P.R. Plan

So how can you apply this definition to your small business? To get started on a P.R. effort, there are three relatively simple steps you can take:

### I. Think through your audiences

Surprisingly, even large corporations often fail to realize who their audiences actually are. I define "audience" as an individual or group who has any interest or stake in the activities of the business. This can reach far beyond just your customers. It's likely that your audiences include the local media, your neighbors and surround-

ing community, current/former employees and their families, vendors/suppliers, government regulators/agencies at several levels and your competitors. And remember, audiences—friendly or not—have the power to communicate information about you.

> "Public relations" is simply accurate, consistent and timely communications that convey the right message to the right audience.

## II. Develop a P.R. Plan

This need not be complex. In simplest terms a P.R. plan consists of a few steps:

- Objectives—identify your goals and what you want to accomplish for your business.
- Positioning—decide how you want to be perceived by your audiences. As the best quality personal tax adviser in town, or the least expensive business tax preparer?
- Key messages—prioritize the most important facts about your business.

Once you have developed these core concepts, you can create:

- Strategy—how you can accomplish your objectives. For example, you may adopt a strategy of marketing your services only to those in a certain age group. Or create the impression that your products are more expensive, but worth their quality. Or position your business as an innovator in a technology instead of just a follower. None of these are new, but remain good illustrations of simple business strategies.
- Tactics—the tools or means to carry out your plan. Speeches, articles, sitting on advisory boards, media outreach are all good tactics for small businesses.

> Small businesspersons should
> never be intimidated by reporters.
> They may need you and what you
> have to say about your field.

## III. Develop a relationship with and use the local media

Small businesspersons should never be intimidated by reporters. Especially at local and regional levels, the media are always on the lookout for a new story, a different angle, a fresh approach and therefore, potentially interested in you and what your business is all about. These media outlets, charged with covering their communities, do not have the vast resources of celebrities, well-known experts and satellite feeds. They may very well need you and what you have to say about your field.

When your business gets a significant new customer, moves from your home to a real office, wins a community award or comes up with a solution to a community problem, don't hesitate to call an appropriate reporter. You may not always get coverage, but you have nothing to lose by cultivating these relationships.

In your small business, what do you know, offer, produce, compile, interpret, provide, market, analyze, understand or do better than anyone else? Whatever it is, someone among those audiences wants to hear more about you.

> P.R. includes community participation,
> bylined articles, public speaking,
> media commentary, relationships with
> local area reporters and development
> of good professional citizenship.

Let's look at two examples of typical small businesses successfully applying some of these steps:

## What One Small Businessman Can Do for Himself

Kenny Dale started his roofing business in Kansas City 30 years ago, getting in on the first profitable stages of a suburban building boom. A beautiful and thriving city, KC's suburbs grew tremendously for 20 years. Competition among builders, contractors, roofers and all types of construction professionals was intense, resulting in many beautiful homes on rolling, wooded sites. All are distinctive, but they have one thing in common: thick "shake" cedar shingle roofs. Enormously popular, more than 90 percent of all new single-family dwellings built in Kansas City each year have shake shingles.

The city is noted for something else: occasionally violent extremes of weather. In every season, intense thunderstorms, hailstorms or heavy ice and snow reduce many shake shingle roofs to splinters.

Kenny had solid business, but eventually was pressured by larger construction firms who brought in whole crews under one contractor, eliminating many traditional subcontracting functions, including roofing. He was known for quality work, but it was also common knowledge that no shake shingle roof would survive baseball-sized hail or the occasional tornado.

Sure enough, an unusually violent combined tornado/hailstorm hit Kansas City a few years ago. Wind damage was significant, but it was huge hailstones that left thousands of shake shingle roofs looking like so many toothpicks.

Demand for roof repairs far exceeded local contractors' abilities to meet them quickly. As roofless homeowners besieged insurance adjusters, they learned it could be weeks before they could get a contractor. Dale Roofing got more than its share of immediate repair business, but Kenny also realized here was a longer-term opportunity to distinguish himself from the large, impersonal firms he had been fighting for so long.

The day after the storm—in a watershed moment for his business—Kenny called all the local television news programs. He described his operations and credentials, indicating he could provide information for homeowners on what to do until permanent roof repairs could be made. Two of the three stations interviewed Kenny at his facility, (with Dale Roofing signs in the background) as he expertly instructed desperate viewers how to use plastic sheeting, heavy wood staples and plywood to create an effective temporary roof.

Without resorting to high-priced agencies, Kenny had become his own very effective public relations consultant. Results? First, while still struggling against larger firms for original roofing contracts, he is now known as the premier shake shingle roof repairer in the city; second, his interviews resulted in new status as an "expert resource" on storm damage prevention and repairs—both in subsequent tv interviews, and in several home repair columns in local newspapers and magazines.

Kenny is a prime example of a small business owner's intrinsic ability to combine his own resources with basic public relations techniques to achieve terrific results.

Let's look at exactly what he did: first, he realized he could provide important information to people far beyond his regular customer base, i.e., the entire shake shingle roof homeowner population in Kansas City—literally tens of thousands of people (increased his audiences); second, he knew he could provide this information where his competitors would not or could not (developed a strategic plan); finally, he used the media to convey his message—in this case, the immediacy of the Six O'Clock News—and was the first to do it (timely and effective media communications). In effect, he positioned himself as a long-term expert, an astute businessman and a provider of solutions in his field.

Kenny's ongoing "expert resource" quotes—particularly in storm seasons—constitute free advertising for Dale Roofing. He remains not only a profitable and successful competitor in the roofing industry, but a well-known and respected local personality.

> People in small businesses actually have opportunities and forums beyond the usual advertising and networking options—and they can learn to be their own best promoters.

## Law Practice in a Small Town

Another success story is from my own midwestern hometown. John Bolling Sr. had practiced law in an old building in our sleepy downtown area for 40 years. It's still a vital community, but a bypass highway built around the western side of town took most of the downtown traffic, business and professional offices with it. As with many other small midwestern cities, the old business district slowly decayed into a collection of mostly vacant buildings. John Sr. made no moves to update the office and eventually did little else but write wills for an elderly, declining client base. Younger clients moved to two newer firms on the highway or to other nearby towns.

When John Jr., at 33, took over the firm, he inherited dwindling profits, cramped, outmoded quarters in an all-but-dead business district and his father's two aging law partners.

John Jr. was essentially a small town guy and immediately dismissed suggestions that he move the firm to a larger city. He wanted Bolling & Bolling to be a dynamic town institution once more, not just a relic from another era. But he had to assess his options quickly.

He first considered building a new office on the highway bypass, but found the best sites already taken. New zoning and environmental restrictions combined with rights-of-way problems virtually eliminated such a move. So it came down to working with the existing site— or nothing.

In addition to site issues, John needed to reach younger clients. Certainly he had excellent professional credentials, but he needed to overcome the outmoded, stuffy reputation the firm had developed. What could he offer? Life in a small town had taught him how important reputation and commitment to the community could be. He hit upon his strategy.

First, he upgraded the old Bolling building, keeping the best of the old elements (it was an historic Art-Deco structure) while modernizing signage, access, parking and interiors. John invited reporters from not only the town newspaper, but from surrounding counties as well, to monitor the progress of his restoration (nothing gets greater notice than construction in one's own back yard). Resulting headlines read "New Life at Bolling Building," "Bolling Law Firm Bucks Migration Trend to Bypass Locale."

> **What do you know, offer, produce, compile, interpret, provide, market, analyze, understand or do better than anyone else?**

Second, John Jr. began to raise his profile in the region. He joined several high-profile community organizations, speaking out for preservation of historic buildings in small towns, arguing that such vision could help improve area towns' ailing economies, foster tourism and even build the tax base.

Third, John added political power to his speaking opportunities by successfully running for City Council. The result is that John Bolling Jr. is known throughout five counties as an astute lawyer and businessman committed to the survival of small town economies. If not the largest, Bolling & Bolling is among the best-known small law firms in the region, comfortably profitable and holding its own against the larger firms on the highway.

John succeeded by employing the same three basic public relations tools that Kenny Dale used: in becoming a small town business preservationist he developed a strategic plan by shrewdly

inviting reporters from several papers to watch him renovate his offices and rebuild his firm, he used media communications effectively; and by reaching beyond his existing client base to create a public platform for himself in his community he increased his audiences.

---

These examples of small business public relations success are neither complicated nor expensive. Their only real cost (other than John Bolling's renovations)was the time, thought and access that the small business owners expended or provided. Yet they are perfect examples of the types of effective public relations strategies and tactics that virtually any small business owner can adopt—if one takes the time to think, to identify and tap existing resources and attributes, and to develop a simple plan to communicate key messages about one's own expertise and the attributes of the small business.

Steve Bolerjack is a business writer/editor and public relations consultant, specializing in small business clients. He developed his expertise in corporate public relations during eight years at Hill and Knowlton, Inc., one of the oldest and largest full service public relations agencies in the world.

As a senior vice president at H&K's headquarters in New York, he managed large accounts, directed editorial teams, wrote and edited a wide variety of documents and publications, and counseled on marketing, media, crisis holds a J.D. from Catholic University and a B.A. in English and Communications from George Washington University. He is a member of the Public Relations Society of America, the New York Advertising and Communications Network and several journalism and service organizations.

# Part Eight

. . . . . . . . . . . . . . . . . . . . . . . . . . . . . . . . . . . . . .

# Understanding the Numbers
# Making a Profit

# Cash is King

*Happiness is a positive cash flow.*

Fred Adler, venture capitalist

Over time, you may hear again and again that "cash is king." Without cash, you can't run your business. In the beginning, you may get that cash by working outside and pumping what you earn into the business. You may even put some business expenses temporarily on your credit cards—anything you can do to keep the business going until it generates cash of its own.

But even when it seems as though you are making money—that is, you've sold quite a bit—waiting for that money to come in can make you panicky. Cash is the only thing that keeps your company going. Your employees want to be paid—although those who believe in you and are able to do it may sit for a little while with un-cashed paychecks. Vendors want to be paid, but you can tell them—for a little while—that you are expecting a check and should be able to pay them by a week from Tuesday.

Cash is more important than profits. Your P&L (profit and loss statement, which you will learn about later) may show a handsome profit, but if you can't collect on those receivables (the money people owe you), your business stops. There was a time (actually a few times) where a big customer owed us quite a bit of money, and they took six months to pay! One time, someone owed us significant money for a year! I was getting desperate and had even spoken to lawyers. It's a long story, but there was essentially nothing I could do that would get us that cash fast. Ironically, our P&L looked the best ever, but that didn't help in the short run. I had to get money and put it into the business. Now we have cash reserves, so when the Five O'Clock Club needs cash, we can advance money from our reserves.

On the other hand, we stay away from customers who don't pay! You can't go on for six months to a year waiting for that cash. You'll need a process for collecting your accounts receivable—and not waiting until the money is *due* before discovering that the person you were dealing with never put your invoice in for payment!

When we've had *plenty* of money, it's been difficult to train our accountants not to pay the bills the day they come in. Yes, we pay our consultants and other individuals quickly because they may be living from check to check. But most major vendors expect to be paid in one month.

Have your accounting person do a cash analysis every day or every week; project when the receivables are expected to come in and also project when certain bills have to be paid. That way, you know whether you have to slow down on paying bills or perhaps tap into your line of credit. You need cash to pay people—or there is no business. When you look at that terrific P&L and then see that you have no cash, you too will understand that cash is king.

If you have cash, you don't have to borrow money and it's great to get to the point where you are debt free and have cash reserves (in a liquid account so you can draw on it when you need to). If you don't have to borrow money, you have no interest expense, and instead have interest *income*. You can use that cash to pay bonuses to employees who have been working hard or who have perhaps been paid under market rates.

*This year I've decided on a whole new strategy... to actually make money*

## Spend *Money* on the Right Things

*Sometimes, the hardest decision made is the right thing to do.*

Yanny Natashah

In the early days, when we had no money, I spent whatever it took for attorneys to protect our trade names and copyrights. Without those, we had no business. It was not cheap, but it was necessary. You too need to legally protect your product or service. Patent all inventions and innovations. Trademark all brands and slogans. Copyright all writing. And then you must vigorously defend your trademarks or you will lose them.

A university thought they were clever and started a job-search group called the "Six O'Clock Club." Unfortunately, that could create confusion in the public about their relationship with us, or what they do could reflect on us, so we wrote them a simple letter that they should "cease and desist" from using that name and they stopped immediately. So spend money—and effort—to protect your most important intellectual property.

But skimp on spending that is not revenue producing. "Revenue producing" could even be software that allows you and your employees to work much more efficiently. It could include hiring talent who will sell your product or service, or new marketing literature that makes you look more credible.

Ask yourself whether an expense will really make a difference in your business. In the early days, people continually told us that the brand name, The Five O'Clock Club, was a stupid name. Changing the company name would have been a tremendous effort and expense. I asked myself: "Is this *really* the problem? Will this make *the* difference and make people flock to our door?" The answer was clearly "no," so I spent time and money on what I thought would have the biggest impact on the business. And it turns out that the name was a great one and has served us well!

## Spend Your *Time* on the Right Things

It's very easy to spend your money and your time on the wrong things. Every morning, I ask myself, "What is the most important thing for me to work on today?" and that's what I focus on. A corollary is to ask yourself, "What is the most important thing for me to spend money on?" and do that—but don't spend money on things that may make you feel good or look good—unless you think it will result in more revenue.

You can get so swamped with the day-to-day tasks that you forget to *guide* the business and instead are working *for* the business. Take some time out to step back and think things through. Get some perspective to make sure you and your staff are all working on the right things. What was important one month turns out not to be so important and you find you have to focus on something else and steer that ship in a different direction.

Delegate tasks and responsibilities you now think can only be done properly by you. In the early days (1978 to 1986), I was the only coach because I was developing the methodology. That time was actually research time while I kept my day job. In 1986, I started to bring in other coaches and people said it wouldn't work: "Clients will only work with you!"

But I knew there were plenty of brilliant coaches who would respect our methodology, and I also knew that there were coaches who were even *better* coaches than I was. I knew that when I found those coaches, our clients would be glad to work with them. And that's what happened. We pride ourselves on assigning the right coach to the right person, and it worked out best for all concerned.

I ran a small coaching group for nineteen years—as just another coach—and loved every minute of it. Eventually, however, I knew I had to spend my time focusing on running the business and not coaching individuals. When I announced that I was "getting kicked upstairs" and would no longer physically be at the Club, people said that clients would not show up. I knew that

wasn't true. Many of our coaches had been with us for a decade or more and some were the most respected coaches in the industry. They carried on without me and it has now been years since I have actually coached anyone privately or in small groups.

As heads of organizations, we all have to delegate. The business can't all be about *us* personally, or you will wind up very tired and the business will be limited to what you can personally handle. Even if someone is not quite as good as we are in certain tasks, it is still better to have those tasks performed by someone else, so we can be free to concentrate on bringing in more business and making the current business run well. Improve the technology. Nurture the people. Increase productivity. That's where your time and money should be invested.

## Identify Your "Nut"

Your nut is your *fixed* expenses that must be covered every month regardless of revenue. Other expenses may vary with revenue. How much do you need to make every month just to stay in business? You must know how much revenue you need to cover all of your costs in a certain time period—usually every month. This is called your "break even." When you know how much revenue you will need, you can translate this into how many *customers* you will need at a certain average revenue per customer to make the money you need just to stay afloat.

## "Quickie" Test Your Idea

I remember one person in my small-business class who wanted to make specialty sunglasses to celebrate the year 2000—not the most inventive idea. But I asked him to take just five minutes to determine his price, his costs, and his profit per sunglass—and how many he would have to sell to make a living. It doesn't matter whether you *really* know the actual numbers at this point. Just plugging numbers into a formula gives you some perspective. He figured if he made a profit of $2.00 per set of glasses—just to name a number—and if he hoped to make $50,000 on the venture, he would have to sell 100,000 sets of glasses. Did he have any idea of how he might do that? Just the number he would have to sell was so staggering to him that he dropped the idea. Ideas are cheap. Execution is everything. And within execution, *marketing* is everything. How would he market 100,000 pairs of eyeglasses? He had no idea and therefore his business was a non-starter. If he thought he could tackle the *marketing* part of the business, then he could focus on developing real numbers to support his business concept.

Here's another example. One of our branches has 50 attendees (job hunters) a week. The average attendee gets a new job within ten sessions. We meet forty sessions per year—allowing time off for holidays. To consistently have 50 attendees a week, knowing that the average person is gone after ten sessions, that branch would have to attract 200 new job hunters per year. The question then becomes: How can the head of the branch attract that many people without spending money (since we charge individuals very little)? Basically, the coaches have to deliver speeches and if they don't do that, the attendance will fall off. If they can't figure out how to market and attract that many people a year, they can't run a branch.

If you don't like the way the numbers are coming out, something has to change. Here are some possibilities:

1. *You are undercharging.* I was scared to death when Richard Bayer came on board as our Chief Operating Officer and immediately raised all of our prices. It was our first price increase in five years, but he knew that we were undercharging. We grandfathered people in at the old price, but I was still afraid that we would lose customers. Instead, revenue went up and we kept all of our customers. They realized what a bargain we still were.

2. *You are not making enough sales calls.* You need to call on lots of people or make sure lots of people know about you before you will get new customers. Get out there and sell.

3. *You are not keeping or growing your current accounts.* Take real good care of your current customers. It's easier to get additional business (or referrals) from current customers than it is to find a new customer.

4. *Your costs have gotten out of hand.* Review all of your expenses. When I was in charge of the budget for a $64 million branch of an advertising agency, it happened to be the most profitable advertising agency branch in the world—not because of me! It was because the budget process included reviewing and budgeting every single line item that was more than $1000. Every small category of expense was examined every year—not at the macro level—but in each of thirteen departments. Yes, they kept their revenue up and got rid of unprofitable accounts. But it takes a lot of revenue to make up for slovenly spending habits.

In the last few years at The Five O'Clock Club, we've changed shipping vendors twice and phone carriers twice—and these are relatively small expenses for us. We send print jobs out for bid. As Richard Bayer says, "All profit is at the margins." Those little savings add up over time.

It's important to know the number of customers you need to attract, and then figure out how you will attract that number of customers. It's pretty easy to come up with a preliminary break-even analysis—look at the sunglasses example. But many people do not put pen to paper to jot down a few numbers. Instead, they focus only on the product idea and ignore the execution of the ideas.

Ideas are cheap. Execution is everything.

## The Basic Numbers

You need to know the average revenue you expect from each paying customer—and the average number of units each customer will purchase. Then, calculate the number of customers you will need to make the revenue you want to bring in. Next, calculate the expected costs—both direct (that is, directly related to the product or service) and indirect (that is, general business expenses such as telephone, rent and so on). The difference between your revenue and your expense number is your profit.

If you can't come up with a reasonable profit number—even on paper and given ideal conditions (after all, these are all theoretical and probably optimistic), then you don't have a business. There's no sense investing a lot in it or even trying to raise funds. No one will fund you: They need to see the numbers.

*"The bad news is we've lost $187,000 this month. The good news is that's nothing compared to what we lost last month."*

## Make Money While You Sleep

If you are a sole proprietor of a store, or a physician, accountant, architect or attorney in private or group practice, you earn money only when you work. I met one Park Avenue doctor who had fabulous space and four or five full-time people in his office where he also had a surgery unit. I said to him, "Gee. All of this depends on you. What happens if you're out sick for a month?" He said, "Well, I guess we'd have to close up shop."

When he stops working, no money comes in. These sole proprietors are in their own businesses to some extent, but they are not really entrepreneurs. Entrepreneurs create a business structure that brings in revenue even when they are not working. Think this through before you start your business. Can you create a business that keeps on churning when you're not? To do this, other people must be working with you, and you must get some income from the revenue they generate.

Can you think of some way to extend your business idea so it turns into a real entrepreneurial venture and not just a small business that makes money only when you work? This is the time to think about that possibility. If your business is of the "If I don't work, I don't eat" variety, maybe you would like to think through a different model. If you don't want to do that, fine. But think of yourself as having a private practice—however lucrative it may be—rather than thinking of yourself as an entrepreneur.

Another test is what your "business" is worth when you are ready to sell it or retire. If you are in your own private practice, the business goes when you go. That Park Avenue physician has no business he can sell when he retires—just the real estate if he owns it. But if you have created something of value that can live on after you go, then you have something to sell.

# Analyzing the Business

*The problem is not that there are problems. The problem is expecting otherwise and thinking that having problems is a problem.*

Theodore Rubin

Every business has key measurable items that can give you a warning of how the business will do in the near future without waiting for the month-end financials to come out. For example, in a retail store, if there is no foot traffic, there is no business. You don't have to wait until the end of the month to realize that no business came in. No customers; no money. If you identify these early indicators, you can take action sooner if things are not going well: stand outside and drag people in; place an ad; run a sale. Do whatever you can to bring business in, and cut expenses at the same time.

Uncover the leading indicators of whatever business you will be running—those statistics that let you know that the business is going along okay. For example, it could be:

- the number of sales calls you make (If you made fewer sales calls this month, less business will come in.)

- the number of times someone calls for information (If the phone isn't ringing, you won't get new business.)
- the traffic to your website (If you depend on the Internet for leads, and traffic has dropped, sales will drop that month too.)

Uncover the numbers that drive the business *you're* interested in. What should you watch month by month to know whether the business is doing well or not? How can you keep your finger on the pulse of what's really happening so you don't get blindsided? Don't buy a business unless you understand the metrics.

If you want to buy a catering business instead of starting your own, for example, you would have to understand the metrics of that business in detail. It's not enough to simply look at the profit and loss statement and the balance sheets. Get underneath the numbers. How many clients do they have? How much of their revenue do they get from each of those clients? Do their lives depend on one big account? What if that account went away? What are their profit margins on each of the accounts they do business with? Are the big accounts squeezing them margin-wise? The questions you actually ask will depend to a great deal on the kind of business and what you need to know!

Once you understand the business, decide what you can do to keep it going and to improve its operations as well as its revenues. This all takes a great deal of work. I would hire a consultant to help me understand the business! If you don't thoroughly understand those numbers, you could get hoodwinked. Yes, you could.

Below is an analysis of two businesses that are extremely "business metrics" (measure)-oriented—the direct mail business and the collections business. Chances are, your business will not be about numbers as much as these two are, but you can still notice the metrics for each of these businesses—the basics of how each business works.

Now, when reading these case studies, don't be intimidated by the numbers. As they say in the business, "It's only zeros." That is, you would use the same basic thought process when thinking about a company that has $60,000 in revenue or $6 million or $60 million. They're just zeros. And a business owner is a business owner, no matter what the size. We're all in the same Club.

Now, let's examine two businesses, a direct mail company and a collections agency.

..........................................

*Some regard private enterprise as if it were a predatory tiger to be shot. Others look upon it as a cow that they can milk. Only a handful see it for what it really is—the strong horse that pulls the whole cart.*

Winston Churchill

## Case Study: Apex Corporation A Computer-Based Direct Mail Operation

Apex is a $6 million revenue business trying to get people to pay bad debts by sending them a notice by mail. It's a typical direct mail company. But, in this case, they are mailing to people who got a parking ticket in New York City. Let's take a look at this operation. It's a numbers business, so I'll throw a lot of numbers at you.

In 2004, Apex made an average profit of $4.60 for every notice they mailed to someone who owed money for parking tickets. Sometimes the person pays the parking ticket, and sometimes they don't. Apex keeps a percentage and the rest goes to the City of New York. Their costs are for things such as name and address acquisition, postage, printing, and so on. For example, in the name and address acquisition area, they have to decide if it's worth it to go after name and address information in certain states. If a state charges Apex $2.00, should they ask for names and addresses in light of their other costs? If the state charges Apex $160 for a database of names and addresses, and Apex has only 10 requests for that state, then it wouldn't make sense to go after names and addresses from that state. But on the whole, in 2004, Apex made a profit of $4.60 for every notice they mailed.

They're always planning ahead. They're always saying: what will we mail in March? What will we mail in April? And, as a rule of thumb, they'll hit their revenue budget if they mail at least 120,000 notices.

But there's more to it than that. A good 50% of those had better be *first* notices. That is, the first notice the person received—because Apex gets a better return on those.

Think of it this way. George from Burbank gets a ticket in New York. In fact, he was in New York for a week, knew that it's best not to drive in the city, drove anyway, and was still irritated because he couldn't figure out how to find a legal parking space. George must have driven around for hours and hours trying to find a legal spot. Why can't it be like Burbank? He wound up with $500 worth of parking tickets. Such grief. For that kind of money, he could have parked in a garage, but he's gone now, on his way home to sunny Burbank, and he has no intention of paying for these tickets.

George tells his friends: "The least they could do is provide a place for decent people to park. I'm going to throw those tickets away."

But in the meantime, Apex is on the job. They've contacted the Department of Motor Vehicles in California and have asked them for George's name and contact information. And Apex tracks him down.

Apex has his address and his phone number, and they send George a little note—not very threatening. It's only their first notice. George is a nice guy, and he's cooled down by now, and he certainly doesn't want to be a law-breaker, so he pays up. Most people pay on the first notice. Only stingy people and scofflaws don't pay.

So, you see, when Apex is projecting its revenues, it's not enough to say they'll mail 120,000 notices. 50% of those had better be people like George who will probably pay. If not, Apex's returns go down and its costs go up.

After 30 days, Apex mails a second notice to those who didn't pay. And 30 days later, Apex mails a 3rd notice.

After the 2nd notice, if the debtor owes more than $400, Apex sends him to a collection agency, which we'll cover next.

There's another factor that dramatically affects revenues, and that's the timing of the assignment information Apex gets from the City of New York. Apex received a new assignment at the end of November, so in December they mailed a lot of first notices and their revenue shot up. In January, they mailed mostly 2nd and 3rd notices. February was even worse. They mailed 3rd and 4th notices to a guy in Iowa and he's laughing at them. To make February marginally better, Apex was forced to go back to assignments they received in July and September and mail 5th and 6th notices to them. They'll mail a lot in February, but the return is a low margin. On the other hand, if they get a lot of names and addresses, the can mail first notices to those people and have a higher return.

To summarize: it's not enough to mail 120,000; it's also the quality of the notices.

So, if you were buying this business, what could you do to increase its revenues? Unless you are really aware of the direct mail industry, there is no way you could know how to think about it.

If you do know the direct mail industry, you may come up with lots of ideas.

In this case, new management tested a 5th notice, a 6th notice, and are now testing a 7th notice. For the 6th notice, they made a profit of $2.60 for each notice mailed. That compares with a $4.60 for the average notice mailed in 2004, but it's still very profitable. What a great idea. The net profit to Apex for the 6th notice was $174,000.

Now they're testing a 7th notice. They plan to mail only 58,000 by regular mail. But they'll also test an attorney letter by certified mail, an attorney letter by regular mail, and a certified regular dunning notice. They feel pretty sure they'll show a profit of $40,000 on this 7th notice—even if the test mailings show no increased effectiveness. That would he a net profit of $1.38 per notice mailed compared with $4.60 for the average mailing in 2004 and $2.60 for the 6th notice. It's still profitable.

Now one thing that happens when you mail a 6th or 7th notice is that costs increase in other areas. For example, costs for correspondence increase. People like George who pay on the first notice, simply pay. But some of the people who don't pay are ignoring Apex because they feel they have a case. So when Apex mails out a 6th notice, it increases the likelihood of getting a letter from someone who says: "I've ignored you all this time, but you keep on sending letters to my father who died in September." So Apex's correspondence costs go up.

The new Apex wants to get even smarter at this. They want to be able to predict the outcome of mailing 12,000 notices: the breakdown of test notices, second notices, etc.

They want to know in advance that they should expect a return of x%, that they should expect so many letters in the correspondence unit, and that they should expect so much in revenue.

They should be able to tell all of that from the quality of the notices they're sending out.

And they want to be able to project this within a variance of 2 to 5%. This is a science—just like any basic direct marketing.

You have to thoroughly understand the industry you're getting into. There's more to it than meets the eye. That's why it's best if you've already worked in the industry or plan to work in it for a few years before having your own business.

## Case Study: Kantor Kollections
## A Collections Agency

Now, back to George. Can you believe it? That guy didn't pay. Boy, was I wrong about him. So Apex sent the information on George to Kantor Kollections.

Let me tell you about the collections business. It's a mature industry: lots of competitors and all of the players know who their competition is. It's a low margin business because it's easy to compare the performance of the collections agencies and clients know what they should be paying. There's not much product differentiation.

It's also a people-intensive business, and the people who work in this business are not like the systems analysts and programmers at Apex. They're bill collectors, but Kantor's are on a higher level than most. They're very smart people who know the law and know how to handle lawbreakers. They collect by mail and phone debts that are over $400. Remember that the people they're calling are not people who forgot to pay their Bloomingdale's bill. They're people who intentionally parked illegally and did it over and over again and are proud of the fact that they got away with it. Some of these people owe thousands of dollars for parking tickets.

This is a very high pressure business and the industry experiences a very high turnover rate—about 50%. People get burnt out in this business, and one of the things Kantor concentrates on is ways to avoid burn-out.

The business owner is doing a real good job here. Kantor used to have a car rental contract that made up 70% of his business. (People rent cars, get parking tickets and don't pay them.

Kantor Kollections tracks them down.) It was relatively easy money, but they lost that contract 2 years ago. Kantor has succeeded in replacing all of that business. He's developed a department that is very well organized, and he's installed a highly sophisticated computerized system. Of course, every collector sits at a terminal.

And there's plenty of room for growth at Kantor Kollections. Consider that only 57% of the plates suitable for the Automated Collections System are actually on that system. Kantor has loaded only the number of accounts that his present staff can reasonably handle well, and he's done the right thing there. If he loaded everything, they would collect all the easy money and ignore the more difficult collections problems.

But as the effectiveness of the average collector increases, then it would make sense to add more people and make more money. But not now, it wouldn't make sense. For the past 5 months, from September '04 through January '05, the average collector brought in $22,886 gross per month. Kantor wants to get the average up from $23,000 to $30,000 per month gross collections for the average collector, and they're on their way. In January, they averaged $26,000 per month gross per collector, but he had to really push to do that.

They can make the $30,000 number. Four collectors passed that number in January, and they've started a Winners Circle for those who do it. The trick for reaching this goal for the average collector and for the department as a whole is:

- to keep the company fully staffed. That's tough, but they've got to keep their turnover down.
- to retain experienced personnel. Kantor now has good people who have been with them for a year or longer. They're got to keep them.
- They've got to continually analyze the effectiveness of each collector and provide constant training. Kantor is doing that right now.
- They've got to stay away from accounts

such as the student loan business and stick with our core—at least until their productivity is better. You see, if they get accounts that have been worked elsewhere, it's harder to collect that money. Right now, they can't afford to handle bad paper (as they say in the business).

- And they've got to encourage the collectors through both monetary and non-monetary incentives. They're doing that through the bonus system and through ideas such as the winners circle, constant training, and things like that.

Kantor has a staff member who analyzes the effectiveness of the collectors on an individual basis and trains them at their stations in addition to the group training they all receive.

Kantor also has an attorney who knows the collections business inside out and is working hard on the attorney network.

Kantor has a network of attorneys throughout the country, even in California where George lives. When a scofflaw doesn't respond to the letters and phone calls from the Kantor Kollections, the collector can recommend that the account be turned over to an attorney in the state where the scofflaw resides.

The Network is doing very well. The analysis of that business showed that it averaged $31,300 per month for the 8 months worked in 2004. Kantor started the Network in May of last year. They're now developing a plan to make the Network even more effective and increase the revenue per month from that effort. For example, they now have 34 attorneys and the plan is to have 46 by the end of '05. And management is working to increase the effectiveness of each attorney in the Network.

But I digress. Back to George. Kantor Kollections sent him 3 collections notices within 35 days. He ignored them. A collector assigned to California called him a number of times on the phone. At first, his wife insisted that he was never home. When the collector finally spoke to him, he promised to pay, but he never paid. Kantor was ready to turn his account over to their attorney in California.

But why do that? I've heard that George is back in town. He has returned to the scene of the crime. He has thwarted Kantor's every attempt to collect from him and he's flush with a feeling of power. He's back in New York, and although he's staying in New Jersey, he has parked his car in New York—on the street—just two blocks from the Grand Hyatt. George likes the Grand Hyatt. The Garden Room. Great food. Nice desserts. George is cool. He's cocky. He obviously doesn't know who he's dealing with. He doesn't know about Kantor Kollections secret weapon—the city towing operation.

Kantor Kollections notified the towing operation, which found George's car and took it away. It was a nice car too.

## The Business Outlook

The collections business is a good operation in a stable industry. With outstanding consumer debt at $1.15 trillion, the United States' 6,300 collection agencies should thrive. Thanks to Kantor's skill and its $300,000 investment in sophisticated computer and telephone equipment, and to its low-cost workforce, it could profitably expand from its relatively small regional base and its emphasis on parking tickets. So it looks like a good business to buy, depending on what you find out when you look at the books, and depending on your experience in this industry. The collections business might look easy if you don't know anything about it, but every business requires some particular knowledge.

# Profits:
# The Bottom Line

*In business, the earning of profit is something more than an incident of success. It is an essential condition of success. It is an essential condition of success because the continued absence of profit itself spells failure.*

Louis D Brandeis

Yes, you need a good product or service. You need good, highly motivated people. You need marketing so people know who you are and value what you offer. The result should be profit. Without a good product or service, good people, and marketing at a profit, you have no business.

Whether you are a manufacturing company or a service business, it takes capital to run that business. You need working capital to cover your receivables and any unsold inventory. You also need capital for leasehold improvements, furniture, computers, and so on.

Most businesses have no outside sources of capital. Profit is your only source. *You need capital to grow.*

If your profit margins dropped from 20% to 10%, your growth would slow. Without profits there can be no investment in better people, greater capabilities, better client service (and more business). The greater your profits, the greater the opportunities for your people and the greater the value of your business.

You need profit not only to make a good living but also to sustain company growth. It takes money—investment spending—to grow.

## The Profit and Loss Statement

*Remind people that profit is the difference between revenue and expense. This makes you look smart.*

Scott Adams

The first and most used profit management report is the profit & loss statement. It is generally published monthly. In many companies, it compares current information against budget and against prior periods.

You must continually compare the current time frame (month, quarter, year, or a certain period year to date, such as year-to-date May) versus prior periods (prior month, quarter, year, or prior year-to-date such as prior year May-to-date.) You must compare against prior periods so you can evaluate your performance.

The P&L won't help you identify the *reasons* for profit improvement or decline but will prompt you to ask good questions by identifying trends and inconsistencies. You may notice, for example, that the postage category has sky-rocketed compared with the prior month and also compared with the same month last year. Now you can ask some questions about this.

Some of the standard analyses which can be performed on the P&L are:

- growth in income versus growth in expense
- growth in the various expense categories versus overall expense growth
- growth in income versus headcount
- growth in expenses versus headcount
- the trend in margins (up or down) This is also known as the profit margin. The profit margin is the percent of income that is retained as profit.

To give you a sense of what can be learned and to help you evaluate P&Ls, let's analyze a few businesses.

At the end of this chapter, you will find the five-year P&L history of three domestic privately-held advertising agencies of similar size. Take a look at those P&Ls now and analyze both companies. Consider:

- How each company is currently performing
- The trends you see (good and bad)
  - ∆ Income growth vs. Expense growth
  - ∆ Expense growth by category
  - ∆ Income vs. Head count
  - ∆ Expenses vs. Head count
  - ∆ Margins
  - ∆ Historical analysis
- Your assessment of the probable causes for each company's performance to date.
- The questions you would ask of the owner.

The exercise gives you a little experience with using the P&L as a management tool—especially with regard to comparing the performance of similar companies.

Here are a few observations—just to get you started:

- In each case, 2008 is an estimate for the current year. 2009 is the budget for next year.
- Look at the incomes of these various companies historically. If company X has been growing at 20% per year, and it's now looking at 6% growth, you can ask yourself why. What's the reason? Is there a fundamental problem or is the situation temporary? If it's a fundamental problem, the business needs to respond accordingly.
- You could take a look at the increase of expenses in various categories year over year. In company A, for example, rents are going up considerably in later years.
- Also calculate the percent of revenue for every expense item and see how one company is doing against another in each category of expenses. For example, one company may be spending much more on travel and entertainment than the others. That's worth noting. How much is income changing each year, and how is each expense category changing with it?
- What is the revenue per employee for each company and for each year?
- Is each company trying to increase profit before tax in the projected year (2009)?
- For company B, the growth is tremendous. Can they keep it up? How are the margins doing as a percent of revenue? (That is, how much of that growth is dropping to the bottom line, or are they spending all of it?)
- What is the payroll sub-total as a percent of revenue for every company? What observations can you make about that?
- For company C, what makes them think the revenue projections have some basis? Revenue declined in 2008, and held relatively steady for many years. What makes them think it will go up 30% next year?
- What is their revenue per person compared with the other companies? Which company is currently most productive (2007)?
- For company C, what is their labor sub-

total as a percent of revenue for each year? If a company's labor expenses are now high, how will that impact future years? What impact will the people expense have on future years? Company C is projecting a huge growth in manpower.

There are no right answers because you can't talk to management. You also do not have all of the information you need to completely analyze a company and tell which company is better run than the others. For example, a company with high revenues and high profits may be getting most of their business from one customer. That is not a strong business. If that one customer leaves, they will have to close. Another business with lower margins and revenue spread over 30 customers may be a much stronger business and may simply need to be a little more aggressive about their pricing.

You have enough information in these P&Ls to raise some questions in your mind. So start thinking. As you may guess, this exercise could take you a significant number of hours. But if you like to "run the numbers," it's fun.

## Investment Spending

*When profit is unshared it's less likely to grow greater.*

Malcolm Forbes

Every year when we have a tremendous profit, we invest much of that back into the business—into revenue-producing items such as an additional sales person, better marketing materials, and so on. Or items that better service our customers, and increase our value in the marketplace.

The best plan for next year is one that shows the combination of continued health and development of the basic business and well-thought-out and justified investments. It's not enough to simply work in your business all day long. You must also *run* your business and that means planning for growth.

## Increase Profits: Volume, Price and Cost

There are three aspects of profitability in every business: volume, price and cost. To increase profits, you can change your volume, your price or your cost.

Volume: The sales volume is driven by new business and growth from existing clients. You need plans for both areas: how to get new business and how to keep your current customers happy and grow those accounts. If your margins are good, increase your volume.

Price: This is a critical component of company profitability that's often overlooked. Too often companies *only focus* on price when cost accounting (which will be covered later) indicates piles of red ink.

The chapter, "Negotiating a Consulting or Freelance Assignment/Pricing a Project" covers pricing for consulting businesses. However, because labor is a major component of the costs for most businesses, many aspects of that chapter may apply to other business as well. And you can see from that chapter just how much *thinking* has to go into pricing your products or services.

Cost: This is the third part of equation. If you've exhausted all opportunities for new business growth and have used every trick in the book to maximize revenues from the business you've got, then the last remaining opportunity to increase profit is to manage the costs (usually focusing first on labor) necessary to support the business. Of course, you should review your costs all along to increase margins and not wait until you have exhausted everything else.

There is, fortunately, one management process that marries volume, price and cost and looks at them as a single idea: *That process is cost accounting.* The same process that establishes the basis for pricing is used to manage and control costs.

*The worst crime against working people is a company which fails to operate at a profit.*

Samuel Gompers

## Cost Accounting

*Cost accounting* is your company's single most important source of financial information if you use it correctly. While cost accounting systems vary by business, they all have the same objective—to find out whether specific accounts, projects or products are profitable. You will learn much more about this in the next chapter.

## Maximizing Price

It's a maxim that you should maximize your price and charge what the market will bear. I should mention, however, that when we were able to dramatically reduce our expenses, we passed those savings on to our customers.

There is no magic formula. A cleverly constructed pricing approach that the customer won't pay is not so clever after all. But if you don't test the upper limits, you never know.

- Isolate as many services as possible from being part of the standard. If you sell candles, and the customer wants them shipped, the customer must pay extra for shipping and handling, to name an easy example. If you run a moving company, and the customer wants packing, he or she must pay extra not only for the packing labor but also for the packing materials themselves. Charge separately for extra items. This is called "unbundling."
- On the other hand, you could bundle the services and throw in a lot of extra items or services that don't cost you very much but increase your margins. For one price, the customer gets all of these things.

You will have to thoroughly understand how pricing is done in your industry so you can think through how to do it yourself.

# Company A

| | 2005 | 2006 | 2007 | 2008 (est.) | 2009 (bud.) |
|---|---|---|---|---|---|
| **Income** | **$1,930** | **$2,837** | **$3,002** | **$3,861** | **$4,453** |
| Payroll | 748 | 1,000 | 1,139 | 1,465 | 1,840 |
| Benefits | 27 | 32 | 44 | 56 | 138 |
| Payroll Tax | 47 | 74 | 81 | 106 | 130 |
| **Sub Total** | **$822** | **$1,106** | **$1,264** | **$1,627** | **2,108** |
| Travel&Transp. | 9 | 9 | 13 | 17 | 16 |
| Entertainment | 24 | 37 | 41 | 45 | 50 |
| Presentations | | 2 | | 2 | |
| Write-offs | 2 | 4 | | 10 | 10 |
| Other | 147 | 139 | 117 | 160 | 240 |
| **Sub Total** | **$183** | **$192** | **$171** | **$234** | **$316** |
| Depr&Amort | 21 | 22 | 22 | 30 | 40 |
| Rent& Util. | 172 | 189 | 197 | 265 | 331 |
| Machine Rent | 1 | 8 | 17 | 21 | 25 |
| Repairs & Maint | 3 | 4 | 4 | 9 | 10 |
| Alt & Mov | | 1 | | 2 | 2 |
| Telephone | 30 | 36 | 43 | 57 | 60 |
| Office Supp | 13 | 23 | 19 | 28 | 30 |
| Misc Tax | 12 | 12 | 13 | 20 | 25 |
| **Sub Total** | **$231** | **$271** | **$293** | **$402** | **$483** |
| Advertising | 2 | 3 | 1 | 1 | 1 |
| Bus Lunches | 2 | 2 | 4 | 5 | 5 |
| Contributions | 1 | 1 | 4 | 5 | 5 |
| Gifts | 2 | 3 | 4 | 5 | 3 |
| Insurance | | | 4 | 5 | 5 |
| Dues | 5 | 9 | 10 | 14 | 10 |
| Messenger | 2 | 1 | 1 | 1 | 1 |
| Shipping | 1 | 3 | 3 | 4 | 6 |
| New Bus | 4 | 3 | 10 | 15 | 15 |
| Prof Services | | 5 | 10 | 75 | 50 |
| Misc | 3 | 2 | 1 | 1 | 1 |
| Management fees | 33 | 45 | 56 | 74 | 89 |
| **Sub Total** | **$56** | **$79** | **$108** | **$205** | **$191** |
| **TOTAL EXP** | **$1,313** | **$1,670** | **$1,858** | **$2,498** | **$3,138** |
| Non-Op Income | 17 | 49 | 67 | 65 | 65 |
| **PBI (profit before emp. incentives)** | **634** | **1,215** | **1,211** | **1,428** | **1,380** |
| Total Incentives | 320 | 525 | 539 | 634 | 340 |
| **PBT (profit before taxes)** | **314** | **690** | **672** | **794** | **1,040** |
| # EMPLOYEES | 30 | 37 | 38 | 48 | 51 |

## Company B

| | 2005 | 2006 | 2007 | 2008 (Est.) | 2009 (Bud.) |
|---|---|---|---|---|---|
| **Income** | **$2,568** | **$3,018** | **$3,702** | **$4,468** | **$4,944** |
| Payroll | $1,346 | 1,487 | 1,667 | 1,773 | 2,132 |
| Benefits | 156 | 230 | 154 | 168 | 184 |
| Payroll Tax | 91 | 105 | 117 | 126 | 136 |
| **Sub Total** | **$1,592** | **$1,822** | **$1,938** | **$2,067** | **$2,452** |
| Travel & Transp | 63 | 64 | 49 | 55 | 67 |
| Entertainment | 34 | 33 | 37 | 35 | 45 |
| Presentations | 5 | 4 | 1 | | 14 |
| Write-offs | 13 | 3 | 21 | 52 | |
| Other | | | | | |
| **Sub Total** | **$115** | **$104** | **$108** | **$142** | **$126** |
| Depr&Amort | 37 | 46 | 63 | 78 | 86 |
| Rent | 91 | 93 | 112 | 130 | 150 |
| C Rent | 5 | 5 | 8 | 5 | 5 |
| Rep & Main | 13 | 17 | 29 | 30 | 32 |
| Telephone | 49 | 50 | 54 | 64 | 60 |
| Office Supplies | 69 | 67 | 73 | 89 | 97 |
| **Sub Total** | **$226** | **$232** | **$276** | **$318** | **$344** |
| Advertising | 5 | 4 | 8 | 5 | 10 |
| Bus Lunches | | 7 | | | |
| Contributions | 7 | 7 | 7 | 8 | 3 |
| Insurance | 12 | 11 | 11 | 12 | 12 |
| Dues | 38 | 39 | 43 | 44 | 46 |
| M & L | 1 | | | | |
| Shipping | 16 | 12 | 22 | 24 | 35 |
| New Business | 18 | 34 | 27 | 35 | 30 |
| Pro Services | 11 | 15 | 19 | 25 | 18 |
| Miscellaneous | 13 | 14 | 19 | 13 | 14 |
| Mgmt. fees | 66 | 78 | 96 | 137 | 162 |
| **Sub Total** | **$186** | **$212** | **$252** | **$303** | **$330** |
| **TOTAL EXP** | **$2,156** | **$2,415** | **$2,637** | **$2,908** | **$3,338** |
| Non-Op Income | 168 | 239 | 289 | 205 | 191 |
| **PBI (profit before incentives)** | **580** | **842** | **1,354** | **1,765** | **1,797** |
| Total Incentives | 277 | 411 | 514 | 541 | 548 |
| **PBT (Profit before Tax)** | **303** | **431** | **840** | **1,224** | **1,249** |
| # Employees | 73 | 74 | 80 | 86 | 90 |

## Company C

| | 2005 | 2006 | 2007 | 2008 (Est.) | 2009 (Bud.) |
|---|---|---|---|---|---|
| **Income** | **$3,239** | **$3,828** | **$3,899** | **$3,609** | **$4,675** |
| Payroll | 1,544 | 1,689 | 1,843 | 1,755 | 2,211 |
| Benefits | 136 | 141 | 166 | 152 | 202 |
| Payroll Tax | 100 | 122 | 134 | 126 | 164 |
| **Sub Total** | **$1,779** | **$1,952** | **$2,143** | **$2,033** | **$2,577** |
| Travel&Transp | 52 | 63 | 90 | 94 | 123 |
| Entertainment | 26 | 33 | 28 | 27 | 42 |
| Research | 48 | 47 | 36 | | |
| Media Meas. | 7 | 4 | 2 | 5 | 30 |
| Presentations | 15 | 6 | 7 | 4 | 6 |
| Write-offs | 21 | 29 | 9 | 11 | 15 |
| **Sub Total** | **$168** | **$181** | **$172** | **$141** | **$216** |
| Depr&Amort | 48 | 100 | 76 | 43 | 57 |
| Rent | 151 | 146 | 155 | 159 | 174 |
| Machine Rent | 22 | 29 | 35 | 28 | 42 |
| Rep & Main | 6 | 7 | 6 | 7 | 11 |
| Telephone | 51 | 62 | 71 | 69 | 70 |
| Utilities | 20 | 58 | 61 | 58 | 80 |
| Office Supplies | 55 | 5 | 59 | 54 | 76 |
| Misc Tax | 4 | | 6 | 6 | 10 |
| **Sub Total** | **$308** | **$372** | **$393** | **$391** | **$463** |
| Advertising | 24 | 41 | 20 | 35 | 64 |
| Bus Lunches | 3 | 3 | 5 | 4 | 5 |
| Contributions | 5 | 8 | 5 | 5 | 10 |
| Gifts | 5 | 6 | 6 | 5 | 5 |
| Insurance | 7 | 7 | 5 | 7 | 6 |
| Dues | 26 | 31 | 20 | 19 | 23 |
| Messenger | 6 | 10 | 12 | 10 | 10 |
| M & L | 11 | 5 | 4 | 10 | 15 |
| Ship | 10 | 11 | 14 | 17 | 21 |
| New Bus | 23 | 24 | 38 | 36 | 36 |
| Pro Services | 37 | 41 | 40 | 52 | 40 |
| Misc | 9 | 7 | 9 | 3 | 2 |
| Management fees | 91 | 107 | 272 | 203 | 157 |
| **Sub Total** | **$258** | **$301** | **$450** | **$406** | **$394** |
| **TOTAL EXP** | **$2,562** | **$2,906** | **$3,234** | **$3,014** | **$3,707** |
| Non-OP income | 97 | 127 | 67 | 60 | 80 |
| **PBI (profit before incentives)** | **774** | **1,049** | **732** | **655** | **1,048** |
| Total Incen. | 306 | 443 | 296 | 298 | 315 |
| **PBT (profit before tax)** | **468** | **606** | **436** | **357** | **733** |
| # Employees | 74 | 79 | 64 | 73 | 93 |

# Cost Accounting: Managing for Profitability

*Companies are not charitable enterprises:*
*They hire workers to make profits*

Paul Samuelson

Cost accounting has been common in manufacturing businesses for a century or more. Service businesses did not even consider using cost accounting until around the 1970s or 80s. Yet, it is something *every* business needs—regardless of how large or small.

In addition to projecting the overall P&L for your company, you need to monitor the profitability of your ___most important accounts, products or projects___. Let's say your overall P&L is just fine, showing a 20% profit margin, which is good for your industry. For example, your business shows a revenue of $360,000; expenses of $288,000 (including your salary) and a profit of $72,000 a year, which is 20% of the revenue. But when you look at your various accounts, here is what you find:

- Citygrowth, one of your largest customers, gives you a lot of business but won't allow you to charge what you need to make a profit. You actually have a 5% annual *loss*

*on* this business—an account that makes up 10% of your revenue!

- The next top account, Pathgreat, shows a 20% profit, helping you to support having Citygrowth on your roster of accounts.
- The next ten accounts when ranked by revenue show an average profit of 30% each, with none showing less than 20% profit. This is where your real money is coming from.

If you only looked at your overall P&L and did not examine profitability by account, you would not know that Citygrowth was a loser. You would probably service them more and more, telling yourself how important they are to your business and how you could not afford to lose them. But now that you know that they are a loser and are actually costing you money:

- You decide to meet with them and review the numbers with them to see how you can get more revenue for the work you're doing.
- Or you decide to put lower-priced people on the account.
- Or you decide to hold back on the extra

service you are giving them without notifying them that you are doing so.

- Or you raise prices on one portion of their business.

Regardless of what you do, you don't need more unprofitable business.

In addition, you go after more of the mid-sized accounts where they are less price sensitive and you can make a fair profit.

You need ongoing account analysis because accounts can slip into losses without your being aware of it.

*Account analysis* is one variation of cost accounting. Another variation is *job or project costing*. You get an order to make dresses for an entire wedding party. As the project goes on, the bride changes her mind, changes the fabric, adds expensive buttons, changes the length of the gowns, and requires three extra fittings. Because you have kept track of your costs for this "job," you know that you have lost money on it. You kept track of every second you spent on this project, every piece of fabric and every button you had to buy, every time you had a long conversation with the bride. Your $2000 in revenue wound up costing you $3000 when you added in your labor.

Now that you know the real numbers, you decide to price your custom clothes differently in the future. Now:

- When the bride changes the fabric, you tell her "a change in fabric will be an extra $100."
- You tell her she can get 1 hour of free consultation, but extra consultation will be billed at the rate of $50 per hour.
- You see what other dressmakers charge and what they do when the customer changes her mind, and
- You make sure you have no unprofitable jobs or projects in the future.

Then there is *product or service cost accounting* so you know which of your products or services are generating the most revenue and which

are generating the most profit. Some items you sell are high margin and some are low margin. For example, a bagel shop knows that they could almost give away the bagels—bagels draw customers into the store—but the bagel shop makes its profit on the deli items. If the bagel-store owner didn't know that, he might forget to cross-sell the deli items when someone bought bagels. But because he knows the deli is where his profit is coming from, he pushes those items very hard, even asking customers what they would like him to carry in the deli, for example.

If your analysis shows that your low-margin items are contributing most of your revenue, you may decide to figure out how to sell more of your high-margin products or services, see how you can increase margins on your low-margin items, or perhaps decide things are fine the way they are (the huge volume makes up for the profitable but low margin items).

## Cost Accounting Profit Planning

The next step is to move from this mode of *reporting* on the profitability of each account (job, project, product, service) to the *managing* of the profitability of each in a regular, methodical way. Then you can see how each project and each account is doing against the plan. This kind of planning is an incredibly powerful tool because it gives you the time to change the way you're servicing a piece of business (and thereby turn around an account that may be losing money) or to develop better plans for the next piece of business. This information can help you to price new business better and also to better manage the way your people are spending their time.

For example, just today an important client called us about providing a $5,000 outplacement package to an employee who earned over $200,000 a year. I told the customer that because they were so important we would provide whatever package they wanted, but we would not make our margins on that $5,000 package for such a senior-level person: A job hunter who earns over $200,000 a year usually gets a $7,500 package. I wrote to her: "With the $7,500 package, your employee would get 18 hours of private coaching versus 14 hours for the $5,000 package and would be in a group of those who earn over $200,000 a year. Because we pay our coaches who coach at that level more than we pay our other coaches, the price for a senior executive package (those over $200,000) is proportionately more than the package for those in the $100,000 to $200,000 range. But, as I said on the phone, we'll do whatever you want."

Because I explained to the customer, in so many words, that we would not make as much profit on the lesser package, they decide to allow the employee to have the $7,500 package and we kept our margins! A good customer wants you to make a decent profit.

Let's take it step-by-step. The first step is to keep track of all time and out-of-pocket expenses (to capture labor and other costs) for this specific job. A very small business can track this on an index card, for example. After accumulating all of these customer-related costs, you can calculate your company's overhead rate. That is, any expense that is not directly related to an account is overhead. It's good to know what your overhead is because it is unlikely to change as your revenue goes up or down. You must make enough money to cover overhead no matter what, and then enough money to cover the costs of the accounts you have, and then enough to make a profit—in that order.

The next step is to *plan* your next project where the end result will be your projected revenue and expenses such as the cost of labor, materials, the cost of travel and entertainment, and so on. Then you will project overhead and profit. *Every* time you get an assignment, you will "run the numbers" to see what you should charge for it or what you can deliver for the money they want to pay you.

Actually, you don't have to wait for a new piece of business. You can start now by planning one project for one customer.

## Managing the Cost of New Business

You may also want to capture the cost of the time your people spend on new business development. Track all out-of-pocket expenses for new business, and keep a separate accounting for each major prospect. Many companies find it helpful to track how much it costs to go after new accounts and, in fact, may budget how much they intend to spend on each major prospect or geographic area. Some prospects may not be worth it. You may, for example, decide not to target a certain geographic area because of the great cost of marketing there.

## Managing the Costs of Large Projects

Large projects can get out of control. The customer asks for more and more and in your willingness to please, you end up over-servicing the account—and losing money. Instead, track every major project. When you realize costs are getting out of hand, you can point this out to the customer and mutually decide what to do. This information could be useful in managing large projects in the future so you can more accurately tell your customers what projects will cost.

## Company versus Account Profit and Loss Statements

### (or Project, Job, Product or Service) Profit and Loss Statements

The management reports you need to run your company fall into two main categories:

1. The basic accounting reports (which includes your company P & L), and
2. The cost accounting reports (which include *account* P & L's)

You need both types of reports, even if the latter are hand-generated.

The company P&Ls are accounting-oriented and reflect the way your books are kept. These reports, by their nature, tend to focus on <u>*admin-*</u>

_istrative and overhead items_, and therefore _tend to encourage cost reduction_. These reports allow a comparison of administrative costs between accounting periods, such as year-to-date this year versus the same period last year, or this month's expenses versus last month's.

The account P&Ls, on the other hand, show a direct relationship between costs expended and the revenue received for the work that was done. These reports, by their nature, tend to _focus on direct expense_ including labor, which is often the largest expense, and _tend to encourage a profit orientation_ by account or by project. Account P & L's are meant to reflect the way your business is run rather than the way your books are kept. We are paid by customers and are supposed to do a certain amount of work for that payment. We are also supposed to make a profit on the work we do.

There is a balance between controlling the costs for your company and managing each account (customer or project) for profitability. A focus on account profitability tends to encourage the optimum utilization of manpower because account or project P & L's will show you over time where you may be providing too much service for the revenue received or where you are not being paid enough for the service you are providing.

You may try to develop the following reports, even if by hand:

Report 1: show all of your customers in descending order by revenue comparing this year to last year. You could compare, for example, the first three months of this year (if that is where you are in the year at the time of the report) compared with the first three months of last year or even compared with all of last year, but annualizing this year's revenue (that is, multiplying the first three months by four).

For example, Citygrowth generated the greatest revenue for this period, so it would be listed first.

On the following page is a sample of that kind of report you would eventually have when your company is bigger. Even if your numbers are smaller and you have only ten accounts, you can still do this kind of report for yourself.

## Revenue (in 000s) By Customer 2008–2007

| | 2008 | $ | % | 2007 | $ | % |
|---|---|---|---|---|---|---|
| 1 | Citigrowth | 247.5 | 19.4% | Citigrowth | 283.6 | 32% |
| 2 | Pathgreat | 243 | 19.0% | Pubnet Hines | 30.5 | 3.41% |
| 3 | Littleneck | 81 | 6.3% | Little League Intl. | 27.3 | 3.05% |
| 4 | Nexless | 27.5 | 2.2% | Tagert Online | 26.0 | 2.91% |
| 5 | Whitment | 26.35 | 2.1% | Advert Group | 15.0 | 1.68% |
| 6 | Advert Group | 26 | 2.0% | Fortune Glazing | 12.5 | 1.40% |
| 7 | Comcast | 20 | 1.6% | Wool Protection Group | 10.5 | 1.17% |
| 8 | Undle Hunt and Crew | 18 | 1.4% | Transadvertsiing | 10.0 | 1.12% |
| 9 | Jackson Associates | 18 | 1.4% | Capital Stock Group | 10.0 | 1.12% |
| 10 | Wool Protection Group | 17.75 | 1.4% | Biorest Algo | 9.5 | 1.06% |
| 11 | Tagert Online | 17 | 1.3% | Dinhill and Green | 9.0 | 1.01% |
| 12 | Biorest Algo | 15 | 1.2% | Dougherty Hines | 9.0 | 1.01% |
| 13 | Hest Inc. | 15 | 1.2% | Healthclutch | 9.0 | 1.01% |
| 14 | Rockland Surprise | 15 | 1.2% | Bidderquest | 7.5 | 0.84% |
| 15 | Science Museum | 14 | 1.1% | Whitment | 7.0 | 0.78% |
| 16 | | | | Uniformed Guards | 6.0 | 0.67% |
| 17 | | | | | | |
| 18 | | | | | | |
| 19 | | | | | | |
| 20 | | | | | | |

| **Total of above** | 801.1 | 62.7% | **Total of above** | 482.4 | 54% |
|---|---|---|---|---|---|
| **Total Revenue** | 1,277.3 | | **Total Revenue** | 893.9 | |

|  47 customers in total  |  |  43 customers in total  |  |
|---|---|---|---|
| 21 customers up to June | | 23 customers up to June | |
| New customers | 30 | New Customers | 30 |
| Used our services more than once | 10 | Used our services more than once | 5 |
| Used our services only once | 20 | Used our services only once | 25 |

*Some observations:*

In the above report we can see that Citigrowth made up too much of the company's revenue in 2007 (32%). 2008 was a much better year In that Citigrowth made up "only" 19.4% (15% from one source is considered the maximum you want), and yet total revenue increased overall. Very little revenue (except for Citigrowth and a few others) came from repeat business, so that's something the company needs to look at.

Pathgreat in 2008 was a one-time assignment that will not be repeated, so that revenue has to be replaced for 2009. So the company's strategy may still be to go after the big accounts, but to shore up the diversity of the business by going primarily after the mid-sized and small accounts, which will make the company more stable in the long run.

By the way, the pricing (and profitability) on large and small accounts is the same in this example, so that is not a variable. If it *were* a variable, then you would need an additional column showing the profitability of each account and observing whether you were losing money on certain accounts. *If your pricing and your profitability vary from account to account, then you must examine account profitability*.

Report 2: a summary P & L by account listed in alphabetical order. It would show the costs of each account, such as the amount spent working on the project (labor costs) or out-of-pocket expenses, such as printing, travel, and so on.

Report 3: a labor summary report by account. It shows the amount of time spent on each account by activity (such as delivering your service or client support), the total cost of that time, and the rate per hour (which tells you the level of people you have working on that activity and on that account).

Report 4: an overview of how your employees are spending their time. You may find that your employees are spending, for example, 53% of their time on direct labor hours (i.e. account-related time) and the rest of your company's labor hours are spent on overhead.

If all the above is too much for you, at least prepare Reports 1 and 2. Those are critically important.

## Next Steps

The next step regarding *account or project P & L's* is this:

- Eventually every account, project or major project should be assigned to someone who will be responsible for the profitability of that account (you'll find that managing by account (or product or major project) is a

lot more fun that simply controlling the expenses for your overall company).

- You will need a budget for every account (for every customer or project within customers). You can *plan for the profitability of each account (or product or major project)*. This is the fun part and the chance to truly plan and manage your business.

## Monitoring Payables

Look at your P&L at least monthly. I actually look at ours just about every day to see how our overall revenue is doing this month, or how various revenue and expense items are doing against the previous month, or how this year-to-date is doing against the same time frame for last year. Then I can jump right in and ask questions and perhaps suggest changes in what we are doing. Pay attention to the expenses you've been charged this year: every single bill by category of expense.

The way to find the proper category is via the "general ledger" account codes. For example, 6200 may be the account for "office expense" and 6205 may be the postage account. Under the number 6200, you will find all of the expenses you've charged to that category for this time period (month or year, for example). We'll tell you more about the General Ledger below.

## Your Check on the Accounting Department

The General Ledger is the Bible of all Accounting reporting. If the General Ledger is wrong, then all other accounting reports (such as your company P & L) are also wrong. For example, if an expense was charged to the wrong category (such as if "rent" had gone into the account for "phones"), the company P & L would be wrong in those categories and so would the account P & Ls if those items were charged against specific accounts.

In addition, it would be impossible to track

trends in either of these categories and these two expense categories would then be essentially "uncontrollable."

The Accounting Department needs to make your General Ledger accurate, but it is ultimately up to your review. It's not that hard for you to print out the General Ledger and look it over. See if everything in one expense category actually applies to that expense. You are the best judge of the accuracy of the expenses charged to each category, and you'll find other errors which accounting can then correct.

Every month, along with your company P & L, review your payables listing. This will put you in a better position to control your expenses because you'll be able to see at a glance and in an orderly fashion every bill charged to your company that month. At the same time, you'll provide a check on the Accounting Department and, believe it or not, they would welcome that. In accounting, accuracy is sacred because without it they cannot give you the accurate information you need to run your business. When you have accurate information, you have the basis for making the right decisions.

### The Key to Accuracy in the Reports You Receive

You need two systems: The basic accounting system and the cost accounting system. As I mentioned, the key to accuracy in all of your accounting reports (which includes your company P & L) is an accurate General Ledger. And the key to accuracy in the cost accounting system (which includes account P & Ls) is accurate time reporting if you are in that kind of business.

## Account Management

Your account managers (or you if you are the only account manager) are responsible for account profitability. Other account management responsibilities may include:

- account relationships
- quality of product or service (quality of the

people assigned to the account, quality of the work done, maintenance, etc.)
- long-term needs of the customer

Account profitability should not be the sole measure of an Account Manager's performance. For example, the best managers could be assigned to the *least* profitable accounts because those managers are best able to improve the situation; on the other hand, management may assign less effective managers to the *most* profitable accounts since some of those accounts would make money no matter who was managing them. Profitability is not the only measure of performance.

So don't let your accounting reports undermine the qualities that will make you a superior company, such as the caring attitude you display to customers, and the "can do" attitude you should have with customers. Attention to account profitability alone cannot make a company great. Continued attention to your company's basic values will truly account for your greatness. However, it's Accounting's job to focus on profitability so your company can grow in a smooth fashion and so your employees can be fairly rewarded for their efforts.

Just remember who manages accounting: *You* do. ***You must understand the numbers.*** Accounting and other outside experts can give you advice, but it's *your* business. Sometimes that outside advice is very aggressive, for example to save on taxes. But perhaps that particular suggestion is not in your company's best interests. You have to call the shots. Ultimately, it all rests with you.

So don't think it's enough for you to be a great salesperson and also good at developing your product and service. The third leg of this stool is good record-keeping and accounting systems, and you are responsible for that.

............................................

*Annual income twenty pounds, annual expenditure nineteen six, result happiness. Annual income twenty pounds, annual expenditure twenty pound ought and six, result misery.*

Charles Dickens

# Managing for Profitability: Some Ideas on How to Do It

## 1. Pricing

In general, the *method* you use to price an account, a piece of business, a product or service, doesn't matter so long as your resulting margins are high. Every pricing method has its benefits and weaknesses and you have to do what's best for the situation you happen to be in. You may be forced to price a certain way, and it's all fine so long as you show a healthy margin when you cost it out.

I have always thought that pricing was one of the most central decisions you can make in your business. It shows that you understand the market *and* understand your costs. Pricing is the result of all other analyses put together. You will test your price in the market, and then reexamine it periodically. Pricing is an art as well as a science.

Take this next part with a grain of salt because accounting systems and pricing approaches vary so much from business to business. Having said that, in general, pricing can be thought of as either fee-based or cost-based—with hundreds of variations. The emphasis is on the word "based."

*A fee-based system* is one where you charge a fee for a project, product or service. With fee-based systems, you can afford higher levels of profitability—so long as you know how to control your costs. You can also have losses if you don't know how to control your costs. With fee-based pricing, the responsibility for control is solely on you, and if you can control costs, you will be rewarded with increased profitability. In addition, with fee-based pricing you run your own show without much interference from the customer, but you had better know how to control your costs.

*Cost-based systems* are where you figure out your costs, mark them up (that is, add a percentage to cover overhead and profit) and charge the result to your customer. The price varies directly with your costs. Cost-based systems reduce risks (for profit or loss) and place the responsibility for cost control on the customer (the more they use of your service, the more it costs them.). These systems are good, for example, when the service requirements are very difficult to define: the requirements can be extremely varied and change frequently, yet you can depend on your margins. But because cost control responsibility is shifted to the customer, the customer usually places far greater *administrative* demands on you (to justify your costs), wants more reporting, and often demands an audit. Since the customer has primary responsibility for cost control, you must make sure the customer is not surprised by expenses. You'll find that customers usually feel obliged to question every bill. However, it's all worth it when it's a major account and you want to reduce risk, guarantee your margins, and handle an account that's extremely complicated.

## 2. Costing

Look at your cost accounting reports to determine how well you've priced in the past. For now, you may need to continue to price as you have, but, simply keep margins in mind. Even a *consciousness* about margins is a step in the right direction. You will become more profitable simply by having that frame of mind. *You don't want revenue at any cost: You want profitable revenue.*

Over time, you'll learn more about strategic thinking related to the costing of accounts. Encourage your staff to be accurate in their cost reporting because that information is what you are using to manage your accounts. If you are in a service business and your employees decide to inflate or deflate the amount of time spent working on a project, for example, they take away the flexibility of management to use the information in a way that will better benefit the company. For example, employees who under-report their time don't allow you to go back to a customer for additional fees. And those who inflate their time can make accounts look less profitable than they actually are. In the long run, honest numbers are the sure way to make a business extremely profitable.

## 3. How Account Managers Can Make Accounts More Profitable

There are two obvious ways to increase profitability: get paid more for the products and service you are delivering, and/or control the costs of the products and services. There are many variations on this theme, and I'm sure you know helpful real-life examples of what can be done. Here are a few for starters, but the best solutions depend on the situation you are in:

- Pass on out-of-pocket expenses to the customer. As much as possible, keep out-of-pocket as a separate issue. Or reduce travel on an account. Or arrange for less expensive travel.
- When possible, use the appropriate level of people for the appropriate work. For example, support staff can handle certain jobs cheaper.

### The Role of Cost Accounting

The purpose of cost accounting is to measure the profitability of' an account and it is a mechanism for matching the workload for a customer (or for a product, service or project) to the income received from that customer.

The systems are meant to make your management job easier. They are meant to bring you past the days when you didn't have the information you needed to do a good job. If the systems are not providing you with the information you need, then develop them.

You have to go step by step so you not only have a great product or service, but also know how to sell that product or service and make money on it!

## A Cost Accounting Example
## The Candle-Making Business

It's easy to do cost accounting—by job, by product or by account. So you will soon do one yourself. If you are in the candle-making business, you could pretend you made 50 candles of a certain type. How much do you expect to sell each one for? That would be your revenue line. (Maybe you pretend you have sold one at $15.00 and one person bought ten candles at a reduced rate, and so on.) Let's say your total revenue is $600.

Then you need to figure out your direct expenses. What are the materials and direct labor that went into making those 50 candles? Let's say the materials for the 50 candles—including packaging—is $300 and you spent 15 hours making the candles.

Keep track of your time. You can either do this exercise by valuing your time at a certain amount (say, $15 per hour), and adding it in as one of your expenses, or you can do the calculation without valuing your time at this point and determine what you were actually paid per hour when you look at your profit divided by the number of hours you spent. THIS IS AN IMPORTANT NUMBER. Even if you lose money at the beginning of your business, it's good to know how much you are losing so you can figure some way out of this situation.

So now you have the revenue from the candles ($600) and the direct labor (15 hours at $15 per hour equals $225.) and materials ($300) that went into the candles. Subtract direct labor and materials from the revenue number. ($600 less $525) equals $75 gross profit *after* you have paid yourself. You always want to look at profit in terms of percentages of revenue. $75 is 12.5% of revenue. That's your profit before taxes and overhead.

Overhead includes all expenses that are not directly related to the making of your product or service. This would include your electricity, telephone, marketing literature, postage, the cost of your space, and so on. Yes, you have these expenses and they have to be accounted for, but when a business is so small, it's difficult to figure out what percentage of your overhead should be allocated to this one batch of 50 candles. Overhead allocation calculations can be complex and are not worth it for a business this small.

If you could figure out your overhead, you would have to allocate a portion of it to this batch of candles. Instead, you can look at the numbers and say to yourself: 12.5% profit would be good but I still have to take out overhead and taxes. So—to be comfortable—I need to make at least 30% profit before taxes and overhead.

Even from this brief exercise, you can see that some changes need to be made to make your numbers work out better. You have a choice: charge more per average candle, reduce the materials cost of each candle, or reduce the labor involved in the making of each candle (maybe you teach students or homemakers how to make candles and pay them minimum wage while you supervise them!).

This candle-making example was for one candle product—one type of candle. The owner definitely needs to know the gross profit (before overhead and taxes) on every type of candle. She may have some very elaborate candles that sell for $50 a piece but require so much in time and materials that her profit margin is only 5%. Let's hope she doesn't sell many of those or finds a way to improve her margins on this kind of business.

## Your Chapter Exercise

Now it's *your* turn to do a cost accounting example—by job, by product or by account.

- If you have a catering business, for example, you could cost out one assignment—that would be called *job or project costing.*
- If you have an office cleaning business, you could cost out one *account*—say a business of 15,000 square feet where you take out

the trash, vacuum and clean every night. When they ask you do to extra work, such as cleaning windows, that costs extra. You will have to set up your hypotheses (your assumptions about this account): how many employees they have working there, how crowded it is, how many bathrooms and kitchens they have, and so on, and then how many people you would need to clean this place, how much you would pay them per hour, how much time you would have to spend to supervise, your cost of cleaning materials, and so on.

- If you have a limousine service, you could cost out one day. Assume you have a certain number of calls that day, log the mileage of each ride, the time you spent traveling to pick the person up, the time you spent in the car with the person, gas and other expenses for the day, and, of course, how much you were paid.
- If you have an accounting business, you could do cost accounting for one assignment, say someone's taxes, estimating the number of hours you might spend and how much you would get paid for those hours.

So pick a business and give this a try. Later, you will be glad you understand the process. Don't worry if the numbers are correct—they won't be. But you will have learned a *process* and you will develop the correct numbers in real life when you actually start your business. The exercise right now, however, could point out some major problems that need to be overcome while you are in the planning stage.

••••••••••••••••••••••••••••••••••••••••••••

*I do not believe maximizing profits for the investors is the only acceptable justification for all corporate actions. The investors are not the only people who matter. Corporations can exist for purposes other than simply maximizing profits.*

John Mackey

# Accounting Basics

*Profits are an opinion; cash is a fact.*

(Unknown)

Now that I've made my case for cost accounting, considered by some to be a sophisticated subject, let's get down to some of the basics of accounting.

Record every transaction in its proper place. You will have money coming in and money going out. When you are very small, you may want to keep a simple record book, but then you can move to a simple accounting system and be more professional about it. Keep accurate business records separate from your personal records.

You records will be kept either on a cash basis or an accrual basis, or perhaps a little of both.

## Cash vs. Accrual

*Cash* accounting (generally the method a very small business will use)—is based on actual cash flow in and out of the business. The cash is handled the same way you handle it in your personal checking account.

- You record income not when you make the sale but when you actually receive the cash.
- You record expenses not when you incur the expense (such as when you charge something on your charge card), but when the cash comes out of the business and you pay that bill.

In *accrual* accounting, income and expenses are recorded when they occur. For example, you land an assignment to clean someone's offices. After you clean the offices, you send them an invoice. In the accrual system you would record the income when you send out an invoice. You haven't gotten the cash into your hands. There is no money in the bank for this project, and your cleaning people want to be paid. The amount you invoiced your customer becomes an accounts receivable and then you have to *collect* on that account.

Expenses are recorded when you actually purchase (order) an item and receive a bill, not when you pay for it. Those expenses are accounts payable—you have to pay them, but probably not now. Chances are, your customers will pay you in thirty days and you'll pay your vendors in thirty days. However, this can vary a lot from business to business. So the accrual system can be tricky for a small business.

Businesses with inventory must use the accrual method. Most small service businesses use the cash method.

# Chart of Accounts

You will need a chart of accounts even if you are keeping your records by hand. To develop a chart of accounts, decide what you want to track in your business, and assign a number to each category. Let's just take the basics for your income statement (profit and loss statement).

## Revenue

On the revenue (income) section, let's use account numbers 400 to 500. Record revenue by *source* so you can keep track of where your money is coming from—which items you are selling more of. For example, if Sheila has a flower and candle business, it does her no good at year end to know only that her revenue was $30,000. Where did it come from? Did she sell mostly candles or mostly flowers? So she would need a separate revenue account for candles and a separate one for flowers. Sheila may find that her real revenue is coming from something else, say the delivery charges, so she may decide to track delivery revenue separately as well.

Sheila's chart of accounts on the revenue side may look something like this:

Account # 410—candles
Account # 510—flower arrangements
Account # 580—deliveries

Let's take a look at the revenue some basic businesses may want to track:

- A cleaning business may want to separate the revenue for corporate cleaning from residential cleaning
- A hair salon may want to track separately

the revenue from cutting, coloring and the sale of hair products
- A laundry/dry cleaner business will want to know how much they are bringing in from the washers and dryers vs the dry cleaning
- A deli may want to know how much they are bringing in from prepared food vs beverages.

The income statements record gross amounts, and you would need other record-keeping to break it down even further. That's where your cost accounting comes in.

So, Sheila will assign a number to each source of revenue for her business:

- Such as, 410—candles
- 510—flower arrangements
- 580—deliveries

In addition, she will **ANNOTATE *each transaction***. That is, she will put a comment next to each transaction. If she records:

- 410—$192.00
  - ∆ she already *knows* it's for candles because the revenue was recorded in 410, the account for candles, but Sheila *doesn't* know whether one person bought $192 worth of candles, or what kinds of candles they bought. So she could write instead:
- 410—$192.00—S. Johnson—6 margaritas and 3 daiquiris (some of the types of candles Sheila makes)

If Sheila annotates *each* transaction, she will be able to analyze her records later to understand how her business is working. At The Five O'Clock Club, I review our accounting records periodically (I used to do it very often) to make sure the accountant is annotating each transaction. After all, accountants do not care about analyzing the business. They just care that the money balances. You, however, must direct your accountant to annotate so you can analyze how things are going in your small business.

In the candle and flowers example, Sheila's used up only three numbers for revenue, so she'll have a lot more numbers she can use later. In developing *your* chart of accounts, keep like things together. That is, keep candle-type revenue categories together and flower-type categories together.

She could even set up a separate category for each kind of candle, if she wants—and only if she has just a few of them. She doesn't want her chart of accounts littered with 15 kinds of candles. It's best to have just *major* categories in your chart of accounts—and annotate them.

## Cost of goods sold

- 550—cost of merchandise sold
- 560—freight expense

Many start ups ignore "cost of goods sold" as a separate category because it can be too complicated for novices. If you can't get good advice about how to record cost of good sold, account for them like this:

## Expense

Let's use 600–799 as our account numbers for expense items:

- 600–659—Labor
  - Δ 610—salaries
  - Δ 620—consultants
  - Δ 630—advisors (lawyers, accountants, etc.) but find free services if you have no money
  - Δ 640—taxes paid having to do with labor
- 660–680—Direct supplies (raw materials) having to do with items you sell (as opposed to office supplies)
  - Δ Purchases of wax, colors, wicks, glasses, yarn, food, cleaning supplies, etc. Must be items directly related to the items sold—that is, the ingredients or packaging.
- 690—Property and equipment (computers, cleaning machine for a cleaning business, office desks)

(When you get to this point, ask your accountant. Some of these items could be subject to depreciation and should be listed as assets.)

- 700—Administrative Expenses
  - Δ Office Supplies (710)
  - Δ Postage (711)
  - Δ Telephone (712)
  - Δ Dues and subscriptions, memberships (713)
  - Δ Insurance (714)
  - Δ Auto expenses; travel (such as subways) (715)
- 730—Space and utilities
  - Δ Rent (731)
  - Δ Utilities (electric, etc.) (732)
- 740—Depreciation (such as on furniture and office equipment; chairs, sinks, etc.)
- 800—Taxes (not labor-related)—Federal, state, local, real estate.

## Other Record-Keeping

In a separate log, Sheila could do the cost accounting (product costing, in this case). For each type of candle, she would calculate and record the number sold, the cost to make that type of candle, the selling price and the gross margin (before taxes and overhead) for each type of candle.

Sheila doesn't have to do this continually. Once she has it figured out, she can update her numbers from time to time to see how she is doing. For example, if one of the ingredients now costs more, that would change her formula.

Figure out where you make high margins. For example, the deli we spoke about can almost give away the bagels because they make their margins on the deli items.

Keep track of your orders so you know how much you expect to have coming in. Accounts Receivables is the term for money people owe you. Accounts Payable is the term for money you owe other people.

## Inventory and Supplies

Track how many items you made, how many you sold and how many are in inventory. Keep your inventory at certain levels, depending on how quickly a certain item is moving. For every product or service, know which ones sold well and which ones make you the most money (margins). Also track your raw materials and supplies so you know when to re-order.

## "The Profit is at the Margins."

If that is your mindset, you will:

- *Pinch pennies*. Watch every dollar. Buy used equipment. Try not to buy on credit (interest rates are a killer.) Save money wherever you can. The Five O'Clock Club still ships via the cheapest way possible, and encourages all staff members to save money every chance they get. (However, we do tip delivery people and other workers well. You are not allowed to cheat people out of fair payment, but can and should cut other expenses.)

- *Wind up debt free*. Then you can develop wealth (instead of debt).

- *Not live extravagantly*. Don't *care* what other people think. Just watch your bank account grow.

- *Not spend money on alcohol or cigarettes*. They cost a lot and they're bad for you. Alcohol causes you to do bad things and takes your mind off the business. You can't be productive the next day. When you get drunk, you take away from your possible success. Instead, get high about your busi-

*Our accountant has informed me that if we moved our company to the bottom of the sea, we wouldn't have to pay taxes. So, each one of your will be outfitted with scuba gear.*

ness. I can't imagine Oprah or Mary Kay Ash or Donald Trump getting drunk and thinking about how to cure a hangover. People trying to grow a business don't walk around with hangovers.

When you have your own business, you have an unforgiving boss: your customers. You have to keep sharp.

# Financial Goals, Ratios and Philosophies

Here are a few miscellaneous hints. They may or may not apply to your business, but they are a starting point for deciding what your key ratios should be.

## Key Ratios and Revenue:

- Do not allow payroll costs (direct labor) for a project to exceed ⅓ of the revenue for that project.
- Observe the ratio of direct expense to overhead. We try to keep ours at 1:1. Then we have direct expense of ⅓, overhead of ⅓ and profit of ⅓. What should the ratios be for your business?
- Aim for a certain pretax margin so you can grow the business.
- Go for margins, not volume.
- Go for margins, not volume.
- Go for margins, not volume.

## Controls:

- Keep accurate, computerized financials to control the business.
- If the margins are so weak that there is not enough money to support growth, the business will fold and will also have large, outstanding debt.
- Go for margins, not volume.

## Debt/Expenses:

- Only incur debt that can be repaid.
- Do you really need investment money? Yes, if you will have large capital expenses, such as in a manufacturing company. Otherwise, try to grow your own investment spending out of profits. That way, you'll keep the business and not have to share it with investors—who actually become your boss.
- Thoroughly analyze alternatives before spending money. Those involved in the business should realize that it's their money too. If you spend money on extravagant lunches and elegant furniture, there is less for profit sharing and investment spending.
- Try to think of ways to do things for free or for little money. For example, public relations instead of advertising, or partnering with a company who will throw in the cash for what you are trying to do.
- To be rich later, conserve spending now—except for rational investment spending.

# 15 Helpful Hints for a Profitable Agreement

Here are a few things to keep in mind when you are negotiating with a customer.

1. **Assume the responsibility for making a fair profit.**
   You know how your business works and it's up to you to come up with an agreement that is as fair as possible and that stays that way. And anyway, 99 out of 100 clients want you to make a fair profit.

2. **Explain the specifics.**
   Don't assume the customer knows that much about the business part of your business. The way you get paid may not be simple, and can be very fragile, so you owe it to your customer to make sure he understands.

3. **Don't be afraid to ask.**
   Your goal is a fair profit and the details don't matter so long as the profit is fair. Ask for those details that will allow you to have the profit you deserve.

   For example, you may ask the client to pay for all packaging material, or make sure the customer knows that it's your policy to have one supervisor on site when an event is happening. The customer may say "no problem" and that saves you the trouble of having to go back to him later to get reimbursed for these items.

   And remember that you will not lose an account for aggressively protecting your interests during contract negotiations, but you are likely to be forced to resign accounts—even big name accounts—because they weren't profitable.

   If you happen to lose an account because you pushed too hard, you're probably better off without that loser anyway.

4. **Change your contract as the situation changes.**
   The current arrangement may not always be appropriate so be sure to point this out to the client in the beginning. It's better if you start with the basic premise that your company should make a fair profit and then change the contract accordingly to decide just how you're going to make that profit.

5. **Review your accounts regularly.**
   There is no set agreement that is right for any one client. Getting paid by people is a dynamic situation, and the parties involved expect the contract to change over time. What's working today may not work five years from now, so review your contracts at least annually.

6. **Know thyself.**
   Make sure new projects or new clients fit in with the way you work best. Don't take on new projects or clients simply to increase income unless you need that income to cover overhead. Often those clients you're not good at handling will eat up more overhead than you had expected—and hurt your company's morale as well. So be choosy.

7. **Consciously drop unprofitable accounts.**
   Go through your accounts and see which ones you should get rid of. When you get that new business you've been hoping for, don't add to staff—resign that loser.

8. **Get your prices into line.**
   Oftentimes companies allow their prices to lag behind cost increases. This means that your company is losing precious margins especially during inflationary times. When was the last time you adjusted your prices? It's an arduous job, so many companies put it off. But if your prices are out-of-line, there's no reason to wait a full year before you adjust them again.

9. **Improve the margins on the accounts you retain by running your existing operations more efficiently.**
   Use improved systems and techniques to make your business run more smoothly and profitably.

10. **Charge for your services.**
    A well-managed company does not economize its way into a profit: it charges for its services.

11. **As your company grows, develop appropriate controls.**
    If your company is growing or has grown dramatically, chances are that your controls are out-of-line. The hands-on type of control that worked when have you have five people will not work when you have 30 or more.
    More formal controls are needed and a new dose of control is needed everyday.

12. **Fix your systems now.**
    Good information is the only basis for growth and decision-making that is based on more than a prayer. What's more, when you finally decide to develop good information, it will take two years (!) before you have accurate data by account that will allow you to compare one year's data to the previous year's.

13. **Make your company profit-conscious.**
    Make sure your employees recognize the significance of what they're doing when they ship something by messenger (very expensive) or send everything overnight and early morning. Make them more conscious of how to get things done quickly as well as accurately. They'll become more conscious of how they spend their time—saving money for the clients and making money for your company.

14. **Examine all accounts—even if your company is very profitable.**
    Don't think that an excellent profitability picture allows you to ignore examining every single account. It's not fair to have reasonable clients carrying unreasonable clients. And besides, companies that face a disaster usually had problems that were many years in the making.

15. **The customer should never refuse to pay for bad work.**
    If the work is bad, they should fire you, but they should never refuse to pay you.

# Negotiating a Consulting or Freelance Assignment/ Pricing a Project

*Hey, no matter what—it's better than working at the post office.*

Jerry Sterner, *Other People's Money*

As I said earlier, I have always thought that pricing is one of the most important decisions you can make in your business. It shows that you understand the market and also understand your costs. Pricing is the result of all other analyses put together. You will test your price in the market, and then reexamine it periodically. Pricing is an art as well as a science. This chapter goes into some detail on the pricing of a consulting or freelance assignment. Consulting businesses are among the easiest to price. However, you can see how much goes into even that kind of business.

You will have to learn the intricacies of the kind of business you are going into so you can price your product and services profitably (so you make money) and effectively (so they are appealing to the market). The thinking that goes into consulting pricing will give you some idea of how much you have to learn. You will see many similarities between consulting work and whatever kind of business you will have.

*Here comes the future, rolling towards us like a meteorite, a satellite, a giant iron snowball, a two-ton truck in the wrong lane, careening downhill with broken brakes, and whose fault is it? No time to think about that. Blink and it's here.*

Margaret Atwood, *Good Bones and Simple Murders*

## Pricing Your Services

There are two numbers you need to start with to determine your consulting fee. One is what you are now making—or have been making most recently or what others are making—in the field you are targeting.

We are assuming your consulting will be in the field where you are now considered an expert. If you want to consult in a new field (perhaps as a way to learn that field), instead of your present base plus bonus, use the rate of those at your level in the new field.

The second number to consider is what the market will bear.

*The amount of money you receive will always be in direct proportion to the demand for what you do, your ability to do it, and the difficulty of replacing you.*

Napoleon Hill, paraphrased by Dennis Kimbro,
*Think and Grow Rich: A Black Choice*

## Calculating Your *Cost Rate*

Take your present base plus bonus. Let's say it's $50,000 a year. Add a factor for benefits, such as health insurance. Let's say 20 percent (this includes health insurance, company-paid Social Security, and so on, but does not include paid time off).

So that's $50,000 × 1.20 = $60,000

Divide that number by the number of hours the average person is available to work in a year. We'll use 2,000 hours, just to keep the calculation simple. (You may want to use 1,600 hours, which allows for 10 holidays and 4 weeks of vacation and sick time.)

$60,000/2,000 = $30 per hour.

Your cost is $30 per hour—which is very different from what you will bill your customer. If you were to be able to bill 2,000 hours a year at $30 per hour, you would stay even with what you are now making. However, not only are you unlikely to bill 2,000 hours a year, you still have to buy your own health insurance, put money aside for your vacations, pay your own Social Security, and arrange for your own training, subscriptions, memberships, and so on.

## Calculating Your Low Billing Rate

To account for some of that expense, increase your cost rate by 20 percent—just so you will come out a little higher than your adjusted cost rate. This allows for benefits and also for paid time off. (See chart: Low Billing Rate)

$30 × 1.20 = $36 per hour (Low Billing Rate)

You would try to bill at your low billing rate if you are just starting out or if you are on a long-term consulting assignment with a guaranteed significant number of hours per week.

## Calculating Your Average Billing Rate

If you need to have more than one customer, you probably won't be able to bill 2,000 hours a year because you will have to spend time marketing your services. A rule of thumb if you have no staff is to spend half your time marketing. So to keep even with what you made before, you would have to bill twice your cost rate.

That's $30 × 2 = $60 per hour. (See chart: Average Billing Rate)

You would try to charge the average billing rate for your salary level if you are in a specialized field and in demand. You would also try this rate if you are a serious independent consultant and want to sell your consulting services long-term.

> **A rule of thumb for short-term consulting fees is twice your cost. You will need to make up for the time you spend marketing.**

..........................................

*Maury had enormous admiration for Bennett's grandfather, a self-made man who had opened the store by himself in 1934, a man who always believed things would turn out in his favor and who made things turn out in his favor.*

Alan Lightman, *Good Benito*

## A MODEL FOR ESTIMATING YOUR BILLING RATE

| Base Salary & Bonus | Adj. Base = Base × 1.20 for benefits | COST (Adj.Base/ 2000) | Low Billing Rate[1] (cost × 1.2) | Aver. Billing Rate[2] (cost × 2) | High Billing Rate[3] (cost × 3) | Aver. per diem rate (aver. billing × 7) | MARKET RATES | My Tentative Rate |
|---|---|---|---|---|---|---|---|---|
| $20,000 | $24,000 | $ 12/hr | $ 14.40/hr | $ 24/hr | $ 36/hr | $ 168/day | | |
| $30,000 | $36,000 | $ 18/hr | $21.60 | $36 | $54 | $252 | | |
| $40,000 | $48,000 | $ 24/hr | $28.80 | $48 | $72 | $336 | | |
| $50,000 | $60,000 | $ 30/hr | $36 | $60 | $90 | $420 | | |
| $75,000 | $90,000 | $ 45/hr | $54 | $90 | $135 | $630 | | |
| $100,000 | $120,000 | $ 60/hr | $72 | $120 | $180 | $840 | | |
| $125,000 | $150,000 | $ 75/hr | $90 | $150 | $225 | $1,050 | | |
| $150,000 | $180,000 | $ 90/hr | $108 | $180 | $270 | $1,260 | | |
| $200,000 | $240,000 | $120/hr | $144 | $240 | $360 | $1,680 | | |
| $250,000 | $300,000 | $150/hr | $180 | $300 | $450 | $2,100 | | |
| $300,000 | $360,000 | $180/hr | $216 | $360 | $540 | $2,520 | | |
| $500,000 | $600,000 | $300/hr | $360 | $600 | $900 | $4,200 | | |

[1] Low Billing Rate. Use this rate if you are just starting out, or if you are on a long-term consulting assignment with a guaranteed significant number of hours per week.

[2] Average Billing Rate. Use this rate if you are in a specialized field and in demand. You may also use this rate if you are a serious independent consultant and want to sell your consulting services long-term. You will need to make up for the time you spend marketing and so on.

[3] High Billing Rate. If you have or are setting up a consulting firm, the rule of thumb is to bill out at three times labor cost to cover the cost of overhead, which includes support staff who are not billable, rent, and marketing.

## Calculating Your High Billing Rate

If you are well-established as a consulting firm with lots of overhead, such as office space and administrative support, two times cost will probably not be enough to cover your overhead. The standard factor for this situation is three times cost. In addition, if you are seriously starting a consulting firm (rather than being an independent consultant representing only yourself), you would most likely charge the three-times rate for every billable member of your staff, or for each person you bring in to work on a project.

Finally, if you are well-known in your field, you may also insist on three times your cost rate—or, lucky you, whatever the market will bear.

$30 × 3 = $90 per hour.
(See chart: High Billing Rate)

Charge this rate if you are well-known in your field, or to cover your overhead if you have or are setting up a consulting firm. Overhead includes support staff who are not billable, rent, and marketing.

• • • • • • • • • • • • • • • • • • • • • • • • • • • • •

*You work Saturdays? Well, you must make good money. Well, so you hate it, I'm sorry, I can't help that. What are your aspirations, in that case?*

Craig Lucas, *Prelude to a Kiss*

## Your *Market Worth* Is Whatever the Market Will Bear

When I'm hiring someone as a consultant, I ask them their hourly rate, multiply it in my head by 2,000, and decide if the person would be worth that much on-staff. For example, if someone wants to charge me $25 per hour, I estimate whether that person would be worth $50,000 on staff including benefits. That way, I can quickly assess whether the person is worth it to me.

If there are plenty of people who can do the same job for less, I can simply find someone else. If, however, this person is a known expert, my friends tell me that he or she is reliable, or if there is some other reason for me to think that this person is special, I may be willing to pay more than the typical going rate.

When you think about the rates you will charge as a consultant, remember that someone-will be deciding whether or not you are worth it. So decide whether you are someone who can be easily replaced or are unique and in demand.

*What the market will bear* will be the most important determinant of what you can charge. What you charge will probably change over time. At first, you simply want to get a few jobs and a few clients. Later, as you become better-known in your field, the amount and the way you charge will change.

You must test the waters. Talk to others in your field and find out what they are charging; network in to see prospective hiring managers and see what they would pay. When all else fails, start negotiating with the hiring manager and observe his or her reaction.

Follow exactly the rules in the *Mastering the Job Interview and Winning the Money Game*. After you are well established and have a name in the market, there is a lot of flexibility. I have counseled clients who have ended up working two days a week for one company and two days a week for another company—getting a flat $100,000 a year from each company! These clients had paid their dues in their respective fields

and deserved what they got. They each worked only four days a week, and if they lost an assignment at one company, they still had the other one to keep them going while they looked for a replacement. Not a bad way to earn a living.

•••••••••••••••••••••••••••••••••••••••••

*In playing baseball, or in life, a person occasionally gets the opportunity to do something great. When that time comes, only two things matter: being prepared to seize the moment and having the courage to take your best swing.*

Hank Aaron, former baseball player, commencement address to Emory University School of Law, May 1995

## Corporate Rates

Although the three-times rate is standard for organizations with overhead, companies use different numbers of hours as the base. That is, instead of using 2,000, they may use 1,600 or even as low as 1,300 to 1,400 hours. This increases the hourly rate. Or they may hike up the direct labor rates by including not only base plus bonus but also all benefits, payroll taxes, estimated raises, car allowances, and so on.

Then they come up with a rate card, which may contain inflated rates. When it's time to negotiate, they may come down quite a bit from their rate card.

For example, one company's *rates to use in pricing projects* are listed below. Use a billing rate of $225/hr. or $1,800/day for:

- Employees with salaries in the $65,000 to $80,000 range
- Outside consultants who cost us more than $500 per day

Use a billing rate of $190/hr. or $1,500/day for:

- Employees with salaries in the $50,000 to $64,000 range
- Anyone not on staff who costs us $300 to $500 per day

Use a billing rate of $150/hr. or $1,200/day for:

- Professional staff with salaries less than $50,000
- Anyone not on staff who costs us $150 to $275 per day

Use a billing rate of $50/hr. or $400/day for:

- Administrative support staff
- All temps assigned to this project

You, too, may want to create a rate card for your consulting firm. But be sure to be realistic about your worth in the market.

## Setting Your Rates

When you are starting out, you will probably use just one system for charging your clients, such as an hourly rate.

When you are experienced, you may still wind up charging every client the same rate or each client a different rate. For example, you may have one or two clients who form a stable core for you, and you may have gotten far enough in your career that you are on a monthly retainer with them. You may charge other clients an hourly fee.

You may charge one client per project, one a low hourly fee, and another a high hourly fee. You may charge a large corporation a higher rate than a small company, a for-profit organization more than you charge a not-for-profit (although not necessarily).

Your rates may differ by geographic area. You may charge a certain rate in the big urban areas and a lower rate in the countryside, or one rate for one part of the country and another rate for a different part.

If you are offering your services to individuals, you may use a sliding scale depending on the person's ability to pay, the way that many therapists do.

Finally, you may charge different rates for different kinds of work. When I am hiring a public relations person, to name one example, I may hire someone who is already working full-time

for someone else and wants to earn extra money on the side. That person may charge me a certain hourly fee for the brainy work, such as developing strategy or writing press releases, and a lower hourly rate for the *mindless* work, such as stuffing envelopes.

> Find out the standard fee arrangements for the industries or fields that you are targeting. The variety is endless.

## Fee Structures

Therapists and attorneys charge per hour. Workshop leaders usually charge per diem. Determine how people in your field charge, and do the same—at least when you are starting out.

The two basic structures are per time (such as per hour or per diem) and per project. There are almost infinite variations on charging structures, from a per-head rate for running a seminar, to a percent of gross billing (as in the old days of advertising). There are certain fields in which a success fee rules (that is, if the project works, you make lots of money; if it doesn't, you don't). And then there are lots of combination fee structures, such as a success fee for completion with a guaranteed nominal base amount. If you are working with a start-up company and already have a full range of consulting assignments, you may be paid in stock. Other common arrangements are retainer, commission, percent of sales, bonus, or a combination. Find out the standard fee structures for the industries or fields you are targeting. The variety is endless.

For now, we will cover the *per time* and *per project* structures. The thought processes behind these form the core of most other billing methods.

When considering the fee structure you want to use for a certain situation, remember that some structures are low risk with a predictable reward. Others are high risk (that is, you may wind up losing money or making no money) but high reward (big bucks if things work out). All fee structures can be analyzed by using this criterion.

........................................

*We are what we repeatedly do. Excellence, then, is not an act, but a habit.*

Aristotle

## Project Pricing versus Time-Based Pricing

The benefit of pricing per project, rather than charging a time-based rate, is that you could make much more money that way. You could also lose money if you price incorrectly or if you do not control your costs while delivering the service.

With time-based pricing, on the other hand, you can be sure of getting paid for every hour you work. As long as you get paid, there is no risk on your part. However, you cannot make a great deal of money.

If you simply want to pick up some consulting work while you search for a full-time job, you may want to stick to time-based pricing so you are not at risk. If you want to have a consulting business, you may want to become very good at project pricing (although actually many consulting businesses charge solely by time-based pricing).

## Out-of-Pocket or Pass-Along Expenses

Depending on the kind of work you are doing, certain expenses may be passed along directly to your client. Out-of-pocket expenses include items such as telephone, postage, and overnight mail expenses. Travel could also be considered an out-of-pocket expense—depending on the situation.

Even entertainment sometimes falls into this category. If I hire a public relations consultant, I expect that person to keep track of out-of-pocket expenses and bill me monthly. This is standard operating practice. However, check with others in your field or industry to be sure that this practice applies.

Pass-along expenses could include the cost of hiring an outside photographer, for example. Established consulting firms often *mark up* the cost of these pass-along expenses, say by 15 percent, to make a profit on them. In many cases, this is acceptable.

Pass-along expenses are not to be confused with the cost of outside consultants you may use as if they were part of your staff. These outside consultants would be billed the same as if they were on your staff, but you would have to think through the multiplier to use: perhaps two or three times the rate they charge you. Of course, you have to do what seems reasonable.

........................................

*"How did I deal with racism?" he asked rhetorically at a speech in San Antonio, Texas. "I beat it. I said, 'I am not going to destroy your stereotype. I'm proud to be black. You* carry this *burden of racism, because I'm not going to.'"*

Colin Powell, former Chairman of the Joint Chiefs of Staff, as quoted in *Time,* July 10, 1995

## Time-Based Pricing

If you are in a field that normally charges an hourly rate, as is the case with a therapist or attorney, you need to find out what you are worth in the field and then develop yourself to the point where you have no trouble saying with confidence, "My rate is $50 per hour."

But if you are doing project work for which you want to be paid hourly, that is another matter. As the hiring manager, I will be afraid of how much time you will spend on the project. If you tell me that your rate is $30 per hour, I will still want an estimate of how much a particular job will cost me. I cannot afford to pay you $30 an hour to do graphic design work, for example, if there is no limit. You may decide to fiddle with a design for 40 hours *just to make it perfect* when all I wanted was something that was *good enough*.

You may stay up all night working at home on your slow computer. Why should I pay you $30 an hour for that work, when you could have gotten it done in half that time if you had worked on my faster computer? You may have decided to make four different sketches for me, but if you were working out of my office instead of yours, I might have told you exactly what I wanted and saved all that extra time.

Therefore, if I am paying you per hour for a project, I want to know the limit on this project. Perhaps you will do 15 hours of work at your regular rate and then come back to me to see if everything is on track before you rack up 50 hours for which you expect me to pay.

If you are willing to do the job on-site, there is less risk that you will go off in a direction I don't want. The on-site work is safer for both of us. You will get paid for every hour you work, and I will know what you are doing for the time you are billing me.

If you are working for an hourly rate, you will charge less for per diem work and even less for a monthly rate. Of course, you must spell out the number of hours you will work for a per-diem rate. If you charge $200 per day and don't specify the number of hours in a day, your employer may expect 10- or 12-hour days. If you charge per month, you must specify that it is an 8.0-hour day (or 7.5-hour day), 20-day month (there are 4.3 weeks in an average month; 21.5 work days in an average month—not allowing for holidays or other time off). If you don't specify the number of days you will work per month, your employer will expect you to be there every day for the agreed-upon monthly rate. You will never have a day off.

If you are charging an hourly rate for on-site presentations or for other work for which you have preparation time, make sure your hourly rate includes your preparation time.

If you are required to be on-site, bear in mind that most consultants charge a 4-hour minimum to make the unbillable travel worthwhile. However, if you are doing a lot of work for a certain client, you may come in for an important meeting and charge only for the time the meeting takes, even if it is only two hours. That's called establishing good will.

If you are straight hourly, you do not charge, of course, when you and your prospective client are discussing a possible assignment or when you both are reviewing the work you did.

## How Long Will the Assignment Last?

Another consideration is the length of the assignment. If you should normally get $86 per hour but the company wants to pay you per diem, you would not normally charge the company $86 × 8.0 hours = $688. If it's likely to be an 8-hour day, you would then charge them, say, $600 per diem ($86 × 7.0 hours). And if the company wants to pay you monthly, you probably would not charge them $600 × 21.5 = $12,900 (because the average month has 21.5 work days). Instead, you would say that your fee is normally about $15,000 ($688 × 21.5), but you will charge them only $10,000 per month for a 20-day month with, for example, a 6-month minimum with 60 days' (or 30 days) notice to terminate. That's still $60,000 for 6 months, with time to search if the contract is not extended.

Your rates are reduced for longer amounts of time because you will have to do less marketing than if you sold your services by the hour.

· · · · · · · · · · · · · · · · · · · · · · · · · · · · · · · · ·

*Man is born with his hands clenched, but his hands are open in death, because on entering the world he desires to grasp everything, but on leaving, he takes nothing away.*

The Talmud

## Billable versus Unbillable Time

Sometimes every hour you spend is billable, and sometimes it isn't. This can be tricky, and you should think about it with regard to the situation you are in. For many of your assignments, you may bill a straight hourly, per diem, or other kind of rate. But if you wind up at a company on a regular basis, you may attend weekly staff meetings, travel on company business, and so on. May you charge for this time at your normal rate? It depends. If you are at a large company, and being paid on a monthly basis, there is no discussion. They are paying you monthly, so that includes everything.

If, however, you are being paid hourly, you may or may not be paid for extraordinary travel time. Large companies may sometimes pay you for travel at half your normal rate (depending on the circumstances), while smaller companies may pay you nothing for travel. This is something you may want to negotiate if you think it could get out of hand.

If you are attending staff or other meetings—where you aren't really *working*—may you charge for that time? Again, it depends. If you are on an hourly basis, you may be able to charge half-time for regular (such as weekly) staff meetings. If the staff meeting is an unusual event, you may be able to charge at your regular rate. If you are attending a training seminar just to learn a new skill, for example, it is unlikely that you will be able to charge anything. However, if you are de-livering a seminar, you would, of course, charge at your full billing rate. After all, you are working to your full capacity.

To keep a good relationship, make sure you do not nickel-and-dime your client to death.

Throw in extra time for free sometimes (and let them know that). Perhaps call in with an idea on days when you are not there—gratis. Give a little to an important client just to keep a good relationship going.

## What Will Your Market Bear?

After all of that, consider what is reasonable and customary in the market and for the company to which you are selling yourself. Would they pay someone like you $86 an hour? Or is that unlikely? If the market tends to pay only $50 an hour, that is what you are likely to get. If you

get that amount, just be sure you understand that you are not making what you used to make—un-less you manage to work 2,000 hours a year (or 1,600

hours, which allows for 4 weeks' vacation and 10 paid holidays).

................................................

*Life is to be lived. If you have to support yourself, you had bloody well better find some way that is going to be interesting. And you don't do that by sitting around wondering about yourself.*

Katherine Hepburn

## Project-Based Pricing

Before you can possibly know what you want to charge a customer, you must figure out how much it will cost you to deliver the project. Go through the following steps:

**Step 1.**
List in detail the services you will provide and who will provide them.

**Step 2.**
Price out these services using the billing rate for each person. This means you must be able to estimate accurately how much time you and/or every other person will spend on the project. Then you will apply your billing rate (perhaps two times cost).

**Step 3.**
Get it in writing.

**Step 4.**
Control your costs.
Now let's examine each step in detail.

### Step 1: List in detail the service you will provide.

List everything you will provide—both labor and out-of-pocket expenses. Be sure to include all planning and project-management time, as well as all clerical and other support time. It is not enough to include just the time you actually spend with your client. For out-of-pocket expenses, be sure to include items such as travel and printing costs.

Then estimate how much of each service will be provided. For example, how many hours do you think this project will take overall, for each component of it, and for each person working on it? How much travel will be involved (apart from routine travel to and from their office)?

## Step 2: Figure out the price of each of those services.

Note the actual person or the level of the person who will be delivering each piece. Then use the billing rate for each person to determine the price of each service.

After you have priced each piece of the project, add up all the prices. This will tell you the total amount of revenue you will need on this project. It will also give you a feel for what goes into your project.

......................................

*You have no idea what a poor opinion I have
of myself—and how little I deserve it.*

W. S. Gilbert

## Step 3: Get it in writing.

Make sure the client understands what is included in the project and what is not. In Step 1, you detailed everything that would be included in the project. Make sure the client understands this.

Put it in writing. As you get into the project, both you and the client will probably think of lots more you could do. Or the client will change the specifications.

All of that is fine as long as the client understands what is included in the project fee and what they must pay extra for (perhaps at your hourly billing rate) because it is outside the scope of what you originally agreed upon.

## Step 4: Control your costs.

You must keep track of the number of hours you and everyone working for you spend on the project—or you most likely will lose money, perhaps a lot of money.

Many consultants are so happy to get the projects that they overdeliver to the extent that they lose money. You must track the number of hours you spend on the project. In Step 1, you detailed all of the services you would deliver.

Now you must see how you did against those projections of what you thought the project would include. I have seen everyone from fine artists to senior executives bid on jobs expecting to spend a certain amount of time on them, and wind up spending twice or three times what they had originally projected. Then they are disappointed that they cannot make money.

......................................

*The amount of money you receive will always be in
direct proportion to the demand for what you do, your
ability to do it, and the difficulty of replacing you.*

Napoleon Hill paraphrased by Dennis Kimbro,
*Think and Grow Rich: A Black Choice*

## Starting Out

When you are starting out, it may be that you have to *give away the store* to get experience. You have to figure out what the market will bear, perhaps take what you can get, build up your credentials, and market yourself to other companies. You may even decide to do a small assignment for free—perhaps for a not-for-profit or for a friend—just so you can say you are doing that kind of work.

On the other hand, you may think you are in a weak negotiating position when in fact you are not. I have worked with many an executive whose initial thought was to undercharge dramatically for his or her services. Follow the rules for basic Five O'Clock Club salary negotiation. If there are lots of people who can do what you do, and if you have no way to separate yourself from your competition, then you are in a weaker negotiating position.

On the other hand, if you are offering a service that is somewhat unique and you cannot be easily replaced, you are in a solid negotiating position.

*Occasionally I would start thinking how such dull people could make money. I should have known that money-making has more to do with emotional stability than with intellect.*

J. P. Marquand, *Women and Thomas Harrow*

# Part Nine

## Putting it All Together

# The One-Hour Business Plan

*Take up one idea. Make that one idea your life—think of it, dream of it, live on that idea. Let the brain, muscles, nerves, every part of your body, be full of that idea, and just leave every other idea alone. This is the way to success, that is the way great spiritual giants are produced.*

Swami Vivekananda

Jared had an idea a week. "My girlfriend and I make soap at night. We want our own soap business." Later, he mentioned ideas for a tourist business, then a dating service: "Some people are making a lot of money running dating services. I like people. I could do that." And on it went.

Jared is just one more American with loads of ideas. But it would take very little to make him someone more serious. It would take a one-hour business plan written on one page. He just needs to write down the key elements of his business idea, and he will actually have a chance of doing something and succeeding at it. Here's the process you can follow with every business idea that occurs to you.

***At the top of the page***, succinctly write down the business concept. Is Jared thinking about a computer-based dating service, a one-on-one matching service, or one of those "meet a person every three minutes at a party" kind of service? What does he mean by "a dating business?" He needs to be more specific, and it will take only a sentence or two.

***In the top third of the page***, describe the market need or want. If no one needs or wants your product or service, it will be difficult to convince anyone to buy. Here, list everything you can about the market: whom you would target, how you would market to them, how you would price your product or service, and so on—including more about your competition.

***In the middle third of the page***, describe your product or service and how you see it as being different from your competitors'. You don't need to write much, but you do need to fill up one-third of a page. And while Jared's doing this, at least he's not blabbering on about another business idea.

***In the third third***, analyze the idea's profit potential. What would you charge? What would your expenses be? How much would you actually make per customer? How many customers do you need to have to make a decent profit from this idea?

Now, that's not hard. Whenever you have a business idea, do this quickie analysis and decide whether it's worth your while to go further with the idea. What you write within one hour on one page will not be entirely correct: it's merely a hypothesis. But it will move you from idea to reality. As I always say: "Ideas are cheap. Execution is everything." Jared will now have to spend a lot of time—the average person spends two years—researching his market and further developing his idea before he is ready to hang out the "open for business" sign. During those two years, he will continually test his market, perhaps even matching up a few people to test his hypothesis and develop his systems.

If you have dozens of ideas, narrow down those that are worth exploring by developing a one-hour business plan. Then select three of them and conduct more intensive research.

And if you meet someone like Jared, who comes up with one brilliant business idea after another, just hand him the worksheet on the following page and ask him to fill it out.

. . . . . . . . . . . . . . . . . . . . . . . . . . . . . .

*An idea that is developed and put into action is more important than an idea that exists only as an idea.*

Buddha

. . . . . . . . . . . . . . . . . . . . . . . . . . . . . .

*Often the difference between a successful person and a failure is not one has better abilities or ideas, but the courage that one has to bet on one's ideas, to take a calculated risk—and to act.*

Andre Malraux

. . . . . . . . . . . . . . . . . . . . . . . . . . . . . .

*Adults are always asking little kids what they want to be when they grow up because they're looking for ideas.*

Paula Poundstone

## The One-Hour Business Plan Worksheet

*The Business Idea*

*The Market* (everything about the market for your product or service)

*The Product or Service* (everything about your product or service)

*The Proof of Profitability* (everything about the dollars)

## Your All-Important Notebook and Hanging Files

The One-Hour Business Plan Worksheet is the exciting beginning of developing your business concept. Remember, you may wind up exploring three, four or even more business concepts before you pick the one you actually want to implement. That's okay. The process of exploring is worth it and will save you a few failures later.

As you start exploring business ideas, you can become more organized. Carry around a notebook like the favorite one you used in school. Ideally, it should be bound, not loose-leaf and small enough to carry—perhaps 5" x 8". Carry it with you everywhere. Jot down things people tell you, ideas that you think of to make your product or service better, even the kind of lifestyle you want to lead, the way you want to treat employees, how people should dress, what the office layout will look like, and the kinds of customers you think you want to work with. When you go to a trade show, chat with people in the subway, see a shop that presents a product the way you want to present yours, jot down your thoughts.

Your notebook will prove invaluable to you in the start-up years of your business. Later on, you will never remember the conversations you had—or find the scrap piece of paper you wrote it on unless you write these down in your notebook. Then, you will be able to refer to your notebook for ideas and inspiration.

In addition, you will gather literature, newspaper and magazine clippings and Internet print-outs. Organize this part of your research as well: use hanging file folders! One file could be for your competitor's brochures, another for other marketing ideas. One could be for trade show literature having to do with some aspect of your idea. Another could contain sources of inexpensive office furniture, equipment or supplies. Others could have to do with small business management, such as licensing and other legal requirements, managing people, financing sources, and so on.

## Build on Your One-Hour Business Plan

Spending one hour to actually think about a business idea is a good start and should fill you with excitement and eagerness to go to the next step. Now you need more. Unless you want outside financing, you don't need to develop a business plan that's as formal as the one presented in the next section, but you *do* need to formally think through much more than one hour's worth. That hour was just to get you over the hump. Most people hate the thought of doing a business plan, but none of my clients has resisted the idea of writing down just one hour's worth. Now, research more and write more. You've read some of the case studies in this book, such as Yadira's. You have to put the same effort into thinking about your business.

Here are some thoughts to inspire you. And be sure to return to the chapters and case studies to help you think of more.

### Description of the Market Need or Want.

- What evidence do you have that there is a market need or want? (Answer in as much detail as possible.)
  △ What problem will your product or service solve?
  △ Have you found any research to substantiate this? (If so, print it out and put it in the appropriate hanging folder.)
- Is the timing right? Do people need it now, or are you too late or too early?
  △ What do people do now to solve this need or want?
  △ What's wrong with that?
  △ How will your product or service better solve their want or need?
- Who will buy your product?
  △ Will you target the corporate or the retail market or some other market?
  △ Specifically, who is your target? How will you identify them?
  △ For example, if corporations—what kind? What is the title of the deci-

sion-maker or influencer? If you want to target, for example, "companies experiencing extreme growth," can you identify the likely purchaser?

△ If individuals, who are they? Are they identifiable? For example, if you say "People who want a cleaner house," how will you find them?

△ Who is your competition? Can you compete against them?

• Is the customer able to buy?

△ Is this something they can afford or justify?

△ Is the market already saturated—or is there room for you?

• What is your targeted geographic area?

• What is the market size and potential?

• What effect will the economy have on buyers' decisions?

△ Is your product or service more likely to sell in a down economy or an up economy?

△ Will you market or price your product differently under different economic conditions?

• Can your prospective customer afford to buy it? If, for example you are targeting administrative assistants within organizations, will they be able to get approval to purchase your product or service? If you are targeting kids, will they be able to get their parents to buy it? Who might you target instead?

△ Is your product or service going to be a difficult sell? What logic would the influencer have to use to get someone else to approve this purchase?

△ How will the influencer or purchaser be able to overcome budgetary restrictions? How can you help with this?

• Is the customer likely to buy?

△ What other priorities must the customer consider before spending money on your product or service?

△ What will influence them to buy?

• What are the perceived benefits of your product or service?

△ How will customers see your product or service versus your competitors'?

• How will you make people aware of differences?

△ What kinds of promotional techniques will you use? Which are the least expensive and most effective?

△ Which techniques do your competitors use? Should you do the same or do something different?

• How will you price your product or service for various markets?

• Are there other products or services you could develop or offer to the same customer base?

• What else should be covered in this "marketing" section?

## Description of Your Product or Service:

• Is there a real product or service here? (Many people come up with "ideas" that can't happen in real life.)

• What, in detail, is your product or service?

• Is it something that can actually be made?

△ How will it be made?

△ What goes into making it?

△ What are the roadblocks—legal, economic, pragmatic—that could stand in the way of actually making or developing this product or service?

△ What don't you know that you ought to know more about?

• Do you have the resources to build and/or deliver the product or service?

△ Do you have experience with this product or service? Can you get the experience? Have you been involved with virtually all areas of knowledge required to build or develop this product or service? What will it take?

△ Are you committed to this concept and do you have the commitment of other necessary people?

△ Do you have the financing or can you finance it yourself as you go along?

△ How long will it take to develop the

product or service—to the stage where you can go out and sell it? (You can start selling it before you have it.)

- Will the market be satisfied with your product or service?
  - △ Can you verify this in the market by testing the idea, the price, the delivery mechanism, and the product literature?
  - △ Will the market find it cost-justifiable?
- Can you support the product or service once it is sold? How?
- What other concerns will the customer have about the product or service? (For example, tangibles such as security, upgradability or integration with other products or intangibles such as prestige, comfort, appearance.)

## Profitability Analysis (price, cost, number of customers needed, etc.):

- Develop your price list.
- Develop a projected P&L for a sensible number of years: projected revenue and expenses as well as overhead.
- How much will the average customer spend? Will you have repeat sales or will a customer buy only once?
- What is your profit margin per customer?
- How many do you need to sell to make a living?
- Include here all other financial considerations, such as quantity discounts, cost of supplies and price-breaks on purchasing quantities.
- Develop your start-up costs and sources of funding.
  - △ If you need a million dollars, for example, is there any chance you will ever be able to raise that money? Would investors give you a million dollars? (I've had too many clients who came up with idea that required serious money, but they had no background in the product or service area. No one would *ever* invest in them. Even if you have a

very credible background, it could take two years or more of constant work to find investors. And then they wind up being your boss! Some businesses sensibly need outside funding, but most businesses are bootstrapped (that is, starting a business with little or no external financing). Don't automatically jump to thinking you need investors. It's great having no one to answer to and you keep all the money yourself!

- △ Can you bootstrap the financing.
- △ Can you sell your product or service before you actually build it and tell the customer that you will have it for him or her in two months (or whatever time it would take)? That way, you won't have upfront development costs, and will have tested your market. If no one is interested in your product, don't invest money in it. Instead, rethink your product offering!
- Now, can you make a living at this?
  - △ What kind of income do you expect to have?
  - △ How long will it take you to get to this level?
  - △ Do you have the mindset to live frugally for many years while you work this out?
  - △ Is it workable? Will this idea ever make money?

You need real, live customers to take this idea out of the theoretical and into the real world. If, for example, you want to have a cleaning service aimed at small businesses:

- Gather competitive information,
- Perhaps even go to work for one (who will not be a future competitor) for a little while to see what it is like on the inside,
- Call some small businesses to ask how they like their current cleaning service,
- Don't be put off when they say they already use someone (*everyone* you will try to sell to already has a cleaning service),

- Tell them how you are better than their current service, and
- See how they respond.

Now you are in business without having invested very much at all. You are now *marketing*, and without customers you have no business.

Do you really want investor money? Thousands of people got investor money during the dot.com boom. The heads of those companies all thought they were geniuses. But they weren't really running companies at all. If you don't have customers, you don't have a company. All they were doing was playing with someone else's money. The "burn rate" (and there were plenty of books written about that subject) referred to the amount of investor money they burned within a certain period of time. What a thing to brag about!!

Later, when their businesses folded and they had to find real jobs again, their arrogance kept them from being hired. They thought they had done so much—managed so many people, bought so many things, had so many commercials developed. They were playing at running a business. Having all that money made them dumb. They didn't have to fight for sales: they simply asked for a second and third round of financing, and each time, the investors wound up with a bigger slice of the pie until there was nothing for them. They never learned to bring in customers or change their product or service to make it more appealing to customers. They kept talking to each other—loudly—and told the rest of us that there was a new day, a new business model, and the old business models were dead.

They were wrong.

Focus on marketing and developing a product or service the market wants and is willing to pay for. Good luck.

# Developing Your Business Plan

*New ideas pass through three periods: 1) It can't be done. 2) It probably can be done, but it's not worth doing. 3) I knew it was a good idea all along!*

Arthur C. Clarke

The One-Hour Business Plan and its off-shoots are more important than a formal business plan. With The One-Hour Business Plan, you are thinking about your business so you can run it correctly and in a satisfying way. Take it as far as you can—without concern for outside funding. A formal business plan is meant primarily to sell your idea to outsiders and can waylay you from thinking about how to really run your business. With a formal business plan, you are in a selling mode, want to impress others and may not be completely honest.

## Developing a Business Plan

You can find plenty of sample business plans online. For example, you can go to Google, and key in "business plans" and the type of business you are interested in. Or get free business plans at www.bplans.com, www.blackenterprise.com or www.entrepreneur.com/businessplan/a-z/. You may find other formats through the Small Business Administration, but they all cover basically the same areas.

After you have developed the One-Hour Business Plan and its offshoots, there are three important reasons to develop a thorough business plan:

1. It provides a systematic evaluation of the feasibility of your business concept and the profit potential of the options that exist for developing the business opportunity.
2. It serves as the primary tool for attracting the financing needed to grow the business in a timely and well—planned fashion.
3. It can be used as a "game plan" for successfully starting and operating the business.

### Parts of the Business Plan.

Generally speaking, there are six basic parts of a complete business plan:

1. The Business Concept

2. The Market Plan
3. The Operations Plan
4. The Financial Plan
5. Risk Assessment and Management
6. Supporting Documents

1. *The Business Concept* pinpoints what the venture intends to accomplish in the marketplace. This section presents a clear and concise statement of the business opportunity and the company's objectives. This includes a description of the products or services being offered, the market need to be addressed, and the unique features ("plus values") of the products or services that will set the company apart in a competitive marketplace.

2. *The Market Plan* shows the strength of the business concept and the way to reach potential customers. This section presents your analysis of the market for your product or service. This includes an evaluation of the competition and your strategy for tapping the market. A careful market plan will form the basis for your sales program, which turns analysis and general strategy into a set of tactics for getting potential customers to become satisfied buyers.

3. *The Operations Plan* shows that the business can be run successfully . . . high quality products and services can be produced and delivered under competent management. This section describes the operations and management requirements to successfully run your business. An important part of the operations plan is a discussion of the management team and its qualifications and responsibilities.

4. *The Financial Plan* shows the feasibility of the business in dollars and cents and its need for capital. This section provides detailed estimates of startup and operating expenses, projected sales and earnings, and the cash flow through the business. It also identifies the types, sources, and uses of capital available.

5. *The Risk Analysis* section removes your "rose colored" glasses by making you work through potential problems and solutions in advance. This section of the business plan discusses the key risks involved in the startup and development of the business, and outlines the steps that can be taken to minimize those risks.

6. *The Supporting Documents* section includes any legal and technical information essential to the business such as contracts, licenses, patents and trademarks, copyrights, insurance policies, leases, warranties, and partnership agreements. It should also include testimonial letters from outside parties about the quality of the company's products and management, and hopefully credible commitments to purchase your products once they are available.

You will find plenty of books written about business plans, and you should buy one or two when you decide you want a formal business plan. However, they don't tell you how to determine whether your idea is a good one or even the right one for you. That's why you need to start with this book.

• • • • • • • • • • • • • • • • • • • • • • • • • • •

*The way to get good ideas is to get lots of ideas, and throw the bad ones away.*

Dr. Linus Pauling

• • • • • • • • • • • • • • • • • • • • • • • • • • •

*Everyone is in love with his own ideas.*

Carl Gustav Jung

• • • • • • • • • • • • • • • • • • • • • • • • • • •

*He was a multi-millionaire. Wanna know how he made all of his money? He designed the little diagrams that tell which way to put batteries in.*

Stephen Wright

*I know quite certainly that I myself have
no special talent; curiosity, obsession and
dogged endurance, combined with self-
criticism, have brought me to my ideas.*

Albert Einstein

........................................

*Nearly every man who develops an idea works
it up to the point where it looks impossible,
and then he gets discouraged. That's not
the place to become discouraged.*

Thomas Alva Edison

# Planning the Stages of Your Organization's Growth

*A journey of a thousand miles begins with a single step.*

Chinese Proverb

As important as it is to have a vision of your future, it's not enough. You need to test it realistically and have a plan for getting there. You may want to hedge your bets and come up with a few scenarios for your future. Then you can explore each one to see which is the most fun for you, as well as the most doable.

Think as big and as long term as you can. Then you have to figure out how to get from here to there, a step at a time. Otherwise, it may seem impossible. But you can develop a plan of what you can and should do first, then second, and so on—until you have planned the steps to developing an organization that fits your long-term vision. For example, to start with you may imagine yourself having "a job and a dream"—a day job to earn money while you pursue your dream on the side.

Whatever your vision, you are more likely to achieve it if it is backed by a plan. Plans, however, are not rigid. As you start to investigate and implement your plan, you will learn things you could not have known before. Then you will adjust your plan going forward.

If you still don't have a goal—a vision for your future—do the exercises in this book to the extent that you can and then take the results to a career coach. Together, you can come up with a vision and a plan for getting there.

Be sure to reads the stages Yadira went through. Each stage is described in detail in the case studies in this book.

> **Think as big and as long term as you can.**

## Case Study: Walter Planned All the Way

Walter had already completed his Seven Stories Exercise and his Forty-Year Vision, as well as all of the other exercises. He had put off doing the Forty-Year Vision for a long time; it seemed so intimidating. Once he finally put pen to paper, it took him only an hour or so to complete it and he felt relieved. In retrospect, he wondered why it had taken him so long to start writing it.

Walter's vision of himself is someday to be the head of a community-based national not-for-profit. Well-educated, dignified, and articulate,

Walter volunteered to help with one organization's Harlem program.

> **Whatever your vision, you will need to learn new things, form helpful relationships, and start acting in a way that suits the position to which you aspire.**

## Walter's Huge Vision

Walter's vision is to head up an educational program in Harlem and get it to the point where it runs smoothly. Later, he wants to move the program to other cities, such as Detroit.

Implementing his vision will take a huge effort and can last his entire lifetime. Walter *can* make this vision happen and it is up to him. Now he needs to flesh it out. He needs a very *concrete plan* about how he will get there.

In this section, you will see one planning method. It does not matter what kind of approach you use. If you are comfortable with any other planning tool, use it. If your planning method uses different definitions for words we use here, such as "goals" or "objectives," do not get hung up on the differences. Just use your own definitions and your own method. What is important is that you actually plan and that you write down your plan.

Your business needs a plan to get where it wants to go, so do you.

*Many people go through life looking for favorable "breaks." Perhaps the biggest break anyone could ever receive is to decide exactly what it is he or He wants and then become obsessed with obtaining it.*

Dennis Kimbro, *Think and Grow Rich: A Black Choice*

## Identifying the Most Important Goals

At a Five O'Clock Club program, the group brainstormed the most important steps Walter would need to take to head this not-for-profit and lead it to the national level. We came up with the following:

Goal 1. Learn how to run a not-for-profit, especially in the area of fund-raising.

Goal 2. Learn about Harlem and form strong bonds in the Harlem community. Work closely with other not-for-profits there.

Goal 3. Recruit and retain the best: volunteers, staff, and members of the board.

Goal 4. Create a program based on the needs and best interests of the community.

Goal 5. Develop processes, an operations manual, and computer and other systems to allow this program to be exported to other geographic areas.

Goal 6. Learn about career development and related areas, including the mentoring process, job development, and so on.

Goal 7. Observe and emulate, where appropriate, the professional behavior of someone who is already the head of a national not-for-profit or similar organization.

• • • • • • • • • • • • • • • • • • • • • • • • • • • • • • • •

*Everything about business comes down to PEOPLE. Where in business can we escape the impact of human care, human creativity, human commitment, human frustration, and human despair? There is no reason for anything in business to exist if it does not serve the needs of people.*

Bruce Cryer, *Re-Engineering the Human System* (a conference presentation)

## The Same Applies to You

Whatever *your* vision, you will need to learn new things, form helpful relationships, and start to act in a way that fits the position to which you aspire.

For example, if you want to rise to a higher level in corporate life, you need:

• appropriate technical and interpersonal skills,

- in-depth knowledge about specific topics,
- a network of contacts, and
- a certain demeanor, vocabulary, and dress.

## The Multiplier Effect: Select Strategies That Satisfy More Than One of Your Goals

Next, you need to come up with strategies for reaching each goal. If Walter needed to learn how not-for-profits work, he could, for example:

- take classes,
- talk to people who are already involved in the not-for-profit world, and/or
- work for a not-for-profit and get some on-the-job training.

If Walter actually decides to work for a not-for-profit, he needs to think this through. He could choose to work for a hospital, an association, a university, or the government. But would these be relevant to what he wants to do?

If Walter could work for a not-for-profit and—at the same time—learn about the Harlem community or the area of education, he should choose that not-for-profit. The more goals a strategy supports, the more multiplier effect it will have.

His strategy could be refined even more. Walter needed to be in a position where he would actually learn *how to run* a not-for-profit himself. Therefore, if he could find a job in a staff function, such as administration or finance, in a not-for-profit that dealt with Harlem or with education, he would achieve a "multiplier effect": one of his strategies would satisfy more than one of his goals.

On his plan, Walter would write this strategy— "Work in a staff function in a not-for-profit dealing with Harlem or with education"—under Goals 1, 2, and 6. As He conducted his research, Walter would decide whether he would get more mileage out of working for an organization related to Harlem, to education, or to both. Achieving a multiplier effect—even in two goals—will save his years of effort to reach his vision.

In your career, you will always do better if you can achieve a multiplier effect: *develop strategies that satisfy more than one of your goals.*

It may take you three or four weeks to come up with a plan with multiplier strategies, but that plan could guide you for the next 20 years or so.

> In your career, you will always do better when you achieve a multiplier effect: develop strategies that satisfy more than one of your goals.

## Goals Are Achieved through Strategies; Strategies Are Achieved through Action Plans

Develop your career plan as if you were planning someone else's business. Don't short-change yourself. Be sure your personal plan is as well thought out as if you were handing in a business plan for a company. If you are serious about reaching your goals, nothing less is good enough. It will affect your whole life.

Even if your goals are not as lofty as Walter's, a plan will help you get there. And those who have written plans are more likely to get there than those who don't write their plans down.

So, <u>*for each goal, develop the strategies*</u> you need to get there. See how often you can come up with strategies that serve more than one goal.

<u>*Within each strategy, develop action plans*</u>. For example, if one strategy for learning about not-for-profits is to take classes, Walter would need action steps to support this strategy. These could include researching various organizations that teach what he needs, deciding which classes would be best, and so on.

...........................................

*There are two kinds of people, those who finish what they start and so on . . .*

Robert Byrne

## Review Your Plan and Set Dates

Now step back and take a look at your plan. Set dates for completing those steps over which you have some control. In my own planning, for example, I can very easily set a date by which I should have a book written. Writing a book is completely under my control. There is a good possibility I will be able to meet the goal if it is what I really want to do.

But if my plan said, for example, "Get a book published by a major publishing house by a certain date," less is under my control. I cannot guess how long the action steps would take—regardless of how long and how hard I work at it. The steps could be: find an agent, write a book proposal, develop a book-marketing plan, wait for the agent to sell the book to a publishing house.

I cannot tell how long it would take me to find an agent. And if I attach a deadline to it, either I will be inclined to work with an agent who is inappropriate for me or I will become discouraged that I did not meet the arbitrary date. However, I could set dates for writing a book proposal and a book-marketing plan, because those two areas are completely under my control.

So if I don't have dates on items beyond my control, what can I do to make sure I do not ignore those uncontrollable areas? How can I make sure I am constantly making progress on my plan?

One technique is to devote a certain amount of *time* to achieving the plan. The second technique is to develop *stages* for the plan.

## Work at Least 15 Hours a Week toward Your Goals

Make sure you spend a certain number of hours a week working toward your goals. If you spend no time implementing your plan, or just a few hours, you will make no progress at all. A rule of thumb is to spend 15 hours a week at it—assuming you are working full-time at a job.

Then you have to make sure you are doing the right things during those 15 hours so you are getting the most from the time you are spending.

## Develop the Stages of Your Plan

After you have developed goals, strategies, and action steps, the plan usually seems very daunting—even if you are working 15 hours a week on it. So it's usually helpful to implement your plan in stages. After all, you can only do so much at one time. You may still be working in your present job. You just want to bite off a chunk of this plan and stay headed in the right direction.

The stages you lay out for yourself are hypothetical: When you start to implement them, you will change things. However, looking at the plan in stages helps you see where you intended to go.

Then, because you are bright and energetic, life will present you with other options that could take you off track. If you have laid out a plan, you can reject those that do not fit in with it, and accept those that fit with the stage you are at right now.

### Stage 1—What can Walter do right now?

Walter has to keep his day job. But there are certain things he can do right away to advance toward his long-term goal. He could:

- take on assignments in his day job to develop skills he will need for the future;
- better develop the plan for Harlem, improve the program somewhat, and think of what he should eventually do to make the program stable and self-supporting; and
- think about how he could eventually move into a job with more of a multiplier effect.

For most people, it is advisable to have a day job that somehow supports their other career-related goals—rather than one completely at odds with their long-term vision.

If your job requires so much energy and brainpower that it will take away from your dream, you are unlikely to achieve your dream.

## Stage 2–Free up time to devote to this vision.

We each have the same amount of time. How can we find the time to do what we need to do to reach our goals? No matter how energetic you may be, there is still a limit to your energy. It's better to think through how you want to spend your time and energy.

What are some of the things that Walter should consider so he is not spending his time and energy on the wrong things?

Certainly he could continue to run the Harlem program. However, he should hold off on growing it. If he increases its size a great deal in Stage 2, he won't have time to learn all the other things needed to eventually reach his long-term goal.

To conserve his time and energy, he could spend some of his time gathering information and other time recruiting people to take over some parts of the program. This would free him up for reaching his long-term goals.

## Stage 3–Grow the Harlem program.

Walter could find out how to raise funds, develop a stronger program, and build the infrastructure he would need to export the program to other areas, such as the manual for running the operation.

## Stage 4–Work on the program full-time.

By this time, the program should be large enough to support Walter. In addition, it would need its own full-time space for classrooms because it is slated to be a six-day-a-week operation.

## Stage 5–Make it into a regional organization.

Walter could plant the seeds for other locations in the region. Getting himself on prestigious boards would help him even more with fund-raising and with running the organization.

## Stage 6–Be a national organization.

Take the organization to other geographic areas.

## Stage 7–Influence national policy.

Walter could sit on national boards and work with those at the highest levels of government. The work he would be doing affects the U.S. and can help narrow the growing gap between the haves and have-nots. He wants to have some say in national policy.

# Deadlines

There are no dates on the "Stages" plan. When Walter develops a plan for himself (as opposed to the one the group came up with), he will implement it as quickly as he can. In real life, the stages overlap. An element from Stage 7 may start when he is only in Stage 4. The timing of the plan depends on his dedication—and his ability to plan and keep on moving the plan along despite other demands in his life.

I never put deadlines on my plan stages. I know I would never meet them, which would discourage me. Or, I would meet them at the expense of quality. The dates are arbitrary. I am proceeding as quickly and sensibly as I can. Putting a date on a stage would not make it happen any sooner in my case. I just keep working toward my plan.

# What If I Don't Achieve My Complete Vision?

If your vision is big enough, you may never fully achieve it, but you won't care. You will be doing what you want, your plan will keep you on track, and you will be having a lot of fun. You will get further with a plan than you ever would have without one.

Some people come up with *plans* beyond their abilities. This is less likely when a person actually writes out the details of what it would take to achieve a plan. For example, a person can easily say: "My plan is to have my own business and earn $100,000 a year."

That's not a plan. That's a dream. When a person actually writes down how he or she will get there, then it becomes more realistic. Either they wind up changing their vision or they develop the steps they need to get there. They stand a better chance of succeeding.

.............................................

*The secret of success is constancy of purpose*

Benjamin Disraeli

## My Own Plan—Dealing with Failure

I wrote my plan for The Five O'Clock Club in 1986. Some of the details turned out differently, but the strategies stayed the same. For example, to get credibility in this field, I had imagined myself teaching at New York University and Columbia. In fact, I wound up at the New School for Social Research, which fit in with my plan very well.

*After* a stage is completed, I write down the month and year—just for the record. Stage 3 of my plan failed completely. Many years ago, I had been running The Five O'Clock Club in my apartment and Stage 3 called for me to move it out of my apartment. I took out ads in local magazines, rented space for a meeting, and otherwise promoted the program. Only 12 people registered. It wiped me out financially and emotionally.

I thanked God for this clear failure. There was no doubt that this effort had failed. It would have been worse if the results had been ambiguous. Then perhaps I would have kept at it.

I rewrote Stage 3. I realized that I needed more credibility before I *went public* with this program. So, I decided to write a book. After the book was written, I moved the program out of my apartment—but more cautiously this time. I moved into a very low-rent location. Everything else in the plan stayed exactly the way it was.

In fact, The Five O'Clock Club failed three times in those early years. Each time, it was a clear failure. Each time, I had to stop the program to recover financially and emotionally. Each time, I thanked God for the clear failure. Each time, I decided that this was still a good vision (to make the highest-quality career coaching available to people at all levels) and that it was what I wanted to do with my life. As the saying goes, I picked myself up, brushed myself off, and started all over again.

Most successful people fail, I told myself, and in my failures I collected more quotations that inspired me. And now I pass them on to you.

.............................................

*It is a time for men and women of courage to assert themselves, to try to find a way to bring together people whose ignorance of one another is profound and whose hatreds are intensifying.*

Bob Herbert, *The New York Times,* October 6, 1995

.............................................

*Running a company is easy when you don't know how, but very difficult when you do.*

Price Pritchett

.............................................

*When we begin to take our failures non-seriously, it means we are ceasing to be afraid of them. It is of immense importance to learn to laugh at ourselves.*

Katherine Mansfield

## Homework Assignment:

Re-read Yadira's case study—especially the stages of her business development. Then write out the stages of your business. What are you doing right now? Reading books, taking courses, researching your competition. That's Stage 1 for you. Now, what can you do after that? That's Stage 2. In my experience, prospective entrepreneurs come up with about seven stages in their business development. Write out seven stages for yourself. Over the next few months, if you are still interested in this business, you can refine the stages.

In the early years of my business, when I was essentially working alone and the phone was not ringing, I kept my Seven Stages taped right next to my computer. Every day I was forced to look at those two pages and focus on getting something done that would advance me in my business. People came up with ideas for me, and some of them were tempting. But if those ideas did not fit in with my Seven Stages, I got back to business and focused only on things that were on my wall.

People ask how exciting the business was in the early years. It wasn't exciting at all! It was pure drudgery. I was continually pushing that boulder up the hill. But after about eight years, it took on a life of its own and now I sometimes have trouble keeping up with it and managing the next stage of growth.

Developing a plan of the stages of your business is very important. Write yours out now.

# Your Exciting Business Idea

*For deep in our hearts We do believe
That we shall overcome someday.*

"We Shall Overcome" African-American freedom song

This is the beginning of an exciting journey, and it never ends. The step you are now taking will probably alter the direction of your life. You have a great business idea—or two or three. And now you know the truth: An idea is a starting point, but execution is everything. To make that idea workable, you need to research, plan, and have the right attitude.

As your business develops and grows, you will need different systems, different techniques and different kinds of support. It's all fun.

You are deciding your own future. It's your story, and it is a story you make up as you go along. You don't know how the story will end, and the ending really doesn't matter. What matters is that you are living your life, enjoying the process of living. It's a journey, not a battle.

• • • • • • • • • • • • • • • • • • • • • • • • • • • • •

*. . . [T]he country demands bold, persistent experimentation. It is common sense to take a method and try it. If it fails, admit it frankly and try another. But above all, try something.*

Franklin Delano Roosevelt, speech, Atlanta, 1932

Sometimes we get so caught up in the path we are on that we think we have no choice. We forget what we would rather be doing. It is easy to lose sight of what would make us happy. We forget we have made choices that have brought us to where we are.

• • • • • • • • • • • • • • • • • • • • • • • • • • • • •

*Resolve to be thyself and know that he who finds himself loses his misery.*

Matthew Arnold

Approach starting your own business with an open mind—be open to the possibilities available to you. It is only by going out into the world and testing your ideas that the possibilities present themselves. Explore. Don't rush to start a certain business just because it's the one in front of you. Don't be rigid about your idea. Check it out. The world may tell you differently. And the *world* will be buying your product or service, so listen to it.

*The purpose of knowledge, and especially historical knowledge, is understanding rather than certainty.*

John Lukacs, *A History of the Cold War*

Expect to be surprised. And think of surprise as a pleasant thing, because it adds interest to your life. Every move you make will open a new range of possibilities.

There is no one way to start your own business; one neat solution cannot answer it all. There are many ways. What you find in your research is neither good nor bad; it is simply information to be observed and thought about. This information is an indicator of the correctness of the direction you are pursuing; the information is not an indictment. Information is not personal; information is the world's feedback to what we are doing.

Information is not good or bad; it is simply information. Things are changing so fast that we each need all the relevant information we can get. We may tend to block out information we find threatening—but that is precisely the information we need to get. Knowing the truth of what is happening around us may help us decide how to move forward. The information is not out to harm us—it is simply there.

*To view your life as blessed does not require you to deny your pain. It simply demands a more complicated vision, one in which a condition or event is not either good or bad but is, rather, both good and bad, not sequentially but simultaneously.*

Nancy Mairs (who has multiple sclerosis), *Carnal Acts*

*To be what we are, and to become what we are capable of becoming is the only end of life.*

Robert Louis Stevenson

There is a place for you, and you must look for it. Do not be stopped when others seem as though they are moving ahead. You, too, have a lot to offer if you would only think about your-self and not them. You are on your own track. Put your energy into discovering what is special about you, and then hold on to it. You will be knocked down enough during your business life. Don't knock yourself; push back. Push past the people who offer you discouragement. Find those nurturing souls who recognize your worth and encourage you.

*It is impossible to enjoy idling thoroughly unless one has plenty of work to do.*

Jerome K. Jerome

Continue to move ahead with your business, but be easy on yourself. Work on it whenever you can and keep track of the time you spend so you can be honest with yourself. Some days you'll feel like doing internet or library research. Other days you'll feel like talking to people. Both are ways of making progress. Take notes in your notebook. Fill up your hanging files. You'll be glad you did. The more you understand what is going on, the less anxious you will be.

### OPTIMISM EMERGES AS BEST PREDICTOR TO SUCCESS IN LIFE

*"Hope has proven a powerful predictor outcome in every study we've done so far," said Dr. Charles R. Snyder, a psychologist at the University of Kansas. Having hope means believing you have both the will and the way to accomplish your goals, whatever they may be. . . . It's not enough to just have the wish for something. You need the means, too. On the other hand, all the skills to solve a problem won't help if you don't have the willpower to do it.*

Daniel Goleman, *The New York Times*, December 24,1991

Develop tricks to nudge yourself along. Find someone to report your progress to. Join a Five O'Clock Club group as well as a group of entrepreneurs; meet with a friend. Talking gives you perspective and gives you the energy to keep on going.

Set goals for yourself. Keep in touch with people. Keep pushing even when you get afraid

—*especially* when you get afraid. On the other hand, if you have been pushing nonstop for a while, take a break completely, relax, and the push again.

Get together with a friend and talk about your dreams. In talking about them, they seem possible. And in hearing yourself say them out loud, you can test how you really feel about them. Then you can discover the central dream—the one that will drive you.

· · · · · · · · · · · · · · · · · · · · · · · · · · · · · ·

*Where I was born and how I have lived is unimportant. It is what I have done with where I have been that should be of interest.*

Georgia O'Keeffe

You will find endless resources inside yourself. Get inside yourself, find out what the dream is, and then do it. Stir yourself up. Go for it. The fact is, if you don't try, no one will care anyway. The only reason to do it is for yourself—so you can take your rightful place in the universe.

The only reason to do it is because we each have our place, and it seems a shame to be born and then to die without doing our part.

· · · · · · · · · · · · · · · · · · · · · · · · · · · · · ·

*We are all controlled by the world in which we live. . . . The question is this: are we to be controlled by accidents, by tyrants, or by ourselves?*

B. F. Skinner

The world is big. There are many options; some people try to investigate them all.

Instead, begin with yourself. Understand that part. Then look at some options and test them against what you are. You can hold on to that as a sure thing. You can depend on what you are for stability.

Most start-ups fail, but you have a better chance than others. You have the benefit of the advice in this book. You now understand yourself better and you can learn from the mistakes and successes of others. You can use advisors, a Five O'Clock Club coach and your small group to help through early difficulties.

You have spent time researching your business concept and have developed your "One-Hour Business Plan" to vet your ideas. Then you have focused on two or three ideas to research in depth and have kept your notes in a bound notebook and kept research materials in organized hanging files. You know that having a winning product or service is nothing unless you can *market* that product or service. You plan to keep your expenses low and spend money on revenue-generating expenses. From this book, you can see in depth the angst people have gone through to select a business idea and the time they have spent researching it. You have laid out the Seven Stages of your business so you will be able to stay focused. You have met with SCORE, the SBA, or some other organizations and advisors who support start-up entrepreneurs, and have gotten feedback not only from the market, but from experts in various functions. You are better off than most people who want to start their own small businesses.

*After you have done all of the above*, then you can decide on your business's legal structure, rent space if you need it, purchase equipment, hire employees, and do whatever else most people do prematurely that causes them to focus on the wrong things and then fail.

· · · · · · · · · · · · · · · · · · · · · · · · · · · · · ·

*Our deeds determine us, as much as we determine our deeds.*

George Eliot

The learning is ongoing. I recently joined the Women Presidents Organization (WPO), a national peer-advisory organization for successful women business owners. I'm not the "type" to join women's groups, but at WPO meetings I get feedback and support from other successful business owners. This organization is right for me at this stage. Get the advice *you* need for the stage you are in. Get insight from other entrepreneurs and from those who support and train entrepreneurs. You will learn things you will never find in a book and colleagues will give you feedback and remind you of what you already knew but forgot.

The world keeps changing. It won't stop. We must continually find out what is happening and change along with it.

Entrepreneurs are living the American dream. We are the lucky ones. We are the dreamers of dreams.

· · · · · · · · · · · · · · · · · · · · · · · · · · · · · ·

*We are the music-makers, And we are the dreamers of dreams . . . Yet we are the movers and shakers of the world for ever, it seems.*

Arthur O'Shaughnessy,"Music and Moonlight"

*Far better it is to dare mighty things, to win glorious triumphs, even though checkered by failure, than to take rank with those poor spirits who neither enjoy much nor suffer much, because they live in the gray twilight that knows not victory nor defeat.*

Theodore Roosevelt

# Part Ten

. . . . . . . . . . . . . . . . . . . . . . . . . . . . . . . . . . . . . .

# What is the Five O'Clock Club?

# How To Join The Club

## The Five O'Clock Club: America's Premier Career-Coaching and Outplacement Service

*"One organization with a long record of success in helping people find jobs is The Five O'Clock Club."* —Fortune

- Job-Search Strategy Groups
- Private Coaching
- Books and Audio CDs
- Membership Information
- When Your Employer Pays

> **THERE *IS* A FIVE O'CLOCK CLUB NEAR YOU!**
> For more information on becoming a member,
> please fill out the Membership
> Application Form in this book, sign up on the
> web at: www.fiveoclockclub.com,
> or call: 1-800-575-3587 (or 212-286-4500 in NY)

## The Five O'Clock Club Search Process

The Five O'Clock Club process, as outlined in *The Five O'Clock Club* books, is a targeted, strategic approach to career development and job search. Five O'Clock Club members become proficient at skills that prove invaluable during their *entire working lives*.

## Career Management

We train our members to *manage their careers* and always look ahead to their next job search. Research shows that an average worker spends only four years in a job—and will have 12 jobs in as many as 5 career fields—during his or her working life.

## Getting Jobs . . . Faster

Five O'Clock Club members find *better jobs*, *faster*. The average professional, manager, or executive Five O'Clock Club member who regularly attends weekly sessions finds a job by his or her 10th session. Even the discouraged, long-term job searcher can find immediate help.

The keystone to The Five O'Clock Club process is teaching our members an understanding of the entire hiring process. A first interview is primarily a time for exchanging critical information. The real work starts *after* the interview. We teach our members *how to turn job interviews into offers* and to negotiate the best possible employment package.

## Setting Targets

The Five O'Clock Club is action oriented. *We'll help you decide what you should do this very next week to move your search along.* By their third session, our members have set definite job targets by industry or company size, position, and geographic area, and are out in the field gathering information and making contacts that will lead to inter-views with hiring managers.

*Our approach evolves* with the changing job market. We're able to synthesize information from hundreds of Five O'Clock Club members and come up with new approaches for our members. For example, we now discuss temporary placement for executives, how to use voice mail and the Internet, and how to network when doors are slamming shut all over town.

## The Five O'Clock Club Strategy Program

The Five O'Clock Club meeting is a carefully planned *job-search strategy program.* We provide members with the tools and tricks necessary to get a good job fast—even in a tight market. Networking and emotional support are also included in the meeting. Participate in 10 *consecutive* small-group strategy sessions to enable your group and career coach to get to know you and to develop momentum in your search.

## Weekly Presentations via Audio CDs

Prior to each week's teleconference, listen to the assigned audio presentation covering part of The Five O'Clock Club methodology. These are scheduled on a rotating basis so you may join the Club at any time. (In selected cities, presentations are given in person rather than via audio CDs.)

## Small-Group Strategy Sessions

During the first few minutes of the teleconference, your small group discusses the topic of the week and hears from people who have landed jobs. Then you have the chance to get feedback and advice on your own search strategy, listen to and learn from others, and build your network. All groups are led by trained career coaches with years of experience. The small group is generally no more than six to eight people, so everyone gets the chance to speak up.

*Let us consider how we may spur one another on toward love and good deeds. Let us not give up meeting together, as some are in the habit of doing, but let us encourage one another.* Hebrews 10:24–25

---

### Private Coaching

You may meet with your small-group coach—or another coach—for private coaching by phone or in person. A coach helps you develop a career path, solve current job problems, prepare your résumé, or guide your search.

Many members develop long-term relation-ships with their coaches to get advice throughout their careers. If you are paying for the coaching yourself (as opposed to having your employer pay), please pay the coach directly (charges vary from $100 to $175 per hour). **Private coaching is *not* included in The Five O'Clock Club seminar or membership fee.** For coach matching, see our website or call **1-800-575-3587** (or **212-286-4500** in New York).

## From the Club History, Written in the 1890s

At The Five O'Clock Club, [people] of all shades of political belief—as might be said of all trades and creeds—have met together. . . . The variety continues almost to a monotony. . . . [The Club's] good fellowship and geniality—not to say hospitality—has reached them all.

It has been remarked of clubs that they serve to level rank. If that were possible in this country, it would probably be true, if leveling rank means the appreciation of people of equal abilities as equals; but in The Five O'Clock Club it has been a most gratifying and noteworthy fact that no lines have ever been drawn save those which are essential to the honor and good name of any association. Strangers are invited by the club or by any members, [as gentlepeople], irrespective of aristocracy, plutocracy or occupation, and are so treated always. Nor does the thought of a [person's] social position ever enter into the meetings. People of wealth and people of moderate means sit side by side, finding in each other much to praise and admire and little to justify snarlishness or adverse criticism. People meet as people—not as the representatives of a set—and having so met, dwell not in worlds of envy or distrust, but in union and collegiality, forming kindly thoughts of each other in their heart of hearts.

In its methods, The Five O'Clock Club is plain, easy-going and unconventional. It has its "isms" and some peculiarities of procedure, but simplicity characterizes them all. The sense of propriety, rather than rules of order, governs its meetings, and that informality which carries with it sincerity of motive and spontaneity of effort, prevails within it. Its very name indicates informality, and, indeed, one of the reasons said to have induced its adoption was the fact that members or guests need not don their dress suits to attend the meetings, if they so desired. This informality, however, must be distinguished from the informality of Bohemian-ism. For The Five O'Clock Club, informality, above convenience, means sobriety, refinement of thought and speech, good breeding and good order. To this sort of informality much of its success is due.

*Fortune, The New York Times, Black Enterprise, Business Week,* NPR, CNBC and ABC-TV are some of the places you've seen, heard, or read about us.

## The Schedule

See our website for the specific dates for each topic. All groups use a similar schedule in each time zone.

Fee: $49 annual membership (includes Beginners Kit, subscription to *The Five O'Clock News,* and access to the Members Only section of our website), **plus** session fees based on member's income (price for the Insider Program includes audio-CD lectures, which retails for $150).

Reservations required for first session. Unused sessions are transferable to anyone you choose or can be donated to members attending more than 16 sessions who are having financial difficulty.

The Five O'Clock Club's programs are geared to recent graduates, professionals, managers, and executives from a wide variety of industries and professions. Most earn from $30,000 to $400,000 per year. Half the members are employed; half are unemployed. *You will be in a group of your peers.*

To register, please fill out form on the web
(at www.fiveoclockclub.com)
or call 1-800-575-3587 (or 212-286-4500 in NY).

## Lecture Presentation Schedule

- History of the 5OCC
- The 5OCC Approach to Job Search
- Developing New Targets for Your Search
- Two-Minute Pitch: Keystone of Your Search
- Using Research and Internet for Your Search
- The Keys to Effective Networking
- Getting the Most Out of Your Contacts
Getting Interviews: Direct/Targeted Mail
- Beat the Odds When Using Search Firms and Ads
- Developing New Momentum in Your Search
- The 5OCC Approach to Interviewing
- Advanced Interviewing Techniques
- How to Handle Difficult Interview Questions
- How to Turn Job Interviews into Offers
- Successful Job Hunter's Report
- Four-Step Salary-Negotiation Method

All groups run continuously. Dates are posted on our website. The textbooks used by all members of The Five O'Clock Club may be ordered on our website or purchased at major bookstores.

# Questions You May Have About The Weekly Job-search Strategy Group

Job hunters are not always the best judges of what they need during a search. For example, most are interested in lectures on answering ads on the Internet or working with search firms. We cover those topics, but strategically they are relatively unimportant in an effective job search.

At The Five O'Clock Club, you get the information you really need in your search—*such as how to target more effectively, how to get more interviews, and how to turn job interviews into offers.* What's more, you will work in a small group with the best coaches in the business. In these strategy sessions, your group will help you decide what to do, this week and every week, to move your search along. You will learn by being coached and by coaching others in your group.

*We find ourselves not independently of other people and institutions but through them. We never get to the bottom of our selves on our own. We discover who we are face to face and side by side with others in work, love, and learning.* —Robert N. Bellah, et al., *Habits of the Heart*

## Here are a few other points:

- For best results, attend on a regular basis. Your group gets to know you and will coach you to eliminate whatever you may be doing wrong—or refine what you are doing right.
- The Five O'Clock Club is a members-only organization. To get started in the small-group teleconference sessions, you must purchase a minimum of 10 sessions.
- The teleconference sessions include the set of 16 audio-CD presentations on Five O'Clock Club methodology. In-person groups do not include CDs.
- After that, you may purchase blocks of 5 or 10 sessions.
- We sell multiple sessions to make administration easier.
- If you miss a session, you may make it up any time. You may even transfer unused time to a friend.
- Although many people find jobs quickly (even people who have been unemployed a long time), others have more difficult

searches. Plan to be in it for the long haul and you'll do better.

- Carefully read all of the material in this section. It will help you decide whether or not to attend.
- The first week, pay attention to the strategies used by the others in your group. Soak up all the information you can.
- Read the books before you come in the second week. They will help you move your search along.

To register:

1. Read this section and fill out the application.
2. After you become a member and get your Beginners Kit, call to reserve a space for the first time you attend.

To assign you to a career coach, we need to know:

- your current (or last) field or industry
- the kind of job you would like next (if you know)
- your desired salary range in general terms

For private coaching, we suggest you attend the small group and ask to see your group leader to give you continuity.

*The Five O'Clock Club is plain, easy-going and unconventional. . . . Members or guests need not don their dress suits to attend the meetings.* (From the Club History, written in the 1890s)

## What Happens at the Meetings?

Each week, job searchers from various industries and professions meet in small groups. The groups specialize in professionals, managers, executives, or recent college graduates. Usually, half are employed and half are unemployed.

The weekly program is in two parts. First, there is a lecture on some aspect of The Five O'Clock Club methodology. Then, job hunters meet in small groups headed by senior full-time professional career coaches.

*The first week*, get the textbooks, listen to the lecture, and get assigned to your small group. During your first session, *listen* to the others in your group. You learn a lot by listening to how your peers are strategizing *their* searches.

*By the second week*, you will have read the materials. Now we can start to work on *your* search strategy and help *you* decide what to do next to move your search along. For example, we'll help you figure out how to get more interviews in your target area or how to turn interviews into job offers.

*In the third week*, you will see major progress made by other members of your group and you may notice major progress in your own search as well.

*By the third or fourth week*, most members are conducting full and effective searches. Over the remaining weeks, you will tend to keep up a full search rather than go after only one or two leads. You will regularly aim to have 6 to 10 things *in the works* at all times. These will generally be in specific target areas you have identified, will keep your search on target, and will increase your chances of getting multiple job offers from which to choose.

Those who stick with the process find it works.

Some people prefer to just listen for a few weeks before they start their job search and that's okay, too.

## How Much Does It Cost?

*It is against the policy of The Five O'Clock Club to charge individuals heavy up-front fees.* Our competitors charge $4,000 to $6,000 or more, up front. Our average fee is $360 for 10 sessions (which includes audio CDs of 16 presentations for those in the teleconference program). Executives pay an average of $810 for 10 sessions. For administrative reasons, we charge for 5 or 10 additional sessions at a time.

You must have the books so you can begin studying them before the second session. (You can purchase them on our website or at major bookstores.) If you don't do the homework, you will tend to waste the time of others in the group by asking questions covered in the texts.

## Is the Small Group Right for Me?

The Five O'Clock Club process is for you if:

- You are truly interested in job hunting.
- You have *some* idea of the kind of job you want.
- You are a professional, manager, or executive—or want to be.
- You want to participate in a group process on a regular basis.
- You realize that finding or changing jobs and careers is hard work, but you are absolutely willing and able to do it.

*If you have no idea about the kind of job you want next,* you may attend one or two group sessions to start. *Then see a coach privately* for one or two sessions, develop tentative job targets, and return to the group. You may work with your small-group coach or contact us through our website or by calling 1-800-575-3587 (or 212-286-4500 in New York) for referral to another coach.

## How Long Will It Take Me to Get a Job?

Although our members tend to be from fields or industries where they expect to have difficult searches, *the average person who attends regularly finds a new position within 10 sessions.* Some take less time and others take more.

One thing we know for sure: **Research shows that those who get regular coaching during their searches get jobs faster and at higher rates of pay than those who search on their own or simply take a course.** This makes sense. If a person comes only when they think they have a problem, they are usually wrong. They probably had a problem a few weeks ago but didn't realize it. Or the problem may be dif-ferent from the one they thought they had. Those who come regu-

larly benefit from the observations others make about their searches. Problems are solved before they become severe or are prevented altogether.

Those who attend regularly also learn a lot by paying attention and helping others in the group. This *secondhand* learning can shorten your search by weeks. When you hear the problems of others who are ahead of you in the search, you can avoid them completely. People in your group will come to know you and will point out subtleties you may not have noticed that interviewers will never tell you.

## Will I Be with Others from My Field/Industry?

Probably, but it's not that important. You will learn a lot and have a much more creative search if you are in a group of people who are in your general salary range but not exactly like you. Our clients are from virtually every field and industry. The *process* is what will help you.

We've been doing this since 1978 and understand your needs. That's why the mix we provide is the best you can get.

## Career Coaching Firms Charge $4,000–$6,000 Up Front. How Can You Charge Such a Small Fee?

1. We have no advertising costs, because 90 per-cent of those who attend have been referred by other members.

A hefty up-front fee would bind you to us, but we have been more successful by treating people ethically and having them pretty much pay as they go.

We need a certain number of people to cover expenses. When lots of people get jobs quickly and leave us, we could go into the red. But as long as members refer others, we will continue to provide this service at a fair price.

2. We focus strictly on *job-search strategy,* and encourage our clients to attend free

support groups if they need emotional support. We focus on getting *jobs*, which reduces the time clients spend with us and the amount they pay.

3. We attract the best coaches, and our clients make more progress per session than they would elsewhere, which also reduces their costs.

4. We have expert administrators and a sophisticated computer system that reduces our over-head and increases our ability to track your progress.

## May I Change Coaches?

Yes. Great care is taken in assigning you to your initial coach. However, if you want to change once for any reason, you may do it. We don't encourage group hopping: It is better for you to stick with a group so that everyone gets to know you. On the other hand, we want you to feel comfortable. So if you tell us you prefer a different group, you will be transferred immediately.

## What If I Have a Quick Question Outside of the Group Session?

Some people prefer to see their group coach privately. Others prefer to meet with a different coach to get another point of view. Whatever you decide, remember that the group fee does *not* cover coaching time outside the group session. Therefore, if you wanted to speak with a coach between sessions—even for *quick questions*—you would normally meet with the coach first for a private session so he or she can get to know you better. Easy, *quick questions* are usually more complicated than they appear. After your first private session, some coaches will allow you to pay in advance for one hour of coaching time, which you can then use for quick questions by phone (usually a 15-minute minimum is charged). Since each coach has an individual way

of operating, find out how the coach arranges these things.

## What If I Want to Start My Own Business?

The process of becoming a consultant is essentially the same as job hunting and lots of consultants attend Five O'Clock Club meetings. However, if you want to buy a franchise or existing business or start a growth business, you should see a private coach.

## How Can I Be Sure That The Five O'Clock Club Small-Group Sessions Will Be Right for Me?

Before you actually participate in any of the small-group sessions, you can get an idea of the quality of our service by listening to all 16 audio CDs that you purchased. If you are dissatisfied with the CDs for any reason, return the package within 30 days for a full refund.

*Whatever you decide, just remember: It has been proven that those who receive regular help during their searches get jobs faster and at higher rates of pay than those who search on their own or simply attend a course.* If you get a job just one or two weeks faster because of this program, it will have more than paid for itself. And you may *transfer unused sessions to anyone you choose. However, the person you choose* must be or become a member.

## When Your Employer Pays

Does your employer care about you and others whom they ask to leave the organization? If so, ask them to consider The Five O'Clock Club for your outplacement help. The Five O'Clock Club puts you and your job search first, offering a career-coaching program of the highest quality at the lowest possible price to your employer.

## Over 25 Years of Research

The Five O'Clock Club was started in 1978 as a research-based organization. Job hunters tried various techniques and reported their results back to the group. We developed a variety of guidelines so job hunters could choose the techniques best for them.

The methodology was tested and refined on professionals, managers, and executives (and those aspiring to be) from all occupations. Annual salaries ranged from $30,000 to $400,000; 50 per-cent were employed and 50 percent were unemployed.

Since its beginning, The Five O'Clock Club has tracked trends. Over time, our advice has changed as the job market has changed. What worked in the past is insufficient for today's job market. Today's Five O'Clock Club promotes all our relevant original strategies—and so much more.

*As an employee-advocacy organization,* The Five O'Clock Club focuses on providing the services and information that the job hunter needs most.

## Get the Help You Need Most: 100 Percent Coaching

There's a myth in outplacement circles that a terminated employee just needs a desk, a phone, and minimal career coaching. *Our experience clearly shows that downsized workers need qualified, reliable coaching more than any-thing else.*

Most traditional outplacement packages last only 3 months. The average executive gets office space and only 5 hours of career coaching during this time. Yet the service job hunters need most is the career coaching itself—not a desk and a phone.

Most professionals, managers, and executives are right in the thick of negotiations with prospective employers at the 3-month mark. Yet that is precisely when traditional outplacement ends, leaving job hunters stranded and sometimes ruining deals.

It is astonishing how often job hunters and employers alike are impressed by the databases of job postings claimed by outplacement firms. Yet only 10 percent of all jobs are filled through ads and another 10 percent are filled through search firms. Instead, direct contact and net-working—done The Five O'Clock Club way—are more effective for most searches.

## You Get a Safety Net

*Imagine getting a package that protects you for a full year or more.* Imagine knowing you can comeback if your new job doesn't work out—even months later. Imagine trying consulting work if you like. If you later decide it's not for you, you can come back to The Five O'Clock Club.

We can offer you a safety net of one full year's career coaching because our method is so effective that few people actually need more than 10 weeks in our proven program. But you're protected for a year.

## You'll Job Search with Those Who Are Employed—How Novel!

Let's face it. It can be depressing to spend your days at an outplacement firm where everyone is unemployed. At The Five O'Clock Club, half the attendees are working, and this makes the atmosphere cheerier and helps to move your search along.

What's more, you'll be in a small group of your peers, all of whom are using The Five O'Clock Club method. Our research proves that those who attend the small group regularly and use The Five O'Clock Club methods get jobs faster and at higher rates of pay than those who only work privately with a career coach throughout their searches.

## So Many Poor Attempts

Nothing is sadder than meeting someone who has already been getting job-search *help*, but the wrong kind. They've learned the traditional techniques that are no longer effective. Most have poor résumés and inappropriate targets and don't know how to turn job interviews into offers.

## You'll Get Quite a Package

You'll get at least 14 hours of private coaching—well in excess of what you would get at a traditional outplacement firm. You may even want to use a few hours after you start your new job.

And you get up to one full year of small-group career coaching. In addition, you get books, audio CDs, and other helpful materials.

## To Get Started

The day your human resources manager calls us authorizing Five O'Clock Club outplacement, we will immediately ship you the books, CDs, and other materials and assign you to a private coach and a small group.

Then we'll monitor your search. Frankly, we care about you more than we care about your employer. And since your employer cares about you, they're glad we feel this way—because they know we'll take care of you.

## What They Say about Us

The Five O'Clock Club product is much better, far more useful than my outplacement package. —Senior executive and Five O'Clock Club member

The Club kept the juices flowing. You're told what to do, what not to do. There were fresh ideas. I went through an outplacement service that, frankly, did not help. If they had done as much as the Five O'Clock Club did, I would have landed sooner. —Another member

## When Your *Employer* Pays for The Five O'Clock Club, *You* Get:

- **Up to 40 hours of guaranteed private career coaching** to determine a career direction, develop a résumé, plan salary negotiations, and so on. In fact, if you need a second opinion during your search, we can arrange that too.
- **ONE YEAR (or more) of small-group tele-conference coaching** (average about 5 or 6 participants in a group) headed by a senior Five O'Clock Club career consultant. That way, if you lose your next job, you can come back. Or if you want to try consulting work and then decide you don't like it, you can come back.
- **Two-year membership** in The Five O'Clock Club: Beginners Kit and two-year subscription to *The Five O'Clock News*.
- **The complete set of our four books** for professionals, managers, and executives who are in job search.
- **A boxed set of 16 audio CDs** of Five O'Clock Club presentations.

# COMPARISON OF EMPLOYER-PAID PACKAGES

| Typical Package | Traditional Outplacement | The Five O'Clock Club |
|---|---|---|
| Who is the client? | The organization | Job hunters. We are employee advocates. We always do what is in the best interest of job hunters. |
| The clientele | All are unemployed | Half of our attendees are unemployed; half are employed. There is an upbeat atmosphere; networking is enhanced. |
| Length/type of service | 3 months, primarily office space | 1 year, exclusively career coaching |
| Service ends | After 3 months—or before if the client lands a job or consulting | After 1 full year, no matter what. You can return if you lose your next job, if your assignment ends, or if you need advice after starting your new job. |
| Small-group coaching | Sporadic for 3 months; Coach varies | Every week for up to 1 year; same coach |
| Private coaching | Coach varies | 14 (or more) hours guaranteed (depending on level of service purchased) |
| Support materials | Generic manual | • 4 textbooks based on over 25 years of job-search research • Sixteen 40-minute lectures on audio CDs • Beginners Kit of search information • 2-year subscription to the Five O'Clock Club magazine, devoted to career-management articles |
| Facilities | Cubicle, phone, computer access | None; use home phone and computer |

# The Way We Are

*The Five O'Clock Club means sobriety, refinement of thought and speech, good breeding and good order. To this, much of its success is due. The Five O'Clock Club is easy-going and unconventional. A sense of propriety, rather than rules of order, governs its meetings.*

—J. Hampton Moore, *History of The Five O'Clock Club* (written in the 1890s)

Just like the members of the original Five O'Clock Club, today's members want an ongoing relationship. George Vaillant, in his seminal work on successful people, found that "what makes or breaks our luck seems to be . . . our sustained relationships with other people." (George E. Vaillant, *Adaptation to Life,* Harvard University Press, 1995)

Five O'Clock Club members know that much of the program's benefit comes from simply showing up. Showing up will encourage you to do what you need to do when you are not here. And over the course of several weeks, certain things will become evident that are not evident now.

Five O'Clock Club members learn from each other: The group leader is not the only one with answers. The leader brings factual information to the meetings and keeps the discussion in line. But the answers to some problems may lie within you or with others in the group.

Five O'Clock Club members encourage each other. They listen, see similarities with their own situations, and learn from that. And they listen to see how they may help others. You may come across information or a contact that could help someone else in the group. Passing on that information is what we're all about.

If you are a new member here, listen to others to learn the process. And read the books so you will know the basics that others already know. When everyone understands the basics, this keeps the meetings on a high level, interesting, and helpful to everyone.

Five O'Clock Club members are in this together, but they know that ultimately they are each responsible for solving their own problems with God's help. Take the time to learn the process, and you will become better at analyzing your own situation, as well as the situations of others. You will be learning a method that will serve you the rest of your life, and in areas of your life apart from your career.

Five O'Clock Club members are kind to each other. They control their frustrations because venting helps no one. Because many may be stressed, be kind and go the extra length to keep this place calm and happy. It is your respite from the world outside and a place for you to find com-fort and FUN. Relax and enjoy yourself, learn what you can, and help where you can. And have a ball doing it.

*There arises from the hearts of busy [people] a love of variety, a yearning for re-laxation of thought as well as of body, and a craving for a generous and spontaneous fraternity.* —J. Hampton Moore, *History of The Five O'Clock Club*

# Lexicon Used At The Five O'Clock Club

Use The Five O'Clock Club lexicon as a shorthand to express where you are in your job search. It will focus you and those in your group.

## I. Overview and Assessment

**How many hours a week are you spending on your search?**

Spend 35 hours on a full-time search, 15 hours on a part-time search.

**What are your job targets?**

Tell the group. A target includes industry or company size, position, and geographic area. The group can help assess how good your targets are. Take a look at *Measuring Your Targets*.

**How does your résumé position you?**

The summary and body should make you look appropriate to your target.

**What are your backup targets?**

Decide at the beginning of the search before the first campaign. Then you won't get stuck.

**Have you done the Assessment?**

If your targets are wrong, everything is wrong. (Do the Assessment in *Targeting a Great Career*.) Or a counselor can help you privately to deter-mine possible job targets.

## II. Getting Interviews

**How large is your target (e.g., 30 companies)?**

**How many of them have you contacted?** Contact them all.

**How can you get (more) leads?**

You will not get a job through search firms, ads, networking, or direct contact. Those are techniques for getting interviews—job leads. Use the right terminology, especially after a person gets a job. Do not say, "How did you get the job?" if you really want to know "Where did you get the lead for that job?"

**Do you have 6 to 10 things in the works?**

You may want the group to help you land one job. After they help you with your strategy, they should ask, "How many other things do you have in the works?" If *none*, the group can brainstorm how you can get more things going: through search firms, ads, networking, or direct contact. Then you are more likely to turn the job you want into an offer because you will seem more valuable. What's more, 5 will fall away through no fault of your own. Don't go after only 1 job.

**How's your Two-Minute Pitch?**

Practice a *tailored* Two-Minute Pitch. Tell the group the job title and industry of the hiring manager they should pretend they are for a role-playing exercise. You will be surprised how good the group is at critiquing pitches. (Practice a few weeks in a row.) Use your pitch to separate you from your competition.

**You seem to be in Stage One (or Stage Two or Stage Three) of your search.**

Know where you are. This is the key measure of your search.

**Are you seen as an insider or an outsider?**

See *How to Change Careers* for becoming an insider. If people are saying, "I wish I had an opening for someone like you," you are doing well in meetings. If the industry is strong, then it's only a matter of time before you get a job.

## III. Turning Interviews into Offers

**Do you want this job?**

If you do not want the job, perhaps you want an offer, if only for practice. If you are not willing to go for it, the group's suggestions will not work.

**Who are your likely competitors and how can you outshine and outlast them?**

You will not get a job simply because "they liked me." The issues are deeper. Ask the interviewer: "Where are you in the hiring process? What kind of person would be your ideal candidate? How do I stack up?"

**What are your next steps?**

What are *you* planning to do if the hiring manager doesn't call by a certain date or what are you planning to do to assure that the hiring manager *does* call you?

**Can you prove you can do the job?**

Don't just take the *trust me* approach. Consider your competition.

**Which job positions you best for the long run? Which job is the best fit?**

Don't decide only on the basis of salary. You will most likely have another job after this. See which job looks best on your résumé and will make you stronger for the next time. In addition, find a fit for your personality. If you don't *fit*, it is unlikely you will do well there. The group can help you turn interviews into offers and give you feedback on which job is best for you.

> *"Believe me, with self-examination and a lot of hard work with our coaches, you can find the job . . . you can have the career . . . you can live the life you've always wanted!"*
> Sincerely,
> Kate Wendleton

## Membership

As a member of The Five O'Clock Club, you get:

- A year's subscription to *The Five O'Clock News*—10 issues filled with information on career development and job-search techniques, focusing on the experiences of real people.
- Access to *reasonably priced* weekly seminars featuring individualized attention to your specific needs in small groups supervised by our senior coaches.
- Access to one-on-one coaching to help you answer specific questions, solve current job problems, prepare your résumé, or take an in-depth look at your career path. You choose the coach and pay the coach directly.
- An attractive Beginners Kit containing information based on over 25 years of research on who gets jobs . . . and why . . . that will enable you to improve your job-search techniques—immediately!
- The opportunity to exchange ideas and experiences with other job searchers and career changers.

All that access, all that information, all that expertise for the annual membership fee of only $49, plus seminar fees.

## How to become a member—by mail or E-mail:

Send your name, address, phone number, how you heard about us, and your check for $49 (made payable to "The Five O'Clock Club") to The Five O'Clock Club, 300 East 40th Street—Suite 6L, New York, NY 10016, or sign up at www.fiveoclockclub.com.

We will immediately mail you a Five O'Clock Club Membership Card, the Beginners Kit, and information on our seminars followed by our magazine. Then, call **1-800-575-3587** (or **212-286-4500** in New York) or e-mail us (at info@ fiveoclockclub.com) to:

- reserve a space for the first time you plan to attend, or

- be matched with a Five O'Clock Club coach.

# Membership Application

The Five O'Clock Club

____**Yes! I want to become a member!**

I want access to the most effective methods for finding jobs, as well as for developing and managing my career.

I enclose my check for $49 for 1 year; $75 for 2 years—payable to The Five O'Clock Club. I will receive a Beginners Kit, a subscription to *The Five O'Clock News*, access to the Members Only area on our website, and a network of career coaches. Reasonably priced seminars are held across the country.

Name: _____

Address: _____

City: State: Zip:_____

Work phone: (____)_____

Home phone: (____)_____

E-mail: _____

Date: _____

How I heard about the Club:_____

**Your Great Business Idea**
The following optional information is for statistical purposes. Thanks for your help.
Salary range:
___$100,000 to $200,000   ___$200,000 to $300,000   ___$300,000 and above
Age: __ 30–39 __ 40–49 __ 50+
Gender: __ Male __ Female
Current or most recent position/title: _____

Please send to:
Membership Director, The Five O'Clock Club,
300 East 40th St., Suite 6L, New York, NY 10016

*The original Five O'Clock Club® was formed in Philadelphia in 1893. It was made up of the leaders of the day who shared their experiences "in a setting of fellowship and good humor."*

# Bibliography

**Basic Business Books:**

- *Black Enterprise Guide to Starting Your Own Business* by Wendy Beech (Black Enterprise Series)
- *Complete Idiot's Guide to Starting your own Business* by Edward Paulson
- *Complete Idiot's Guide to Law for Small Business Owners* by Stephen Maple
- *Home-Based Business For Dummies* by  Paul Edwards
- *Running a 21ˢᵗ-Century Small Business: The Owner's guide to Starting and Growing Your Company* by Randy Kirk
- *Sister Ceo: The Black Woman's Guide to Starting Your Own Business* by Cheryl D. Broussard
- *Small Business for* Dummies by Eric Tyson and Jim Schell
- *Smart Marketing: 10 Easy Steps to Promoting Your Small Business Like a Pro* by Victoria Garcia
- *Start Your Own Business* (Entrepreneur Magazine's Start Up) by Rieva Lesonsky
- *Starting an eBay Business for Dummies* by Marsha Collier
- *The Ernst & Young Business Plan Guide* by Eric Siegel
- *The Entrepreneur's Guide: Experience-Proven Advice* by Deaver Brown
- *The Everything Home-Based Business Book: Everything You Need to Know to Start and Run a Successful Home-Based Business* by Jack Savage
- *The Young Entrepreneur's Guide to Starting and Running a Business* by Steve Mariotti
- *What No One Ever Tells You About Starting Your Own Business: Real Life Start-Up Advice from 101 Successful Entrepreneurs* by Jan Norman

## Advanced Business Books:

- *Blue Ocean Strategy: How to Create Uncontested Market Space and Make the Competition Irrelevant* by W. Chan Kim and Renee Mauborgne
- *Corporate Turnaround: How Managers Turn Losers into Winners* by Donald Bibeault
- *How to Make Big Money in Your Own Small Business* by Jeffrey Fox *Shortcut Your Search: The Best Ways to Get Meetings* by Kate Wendleton
- *Pricing Strategies* by Alfred Oxenfeldt
- *The Franchise Option: How to Expand Your Business Through Franchising* by Kathryn Boe
- *The Mind of the Strategist* by Keniche Ohmae

## Small Business Accounting, Finance and Taxes:

- *Alpha Teach Yourself Accounting in 24 Hours* by Carol Costa
- *Bootstrapping Your Business: Start and Grow a Successful Company with Almost No Money* by Greg Gianforte with Marcus Gibson
- *Financing the Small Business: A Complete Guide to Obtaining Bank Loans and All Other Financing* by Robert Sisson
- *Keeping the Books: Basic Record Keeping and Accounting for the Successful Small Business* by Linda Pinson
- *The SBA Loan Book: Get A Small Business Loan--even With Poor Credit, Weak Collateral, And No Experience* by Charles H. Green
- *Small Business Accounting Simplified* by Daniel Sitarz
- *Small Business Taxes Made Easy: How to Increase Your Deductions, Reduce What You Owe, and Boost Your Profits* by Eva Rosenberg *Small Business Bookkeeping System* Simplified by Daniel Sitarz
- *The Accounting Game: Basic Accounting Fresh from the Lemonade Stand* by Darrell Mullis, Judith Handler Orloff, and Educational Discoveries

## Books related to businesses you are interested in:

Look on the internet for books related to the specific business idea you are researching. For example, if you want to open your own restaurant, Google "Restaurant small business plan" and see what you find. Go to Amazon and key in "restaurant business," and see if there are books that specifically apply to your business idea. You may be surprised.

## Biographies of people who started their own successful business:

- *Against All Odds: Ten Entrepreneurs Who Followed Their Hearts and Found Success* (Black Enterprise Series) by Wendy Harris
- *iCon Steve Jobs: The Greatest Second Act in the History of Business* by Jeffrey S. Young and William L. Simon
- *Oprah Winfrey* by Katherine Krohn

- *Madam C.J. Walker (Black Americans of Achievement)* by A'Lelia Perry Bundles
- *Miracles Happen : The Life and Timeless Principles of the Founder of Mary Kay Inc.* by Mary Kay Ash
- *Only the Paranoid Survive: How to Exploit the Crisis Points That Challenge Every Company* by Andrew S. Grove

## Books to inspire you and keep you motivated:

- *Good Business: Leadership, Flow and the Making of Meaning* by Mihaly Csikszentmihalyi
- *Seeds Of Greatness* by Denis Waitley
- *The Psychology of Winning* by Denis E. Waitley
- *Live Your Dreams* by Les Brown
- *Think and Grow Rich: A Black Choice* by Dennis Kimbro
- *Think and Grow Rich* by Napoleon Hill
- *The Purpose-Driven Life: What on Earth Am I Here For?* by Rick Warren

## Books to build the character needed for your own small business:

- *Adaptation to Life* by George Vaillant
- *Fierce Conversations: Achieving Success at Work & in Life, One Conversation at a Time* by Susan Scott
- *Flawless! The Ten Most Common Character Flaws and What You Can Do about Them* by Louis Tartaglia
- *Habits of the Heart: Individualism and Commitment in American Life* by Robert N. Bellah
- *How to Win Friends & Influence People* by Dale Carnegie
- *Learning at the Speed of Growth: Over 500 Entrepreneurs Reveal the Secrets of Successful Leadership and Sustained Growth* by Katherine Catlin & Jana Matthews
- *Rich Dad's "Before You Quit Your Job"* by Robert Kiyosaki
- *Rich Dad, Poor Dad: What the Rich Teach Their Kids About Money--That the Poor and Middle Class Do Not!* by Robert T. Kiyosaki
- *The Five Dysfunctions of a Team: A leadership Fable* by Patrick Lencioni
- *The Millionaire Mind* by Thomas J. Stanley, Ph.D. (author of the best-seller *The Millionaire Next Door*)
- *The Progress Paradox: How Life Gets Better While People Feel Worse* By Gregg Easterbrook

# Appendix: The New Outplacement Model

The following pages show how the Five O'Clock Club differentiates itself from its competitors. It forms the basis for our corporate sales calls and helps the prospect understand why these should use a different model form the one they have been accustomed to.

# The Five O'Clock News®

from America's Premier Career-Coaching and Outplacement Service

$4.95

A Publication of The Five O'Clock Club®—www.FiveOClockClub.com

**"One organization with a long record of success in helping people find jobs is The Five O'Clock Club."**

*FORTUNE*

# The New Outplacement Model

## Giving job hunters what they need most: personal coaching and a proven methodology.

by Kate Wendleton
Founder and President of The Five O'Clock Club

# THE NEW OUTPLACEMENT MODEL

The *new* model of outplacement emphasizes a *personal, one-on-one* approach to career coaching. The *old* model gives job hunters a cubicle and a phone and substitutes technology for human interaction. Job hunters learn from webinars and use databases, but have very little interaction with real, live career coaches—the component job hunters need most.

## The Evolution of Outplacement

The outplacement industry has changed dramatically over the past 30 years.

The old, space-based model (cubicle and phone) was developed in the 1970s. It made sense then. Employees didn't have home computers or answering machines. They *needed* an office to have their messages taken and get their letters typed.

Back then, most displaced employees had been with their employers for 20 or 30 years and had never searched for a job before. They needed lots of help. The services lasted until the job hunter found a new position. Employers paid dearly for these services: packages cost 10 to 15 percent of the person's prior W-2.

## The Situation Today

Today, the average American has been in his or her job only four years. But simply getting *another job* is no longer the issue. The issue is finding the *right* job: The one that positions the person for the one after that—because most job hunters will have to search again in an average of four years! The emphasis needs to be on *career development*, not just job search.

---

**The service job hunters need most is personal coaching, not webinars, e-learning and useless job banks.**

---

The churning in organizations is here to stay. Companies now routinely restructure to keep pace with changing international, market and economic forces. With the emphasis on reducing costs, employers have had to *reduce the amount they spend*

*per person on outplacement.* Instead of one-year packages, employers offer three-month or six-month packages that provide, *primarily,* a cubicle, a phone, and a database—and little coaching.

---

**Old-model outplacement firms are saddled with overhead, especially rent. Coaching is curtailed.**

---

### SUPPORT FOR JOB HUNTERS

**Personal Contacts** through the small group

**Network** with Five O'Clock Club Alumni

**Set of Books** and other materials

**Audio CDs** listen many times

**Career Coaches** private & small group

**Job-Search Buddies**

**At the Five O'Clock Club, the emphasis is on personal coaching — what the job hunter needs most. All packages are for a minimum of one year.**

## The Old Business Model

With plummeting outplacement revenues per person, the old-model firms could be profitable only if they charged the expense side of the ledger. With space as a fixed expense, they had to reduce labor in the form of career coaching, replacing it with the webinars, e-learning and databases.

Old-model firms have been forced to *increase the client load of their coaches,* who now may be expected to help 50 to 70 job hunters at once! The coaches remark that they can no longer remember their clients' faces let alone their names. They cannot do the heavy up-front assessment that would help the person to develop his or her *career* (as opposed to just finding another job). Job hunters may find it difficult to get on a coach's calendar, and are forced to schedule meetings every three

weeks or so. During the course of a typical three-month outplacement package, a job hunter may see a coach privately for a couple of hours. Some old-model firms admit that their profitability depends on *half* of the job hunters *not showing up* to use the service at all! It's like the gym membership model: Gyms sell far more memberships than they have the facilities to handle.

At the old-model firms, the pressure from the coach is to declare victory. If the job hunter gets an offer, the coach is tempted to encourage the person to take it — even if it is a mediocre job: After all, the service will end shortly anyway, and it would be better to mark this person as "landed" rather than "not employed yet."

What about the beloved space that is the centerpiece of the old model? One HR executive, who had paid $25,000 for a senior executive's outplacement, was distressed that the former employee didn't use the space at all! This is common. Typically, in the beginning, some rush to grab a cubicle and sit with other unemployed job hunters, but few are disciplined enough to ignore an emotionally depressing (but physically attractive) environment, and get on with their searches. They may engage in continual negative talk about the job market, which further decreases their productivity.

---

**Those in three-month, old-model programs end up with lower salaries and lower job satisfaction than those in longer-term programs.**

---

## THE COMPONENTS OF A SUCCESSFUL, MODERN OUTPLACEMENT SERVICE

What job hunters need most is the coaching, *not* the cubicle. Yes, they need to get out of the house, and there are ways

## THE NEW OUTPLACEMENT MODEL

to do that while still getting the coaching they need. When The Five O'Clock Club developed its outplacement business model, we wanted something that would work in the best interests of today's job hunters while helping HR remain within budget constraints. We started with a clean slate and tested various hypotheses.

### All Five O'Clock Club Outplacement Packages are for a Minimum of One Year.

Why does this work best?

• Job hunters who get three months of outplacement feel like they have been fired all over again when those three months are up. What's more, they tend to shortcut aspects of the job-search process (such as a thorough assessment), because they feel the pressure of having to land a job, *any* job, quickly. Counter-intuitively, those who have a one-year package *get jobs more quickly than* those with a three-month package because they are less likely to skip the important early steps. (In fact, job hunters at The Five O'Clock Club find new employment within an average of ten weeks!) People who feel the three-month pressure are more prone to make errors and take inappropriate jobs. They are encouraged to take jobs in the same field or industry because going for career continuation means a quicker search. But at The Five O'Clock Club, job hunters have a chance to *explore* career options. Because of the in-depth assessment process, 58% of the people who come to the Club decide to change careers and get into a field or industry they find more satisfying.

• Our one-year packages are a safety net. Sometimes a new job may not work out. It is a great comfort to a job hunter to know that he can come back to the Club should he lose the new job, or get advice so he does well with his new employer. He can also accept a lengthy consulting assignment, or try to start his own business. We work with each person for a year minimum *no matter what,* and that makes people feel grateful to the former employer who provided a Five O'Clock Club package.

• Academic research supports the one-year package. Columbia University conducted a study of 1,880 managers and executives who received three-month, six-month and unlimited service programs. (James D. Westaby, *Journal of Employment Counseling,* March 2004). Not surprisingly, those who received higher levels of outplacement support had a greater likelihood of reemployment, and had higher salaries in new jobs than individuals participating in programs with lower levels of outplacement support. Those who are in lower-support programs feel the pressure to take jobs more quickly, and are more likely to take the first job offer, however inappropriate.

Surprisingly, however, **the results for the three-month and six-month programs were essentially the same**, producing no additional benefit for job hunters. Perhaps job hunters feel the same pressure whether they are in a three-month or six-month program.

As the author says, "Organizations providing these [supportive, *unlimited* outplacement] services could reassure their displaced managers and executives that this type of outplacement assistance can help them achieve beneficial outcomes."

### A Mix of Employed and Unemployed Job Hunters

• Half the people attending The Five O'Clock Club are employed; half are unemployed. We work hard to maintain this balance. It's not good if *everyone* is unemployed. The depressing emotional atmosphere at many old-model firms works *against* the good of the participants. Most attendees at The Five O'Clock Club *choose* our services, or are referred by employers who really care about them, which creates a healthy spirit at the meetings. Furthermore, those who land jobs and want to search three or four years later come back to The Five O'Clock Club on their own. They are charged a nominal fee (only a few hundred dollars), and this keeps the atmosphere upbeat and hopeful. The employed people add hope and the unemployed people add the sense of urgency that is also necessary for a successful job hunt. In fact, those who are unemployed find jobs more quickly than those who are employed because they have more time to search!

• Most job hunters who are searching while unemployed assume they'll be forced to take a pay cut when they do

land their next position. But, 73 percent of the unemployed job hunters using The Five O'Clock Club approach have found jobs that paid more than (or at least the same as) their previous positions. Even during the recession from 1987 to 1992, Club members who had been unemployed for 9 to 18 months before they came to us still found jobs in an average of ten weeks at market rates. The Five O'Clock Club has a proven methodology for every aspect of the job-search process, and those who follow our methodology do better (more about that later).

---

Surprisingly, those in six-month programs received the same low salaries as those in the three-month programs.

---

### A Tremendous Amount of Support

• Guaranteed hours of private coaching over the course of a year.

The cost of a typical three-month program at an old-model firm could provide the job hunter with one year of service and a guaranteed 14 hours of private coaching at The Five O'Clock Club. This means the job hunter can spend a number of intense hours up-front with his/her private coach to go through an assessment process, write a résumé and develop a job-search plan. Then the job hunter can meet with his or her coach privately throughout the process. This is good for both the job hunter as well as for the HR purchaser.

---

All Five O'Clock Club programs are one year and cost the same as a three-month program elsewhere.

---

At the old-model firms, the coaches are over-burdened. Most are paid at a very low hourly rate. Five O'Clock Club coaches, on the other hand, are paid very well (three or four times the hourly rate of the typical old-model coach). Since they are paid *by the hour,* it is in their best interest to encourage the job hunter to use every hour he has coming to him — even

## THE NEW OUTPLACEMENT MODEL

if he has already landed a job! In fact, when a Five O'Clock Club member gets his first (perhaps bad) offer, the coach is likely to say, "That's just your *first* offer. Is it really the one you want? We prefer that you get three concurrent job offers so you can pick the one that positions you best for the long term." This is the difference between **the Club's emphasis on** *career development* **vs. the old-model firms' urgency to get job hunters out the door.**

### One Year of Small-Group Coaching

Five O'Clock Club research shows that those who participate in a *small strategy group* of their peers (those at the same salary level), headed by a senior Five O'Clock Club coach, get jobs faster at higher rates of pay than those who simply work with a private coach alone. That's because the job hunter and coach can test ideas and strategies with the small group and the job hunter wins by gaining a new understanding of what the coach asks him or her to do. Five O'Clock Club small groups are not support groups or even discussion groups, in the traditional sense. They are *job-search strategy groups:* Each person is coached indi-

vidually in a small-group setting. For our coaches, it is the most difficult coaching hour of the week. Some say the pace is as fast as a TV reality show. Each job hunter is the focus of attention one at a time. The coach and the other job hunters give each person feedback on his or her search, deportment, and presentation. Everyone is following The Five O'Clock Club methodology, so there is no time wasted debating the best résumé techniques or how to manage a networking meeting. They already know the answer. What's more, each person in the group goes away with an assignment: The most important things to do this very next week to move the search along.

---

**Half of the people who attend The Five O'Clock Club are employed, making for a healthier environment.**

---

The peer pressure is on! Everyone in the group hears what each person agrees to do during the next week. The job hunter is expected to do what needs to be done before the next meeting, and this

keeps the job hunter going. It's difficult to ignore peers (monitored by a coach) who all agree on what you should be doing.

Each person is assigned to a small group based on his or her salary history and expectations. This ensures that job hunters receive advice and encouragement from those who understand their position.

Job hunters get support from a private coach, a small group coach, and the seven to ten members of the small group. Every person in the small group gets everyone else's phone number, e-mail address, résumé, cover letter and Job-Search Marketing Plan. The job hunter can rely on the members of his or her small group to give him feedback and support.

### Job-Search Buddies

Each person has one to three job-search buddies, usually members of his or her small group. The job hunter can select his or her job-search buddies, or the coach can help in this process. Job hunters can talk to their buddies every day to exchange information on what they are each planning to do and then follow up to make sure they each did it! They can talk

---

## Employer-Paid Outplacement Services

### All Five O'Clock Club *Employer-Paid* Outplacement Packages are for ONE YEAR!

### Comparison of an *Employer-Paid* $5,000 Package

| | Old-Model Outplacement | The Five O'Clock Club |
|---|---|---|
| Who is the *Client?* | The organization. | Job hunters. Retail attendees *choose* our services, which means that we have an employee advocacy mentality. We *always* do what is in the best interest of job hunters. |
| The Clientele | All are unemployed. | Less than half of our members are unemployed; the rest are employed. There is an upbeat atmosphere; networking is enhanced. |
| Length & Type of Service | 3 months, primarily space. | 1 year, *exclusively* career coaching. |
| Service Ends | After 3 to 6 months—or *before* if job hunter lands a job or consulting assignment. | After one full year. The clients can return if they lose their next job, if their consulting assignments end, or if they need advice after starting their new job. |
| Small Group Career Coaching | Sporadic; up to 3 months. Coach usually varies. | Every week for up to 1 year; same coach. In a group with peers. Provides a job security buffer. |
| Private Coaching | 5 hours *maybe*. No time guarantee at all. | 14 hours **guaranteed** to determine a career direction, develop a résumé, plan salary negotiations, etc. — for a whole year. |
| Support Materials | Generic manual. | • 4 textbooks based on over 25 years of job-search research. • A set of 16 38-minute lectures on CDs. • Beginner's Kit of Search Information. • 2-year subscription to the *Five O'Clock News*, a magazine devoted to career management articles. |
| Facilities | A cubicle, phone, shared computer workstations. | None. Use home phone and computer. |

## THE NEW OUTPLACEMENT MODEL

about their anxieties or personal situations, and help each other to move along. This works even at the most senior levels!

> ## We can tell our job hunters exactly where they are in their searches and what they need to do next.

### The Five O'Clock Club Alumni Network

Over 1,000 successful and enthusiastic Five O'Clock Club graduates have volunteered to help those who are still searching. A job hunter who has attended at least four weekly meetings may access the alumni database, type in a key word, such as "accounting" or "publishing," and get up to 25 names of people to contact by phone or e-mail. This is a great boon to current job hunters.

> ## The Five O'Clock Club methodology is the key to our job hunter's success.

### Following a Methodology Based on Research

"It's the methodology." That's what David Madison, the head of the Five O'Clock Club's Guild of Career Coaches, says when asked to what he attributes The Five O'Clock Club's success in helping people find good jobs quickly. Yes, it's the methodology, based on 25 years of continual research into who gets the best jobs fastest and at the best pay. No other firms conduct such research. So our fundamentals are anchored in reality.

For example:

- Have six to ten job possibilities in the works. Our research shows that five of those will fall away through no fault of the job hunter: The employer may decide to hire an accountant instead of a marketing professional, may hire no one, or may hire the CFO's cousin. It's not the job hunter's fault!
- It takes an average of eight follow-up phone calls to get a meeting. We have a detailed write-up on how to conduct those calls (one rule is, "Leave only one message").
- Job hunters rely too much on net-

working, search firms and ads, and not enough on direct contact. Our survey of professionals, managers and executives clearly shows that job hunters get more meetings for the time spent through "direct contact" than through any other single technique. Yes, networking is important. "Networking" means using someone else's name to get a meeting. "Direct contact" means pursuing association members, or people identified on the Internet, through newspaper or magazine articles, or from library research. There's a myth out there that executives rely only on networking to get in to see people more senior than they are. At the Five O'Clock Club, even executives get almost one-third of their meetings through direct contact.

### Measuring Job-Search Effectiveness

At the old-model firms, job-search progress is usually measured by activity level: How many search firms were contacted? How many ads answered? But this approach doesn't measure the quality of those efforts; job hunters often *waste time* on ineffective techniques.

It took The Five O'Clock Club four years of research to develop a *measure* of job-search effectiveness to enable job hunters to know how well they were doing in their searches. Now, job hunters talk in terms of being in Stage 1, 2 or 3, and they know exactly where they are in their searches. In fact, when a Five O'Clock Club coach meets a client in the small group for the first time, it takes the coach only minutes to figure out where that person is in his or her search — and what needs to be done this very next week to move the search along.

Because the Five O'Clock Club has quantified every aspect of the job-search process, job hunters can be more objective about their searches and are encouraged to do the *right* things, *i.e.*, the things that *work*.

> ## We don't use the job-search approaches taught at the old-model firms. Our methods are based on over 25 years of research.

### The Best Materials

The Five O'Clock Club does not endorse the vanilla job-search techniques taught by the old-model firms (network, network, network). Our CDs and books show that research is behind every technique. Each professional, manager and executive in our outplacement program gets:

- A set of four books covering every aspect of The Five O'Clock Club methodology
- A boxed set of 16 38-minute presentations on audio CDs. These, too, cover every aspect of The Five O'Clock Club methodology. Job hunters listen to them over and over so that key words and terms naturally flow out of their mouths when they are in a job interview or are negotiating salary.
- A two-year subscription to our magazine, *The Five O'Clock News*, to help people remain current on job search and career management — who knows when they'll need help again!

So, the Five O'Clock Club methodology, combined with supportive coaching — both in small groups and privately — constitute the best outplacement package possible at affordable prices. ●

---

### Why Provide Outplacement?

- **Improves retention and recruitment.** Companies that demonstrate a strong commitment to the welfare of their employees find it easier to retain and recruit key talent. Those who leave are less likely to say bad things about the firm.
- **Improves employee morale.** Outplacement programs demonstrate your concern for your employees' welfare. This boosts morale for individuals in transition, and *those who remain* see how well you treated those who are let go.
- **Reduces likelihood of legal problems.** Individuals offered outplacement are more inclined to feel they were treated fairly and are less likely to sue. The outplacement coach can redirect anger, focus on the future and help the client to get on with life.

---

## HOW TO TERMINATE EMPLOYEES WHILE RESPECTING HUMAN DIGNITY

"Termination with Dignity" helps both the employee and the organization to move forward.

### A Kind Word Helps

If you lay off one or more staff members, what impact will that have on those who remain? Will productivity—and the bottom line—suffer? Are you likely to lose your best people who will worry about their positions? Or will morale increase because you handled the terminated employees with dignity?

Call for our free booklet, *Termination with Dignity*. Here are a few points to remember:

• Allow separated employees a "decompression period" in familiar surroundings. Let them have some control over how they leave. If possible, let them finish tasks they want to finish and make arrangements for keeping in touch with co-workers.

• A kind word helps during the dismissal meeting. For example, "George, you've been a trooper. I'm sorry that the organization has moved in a different direction."

• Give your employees the kind of outplacement that gives them dignity while positioning them for the future. ●

---

## The Way We Are

*The Five O'Clock Club means sobriety, refinement of thought and speech, good breeding and good order. To this, much of its success is due. The Five O'Clock Club is easy-going and unconventional. A sense of propriety, rather than rules of order, governs its meetings.*

J. Hampton Moore,
*History of The Five O'Clock Club*
(written in the 1890s)

Just like the members of the original Five O'Clock Club, today's members want an ongoing relationship. George Vaillant, in his seminal work on successful people, found that "what makes or breaks our luck seems to be . . . our sustained rela-

tionships with other people." (George E. Vaillant, *Adaptation to Life*).

Five O'Clock Club members know that much of the program's benefit comes from simply showing up. Showing up will encourage you to do what you need to do when you are not here. And over the course of several weeks, certain things will become evident that are not evident now.

Five O'Clock Club members learn from each other: The group leader is not the only one with answers. The leader brings factual information to the meetings, and keeps the discussion in line. But the answers to some problems may lie within you, or with others in the group.

Five O'Clock Club members encourage each other. They listen, see similarities with their own situations, and learn from them. And they listen to see how they may help others. You may come across information or a contact that will help someone else in the group. Passing on that information is what we're all about.

If you are a new member here, listen to others to learn the process. And read the books so you will know the basics that others already know. When everyone understands the basics, this keeps the meetings on a high level, interesting, and helpful to everyone.

Five O'Clock Club members are in this together, but they know that ultimately they are each responsible for solving their own problems. Take the time to learn the process, and you will become better at analyzing your own situation, as well as the situations of others. You will be learning a method that will serve you the rest of your life, and in areas of your life apart from your career.

Five O'Clock Club members are kind to each other. They control their frustrations—because venting helps no one. Because many may be stressed, be kind and go the extra length to keep this place calm and happy. It is your respite from the world outside and a place for you to find comfort and FUN. Relax and enjoy yourself, learn what you can, and help where you can. And have a ball doing it.

*There arises from the hearts of busy [people] a love of variety, a yearning for relaxation of thought as well as of body, and a craving for a generous and spontaneous fraternity.*
J. Hampton Moore
*History of The Five O'Clock Club* ●

## What HR Executives Say

"**This thing works**. I saw a structured, yet nurturing, environment where individuals searching for jobs are able to position themselves for success over the long term. I saw 'accountability' in a non-intimidating environment. It isn't just about getting a job; each individual was gaining self-confidence. It was particularly notable to observe the support and willingness to encourage those who had just started the process by the group members who had been there for a while."
— Employee Relations Officer, financial services organization

"**Wow! I was immediately struck by the electric atmosphere** and people's commitment to following the program. Job hunters reported on where they were in their searches and what they had accomplished the previous week. The overall environment fosters sharing and mutual learning: A very interesting approach for a group of people who had clearly been 'burned' by the establishment and were now involved in a cooperative effort."
— Head of Human Resources,
    major law firm ●

---

HR executives can observe
The Five O'Clock Club
**COACHING IN ACTION**
and see for themselves why
our job hunters get better
jobs faster.

We would like to invite you—or someone on your staff—to attend a Five O'Clock Club outplacement coaching session in person. You'll feel the excitement and see how we're different! And you'll see why more companies are selecting The Five O'Clock Club as their outplacement provider.

This is an opportunity to observe the small group meetings for professionals, managers and executives who are in job search. These sessions are held weekly on Monday evenings at the Roosevelt Hotel on Madison at 45th Street, and on Wednesday evenings at 11 Penn Plaza.

**Just call David Madison (212-286-4500)**

# When employees are given a choice,

they choose the **Five O'Clock Club**

for their outplacement program.

*"The Five O'Clock Club program is far more effective than conventional outplacement. Selecting the Five O'Clock Club was one of my best decisions this year."*
*SVP, HR, consumer products company*

## Old-Model Outplacement:

- Saddled with real estate costs
- Very limited one-on-one career coaching
- Overburdened coaches
- Started in the 1970s when people did not have computers and answering machines at home
- Vanilla career coaching methods developed in the 1970s

## Five O'Clock Club Outplacement:

- **We work with each person for one full year,** even if the person lands a job quickly – a great benefit to offer to your employees. Our one-year package means that we will continue working with him/her even if he loses his next job, decides to do consulting work for a while, or needs help handling the political situation in a new job – months later! We're not trying to rush clients out the door!

- One year of outplacement, with no extra cost to you.
- **Guaranteed number of hours of private coaching** coupled with weekly small-group strategy sessions headed by a senior coach.
- **A method based on 25 years of job-search research.** This is not vanilla job-search coaching. Our average job hunter in the $40,000 to $400,000 range has a new job **within just ten weeks.**
- **One-year premium packages cost** only $3,000 for those earning under $100,000 a year, $5,000 for those earning over $100,000 a year, and $7,500 for those earning over $200,000 a year. (Less expensive packages are available.)
- **When employees are given a choice, they choose us.** Who wouldn't choose a one-year package? We don't provide space, but we do provide what the job hunter needs most: first-rate and significant career coaching!

## The Best Job-Search Materials Anywhere

Finally: a proven methodology based on two decades of research that can be followed for job hunting, changing careers, consulting and freelance. Used by thousands of members of The Five O'Clock Club — a national career coaching and outplacement firm.

**All Five O'Clock Club packages include:**

- Guaranteed private coaching
- 1 year of small group coaching
- 2 years of Club membership
- The set of 4 books
- A boxed set of 16 lectures on CDs.

The Five O'Clock Club's job-search techniques are covered in **four books** and **sixteen 38-minute lectures on audio CDs.** Five O'Clock Clubbers are urged to study the books as if they were in graduate school.

Each job hunter gets:

- The set of 4 books
- 2 years of membership, including a subscription to our monthly magazine, *The Five O'Clock News*
- A boxed set of 16 lectures (40 minutes each) on audio CDs.

We work with an impressive list of financial service, law and health care organizations, among others: public companies such as Time Warner and not-for-profits such as PBS. We work with single individuals or handle major downsizings. All downsized employees hear from us within 1/2 hour.

### ALL OF OUR PACKAGES INCLUDE
### AT LEAST ONE FULL YEAR OF COACHING

Invariably, therefore, when employees are given the choice of working with old-model outplacement firms or The Five O'Clock Club, they chose us. This is because we offer first-rate and significant career coaching for a year, instead of office space.

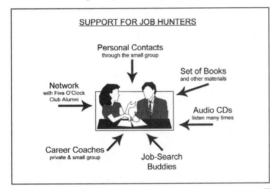

SUPPORT FOR JOB HUNTERS

message every time). They know they must spend 15 to 35 hours a week on their job searches, depending on whether they are employed or unemployed. They know that when they are negotiating they should first settle on the job, then find out about their competition, get the offer, and *then* negotiate the compensation. They know that networking is a process of forming lifelong relationships, and not a hit and miss process for finding someone who needs to hire right now. And they know that they must work to get six to ten concurrent job possibilities in the works — because five will fall away through no fault of their own.

Much of the success of those who attend The Five O'Clock Club can be attributed to learning these unusually realistic and research-based approaches. **The average person in the Club finds a new position in just 10 weekly sessions—a record unheard of in the industry.**

**Guaranteed private career coaching!** (Hours listed below.) If the employee needs help in the new job or loses the next job, he or she can come back to us. Or if he can try consulting work and continue with us.

We would be happy to come to your office to describe our services in detail. **Call David Madison, Senior Vice President, at 212-286-4500. Or email David @FiveOClockClub.com.**

The Five O'Clock Club, 300 East 40th Street
New York, NY 10016      www.FiveOClockClub.com

### The Five O'Clock Club Job-Search Techniques
### — based on 25 years of research

The Five O'Clock Club job-search techniques upset common assumptions about job-hunting today. The common myth is that people get jobs through networking—or through answering ads, directly contacting companies, or through search firms. Actually, those are techniques for getting *interviews*—not jobs, and the distinction is an important one. It means that—contrary to what most firms teach —a job hunter's work *begins* when they get the interview. It's a difficult process to *turn those interviews into offers*, but The Five O'Clock Club shows its members how. No other organization does that.

Or consider how people get meetings: Most people assume that search firms, ads and networking are the way to go. Yet our members get 31% of their meetings by contacting employers directly. We show them how to do it.

They know, based on our research, that it takes an average of eight follow-up phone calls to get a meeting (without leaving a

### Five O'Clock Club Outplacement Prices

|  | Price | Private Hours |
|---|---|---|
| **Senior Executives earning over $200,000 / yr** | | |
| Tailored Program (2-year coaching program & office space, administrative services, etc.) | $25,000 --- $20,000 | 40+ |
| Platinum (2-year program) | $15,000 | 40 |
| **Premium** (15-month program) | **$10,000** | **28** |
| Standard | $7,500 | 18 |
| **Executives earning $100,000 to $200,000 / yr** | | |
| **Premium** | **$5,000** | **14** |
| Standard | $4,000 | 9 |
| Bare-bones | $3,000 | 5 |
| **Professionals / managers: under $100,000 / yr** | | |
| Long-Term Care (for long-service employees) | $4,000 | 12 |
| **Premium** | **$3,000** | **8** |
| Bare-bones | $2,000 | 3 |

# Index

Aaron, Hank, 300
account analysis, 280
accountants, 121
accounting, 289–93
    cost accounting, 274,
      279–88
    profit and loss statements
      in, 271–73
    sample profit and loss
      statements, 275–77
accounting departments,
  284–85
accounting systems, 170
account management, 285, 287
account profit and loss statements, 281–84
accounts receivable, 259, 260
accrual accounting, 289–90
activities, in Ideal Business
  Environment exercise worksheet, 71, 73
Adams, Douglas, 104
Adams, Henry, 228
Adams, Scott, 271

Adams, Thomas, 229
Adler, Fred, 259
advertising, 178
    samples, 212–13
    speeches and demonstra-
      tions as alternative to,
      237–38
    in Yellow Pages, 179
advice
    in buying businesses, 125
    getting, 106–7
    unhelpful, 119
    universities for, 189
age, in starting new businesses,
  24–25
aged, services for, 24
Agesilaus, 102
agreements, hints for negotiating, 295–96
alcohol, 292–93
Alcott, Louisa May, 162
Allen, Robert, 184
altruism, 96
ambition, 97–98

American Management
  Association, 162
Andersen, Hans Christian, 39
anticipation, 96
appearances, in failures of
  small businesses, 9
Arcaro, Eddie, 97
Aristotle, 95, 302
Armstrong, Lance, 97
Arnold, Matthew, 329
arts businesses, 132
Ash, Mary Kay, 131, 141
assessments, in case study, 29
associations, 187–88, 190
    locating and contacting,
      240–41
    speaking before, 239–40
Associations on the Net, 188
attorneys, 121
    intellectual-property, 209
    public relations for, 254–55
Atwater, Lee, 48
Atwood, Margaret, 297

Bach, Richard, 229
Baldwin, James, 83, 235
Ball, Lucille, 107
bankers, 121
bankruptcy, 106
basic accounting system, 285
basic research, 186–87
Baskin-Robbins, 127
Bates, Marston, 188
Bayer, Richard, 9, 198, 262
beauticians, 16
Bellah, Robert N., 339
Benjamin, Keith, 60
Bennis, Warren, 25
billable versus unbillable time, 303–4
blackenterprise.com, 317
Bloch, Robert Albert, 107
Bolerjack, Steve, 251–55
Bolling, John, Sr., 254
Bolling, John, Jr., 254–55
Bond, Edward, 190
bookkeeping
    as business, 16
    marketing, to corporate clients, 217–18
books, researching in, 185–86
borrowing money, 259, 260
bosses exercise, 48
    worksheet, 51
bplans.com, 317
brainstorming, 208
Brainstorming Possible Businesses exercise, 75–76
    in case study, 83, 85
    worksheet, 77
Brandeis, Louis D., 271
branding
    of Five O'Clock Club, 19
    of franchises, 128
    names and logos for, 207

trademarks for, 208–9
Branson, Richard, 23
breakfast seminars, 220–21
Bridges, William, 83
brochures, 159, 211
    for corporate sales, 217
    in meetings with organizations, 226
    sample, 160–61
    tagline in, 196
Buddha, 110, 310
burn-out of employees, 268
Bush, Vannevar, 106
Bushnell, Nolan, 105
business.com, 187, 188
business concepts, in business plans, 318
business cycles, 170
businesses
    analysis of, 265–69
    Brainstorming Possible Businesses exercise, 75–77
    buying existing businesses, 117–25
    corporate scandals, 104
    employment by, 3
    growth, starting, 131–35
    Ideal Business Environment exercise, 71–74
    Ideal Businesses exercise, 67–70
    inventing, 54
    market worth calculated for, 300–301
    names for, 207–9
    Preliminary Businesses Investigation, 88–89
    profit and loss statements for, 271–73
    service, 15–17
    see also small businesses

business plans, ix
    for buying existing businesses, 118
    developing, 317–19
    failures and, 7–8
    for Five O'Clock Club, xvi
    One-Hour Business Plan, 132–34, 309–15
    in selecting businesses, 34
Butler, Samuel, 22
buying existing businesses, 117–18, 121–25
    case studies in, 118–23
    franchises, 127–28
    research on, 183
Byrne, Robert, 323

cake baking and decorating, 16
Camus, Albert, 87, 113
Canin, Ethan, 63
Career Buddies, 68, 71
career coaching, see coaching
caretaking, 16
Carnegie, Dale, 237
cash, 10
cash accounting, 289–90
catering services, 16
Chambers of Commerce, 118, 119, 122, 188
character traits, for entrepreneurship, 95–98, 103–11
Charell, Ralph, 189
charts of accounts, 290–91
Chesterton, G.K., 249
Child, Julia, 25
Child, Paul, 25
child care, as business, 16
China, 169–70
Churchill, Sir Winston, 97, 106, 266
cigarettes, 293
Clarke, Arthur C., 317

cleaning services, 16
clients (customers)
    agreements with, hints for
      negotiating, 295–96
    in buying existing busi-
      nesses, 120
    of consulting practices,
      155–56
    corporate, 215–21
    dissatisfied customers, 181
    of Five O'Clock Club, 18, 20
    follow-ups to, 181–82
    keeping, 262
    leads databases of, 162–63
    market research on, 177
    rejecting, 4
    setting rates to charge,
      300–303
    in target market, 193
clothing making, 16
coaching, xv
    as business, 16
    decision-making styles, 138
    diversity in, 9
    executive leadership coach-
      ing, 168–69
    by Five O'Clock Club, 340,
      341–42
    in history of Five O'Clock
      Club, 261
coaching, by Five O'Clock Club,
  336
coal, 148
Coffin, Harold, 99
Cohen, Claudia, 245
cold calls, 243–44
collection agencies, case study
  in, 268–69
communications, of Two-
  Minute Pitches, 203–4
company culture, 121

company profit and loss statements, 281–84
competition, 18
    in choosing businesses, 34
    in growth industries, 21
    in meetings with organiza-
      tions, 227–28
    outworking and outthink-
      ing, 108–9
    research on, 177, 185
    sending dissatisfied cus-
      tomers to, 181
compound growth, 101–2
Compton, Ronald, 186
computer-assisted instruction,
  23
computerized shopping, 76
conflicts, in case study, 82–83
Confucius, 67, 101, 105, 178
consulting and consultants, 22
    age as positive factor in, 25
    becoming, 153–54
    clients starting businesses,
      137
    creating jobs, 167–70
    executive leadership coach-
      ing as, 168–69
    for existing businesses,
      120–21
    Five O'Clock Club assis-
      tance for, 342
    in health care, 168
    management and financial
      consulting business, 132
    negotiating assignments for,
      297–306
    research on, 183
    speeches for promotion of,
      238
    starting businesses in,
      155–65

technical, as business,
    16–17
contracts, hints for negotiating,
  295–96
conventions, of trade associations, 188
co-promotions, 180
copyrights, 6, 260
corporate sales, 177–78, 215–16
    Five O'Clock Club market-
      ing plan for, 220–21
    getting meetings for,
      223–30
    leads databases for, 219–20
    marketing plans for, 217–19
    measuring effectiveness of
      sales campaigns, 231–33
    target markets for, 216–17
corporate scandals, 104
corporations
    corporate worth calculated
      in, 300–301
    *see also* businesses; small
      businesses
cost accounting, 274, 279–80
    account management in,
      285
    company versus account
      profit and loss state-
      ments, 281–84
    example of, 287–88
    managing for profitability,
      286–87
    for profit planning, 280–81
cost accounting system, 285
cost-based pricing systems, 286
costing, 286–87
Costner, Kevin, 177
cost rates, 298
costs, 273
    of goods sold, 291
cover letters

in marketing consulting and consultants, 158
pitch in, 200
Covey, Stephen R., 223
creative visualization technique, 67–68
credibility, 193–94
in corporate marketing plans, 220
image building for, 176
websites for, 179
credit, 103
credit cards, 10
cross-selling, 174
Cryer, Bruce, 322
culture, company, 121
customers, *see* clients

Dale, Kenny, 253–54
Daniel, Don, 165
Danielson, C. Archie, 98
databases, *see* leads databases
deadlines, 325
Deanna Dell Associates, 168
de Bono, Edward, 191
debts, 103, 293
case study in collection agencies, 268–69
decision making, 12
styles and manners in, 138
de Geus, Arie P., 188
Dell, Deanna, 167–68
DeLuca, Joel M., 199, 245
demonstrations, 178, 180, 237–38
dentists, marketing by, 174–75
DependableStrengths.org, 36
depression, 113–14
diaries, 59
Dickens, Charles, 109, 286
direct contacts, 224
direct mail, case study of business in, 266–68
direct mail marketing
for consulting and consultants, 157–59
sample brochure for, 160–61
discipline, 105–6, 108
discounts, 180
Disraeli, Benjamin, 326
dissatisfied customers, 181
distribution, alternative means of, 24
Dittbrenner, Jim, 168
diversity, among clients of Five O'Clock Club, 9
Dobbs, Robert, 15, 147–49, 169–70
documentation of systems, 107
drinking, 105
Drucker, Peter F., 23, 110, 186, 187, 215
Dubois, Charles, 94

Eastern Europe, 18
eBay, 179
Edelman, Marian Wright, 149
Edison, Thomas Alva, 319
education
as growth industry, 15, 23–24
technological change in, 23
Edwards, Harry, 235
Einstein, Albert, 29, 107, 138, 319
Eliot, George, 76, 331
email, for marketing, 179–80
Emerson, Ralph Waldo, 15, 143, 180, 190
emotional health, 12
emphasis, in Two-Minute Pitches, 204
employees, 6
burn-out of, 268
of existing businesses, 120
employment
bosses exercise, 48, 51
entrepreneurship versus, 11
Five O'Clock Club services for finding, 341–42
on path toward future business, 94–95
satisfiers and dissatisfiers exercise, 48, 50
by small businesses, 3
while buying businesses, 122
Encyclopedia of Associations(EOA), 187, 188, 240
Encyclopedia of Business Information Sources,186–87
enthusiasm, in Two-Minute Pitches, 205
entrepreneur.com, 317
entrepreneurship, 11–14
character traits for, 95–98, 103–11
jobs leading to, 94–95
reading books on, 185
sole proprietors, 263
environmental growth industries, 23
environments
Ideal Businesses Environment exercise, 71–74
in selecting businesses to start, 138–39
Epictetus, 106, 139
ethics, 20
ethnically-oriented businesses, 17
evaluation forms, 248
events planning business, 132

executive leadership coaching, 168–69
expenses, 293
  in charts of accounts, 291
  in failures of small businesses, 9
  fixed ("nut"), 261
  out-of-pocket or pass-along, 302
experience
  lack of, as reason for failure, 8
  in Two-Minute Pitches, 201, 202

fads, 81
failure, dealing with, 326
family life, 13
  in case studies, 139
  views of spouses, 110–11
Faraday, Michael, 107
fee-based pricing systems, 286
fee negotiations, 230
Fifteen-Year Vision, 55–56
  in case studies, 138
  Madison on, 59–61
  worksheet, 57–58
filings, 6
finances, 259–63
  accounting systems, 170
  debts and, 103
  learning, 13
financial plans, 318
financing small businesses
  in buying businesses, 123, 124
  consulting and consultants, 154, 156–57
  failure risks in, 7
  family life and, 13
  Five O'Clock Club, 20
  lack of, as reason for failure, 8

in One-Hour Business Plans, 123
in successful businesses, 14
Fisher, Carrie, 103
Fisher, Geoffrey, 88
Five O'Clock Club, 335–38, 347–48
  business plan for, 326
  clients of, 18
  consultants counseled by, 153
  corporate marketing by, 220–21
  history of, 337
  HR Network of, 196
  lexicon of, 349–51
  membership in, 350–51
  membership application for, 352
  name and logo of, 19, 207, 208
  origins of, xvi
  pricing and staff of, 20
  program of, 19–20
  speeches to promote, 175
  topics of meetings of, 245–46
  trademarks owned by, 209, 260
  weekly job-search strategy groups of, 339–45
fixed expenses ("nut"), 261
flex-time, 4
flyers, 180
focus, 108, 114
follow-ups
  after meetings, 228–29
  after sales calls, 230
  cold call follow-up letters, 244
  on contacts with associations, 241–43

with past clients, 181–82
food businesses, in case study, 140–43
Forbes, Malcolm, 273
Ford Motor Company, 106
Forty-Year Vision, 55–56
  in case studies, 28–29, 83, 138
  Ideal Scene exercise and, 64
  life expectancy and, 24–25
  Madison on, 59–61
  worksheet, 57–58
Foster, Willa A., 104
franchises, 127–28
Franklin, Benjamin, 226
Fraser, Don, 110
freelancing
  negotiating assignments, 297–306
  see also consulting and consultants
Fromm, Erich, 93
fun, scheduling, 235
furniture, 103

Galileo Galilei, 34
Garfield, James, 98
Gates, Bill, 167, 181, 185
Geneen, Harold S., 179
General Ledger, 284–85
geography, in locating business, 22
Gide, André, 21, 27
gift basket businesses, 16
Gilbert, W.S., 305
Glasow, Arnold H., 25
Gluck, Fred, 156
goals
  achieved through strategies, 323
  identifying, 322
  setting, 53–54

wealth as, 99–102
working towards, 323
God, 109
Golas, Thaddeus, 35
Goleman, Daniel, 330
Gompers, Samuel, 273
Google, research using, 187, 188, 239
Gouillart, Francis, 22
Gracian, Baltasar, 201
growth
in failures of small businesses, 9
planning stages of, 321–27
growth businesses, starting, 131–35
case studies in, 137–45, 147–50
research on, 184
growth industries, 23–24

Hafner, George, 36
Haldane, Bernard, 36
Halper, Jan, 79
handouts, 162
hanging files, 142, 177, 312
Hastie, William, 63
health, physical and emotional, 12, 105
health care businesses, 16, 17
consultants in, 168
as growth industry, 23
marketing to, 218–20
Hearst, William Randolph, 182
Henderson, Bruce, 18, 142
Hepburn, Katherine, 304
Herbert, Bob, 326
Herbert, Jack, 107
Herodotus, 27, 137
high-growth industries, 21
Hill, Napoleon, 103, 108, 298, 305

Holmes, Oliver Wendell, 68
home renovation services, 16
hours
billing by, 301–3
in market worth calculations, 300
HR Network, 196
Hubbard, Elbert, 108
Hughes, Howard, 100
humor, sense of, 96

Ideal Business Environment exercise, 71–74
worksheet, 73
Ideal Business exercise, 67–68, 70
Ideal Business Environment exercise, 71–74
worksheet, 69
Ideal Scene exercise, 62–64
in case studies, 139
worksheet, 65–66
Ilhan, John, 192
image building, 176
insurance business, 132
integrity, 104
intellectual capital, 125
intellectual-property attorneys, 209
interests exercise, 47
worksheet, 49
International Franchise Association, 127
international growth industries, 23
Internet
researching associations on, 240
in researching buying businesses, 123
research on, 187–88
searching for trademark

infringement, 209
selling on eBay, 179
websites on, 176, 179
interviews, 350
inventories, 292
investments, 101–2
investment spending, 273
investors, 20
Irving, Washington, 199
isolation of owning businesses, 5

jargon, 199
Jerome, Jerome K., 330
job (project) costing, 280
job profit and loss statements, 281
Jobs, Steve, 59–60, 185
jobs, see employment
Joel, Billy, 145
Johnson, Samuel, 102
Jordan, David Starr, 109
Jung, Carl Gustav, 318

Kafka, Franz, 86
Kaplan, Harvey, 167
Kennedy, John F., 96
Khrushchev, Nikita S., 219
Kierkegaard, Sören, 70
Kiev, Ari, 55
Kimbro, Dennis, 229, 322
King, Martin Luther, Jr., 53–55, 202
Kingsley, Charles, 144
Kotler, Philip, 194
Kotter, John, 147
Krispy Kreme donuts, 127
Kundera, Milan, 173

Labor, U.S. Department of, 187
large projects, managing costs of, 281

laundromats, 122–23
law of large numbers, 240
Lawrence, D.H., 217
lawyers, *see* attorneys
lead generation, 176–77
leads, tracking, 197
leads databases, 162–63, 178, 181
   audiences at speeches added to, 238, 247
   in corporate sales, 219–20
Leno, Jay, 109
Lerner, Diane, 245
Levinson, Jay Conrad, 194
Lewis, George H., 251
Lewis, Michael, 50
library research, 186
licenses required for some businesses, 140–41
licensing, 6
life expectancy, 24
Lightman, Alan, 298
Lincoln, Abraham, 110
literature
   distributed at speeches, 238
   marketing, 211–13
location
   in failures of small businesses, 9
   geography, in locating businesses, 22
   in Ideal Business Environment exercise worksheet, 71, 73
   researching, in buying existing businesses, 118–19
logos, for Five O'Clock Club, 19, 207
Lohr, Steve, 60
Longfellow, Henry Wadsworth, 201, 228
long-term planning, 106

Lucas, Craig, 299
Lukacs, John, 67, 330
Luther, John, 51, 183

Mackey, John, 288
Madison, David, 238, 246
   on creating consulting jobs, 167–70
   on Forty-Year Vision, 59–61
magazines
   publishing, in corporate marketing plans, 220
   researching in, 185
   trade magazines, 187, 188
Maguire, Jack, 89, 114
Mailboxes Etc., 128
mailings to target market, 225, 241
   for consulting and consultants, 157–59
Mairs, Nancy, 330
Malraux, Andre, 310
management, in successes and failures of small businesses, 8–9
management and financial consulting business, 132
Mandel, Michael, 10, 17, 188
Mansfield, Katherine, 326
marketing, 7–8, 262, 315
   for consulting and consultants, 153, 155, 157–61
   in failures of small businesses, 10
   literature developed for, 211–13
   measuring effectiveness of, 231–33
   in One-Hour Business Plan, 133
   sample brochure for, 160–61

   small businesses, 173–82
   Two-Minute Pitch in, 195–206
marketing campaigns, 226–30
marketing plans, 164
   in business plans, 318
   for corporate sales, 216–19
   detailed, 223–25
market rates, 304
market research, 177, 189–90
markets
   determining need of, 312–13
   in high-growth industries, 21
   research to decide upon, 184
   in retrenching industries, 21
   *see also* target markets
market worth, 300
Marquand, J.P., 306
Mascall, Eric, 206
Maugham, Somerset, 225
Mays, Benjamin F., 216
McGinley, Phyllis, 96
McGlaughlin, Flint, 211
media, in public relations campaigns, 252
meetings, charging for time spent at, 304
meetings, in corporate sales, 215–16, 227–28
   developing marketing plans for, 223–25
   in Five O'Clock Club's marketing plan, 220–21
   follow-ups on, 228–30
   planning, 225–26
men, less successful in small businesses than women, 111
Miller, Arthur, 75, 86

Miller, Henry, 74
Miller, Margaret, 179
Miller, Olin, 99
millionaires, 4–5
Millman, Dan, 108
Mr. Holland's Opus(film), 237
money, spending on right
    things, 260
Montagu, Ashley, 225
Moore, J. Hampton, 347, 348
motivated skills, 35–36, 38
motivation, 12
Mullen, Jeanniey, 179
multiplier effects, 323
names for businesses, 207–9
    for consulting firms, 159
    of Five O'Clock Club, 19
nano-technology, 15, 147–49
Natashah, Yanny, 260
National Aeronautics and Space
    Administration (NASA), 169
negotiating
    agreements, hints for,
        295–96
    consulting or freelance
        assignments, 297–306
    fees, 230
Nelson, Willie, 97
networking, 169, 189
    at conventions of trade
        associations, 188
    for getting known in target
        areas, 224–25
    in marketing plan, 223
new business, managing costs
    of, 281
newspapers, 188
    trade, 187
Nicholson, Jack, 113–14
Nietzsche, Friedrich, 220
Nobel, Alfred, 54
Noble, Charles C., 76

Nolte, Nick, 96
non-disclosure agreements,
    123–24
notebooks, 95, 312
    in starting businesses, 142
not-for-profit organizations, 218

obituaries, 53–54
office furniture, 103
O'Keeffe, Georgia, 331
One-Hour Business Plan,
    132–33, 309–15, 317
    research leading to, 189
    worksheet, 134, 311
on-site sales, 246–47
operations plans, 318
optimism, 13, 107
O'Shaughnessy, Arthur, 332
out-of-pocket expenses, 302
outplacement businesses, 18
    Five O'Clock Club, 19–20
overhead, 287–88

Pacal, Blaise, 231
panic, 106–7, 145
partnerships, 14
    strategic, 179, 248–49
party favors, 131–32
pass-along expenses, 302
Pasternak, Boris, 46
patents, 260
Pauling, Linus, 318
Pavese, Cesare, 219
payables, 284
Peale, Norman Vincent, 16, 43, 249
people, in Ideal Business
    Environment exercise work-
    sheet, 71, 73
people skills, 105
Perot, Ross, 192
pet grooming, walking and
    sitting, 16

phone calls
    cold calls, 243–44
    follow-ups to contacts with
        associations, 242–43
    to locate and identify as-
        sociations, 240–41
physical health, 12, 105
Pittman, Sir Brian, 163
Pixar, Edwin, 60
planning
    cost accounting profit plan-
        ning, 280–81
    developing business plans,
        317–19
    essential for entrepreneur-
        ship, 12
    events planning business,
        132
    in failures of small busi-
        nesses, 7–8
    growth stages, 321–27
    long-term, 106
    One-Hour Business Plan
        for, 309–15
    see also business plans
Poe, Edgar Allen, 195
positioning businesses, 198–99
positioning statements, in Two-
    Minute Pitches, 201, 202
positive attitudes, 107
Possible Businesses exercise,
    75–76
    worksheet, 77
Poundstone, Paula, 310
Powell, Colin, 302
prayer, 109
Preliminary Businesses
    Investigation, 88–89
    in case study, 76
    worksheet, 89
Preliminary Target
    Investigations, 193, 216,
    231–33

premiums, 180
present, exercise in, 55–56
press (newspapers and magazines), 187, 188
price, 273
    maximizing, 274
    in negotiating agreements with clients, 296
pricing, 286
    consulting or freelance assignments, 297–306
    Five O'Clock Club's, 20
    in profit and loss statements, 284
    project-based versus time-based, 302–3
primary research, 189–90
Primet Precision Materials, Inc., 147–49
prisoners, 94, 131–32
Pritchett, Price, 141, 326
private coaching, 336
procedure manuals, 107
product (service) cost accounting, 280
product profit and loss statements, 281
products
    deciding on, in starting businesses, 143–44
    description of, in One-Hour Business Plan, 313–14
    marketing, 173–82
    offered by consultants, 156
    in One-Hour Business Plan, 133
professional referrals, 174–75
profitability
    account management and, 285
    analysis of, 314–15
    managing, 286–87

in profit and loss statements, 284
profit and loss statements (P&L), 259, 271–73, 279
    company versus account, 281–84
    samples, 275–77, 283
profit planning, 280–81
profits, 271
    increasing, 273
    maximizing price in, 274
    in negotiating agreements with clients, 295, 296
    in profit and loss statements, 271–73
project-based pricing, 304–5
    time-based pricing versus, 302
project (job) costing, 280
project profit and loss statements, 281
promotions, 175
    co-promotions, 180
publicity, 178
public relations, 178
    for small businesses, 251–55

Quinn, James, 137

raffles, 247
Ramadan (Muslim holy month), 9
Rappaport, Herbert, 93
ratios, financial, 293
Read, Leonard E., 27
real estate businesses, 17–18
recognition and rewards, in Ideal Business Environment exercise worksheet, 71, 73
recruiting firms, 17
references, in corporate market-

ing plans, 217
regulations, 6
reporting (accounting), 280
research
    on associations, 240
    basic, 186–87
    books and magazines for, 185–86
    in buying existing businesses, 118–19, 123
    on competition, 185
    information sources for, 187–90
    in libraries, 186
    on new business ideas, 183–85
    in starting businesses, 141, 142
    on trademarks, 209
restaurants, 18
retirement, 101–2
retrenching markets, 21
revenues, 290–91, 293
Revson, Charles, 211
Rickenbacker, Eddie, 201
Rilke, Rainer Maria, 37, 71
risk analysis, 318
risks, 106–7
Roddick, Anita, 18
Romero, John, 177
Roosevelt, Franklin Delano, 329
Roosevelt, Theodore, 105, 155, 332
Ross, Steven J., 75
Rothschild, William E., 157
Rubin, Theodore, 265

safety and security industries, 23
Saint-Exupéry, Antoine de, 20, 178
sales

corporate, 215–21
in failures of small businesses, 10
at sites of speeches, 246–47
sales calls, 178, 262
to corporate clients, 215
follow-ups after, 230
*see also* meetings
sales campaigns
managing, 226
measuring effectiveness of, 231–33
refining, 234–35
sales meetings, 200
Salter, James, 62, 64
samplings, 180
Samuelson, Paul, 279
Sarnoff, David, 185
satisfiers and dissatisfiers exercise, 48
worksheet, 50
Schwartz, David Joseph, 110
Schwartz, Peter, 64, 188
Schwartzkopf, Norman, 150
SCORE (Service Corps of Retired Executives), 188
Scorsese, Martin, 96
Scott-Maxwell, Florida, 24
script books, 197–98
scripts
for cold calls, 243–44
for follow-up phone calls, 242–43
for selling items at speeches, 247
Scully, John, 59, 80
search firms, 132
seasonal businesses, 118
secondary research, 189–90
self-confidence, 13
self-discipline, 105–6, 108
self-esteem, 113

selling businesses, 263
service businesses, 15–17
consulting as, 156
marketing, 173–82
One-Hour Business Plan for, 133
service (product) cost accounting, 280
service profit and loss statements, 281
services
descriptions of, in One-Hour Business Plan, 313–14
pricing, 297–99
Seven-Stage Plan, 108
Seven Stories Exercise, 35–39
in author's life, 29
in case study, 27–28, 79–82
in starting businesses, 132
worksheet, 40–44
Shakes, Ronnie, 29
Shakespeare, William, 17, 56, 176
Sheldon, Arthur F., 153
short-term projects, 81
signatures, on email, 180
sign-up sheets, 247
Singer, Isaac Bashevis, 88
Skinner, B.F., 331
sleep, need for, 105
Slim, W.J., 249
Small Business Administration, U.S., 188, 317
small businesses
benefits of owning, 3–5
buying existing businesses, 117–25
choosing, 33–34
disadvantages of owning, 5–7
employment by, 3

factors in success of, 14
franchises, 127–28
marketing, 173–82
own boss in, 3
partnerships as, 14
public relations for, 251–55
reasons for failures of, 7–10
selling, 263
service businesses, 15–17
starting, 131–35
women more successful than men in, 111
smiling, in Two-Minute Pitches, 204–5
Smith, Walter ("Red"), 231
socioeconomic level of target market, 192
sole proprietors, 263
Sonner, Donald, 5
space exploration, 169
Spark, Muriel, 36
specialty party favors, 16
speeches, 162, 237–39
audience reactions to, 248
choosing topics for, 245–46
finding audiences for, 240–45
in marketing, 174–77, 178
sales of books or items at, 246–47
techniques for giving, 246
sports, visualization techniques used in, 67
spouses, 110–11
staffing, of Five O'Clock Club, 20
Stanley, Thomas J., 4–5
starting businesses
case studies in, 137–45, 145–50
in consulting, 153–54, 155–65

growth businesses, 131–35
    research on, 184
    setting rates when, 305–6
Star Trek,138
Sterner, Jerry, 297
Stevenson, Robert Louis, 109, 330
Stine, Gary, 168–69
Stowe, Harriet Beecher, 111
strategic partnerships, 179, 248–49
structured marketing, 232
style, in Ideal Business Environment exercise worksheet, 71, 73
sublimation, 96
subtargets, 218–19
suburbs, 22
Sun Tzu, 18, 139
supplies, 292
supporting documents, in business plans, 318
surveys, 180
sustainable competitive advantage (SCA), 21–22
systems, development of, 107

taglines, 196
targeted mailings, 225, 241
    sample brochure for, 160–61
targeting, 191–94
target markets, 163–64, 177, 191–94
    for corporate sales, 215–17
    detailed marketing plans for, 223–25
    Preliminary Target Investigations for, 231–33
    refining sales campaign for, 234–35
Taubman, A. Alfred, 177

taxes, 4, 6
technical consulting, 16–17
technological change, 22–23
technology, in growth industries, 23, 24
telecommunications, 23
television, 203
    used in marketing, 175–76
tempo, in Two-Minute Pitches, 204
Teresa (Mother Teresa), 64
testimonials, 217
testing target markets, 194
Thoreau, Henry David, 39
Thurow, Lester C., 114
time
    billable versus unbillable, 303–4
    billing by, 301–3
    in calculating market worth, 300
    spending on right things, 261
Tolstoy, Leo, 87
Townsend, Robert, 33
tracking leads, 197
Tracy, Brian, 103
trade associations, 187–88
trade magazines, 187
Trademark Electronic Search System (TES), 209
trademarks and copyrights, 6, 208–9, 260
    for business names, 207
trade shows, 180
training
    in collection agency case study, 268–69
    in operating franchises, 128
travel services, 16
travel time, 303, 304
Trotsky, Leon, 155

True, Herb, 184
Truman, Harry S., 141
Trump, Donald, 36
Twain, Mark, 145
Two-Minute Pitches, 195–206, 226–27, 350

unbundling extra services, 274
undercharging, 262
universities, 189
uspto.gov, 209

Vaillant, George, 96, 347
valuation of existing businesses, 124
value-added pieces, 159
values
    conflicts in, 113
    work-related, 45–46
Values exercise, in case studies, 28, 82
van Dyke, Henry, 101
Ventura, Michael, 64
Viorst, Judith, 87
visualization techniques, 67–68
Vivekananda (swami), 309
voicemail, 242
volume, of business, 273

Wachtler, Sol, 225
Waitley, Denis, 108
Walker, C.J., 95
wealth, 99–102
Webb, Dennis R., 62
websites, 176, 179
wellness, businesses in, 16
Williams, Tennessee, 95
Wilson, Orvel Ray, 211
women, more successful in small businesses than men, 111
Women Presidents

Organization (WPO), 331
word of mouth, 178
work hours, in market worth
  calculations, 300
work-related values, 45–46
worksheets
  bosses exercise, 51
  Brainstorming Possible
    Businesses exercise, 77
  Fifteen-Year Vision, 57–58
  Forty-Year Vision, 57–58

Ideal Business Environment
  exercise, 73
Ideal Business exercise, 69
interests exercise, 49
One-Hour Business Plan,
  134, 311
Preliminary Businesses
  Investigation, 89
Seven Stories Exercise,
  40–44
Wright, Stephen, 318

writing articles, in marketing,
  in image building, 176

Yang Liwei, 169
Yellow Pages, 179

Ziglar, Zig, 96, 193

# About the Author

Kate Wendleton is a respected authority and speaker on career development, having appeared on the Today Show, CNN, CNBC, The Larry King Show, National Public Radio, and CBS, and in The Economist, The New York Times, The Chicago Tribune, The Wall Street Journal, Fortune magazine, Business Week, and other national media. She was a nationally syndicated careers columnist for eight years.

She has been a career coach since 1978, when she founded The Five O'Clock Club and developed its methodology to help job hunters and career changers of all levels in job-search strategy groups. This methodology is now used by branches of The Five O'Clock Club that meet weekly in the United States and Canada.

Kate also founded Workforce America, a not-for-profit affiliate of The Five O'Clock Club that ran for 10 years. It served adults in Harlem who were not yet in the professional or managerial ranks. Workforce America helped adults in Harlem move into better-paying, higher-level positions as they improved their educational level and work experience.

Kate founded, and directed for seven years, The Career Center at The New School for Social Research in New York. She also advises major corporations about employee career-development programs and coaches senior executives.

A former CFO of two small companies, she has 20 years of business-management experience in both manufacturing and service businesses.

Kate attended Chestnut Hill College in Philadelphia and received her MBA from Drexel University. She is a popular speaker for associations, corporations, and colleges. When she lived in Philadelphia, Kate did long-term volunteer work for the Philadelphia Museum of Art, the Walnut Street Theatre Art Gallery, United Way, and the YMCA. Kate currently lives in Manhattan with her husband.

Kate Wendleton is the author of many books on job-hunting and career development.

# About The Five O'Clock Club and the "Fruytagie" Canvas

Five O'Clock Club members are special. We attract upbeat, ambitious, dynamic, intelligent people—and that makes it fun for all of us. Most of our members are professionals, managers, executives, consultants, and freelancers. We also include recent college graduates and those aiming to get into the professional ranks, as well as people in their 40s, 50s, and even 60s. Most members' salaries range from $30,000 to $400,000 (one-third of our members earn in excess of $100,000 a year). For those who cannot attend a Club, *The Five O'Clock Club Book Series* contains all of our methodologies—and our spirit.

## The Philosophy of The Five O'Clock Club

The "Fruytagie" Canvas by Patricia Kelly, depicted here, symbolizes our philosophy. The original, which is actually 52.5" by 69" inches, hangs in the offices of The Five O'Clock Club in Manhattan. It is reminiscent of popular 16th century Dutch "fruytagie," or fruit tapestries, which depicted abundance and prosperity.

I was attracted to this piece because it seemed to fit the spirit of our people at The Five O'Clock Club. This was confirmed when the artist, who was not aware of what I did for a living, added these words to the canvas: "The garden is abundant, prosperous and magical." Later, it took me only 10 minutes to write the blank verse "The Garden of Life," because it came from my heart. The verse reflects our philosophy and describes the kind of people who are members of the Club.

I'm always inspired by Five O'Clock Clubbers. They show others the way through their quiet behavior ...their kindness ...their generosity ...their hard work ...under God's care.

We share what we have with others. We are in this lush, exciting place together—with our brothers and sisters—and reach out for harmony. The garden is abundant. The market is exciting. And Five O'Clock Clubbers believe that there is enough for everyone.

## About the Artist's Method

To create her tapestry-like art, Kelly developed a unique style of stenciling. She hand-draws and hand-cuts each stencil, both in the negative and positive for each image. Her elaborate technique also includes a lengthy multilayering process incorporating Dutch metal leaves and gilding, numerous transparent glazes, paints, and wax pencils.

Kelly also paints the back-side of the canvas using multiple washes of reds, violets, and golds. She uses this technique to create a heavy vibration of color, which in turn reflects the color onto the surface of the wall against which the canvas hangs.

The canvas is suspended by a heavy braided silk cord threaded into large brass grommets inserted along the top. Like a tapestry, the hemmed canvas is attached to a gold-gilded dowel with finials. The entire work is hung from a sculpted wall ornament.

Our staff is inspired every day by the tapestry and by the members of The Five O'Clock Club. We all work hard—and have FUN! The garden is abundant—with enough for everyone.

We wish you lots of success in your venture. We—and your fellow members of The Five O'Clock Club—will work with you on it.

—Kate Wendleton, President

*The original Five O'Clock Club was formed in Philadelphia in 1883.*
*It was made up of the leaders of the day, who shared their experiences "in a spirit of fellowship and good humor."*

 **THE GARDEN OF LIFE IS** abundant, prosperous and magical. ❦ In this garden, there is enough for everyone. ❦ Share the fruit and the knowledge ❦ Our brothers and we are in this lush, exciting place together. ❦ Let's show others the way. ❦ Kindness. Generosity. ❦ Hard work. ❦ God's care.

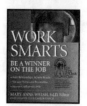